Laughing in the Dark

Also by Laurie Stone
Starting with Serge, a novel

Laughing in the Dark

A DECADE OF

SUBVERSIVE COMEDY

Laurie Stone

THE ECCO PRESS

THE ECCO PRESS
100 West Broad Street
Hopewell, New Jersey 08525

Published simultaneously in Canada by
Penguin Books Canada Ltd., Ontario
Printed in the United States of America

Photograph credits: "Richard Pryor" © Bettmann; "Joan Rivers" ©
Catherine McGann; "Sandra Bernhard" and "Members of Slant" ©
Richard Mitchell; "Emo Philips" and "David Letterman" © Sylvia Plachy;
"Danny Hoch," "Holly Hughes," and "Lois Weaver and Peggy Shaw" ©
Dona Ann McAdams. Cover photo of Reno by Dona Ann McAdams: 1991
Benefit Performance for Planned Parenthood at P.S. 122, New York, NY, ©
1996 Dona Ann McAdams/*Caught in the Act*, Aperture. All photographs
printed by permission of the photographer.

Library of Congress Cataloging-in-Publication Data
Stone, Laurie.
      Laughing in the dark : a decade of subversive
    comedy / Laurie Stone.—1st ed.
          p.   cm.
      Includes index.
      ISBN 0-88001-474-1
      1. Stand-up comedy—United States. 2. Comedians—United
    States—Biography. 3. Comedy—History and criticism.   I. Title.
    PN1969.C65S76   1997
    792.2'3'0973—dc21   96-37636

Designed by Barbara Aronica
The text of this book is set in Baskerville
9 8 7 6 5 4 3 2 1
FIRST EDITION 1997

For Gardner

Thanks to the comedians who made me laugh; to my witty, attentive editors at the *Village Voice*: Vince Aletti, Erika Munk, Richard Goldstein, Jeff Salamon, and Ross Wetzsteon; to Alan Turkus, my bright, encouraging editor at The Ecco Press.

CONTENTS

INTRODUCTION   Cracking Up   xi

One   Comedy Veterans: Classic, Still Trucking,
and Sometimes Forgettable   3

Two   Modern Wild Cards: High-Wire Iconoclasts,
Risk-Surfing Hipsters, and Political Provocateurs
24

Three   Lunatic Fringe: Clowns and Character Assassins
Who Detonate from Inside a Persona or a Series
of Alters   57

Four   Performance Trance Channelers and Puppet-
Masters of the Character Gallery   93

Five   Comedy Confessors: Stand-up Analysands, Auto-
biographers, and Reporters from the Gut   125

Six   Outstanding and Outwitting: Gay Stand-ups,
Troupes, Soloists, and Drag Racers   157

Seven   Postmodern Clowning: Spiking Simple Pleasures
199

Eight   TV: Comedy Tubular and Wired   238

Name Index   283

INTRODUCTION

Cracking Up

Richard Pryor

It's 1980something, and I'm in a small, art-friendly theater in New York—say La MaMa, or P.S. 122, or Dance Theater Workshop. The lights come up on a lone figure, perhaps a woman wearing a cowboy hat and sitting on a stool, or a guy in black with a rubber nose. There are props in the background, maybe a map, or a screen for projections, or a clown's trunk, or a clothesline hung with costumes. The lighting is stark and atmospheric, the electronic tape pulsing intriguingly, the haircuts clipped as topiaries, the movements razor edged.

Soon begins a rap about daddy's drinking, or the slim pickings in arts grants, or the way lovers get sadistic after they move in. The bleating is uttered in italics, as if copping to complaining turns it into commentary, or into theater, and the performer starts to give off a nervous tang, realizing no one is fooled. I stay, because I'm reviewing for the *Village Voice*. I don't feel aggrieved, because, hey, I'm getting paid, but I shift into flotation-tank mode and think: There are comedians in clubs doing better monologues than this.

I suggest to my editors that I treat stand-up comedy as solo theater, saying I want only to cover people who make me laugh. My editors say go ahead. I begin filing pieces about Sandra Bernhard, Emo Philips, and Judy Tenuta when they're relatively unknown, and soon talent bookers are calling to clue me to innovative acts.

I'm still writing about theater, seeing performance artists and character actors and one-person shows, and, amateurism notwithstanding, it's a yeasty time, the downtown clubs wafting a democratic, unregulated atmosphere—like the freedom of early internet and public access TV, where anyone can publish fantasy and opinion, anyone can beam a version of *Wayne's World* from their bedroom. Part of the surge in solo work is fueled by economics. Solo shows are cheap to mount and transport, and they don't depend on producers. It's no accident that they multiply during a time when public money for theater companies is drying up and when New York City's Mayor Koch, rather than subsidizing small theaters, makes it possible for developers to devour their property.

Downtown performers create or plug into hole-in-the-wall outlets like WOW Café, 8BC, Limbo Lounge, and the Pyramid Club. These artists would not otherwise find backing, because they are females and minorities, or their work isn't commercial, or it's deemed untouchable because it's gay, or repellent for injecting pain and violence in the raw forms of self-mutilation and simulated shit-tantrums, using slathered chocolate and yams. A lot of this work is infantile and desperate, a kind of group diary of primaling and flashing, but every art form needs a playpen.

At the same time, the Lower East Side hosts image theater groups and other eruptions rumbling around the globe. At La MaMa, especially, international soloists and ensembles appear, infusing downtown with Asian and African theater and dance, European and Chinese circus, and avant-garde forms inspired by Artaud and Grotowski—among them the wildly personal dream plays of Thadeusz Kantor. Over time, performance artists who have entered the ranks from dance and visual art figure out that they need writers, and performers whose bent is autobiography learn to move while talking. There is a dawning sense that rants are self-indulgent and that shock is one-minute theater.

The growth in comedy, on the other hand, is driven not by a grassroots initiative but by money. The organizers are club owners and producers scouting product. Comedy is showbiz, which means bucks. In the late seventies and early eighties, comedy expands, boosted as the new rock 'n' roll—at a time when rock isn't snarling and won't grow fangs again until new wave and grunge. People go out to laugh and get wasted. Comedy spaces mushroom around the country, so that where once there were only scores of rooms, thousands crop up on strip malls, in shopping centers, in the back rooms of pizza joints.

Now being a stand-up isn't a vestige of vaudeville and Borscht Belt tummling, as it was for Alan King and Buddy Hackett, nor, for the most part, is it an impassioned calling, as it was for Lenny Bruce and Richard Pryor. It becomes a career choice, a way to package talent—to nail a development deal, a sitcom part. Stand-up at this time does share with early performance a freewheeling, anyone-can-get-up energy, and there's some truth to the adage that everyone has five minutes of material. In stand-up, while there's more cloning than experimenting, as the numbers swell, so does the crop of originals.

In searching for talent, I put aside the categories performance art, one-person theater piece, and stand-up; don't care if the venue is a performance space, a theater, or a nightclub. Sass and craft are my criteria, and in addition to finding them in performance I see them regularly with stand-ups, few of whom have captured critical attention, all of whom yearn for their skills to be acknowledged.

In my column *Laughing in the Dark,* begun in 1987, I primarily champion stand-up, but I write about performance in the *Voice*'s theater section and follow TV and movies in their respective domains. Like most popular entertainment, the majority of comedy reassures rather than frightens or arouses—and has no other ambition—so I don't cover it routinely. In the column I mostly report on live acts, where comedian and audience riff off each other, creating a frisson that heightens the power dynamic existing in all theater—the actor at once commanding and naked. I don't write as an expert or as a guide for consumers. I try to re-create my experience on the page, letting readers decide if they'll be similarly juiced. I cheer candor and foolishness. I seldom annihilate, though I do bite the ankles of a few scoundrels with clout.

This book, which collects my pieces, isn't a survey of stand-up, solo, or satire but something closer to what all heartfelt criticism probably amounts to: autobiography. It tracks my tastes and enthusiasms through a decade of comic performance, follows my inclinations as I scope performers, talk with downtown presenters in their scruffy T-shirts, and with uptown power brokers wearing Rolex watches and Armani suits. I am in New York at exactly the time when stand-up and solo not only blossom but cross-pollinate. Performance artists learn timing and delivery from stand-ups, and comedians develop solo evenings, structured around themes rather than rat-a-tat joke sprays. When HBO and Comedy Central enter the scene with so much air time to fill, they become voracious and adventurous presenters, the first to broadcast gay and minority talent in a concerted way—producing specials for, among others, Reno, Marga Gomez, and John Leguizamo. Increasingly, there is a healthy blurring of boundaries between the avant-garde and showbiz, an openness to queers, an uncensoring of language and outlaw subjects.

■ ■ ■

My theory of comedy is simple: You laugh, you don't laugh. For me, the goals inspiring the richest comedy are the same steering all art: to say what is usually suppressed and also speak truthfully. The words that are usually muzzled are those that defy established values and undermine bases of power. To speak truthfully, a performer has to strip off defenses, in other words, forgo his or her alliance with authority. Watching such acts, we're given license to admit our own puniness, terror, and dreams. Laughter, like a sneeze, isn't deliberated but bursts forth, almost always from a sense of wickedness. Laughing, we trip over our own muffled desires and aggressions—like the kick of seeing another shmendrik in pain. As Mel Brooks puts it, "Comedy is when you accidentally fall off a cliff and die. Tragedy is when I have a hangnail."

We want to see lunatics running the asylum, those who've been kicked doing the stomping. Through irony, the distasteful and dangerous become approachable, even palatable. But vulnerability is missing from a lot of material presented as taboo-bashing. "Goy" jokes told by Jews, black jokes by whites, gay jokes by straights may generate sadistic glee, but this material is really safe and conventional, inviting audiences to cozy up to authority and cave in to, rather than recognize, their fears. The same is true of comedy that sneers at everything, serving sarcasm as satire, emissions from a school-yard bully with no point of view, no knowledge. Nonetheless offensiveness is always, in a way, what excites us: to hear unsettling truth we can't fend off. The most stirring comedy mixes pain with pleasure, its pleasure in part de-riving from its pain.

Like sex, comedy is irrepressible, laughter libidinous, though comedi-ans themselves are often sexually masked, funneling aggression through language rather than their bodies. They need to brandish the riding crop of their aggression, lest the audience—always potentially a heckling mob—goes for their throats. Sex fuels on fantasy, comedy on anxiety. Overt sex mostly dissolves comedy, and comedy reroutes sex. Name a really id-rock-ing comedian, male or female. Maybe Dennis Miller, who is as helplessly vain as he is acerbic. Libido rises off him, but in most comedians it's shad-owy, and sexual starving is part of their bond with us. They admit they don't get no satisfaction, and we let them stand apart, assume control, make us come—in the way that laughing is a little like getting off: the spasm, the exhalation of air, the squealing.

Plenty of performance art isn't comic, and I don't include that work here. At the *Voice,* usually my colleague C. Carr covered it with wit and in-sight in her column *On Edge.* Among the omitted work is body art, where performers mutilate themselves or otherwise subject themselves to extreme duress. In one performance piece, Chris Burden had himself shot in the arm by a friend. The artist Stelarc, in a series of "suspension" pieces, had eighteen fishhooks inserted into his flesh, to which were attached ropes and pulleys, and he would have himself hoisted in the air—in one event, out a window over East 11th Street. The performer Ulay sewed his mouth shut with a needle and thread. Linda Montano and Teching Hsieh remained tied together by an eight-foot rope for a year. Ron Athey, who is HIV posi-tive, stages rituals in which he carves his skin and that of other participants with a knife, drawing blood, blotting the designs on paper, and pinning the monoprints to a clothesline.

Though comedy encompasses pain, sometimes pain doesn't admit comedy. The gore in these enactments is closer to the horror of torture and the trance states of erotic surrender and dominance, aggression channeled through eros rather than a variety of libidinous streams. In his smart, richly researched history of laughter *Sudden Glory,* Barry Sanders posits two see-sawing strains of social control in medieval culture that continue to resonate: carnival and Lent. Carnival, a primary source of subversive comedy, is, in Sanders's words, "a festival of fools, organized by peasants, of the sort that constantly threatened to flip the medieval world topsy-turvy by sending boys to the throne as bishops, and by handing women the scepter as rulers of the realm." Carnival is a fart in the face of established rule, but it serves church and government by providing a safety valve for grievance. Needing to contain the fart—to curb its sting and range—the church contrives Lent, a period in which meat is forbidden and eating curtailed. The result, literally, is a lot less shit.

Body art evokes Lent rather than carnival. It is hunger art, a theater of anorexia, piercing, and marking, where feelings of powerlessness are reversed so that the sufferer calls the shots. Whether or not specific artists mean to convey this, body art acknowledges the erotic satisfactions of pain and reclaims them from religion, which routes sacrifice and torture away from horniness into holiness. Athey acknowledges the sideshow appeal of his pieces, describing a show called *4 Scenes in a Harsh Life* "as an exploration into fetishism" taken from "tattoo obsessions, scarification, terminal illness, and primitive ritual juxtaposed against leather daddies, sexism, white weddings, IV drug use and evangelism."

Laughter in such a context perhaps cancels its transgressive thrust, but it isn't unprecedented and was woven with startling doubleness into the work of Bob Flanagan. Flanagan, who died recently of cystic fibrosis, was born into a life of painful medical invasions due to his disease, and turned his stage into an operating theater, impaling himself with needles and nails and reaping erotic goodies from his suffering, as a form of mastery. Freely admitting to his masochism, Flanagan could include it among his motivations. In a piece he wrote called "Needles," he describes sticking pins in his penis, "thick and purple, bobbing in front of me like a festive party balloon just begging to be popped." Though Flanagan lent his edge play an antic air, most of his self-tortures were not intentionally funny, and yet, in his case, pain skitters on the edge not only of pleasure but of irony.

For the most part, the theater of starving and hurting seeks transcendence from limits. It strives for resurrection and remodeling, railing against death, packaging, boundaries, the human suit requisitioned at birth. Extreme acts describe a yearning to bust out of categories that shrink us, allotting, let's say, only one gender or sexuality per grunt. Body art seems allied with transgender warriors, who disclaim their gender assignments, and with cheerleaders for pansexuality, who think the labels gay and straight false. In a sense, tattoo heads, piercing junkies, transsexuals, and cross-dressers enact a kind of performance simply by exhibiting their tastes.

Comedy is just as interested in multiplicity, snuffling out the labile nature of our moods, but comedy does not believe all limits can be transcended. Instead it embraces ambivalence that can't be resolved. Comedy knows that body artists, no matter what they claim and whatever else they express, are getting off on peril and harm. Comedy accepts that we are divided—beasts with minds—and sees that deviousness, selfishness, and our other drives and appetites will ultimately exhaust our puny human restraints. Comedy thinks it's sad and hilarious when something can't be controlled. Comedy accepts tragedy, knowing that life is finite, that death—not resurrection—is breathing down our necks at every turn.

■ ■ ■

What we laugh at during any period is a soulprint of the age. The pieces I've collected chronicle satiric targets during Reagan/Bush, Clinton, the age of AIDS, the Cold War's finale, the intensifying culture wars, the rise of global net surfing, the infotainment meltdown, the O.J. blitz, and on and on. Comedy expands during the Reagan/Bush years, a time when minority ills worsen. Comedy can function as bread and circuses, a distraction from the real. But I named my column *Laughing in the Dark* because, in addition to honoring Nabokov, the laughter reverberating off this often bleak landscape sounded nervous.

While the poor are struggling for food and housing, in entertainment the center becomes more accommodating to the margins. Increasing numbers of minority artists throw shade over the culture—among them Richard Pryor, Whoopi Goldberg, Marsha Warfield, Eddie Murphy, Chris Rock, the brothers Wayans and Wynans, John Leguizamo, Culture Clash, Marga Gomez, and Dael Orlandersmith. Of the group, Pryor and Goldberg carve the scene with the most originality. Although by the mid-eighties, Pryor has already leaked his genius into drugs, self-loathing, and limp movies, his influence on comic performance—his combination of rage, vulnerability, and ironic detachment—can't be overstated. His concert films of the seventies, *Wanted: Richard Pryor Live in Concert* and *Live on the Sunset Strip*, sway over the scene of subversive comedy like sheltering palms.

Coming up in the black and tan clubs of the Midwest, where blacks and whites mingle, Pryor sees forerunners in Redd Foxx, Dick Gregory, Godfrey Cambridge, and Bill Cosby. But in 1963, working in New York for the first time and meeting George Carlin, he's turned on to Lenny Bruce, and Pryor feels unleashed to throw over censors, both in the tribe and in himself. He evolves a comedy of wounds and nakedness, exposing social cons and his own deviousness, the persona sweet and wild, crazy like a fox and like a kid who has never been loved enough.

"Tricks used to come through our neighborhood," he says in one routine, evoking his childhood in Peoria, where his grandmother ran a whorehouse. "That's where I first met white people. They came down to our neighborhood and helped the economy. I could've been a bigot, you know what I mean? I could've been prejudiced. I met nice white men. They said, 'Hello, little boy. Is your mother home? I'd like a blow job.' I wonder what would happen if niggers went to white neighborhoods doing that shit. 'Hey, man, your mama home? Tell the bitch we want to fuck!' "

Goldberg, a generation younger than Pryor, first gains attention in performance, with a gallery of characters. The freshest is Fontaine, a black male ex-junkie with a Jewish stand-up mouth, a gruff rasp, and a street swagger, who plays a bold game of chicken with gender, sexuality, class, race, and ethnicity. Goldberg has models: Mae West and Bessie Smith, also Barbra Streisand and Bette Midler, phenoms who, above all, remain true to idiosyncrasy. But Goldberg also seems like nothing we've seen before: a black woman who isn't beautiful declaring her animal magnetism, brains, and acting power.

Like Madonna, Goldberg is more incendiary as a cultural figure than as an entertainer. In Goldberg's case, this is less for lack of talent than a scarcity of vehicles as racy as she is. She hosts award shows, ad libs cleverly, and declares her left-wing alliances as if it were her citizenly right. Her life is her edgiest performance, including her show-stopping romance with Ted Danson, who is cast as her white goddess, snared and paraded the way that Richard Pryor and Sammy Davis, Jr., flashed their babes. But Goldberg spins the history anew, not only because she's female, but because she doesn't look taken.

When a skinny black guy wins a gorgeous blonde woman, the assumption—maybe racist, or sizist, or accurate—is that he bought her. In some sense the joke is on the man. Danson is already rich and famous; he's with Whoopi only because he loves her. She works the media so she's scoring not a white guy but a cute guy—the ugly duckling, having morphed into an eagle, claiming her due. If ever she felt self-hatred about race, she has been freed of it. Race makes her wry about the world: the division between how we are seen and how we see ourselves.

During this period, the mainstream is queered, too, thanks to the chutzpah and ingenuity of performers such as Bloolips, Reno, Sandra Bernhard, Pomo Afro Homos, Funny Gay Males, the Five Lesbian Brothers, Lea DeLaria, John Epperson, and Split Britches. AIDS colors everything, as it does for many straights in this age, the illness working as a raw space for projection. For some it's a new cover for homophobia, for others a bridge to identifying.

Performance artists dive into the subject. Karen Finley mourns and rages in her dirge, *We Keep Our Victims Ready.* Tim Miller, in his solo *Naked Breath,* strolls a street on the Lower East Side and flashes to "a thousand beds, the flow of blood, and the possibilities of connection." In Michael Rush's piece *Here Everything Still Floats,* AIDS isn't mentioned, and yet it is the medium in which this eerie, touching movement-theater collage undulates and strokes. "And what else do you remember about that visit to the man you called your friend?" asks a voice, prompting a flood of detail about a man with a blue blanket "which covered most of his body, including half his face."

The ruminations aren't all somber. Michael Klein's powerful memory solo, *10,000 Hands Have Touched Me,* by turns lyrical and raw, treks sex shadowed by the in-your-face mortality of AIDS. "Dogs made me queer, I'm sure of it, loving dogs is effortless, my early loves of men were effortless," he purrs in this cagey exploration of erotic nature. In *Virgins and Other Myths,* Colin Martin recalls being told he has AIDS—because he's sick, and he's slept with guys, and he's in Pittsburgh during the early stages of the epidemic, this is what his doctors conclude. He doesn't learn that the diagnosis is wrong for several months, but the reprieve makes no dent on his career as a sexual obsessive . . . or does it? he wonders in his poignant, raucous monologue.

Because of AIDS and despite AIDS, there is an urgency to out gay experience in performance and comedy. Queer Theater forebears Jack Smith, the director of the avant-garde film classic *Flaming Creatures,* and Jimmy Camicia, impresario of the ragtag troupe Hot Peaches, raise the postshame curtain on a carnival of gender-bending and genre-crunching clowns, foremost among them Charles Ludlam, the innovative founder of the Ridiculous Theatrical Company. Ludlam begets such divine demon spawn as Charles Busch and Holly Hughes.

Busch, a dreamy Long Island kid addicted to *The Million Dollar Movie,* on afternoon TV—where he mainlined Barbara Stanwyck, Bette Davis, and Joan Crawford, begins in the East Village at the Limbo Lounge and quickly blossoms—with the long-running shows *Vampire Lesbians of Sodom* and *Psycho Beach Party*—from cult guy to mass cult guy. Busch doesn't slum in femininity like the majority of pre-Stonewall dragsters. He plays feisty feminists, and his portrayals are affectionate. He not only enjoys the femme part of himself, he sees it as the source of theater, emotional expressiveness. His costumes don't disguise that he's a man, for in his art, to go from boy to girl or girl to boy is not an Outward Bound experience, an act of slumming, or a chance to go native; it's a pass through a door inside the self.

Hughes hits the Village from Saginaw, Michigan, a geography she describes as Republican, straight, and tight-lipped. Knowing early that she is bent gives her a *Blue Velvet* vantage point, so she spies deviance between virgin blades of grass. Eventually escaping to New York, she waitresses at WOW, that home for wayward girls who like other girls and who come out into a life of double crime: homosexuality and theater. As a writer and performer, Hughes devises an original idiom of noir slapstick and pulp punning that permits longing and melancholy. She hits the performance scene in the early eighties, when, as C. Carr observes in her book *On Edge,* "lesbians are trying to create something out of the nothing that is their birthright. And do it with verve instead of the sappiness that runs rampant in Womyn's Culture."

Hughes's definition of performance art, supplied in *Clit Notes,* her collected plays and monologues, aptly applies to the collage form she helps shape. It generally includes "pop culture, high art, spectacle, big hair, substance abuse, and pussy." In order to appreciate the action, she advises, "you've got to imagine yourself sitting . . . far enough back so that what's happening in the audience and what's going on onstage are all part of the show."

Capturing WOW's flavor, she writes, "Most of us were refugees from lesbian feminism who had gone AWOL from other collectives. WOW was safe not only from the male gaze but also from a feminism convulsed by

the sex wars. No one had to reclaim butch and femme; no one had re-
nounced it. No one worried about losing funding; no one got any. . . . No
one made work that tried to convince straight people how nice we were.
In fact, a lot of the characters onstage have been stolen from heterosexual
nightmares: lesbians as hypersexual, as unrepentant outlaws, vampires,
shameless . . . perverts."

In *The Well of Horniness,* Hughes invents Garnet McClit, "seasoned
sapphic flatfoot." In *Dress Suits to Hire* and *World Without End,* she charts the
country of brazen outcasts—of butches and femmes in smoldering
clinches—saluting defiance as this queer nation's banner without soft-pedaling damage. When she sounds Freudian notes, they come out as if delivered by Groucho.

In the eighties, the stand-up team Funny Gay Males, consisting of Bob
Smith, Jaffe Cohen, and Danny McWilliams, and out lesbians such as Lea
DeLaria and Suzanne Westenhoefer don't have a prayer of bookings outside gay venues. Now they appear on cable TV and aren't defanged. They
break through to network, too, where they're more likely to be censored, but
even truncated exposure creates a conversation with the culture—enlarging
the framework of who is allowed to laugh, who is included in the joke.

Activists, who've for decades championed art that represents society's
actual diversity, grease these changes. And the changes, in turn, heat the
culture wars waged against this diversity by Jesse Helms, Pat Robertson,
Donald Wildmon, and their ilk. Theirs is a crusade to reconsecrate repression—remuzzle carnival. Robert Mapplethorpe, who photographs flowers
as if they are sexual organs and S/M acts as if they are flowers, is branded
the Antichrist. It isn't a slander but it does get a planned exhibit of his work
canceled by the Corcoran Gallery in Washington, D.C., and an exhibition
of his photographs in Cincinnati raided by local police.

The National Endowment for the Arts suffers, as do artists and presenters supported by public money. Hughes becomes one of the "NEA four,"
along with performers Tim Miller, Karen Finley, and John Fleck, whose arts
grants are revoked in 1990 by then NEA chairman John Frohnmayer.
Frohnmayer plays hit man for the right's campaign against art that unclosets
the body, especially the body that belongs to queers, women, and people of
color. There is no minimizing the lasting damage of this chilling effect, but
like sex and comedy the multiculti wave, once it begins to rise, isn't crushed.

Performers bare not only their bodies but their lives: They not only

come out sexually, but also out family secrets, producing a theater of autobiography and self-disclosure. Dishing and peeping are hardly new, but an
unprecedented disinhibiting is afoot, coupled with a yearning for first-per-
son stories. Performance art and confessional comedy are smelling salts for
this awakening and are, in turn, shaken to a new alertness by the Oprahiza-
tion of America and by a flood of memoirs that begin swelling bookstores.

Many of the disclosures splashing from performance art are more
drainage than revelation. It's not enough that creepy things have happened, since everyone's life, poked at enough, looks like a tabloid horror
show. What matters is the degree of insight and drama presented.

The best pieces in this genre tell stories about how we live now and are
devoted to their truths, not merely to self-display, though that is part of the in-
centive, the excitement of going public with secrets and shameful emotions.
Perhaps every story worth telling is a dare, a kind of pornography, composed
of whatever we think we're not supposed to say, for fear of being drummed
out, found out, pointed at. The challenge is to enter an ego-free zone, cleared
of self-importance and whining, to walk out naked and speak intimately.

Over the years, Hughes, Pryor, Spalding Gray, Josh Kornbluth,
Marga Gomez, John O'Keefe, and Lisa Kron have learned to do this.
These artists set up the self as a lab rat and mount folly and error as exhib-
its that can be examined. With candor, these tellers transform blunders into
the only shapely and reliably honorable offering that can be made of such
material: art.

It's no wonder that the most accomplished work in this genre is comic,
for comedy is what sounds after psychological mulching and detachment
are achieved. Still, the range of personal stories is wonderfully diverse. Josh
Kornbluth's *The Mathematics of Change* is rollicking narrative, mapping his
career as a math prodigy and his fateful intersection with "the wall" of be-
fuddlement during his freshman year at Princeton. In *Spoke Man*, John
Hockenberry, rendered paraplegic from an auto accident at nineteen,
views his predicament as a kind of Outward Bound challenge. By turns
cocky, poetic, and vulnerable, he rolls so deeply into his personal story—becoming a Middle East frontline reporter for NPR, ABC and now NBC—
that it becomes large.

Spalding Gray's *Gray's Anatomy*, an installment of the monologuist's
autobiography, is hilarious, harrowing, and masterful, as our guide, stricken
with a serious eye ailment, transports us to medical hell. With his eyesight

ablur, he sees surfaces and their underbellies more clearly than ever before. Though for Lisa Kron, pride and appetite present irresistible dares, tangling her in spaghetti strands of desire, she transforms her mortifications into studies in irony. In *Some Notes from the Midwest and Abroad,* she juggles big and little horrors, alternating between a visit to Auschwitz with her father, whose parents were killed there, and a Kafkaesque episode with her frustrating extended family as they visit an amusement park.

■ ■ ■

The past ten years witness not only a boom in live comedy but, recently, a thinning of venues, as new attention-candies—cable TV, videos, and virtual entertainments—lure screen junkies. Late-night is decentralized with the retirement of Carson—not a minute too soon, his show having calcified at the time it sailed off on an ice floe. Letterman and Leno stage a pissing match for top dog but manage at least for a while not to drown alternatives: the fawning-but-original Arsenio Hall and the goofy/sexy hosts Jon Stewart and Greg Kinnear.

While performance artists showcase themselves in five-dollar productions, showbiz grosses more from big-budget comedy films and from TV sitcoms than any other genres. The films tailored for Robin Williams, Chevy Chase, Steve Martin, and Mike Myers make bucks, but the performers lose out artistically. Martin exercises his stand-up persona in such gems as *The Man with Two Brains* and *All of Me,* but in most of his movies his sublimely eccentric, dark comic presence isn't around. Compare Martin's films to those of Chaplin and Keaton—Woody Allen, too—where the performer's style is honored above everything else. The same bucks-driven spirit wastes other comedians, their movies dulling the comic edge that defined them. Bill Murray fares better than most, especially working with writer/director Harold Ramis, who in *Ghostbusters* and *Groundhog Day* clothes Murray's needy weasel in inspired motley.

With Hollywood movies so often churning out inoffensive product and trading heart for the bottom line, biting comedy sharpens in independent films, on live stages, and on TV. It's difficult to generalize about why some comedians register on medium cool and others need to work live. The comics who are clever in small bytes—Jay Leno is a good example—tend to evanesce on live stages, and stand-ups like David Steinberg, who thrives on audience give-and-take and spends time developing his themes, appear muted on the small screen.

For other comedians, leaving stand-up and sketch comedy proves a boon. While Tim Allen is grittier in stand-up than on his sitcom, *Home Improvement,* the opposite is true for Jon Stewart, who, as a stand-up, showed only a sliver of the sexual mischief he served up nightly as host of his now-defunct talk show. The same is the case for Roseanne, Jerry Seinfeld, and Garry Shandling. Seinfeld's competent but uninspired club act gave no hint of the brilliantly rendered, phobic solitary into which he would morph, in collaboration with Larry David, on his sitcom.

Seinfeld evolves into a great antiromance, arguing against coupledom, marriage, parenthood—all the conformist pressures to be happy and normal. Which doesn't mean its crew of arrested singles is protected by their creators. *Seinfeld* remains trained on their feelings of failure, their yearnings, their relentless humiliations. This is a world in which the smallest desires subject one to terrible risk: It's unsafe to park your car, buy soup, throw away a wristwatch, give your parents a present.

But probably nothing more boldly turns TV comedy into art than *The Larry Sanders Show.* Shandling's character knows how fear of humiliation can turn into a bludgeon—knows how good it feels to sneer and pull ahead in the power derby and how bad it feels, too, how empty. This insight drains Shandling's own anger and doubt, turning them into comic targets. His series, pumped by a dazzling ensemble cast, is a shrewd satire of talk shows and presents what well may be the hippest and most savage take anywhere on the pecking order of the workplace.

Sanders is HBO's most exuberant fuck-you to the networks—no more Kremlin, no more all-mighty big-three networks, no more Carson. The show probably couldn't have been made five years before its 1992 debut; the players wouldn't have risked mauling the only hands with kibble. Remember, Shandling used to sub regularly when Carson vacationed, and his name was much bruited as Carson's successor. Good thing he chose not to do the real thing and opted for the true thing.

■ ■ ■

In these pages I visit several Just For Laughs festivals, North America's biggest talent supermarket and summer camp for major players. Power in comedy is concentrated in a remarkably small number of people, among them agent Sam Cohn; movie producers Rollins & Joffe; Budd Friedman, founder of the Improv; Bob Morton, longtime producer of the Letterman show and now an executive of Worldwide Pants, and host and taste-maker Dave himself. Clubs teem with male and female Letterman clones, all equipped with sneers and smug detachment. The money in comedy is a double-edged sword, promoting copycat conservatism but also adventurousness—at least on cable TV, where programmers gamble on fringe artists and introduce them to mass audiences.

The scene has never been more varied, especially since solo performance and stand-up have leaned toward each other and reanimated comedy traditions. A breed of zanies that includes Robin Williams (a spiritual offspring of Jonathan Winters), Steve Martin, and Jango Edwards, the founder of Europe's Festival of Fools, rescues slapstick from innocence while preserving its childishness. Pratfalling nearby are neo-drag actors Charles Busch, La Gran Scena Opera company, Lois Weaver, Peggy Shaw, and Carmelita Tropicana. These performers can imagine anything and not despise themselves for it. Their drag personas, symbolizing the forbidden leap for everyone, invite audiences to indulge their fantasies of otherness without minimizing the terror.

The portraits drawn by character actors Harry Shearer, Catherine O'Hara, Janeane Garofalo, and Martin Short are so nuanced, they play like living Daumiers. (You'd need a heart of stone not to chuckle at Short's self-important Katharine Hepburn—"Booore, booore, booore.") Other comics inhabit a single character. As Cliff Arquette once portrayed the foxy yokel Charlie Weaver, Don Novello tweaks orthodoxy and ritual inside the celebrity-adoring, media-hip priest Father Guido Sarducci. Stand-ups Emo Philips, Judy Tenuta, and Gilbert Gottfried shape single personas, too—respectively the sadistic nerd, the fey dominatrix, and the young old Jew—but these characters bear the same names as the performers, a comedy style harking to Mae West, W. C. Fields, and the Marx Brothers. The Dada depressives Steven Wright, Margaret Smith, and Rodney Dangerfield come closer to presenting unvarnished selves, but for them surrealism maintains a thin fourth wall.

On the other hand, high-wire comics like Richard Pryor, Sandra Bernhard, Richard Belzer, Bill Hicks, Joan Rivers, and Will Durst—all children of Lenny Bruce—strip without the net of any apparent characters.

Pryor and Bernhard work confessionally, exposing their vanity, sexual rage, and solipsism; their frankness startles to consciousness anyone veiling similar frailties. Belzer and Durst are among today's few articulate and passionate political comedians. Others are Harry Shearer, Jimmy Tingle, Reno, Dennis Miller, Jim Morris, Lewis Black, and the late Bill Hicks. Belzer and Durst hiss like populist rattlers, spraying democratic vitriol. Their sets depend on their ability to seduce and threaten, and when they fly—one-upping hecklers and invading privacy like kamikaze voyeurs—the results are as electric as soaring jazz improvs.

Chapters in this book cheer, as well, storytellers like John O'Keefe, monologuists like Reno, character channelers like Danny Hoch, Dael Orlandersmith, Eric Bogosian, and Jeffrey Essmann, ingenious new vaudevillians like Penn & Teller, *comedia* clown Geoff Hoyle, and mesmerizing uncategorizables like juggler/dancer/sculptor Michael Moschen and physical comedy genius, the lip-synching drag performer John Epperson a.k.a. Lypsinka. With his Dada phone calls, Arlene Dahl wig, and Vera-Ellen nothing body, Epperson launches lip-synching into satire that admits infatuation, his features dancing through the Kabuki makeup, his physical control as dazzling as that of great jugglers and clowns.

One of the pleasures of writing about comedy is coming upon relatively little known talents, such as Jango Edwards and Gilbert Gottfried (before he became a Disney voice). Often, they're too disturbing to be packaged for mass consumption. The clowning of Edwards, who works with a four-piece rock band, ranges from neo-Marceauean mime pieces to raucous stripteases, lurching toward the invasive antics of the Kipper Kids. Some of his bits are ancient: paper that sticks to one hand, then the other; cups with wills of their own. He offers a gob of chewed food to a woman in the audience, his face bright with hope and malice, his giant baby-brain calculating its next lunge toward pleasure, foreseeing its next defeat. Edwards levitates the pain of our subservience to body parts. He butts against the limitation of having only one gender, revealing the uncomfortable messiness of boundary-blurred existence and the clean coffin-space of order and certainty.

While Edwards draws a psychological landscape, strewn with impulses and drives, Gottfried presents inspired comedy of manners. A small, rumpled guy in his forties, he twists the mike stand, narrows his eyes to slits, and turns into an old Jewish crank. Like Jackie Mason, Gottfried makes the

world into an old Jew. Serving time in a minimum-security prison, the con-
vict's punishment is to be called each day, "We're coming to deliver the
couch. Will you be there?" Like Mel Brooks's two-thousand-year-old man,
Gottfried's character goes way back in time. He says that if you flip the
pages of the Old Testament in one direction you get Jesus riding a horse
and in the other direction a fat lady with a hula hoop. "Back then, everyone
thought *she* would be the famous one." Like Billy Crystal, Gottfried identifies with the vulnerability and anxiety of being outside—the sense of events
eluding one's control. In South America, Gottfried's Jew is in a shop when
Hitler enters. He signals a photographer not to snap his picture, but it's too
late and he's captured with his arm in a *heil* salute. "That's the shot they *always* use," he whines.

    Gottfried reveals the poison of ethnocentrism. He dissects not only
Jewish racism but the impulse driving all bullies: including bully performers
like Andrew "Dice" Clay and Eddie Murphy in his gay-bashing days. Gottfried's device doesn't boomerang into anti-Semitism, because he goes after
hysteria, not Jews per se.

■ ■ ■

The pieces in this book grew as a conversation with readers and performers, like journal entries, where I would go back to themes and chew on
them. Many—like the ones about Richard Lewis and Garry Shandling—
capture an artist at a moment that is simultaneously particular and em-
blematic. They don't need elaboration. In other cases, I've updated or
situated a performer. It's exciting to discover stars in the raw. Some of the
now-famous performers you'll read about are recorded in debut outings—
John Leguizamo is one. It's interesting to compare his vision of his future
with what has come to pass.

    I've used the introductions to the chapters to continue kibitzing about
performers I did cover, and to add comments on some I didn't have a
chance to write about previously. I've added pieces down to the wire, including one on the debut of Rosie O'Donnell's refreshing talk show and a
review of Spalding Gray's latest monologue, *It's a Slippery Slope*. I've arranged the chapters by looking first at performers who occupy distinct
niches, such as stand-up, or performance art, or new vaudeville. The chapters progress into categories that reflect the blurring of these boundaries. A

performer like Ann Magnuson, for example, freely swims between hard-edged satire in downtown venues and a part on a sitcom—she played ultra-hip Catherine, Richard Lewis's boss, on *Anything But Love.*

The book maps the intermingling of stand-up and solo performance. We've arrived at a point when the bookstore A Different Light hosts performance evenings, when the 92nd Street Y, long a bastion of reserved, intellectual programs, includes nights with Joan Rivers, Joy Behar, and Reno, when Borscht Belt vet Mal Z. Lawrence plays Broadway and does cabaret at Tavern on the Green, when the Jewish Museum and the Whitney regularly schedule monologuists such as Deb Margolin, Richard Elovich, and Carla Kirkwood; when Julie Halston, a longtime member of Charles Busch's ensemble, now does a cabaret/stand-up act and is booked at Caroline's nightclub, when venerable Dixon Place, which started as presenter Ellie Covan's actual living room, is staging not only performance but plays.

The book provides a social history—albeit shaped by my sense of humor—of what we laughed at and who laughed at us during the past ten years. You don't have to read the entire thing cover to cover to catch these currents. Dip in, have a laugh, revisit a favorite performer or discover an innovator who never got hyped.

Originality and depth are as rare now as they have always been. There was only one Chaplin, one Jack Benny, one Lenny Bruce. Among younger performers, Danny Hoch looks like he has the heart and energy to keep challenging himself. I remember seeing him for the first time in 1993, at P.S. 122, where he did his solo *Some People.* Hip-hop music is blaring before the curtain, and then the lights go down, and in the dark we hear a radio DJ from the Caribbean inviting callers in a voice smooth and mellow as coconut milk, and the accent is perfect, every note, and when the lights come up there is this tall, gawky white kid, who is still convincing playing a black man. In another monologue, he is a Polish fixit-guy, fresh off the boat, trying desperately to communicate with the woman whose sink he is repairing. She has a cat, and he wants to tell her a story, but he has so few words his inarticulateness becomes the tale, and it is plangent with his hopes and the Dada nature of his transplanted existence.

Hoch grew up in Queens, a Jewish kid living in a section encompassing more than a dozen ethnic enclaves, and he picked up the various accents and styles, identifying with black and Latino culture, becoming a graffiti punk, a b-boy hanging in Washington Square Park. He comes by the identification authentically, but Hoch doesn't accept that at face value. He's interested in his Jewish roots, which go back to the Lower East Side, and he's lately been pondering the allure of minstrelsy—of race drag—and how the politics work when a white person plays someone of color and the other way around. Inevitably questions arise about boundaries, going native, colonization, passing—all of our desires to look inside each other's pants—the justice of which comes down to: I'll show you mine if you show me yours.

Hoch is a great mongrel: He fuses and remixes influences without blanding them out. Not just in terms of his ethnic embrace but also his grasp of performance styles—from Catskill's tummling, to stand-up, to dialect comedy, to Latin American and European clowning. Hoch and I talked after he returned from a trip to Cuba, where he performed his show, partly in Spanish, to acclaim. After that he was cast for a part on *Seinfeld* and wound up walking out. He was asked to play a character with a Latino accent, and in this context he thought it wrong, suggesting the show hire a Latino actor. I include our conversation, as well as two others with members of the performance community I find especially thoughtful. One is Mark Russell, who has been artistic director of P.S. 122 since it became a performance venue in the early eighties. There is also a conversation with Peggy Shaw, part of Split Britches and a queer theater stalwart from word one.

I started writing about comedy because I like to laugh. What a job. I'm still awed by the nakedness of the solo act. Since I began this trek, the culture's atmosphere has grown more tabloid. The upside is the zapping of sacred cows, but tabloidism is also cynical, making no distinction between the notable and the notorious and subjecting celebrities, regardless of what they stand for, to heedless exposure. Gleeful this may be, but it is knownothingism. Satire is the opposite of cynicism, because it thinks about its targets.

Laughing
in the
Dark

CHAPTER ONE

Comedy Veterans:
Classic, Still Trucking,
and Sometimes Forgettable

Joan Rivers

The veteran stand-ups playing Vegas, Tahoe, and Atlantic City trail min-strel shows, burlesque, vaudeville, music halls, the Borscht Belt, nightclubs. They are keepers of the monologue that is as old as cave schmoozing—reciting headlines about the day's bear hunt or giving a thumbs-up or -down to the latest antelope frieze. Inside stand-up are Shakespeare's confidential asides, Dickens's hamming, Wilde's camping, Twain's ironies, Ruth Draper's character studies, Noël Coward's talk-stories, Will Rogers's politi-cal takes, and Lord Buckley's jazz riffs. Stand-up is observation, confession, and the risk of waltzing out on a limb.

The advent of TV lofted comedians from radio and live stages to a new level of visibility, and many of the stand-ups gaining access after the war were Jews. Plenty of Jewish comedians had made it into the movies—Chaplin, Jack Benny, George Burns, the Marx Brothers—but they didn't play Jews. Maybe because of the war and the acknowledgment of anti-Semitism, postwar Jewish comics didn't mask their ethnicity, rather injected it into the mainstream. *The Ed Sullivan Show* served a smorgasbord of Jewish types, from tribal translators like Myron Cohen and Jackie Mason, to one-line joke machines like Henny Youngman, to antic physical clowns like Sid Caesar and Jerry Lewis, to Dada free-associators like Mel Brooks and Carl Reiner, to cerebral kvetchers like Shelley Berman and Woody Allen.

It was a rich brew, mixing with black comedians like Godfrey Cambridge and Dick Gregory, and with hip white guys who weren't Jewish, among them Jonathan Winters and George Carlin. Their music ripples through everyone now wielding a mike, and a lot of ancient shtick still sings. The anthology *20 Years of HBO Comedy* culled hilarious clips. Myron Cohen replays a conversation between two *alte cockers*. She: "What's by you the sex situation?" He: "Infrequently." She: "Is that one word or two?" Sophie Tucker has a man remark during sex, "You have no tits and a tight box." She: "Get off my back."

But most of the old crew still on the boards are museum pieces, their sets fueled by nostalgia, their audiences laughing at the memory of once having cracked up spontaneously. Their acts are church service and tent meeting, wafting ritual, call and response.

A couple of years ago at Michael's Pub, Sid Caesar and Imogene Coca revived routines from *Your Show of Shows*. The spectacle was sad, Caesar's gaunt cheeks showing the strain not only of his years away from comedy but of dying with gags that had once resounded. The team had nowhere new to go. Another night, at the New School, a panel of writers who had worked for Caesar—among them Brooks, Neil Simon, and Larry Gelbart—described the antic joy and sweating competition of those days. The clips aired were funny still, Caesar coming across as a bull, a dangerous id creature jabbering in nonsense languages and flipping facial takes like a master magician a deck of cards. As John Belushi would later, Caesar teetered on an edge of anxiety and aggression that was funneled into performing but threatened to explode into violence or deflate into depression.

I watched George Burns at ninety-three do a live set. He could still fire off zingers. He said the standing ovation at his entrance made him nervous.

"It should come at the end. Makes me wonder if you think I'll make it." He talked about reigniting his acting career at seventy-nine when he made *The Sunshine Boys*: "The most important thing about acting is honesty; if you can fake that, you've got it made." And he was wonderfully odd doing those arcane songs only he knew, crowding the words as if he were about to get the hook.

But his observational shtick died, based as it was on a framework that had curdled. In his world, females were dumb, and men liked them that way, so their sexual innuendoes could pass over the target's head. Burns's longtime partner Gracie Allen—like Lucille Ball after her—could command laughs because she was infantile, no threat. In his sense of sex, Burns came across coy, smutty, swooping under tables, peeking into toilets and under women's dresses.

His close friend Jack Benny, on the other hand, agilely surfed a myriad of eras, because he was always the fool, and his partner wasn't a dumb woman but a smart black man, Rochester, played brilliantly by Eddie Anderson. The two carved a variant on a classic bit from Roman comedy and Restoration farce: the wily servant and the vain lord. To me Benny is a lynchpin of subversive comedy. In one bit he gazes into the mirror wordlessly, after a long time declaring, "Gee, my teeth are beautiful." He perfected the art of using silence as a punch line, as in the classic routine where a robber demands, "Your money or your life," and Benny stands there, unruffled, until the thief pushes, and Benny sulks, "I'm thinking it over."

Benny didn't break character to wink that he wasn't really foppish and cheap. He endured his personality, as if the reward would be salvation from it. Groucho, too, transcended his time, because his clown, though lecherous, expected the disappointment he mostly reaped in romance and because his anarchy was mainly aimed at wealth and social pretension.

Most vets are dated by their visions of power and sex. The night I saw Burns he did Japanese jokes—"Sony is buying Columbia; they'll have to change the name to Corumbia. Washington's eyes will be getting narrower on the dollar bill." Bob Hope, on the program with Burns, weighed in with Japanese shtick, too: "An eye doctor tells a Japanese patient, 'You have cataracts.' 'No,' he says, 'I have a Lincoln Continental.'" Hope did gay jokes: "Two guys want to be cremated when they die and have their ashes mixed. Where will they go . . . in a fruit jar?"

The show *Catskills on Broadway* ran a few years, featuring Borscht Belt stalwarts. The high point was the set by Mal Z. Lawrence, who told a great joke: "A rabbi invites a blind priest to Passover dinner and places a piece of matzo on his plate. The priest runs his fingers over it—'Who wrote this shit?' " Lawrence was dead on detailing eaters at mountain resorts: men the size of sumo wrestlers favoring warm-up suits; women loading their handbags with Danish pastries, "for later." But like Jackie Mason's spiels, the evening was rife with Jewish complacency and contempt for women and minorities. Jews had foibles but were always adorable. Even Italian Dick Capri, a fixture on the Jewish circuit, treated Jews as the known world, while Others were unchartered, untrustworthy, unreal. The men spewed ugly women jokes, which would have been smug if they had been handsome but seemed reckless, considering they were, variously, bug-eyed, paunchy, and balding.

Mainly the vets still with us are men—Alan King, Don Rickles, and Carson (though he seldom performs these days), to name three with enduring careers. In their acts they talk to men. Women can listen, and women are invited to laugh if they can stomach chuckling at their own humiliation. King, Rickles, and Carson are like husbands who insult their wives at dinner parties, then nail the woman as a bad sport if she doesn't play along. To these men, wives are manipulative and grasping; women control the world. The kind of woman they boost (as well as impale) lacks the brains to want anything. She is all tit—like the procession of big-bosomed blondes who played the Matinee Lady to Carson's cheesy pitchman, Art Fern.

Carson receives no end of adulation, and a good deal of it is deserved. He introduced Barbra Streisand, Joan Rivers, and Bette Midler to the world, and he backed plenty of other talent. He is really funny with a monkey on his head or a cockatoo eyeing him down. But he ran an old boys' club—with sidekicks Ed McMahon and Doc Severinsen pretending to be stupider than they were, in order not to outshine him. He is a godfather in Tom Sawyer's clothing: cold and reserved, quick to take offense, demanding deference. To him sex is embarrassing, hence he loves dirty jokes. He wielded influence over comedy for thirty years, essentially a conservative, emotionally masked, more a recycler than an innovator, mediating eccentricity for the audience with his shocked—"Now that's *wild*"—indulgence of it. His politics weren't oppositional, rather tweaking of whatever policy prevailed, and he didn't book comedians with sharper fangs.

One night in June '88, when his writers were on strike, he hatched an idea. He had an armored car driven onto the stage, filled with small bills: a cool million. With eyes the size of saucers, he explained what a million was: "If you gave your wife a thousand dollars every day for spending money, she wouldn't come back for three years. A *billion* is when she wouldn't come back for three thousand years." Carson had a lottery, calling forth members of the audience. In a voice crackling with excitement, he told the men guarding the money to toss it on the stage, and to the first winner, a woman, he said, "You can pose next to it." To the second, a man, he said, "You can walk through it barefoot." And to the third, a blonde woman in a short dress, he quipped, "You can roll around in it naked. Ha, ha, just kidding. You can sit in it and *touch* it."

The winners, ensnared by the media moment, complied, but they were joyless. They looked appalled, embarrassed, disbelieving that Carson could so baldly flash his kinky fantasies.

Figures far more compelling than Carson didn't get to be king. Compare Carson to Steve Allen, who didn't mute his intelligence and who got down with, rather than presided over, his crew of zanies. Or Jack Paar, who was disturbing, spraying anxiety and longing—as Charles Grodin does now. Or the supremely wry and inventive Ernie Kovacs, a comedian who rode his taste for the surreal without truckling or translating. Not until early *Saturday Night Live,* in some inspired sketches with John Belushi and Bill Murray, would we see Kovacs's brand of irreverence regularly on the tube.

Lenny Bruce died of a heroin overdose on August 3, 1966, a few years after Carson assumed the reins of *The Tonight Show*—not that Bruce would ever have landed the job. Imagine it. Bruce entering bedrooms every night during the Vietnam War, wondering if the Pentagon isn't lying just a teeny bit with its inflated stats on Viet Cong casualties and deflation of U.S. deaths. Or Bruce reviewing new drugs as they hit the streets, or reporting live from Chicago during the '68 Democratic Convention, or mourning the deaths of the Kennedys and Martin Luther King, or booking Abbie Hoffman, Bobby Seale, and Angela Davis—or Patty Hearst in her incarnation as Tanya. She comes out with a machine gun and beret, and Bruce twists his neck stiffly and chuckles, "Now that's *wild.*"

Bruce's humor is the opposite of Carson's. It is unofficial, autobiographical, unconsoling. It is a concert from the margin, in his case Jewish and 'hood. It is about sexual wonder and admitted self-disgust. In one routine Bruce riffs on horniness, how it monsters up without regard to convenience or even pleasure. He's in an ambulance after an accident. He's bleeding, and his leg is hanging by a thread. But he notices the nurse, her breasts, the rest, and he has an erection. She's aghast, asking how this can be, and he bleats, as uncomprehending as she is, "I got hot. I got hot."

On the cover of an album from the early fifties, *The Sick Humor of Lenny Bruce*, the comedian is posed at a solitary picnic in a cemetery. He looks young and fresh, devilish and slim, in slacks and a sweater and an odd pair of thong sandals. The comedy holds up. In an airline routine, pilots too loaded to fly discuss their plight. "I don't dig heights," admits one. The other wonders where they are. "Why does it matter where we are?" To which his partner shoots, "Oh, stop with that existential crap." They plot to jettison the passengers but feel it's cruel to kill them while they're awake.

In another sketch, doctors concoct a new disease in order to make money. In a hilarious dialogue, Eisenhower browbeats Nixon into going on propaganda tours, knowing he's going to be trounced. "They spit on me in Caracas," whines Nixon. "Look, I didn't clean the suit." Under his breath Eisenhower cajoles, "I capped your teeth." He encourages, "You did well in Biloxi," meaning suppressing integration. Nixon admits, "I had Father Conklin on my side."

From the headquarters of Religions Incorporated, a prelate, who has booked the Pope for an appearance on Ed Sullivan, is on the phone catching up—"They want us to ban the bomb. No, they're not going for the Bible shit. They want us to get involved with integration. We got 'em a bus, but we put two toilets on it. By the way, Billy wants to know if you can get him a deal on one of those dago sports cars. Okay, sweetie, for Sullivan wear the big ring. About Spellman? No, nobody knows he's Jewish."

Among the comedians who succeeded Bruce, Richard Pryor most conscientiously extended the line. He grew up under the wing of his protective and domineering paternal grandmother, who ran a brothel and who, when Pryor was a young boy, manipulated him into rejecting his mother—Richard was coached to tell a judge he didn't want to live with her. It was a wound from which he perhaps never recovered, but there was plenty of other brutality in his early life. As a kid he found a dead baby in a box and thought, as he reports in *Pryor Convictions*, "at least my mother didn't do that to me." Later he was molested by a neighborhood bully and forced to suck him off.

Before the pain used him up, he explored his damage and drives, gauging the world's bullshit by his own penchant for meanness and self-deception, propelling the issues of race and class into mainstream culture.

In a bit from the seventies, he sees the movie *Logan's Run*, which is set in the future, and observes there aren't any blacks—"White folks aren't planning for us to be there. Whites know about pimping, because we're the biggest whores they got." At his father's funeral, which he attends as a grown man, his Aunt Maxine tells him, "Your father fucked everything. Just be glad he didn't fuck you." Pryor's reaction: "Okay. Tender thought."

In addition to Benny, Bruce, and Pryor, Woody Allen drives the subversive comedy of our time. I saw him in the sixties, at the Village Gate, when he was still doing stand-up, and he was funny, draping himself over the podium to confide his woes, cupping his chin in mock fatigue with his frustrations, although, with his razor rejoinders to humiliation, he never came off a schlemiel. (Someone once explained the difference between a schlemiel and a schlimazel: The schlemiel is the one who spills the coffee; the schlimazel is the one who gets it spilled on him.)

It had taken Allen a while to get good at the monologue. A friend of mine had seen him years earlier, during his virgin gig at the Blue Angel, and he'd died. The character he created combined the surrealism and moral musing of I. B. Singer, the literary hunger, neurotic introspection, and Jewish self-consciousness of Philip Roth, and the madcap zaniness of Groucho. In what seemed like five minutes—but was years of writing and performing—Allen projected his persona into movies.

For me his important influence on comedy is in the early films—*Take the Money and Run, Bananas, Love and Death, Sleeper, Annie Hall*. They are built on stand-up ideas elaborated with the inventiveness of Bach at the fugue. I'm a fan of the later movies *Crimes and Misdemeanors* and *Manhattan Murder Mystery*, but in much of the work in between he pretends to self-knowledge that's absent, promoting himself as a moral pilot fish in a sea of self-interested sharks. He tones down psychological darkness, reducing it to shtick, and in *Hannah and Her Sisters* his comedy devolves to bourgeois tales in the city. It is cut off, solipsistic, a kind of triumph of the neurotic over the anarchic.

■ ■ ■

The pieces in this section speak for themselves, and the figures profiled haven't changed much since I saw them. I'm more ambivalent about the performers in this section than in any other, because, bridging old comedy and new, they are at times throwbacks. Overall, I'm more tickled than tired by them, and they've been strongly influential—by example and counterexample—to the comedians who follow. I met Joan Rivers after I wrote about her, and to her credit she wasn't insulted by my criticism. A few years later I was a guest on her daytime talk show, to weigh in on sex in movies. (I voted for more.) I was part of a panel, and I could see that to get in a word you had to maneuver like a cabbie—cut in without hitting any fenders. Rivers was delighted she had talkers and no dead air. In my piece, written in 1988, I carp that she's becoming politically conservative. Call me a prophet. In *New York Magazine* dated August 19, 1996, it's reported she donated $1,000 to Steve Forbes's campaign. A worthy charity if ever there was one.

Joan Rivers: Female Trouble

September 1988

Joan Rivers's gig at Michael's Pub is preparation for her new club act, following what Fox executives deemed her disastrous failure on *The Late Show*. Her show wasn't a flop—certainly no more plug-filled and platitudinous than other talk shows. Her bluntness was refreshing. She and her husband surely made enemies in their business dealings, but the pleasure in her cancellation taken by so many in the press and in Hollywood was inordinately gleeful, full of relief that a woman who'd challenged the male bastion of evening talk shows hadn't been able to maintain her standing there. Joan has done nothing requiring a comeback. She just got fired from a job.

Nonetheless, she took it very badly, and the additional trauma of her husband's suicide last year gave her cause, as she's said publicly, to reconsider her career. Back on stage, she's as outrageous and gutsy as she's been since her first, sharp-witted shot on Carson.

She invites the audience to binge, confess, get mean and dirty. She hits on Cheryl Tiegs. "Those *clothes*! She sells them in Sears? Penney's? *Synthetic*. Oh, *yes*. Richard Pryor called me and said, 'Don't smoke in those clothes.' " She accelerates to tougher game: Leona Helmsley. "She made her money in exact-change ambulances." Then Queen Elizabeth. "At a command performance, she was wearing soap-on-a-rope for jewelry." Joan counsels an engaged woman in the audience: "If he wants the ring back, you swallow the stone. No man will look through shit for a diamond." Eyes level. "I got that from Nancy Reagan."

The delight Joan takes in investing everyone with bodily functions is Swiftian, wild. She thumbs her nose at the proper and snooty. She says Jackie Onassis's head darts like a lizard trying to spot "single, rich men." Eyes wide, a glance under a table. "Is she here?" Joan is masterfully intrusive. "So what size Tampax do you wear?" she asks a woman, matter-of-factly. The woman tells her, with a mixture of embarrassment and pleasure. Joan airs all the secret moments women usually conceal. "Before deciding whether to wash panty hose, you sniff the crotch, right? I always do."

Arguably, Joan is still the highest-paid, most watched and talked-about woman stand-up in the country. The problem with her work, however, is that it hasn't developed. Her mode is attack, and without some larger context, this kind of comedy devolves to bullying, dyspepsia.

Inside Joan is a tangle of confusion about self-worth, work, and males that eventually takes over her show. Again and again, she puts splayed fingers to her forehead and laments, "My body's so terrible." She inventories its defects, decrying body hair, breast-feeding, and pleasure in sex. "Do you fake orgasms?" she asks a young woman. "Well, you better learn. *Never* have fun in bed. It gives you a chance to think while he's busy." Women are always "bitches" and "sluts." The only proper use of brains is scheming to marry. She asks women in the audience if they're married or have boyfriends, then asks what these men do. Once, when she inquires about a woman's work and gets the answer "I'm in law school," she shoots back, "*Just* what you need. Become a stewardess or a nurse; they marry rich."

Joan might seem to be satirizing feminism, but the comedian, who works practically every day and whose daughter Melissa is being educated at an Ivy League college, means these words. Her message is that relentless, that resistant to her own experience. She calls herself ugly, refusing to take in that, through diets, trips to the surgeon, and the help of haute couture, she looks glamorous.

Does she really value men more than women? Yes and no. In interviews, she used to pride herself on not making fun of her husband. In fact, she seldom mentions specific men in her act, and she almost never addresses males in the audience. Men are a single thing: creatures with the power to humiliate women because all they care about is how women look. Joan stays clear of men, because she can't find anything funny in her contempt for and anger at them. The fury is all unleashed at women, especially women who, because they are pretty, make her feel worthless. But with women she can at least compete—her mouth and brains against their looks and classiness. She doesn't grant women the same power as men to recognize or hurt her.

If anything has changed since her husband's death, it may be that a part of her is tired of this spiel. Long before her set is finished, she looks strained, bored. She solicits questions from the audience. She repeats herself, going back to her horrible body, always the body. The more exhausted she gets, the shriller she sounds, just as, over the years—disappointed that good looks and material success haven't made her like herself—she's become snobbier, more vengeful, and more conservative. When she started in comedy, she lent her name to feminist and other liberal causes; in recent years, she's boasted of invitations to the Reagan White House and, at one point in her act, says she's considered voting for Bush.

With all Joan's success and visibility, she now has virtually no influence on the material of other women comics; even the most derivative are beyond her brand of self-loathing. She lies about the meaning of work, which, right before our eyes, is saving her life—she's like a woman who *has* orgasms and *says* she fakes them.

She is still raging at the girls with slim hips and jock boyfriends, who sat conspiratorially in the lunchroom and seemed to possess all the secrets of life. She directs her disquiet about power at women, refraining from violating the riskier taboo of male privilege. She sniffs the crotch of her panty hose and hates herself for the charge. And even while mooning icons, she goes on longing for respectability, apparently unaware she's better than that.

Phyllis Diller: About Face

August 1989

Phyllis Diller, honorary guest of the Just For Laughs Festival in Montreal, performs at one of the galas, wearing her trademark Halloween garb: sparkling sack dress and glitter gloves, clothes that make her look sexless, so her barbs shoot from a hag. Her timing is still methodical, scattershot, echoing that of her mentor, Bob Hope, and for the most part she adopts Hope's cozy relationship to the establishment. Personal foibles of Reagan and Bush are lampooned, but scandals are coyly skirted. The one notable difference between Hope and Diller is that Hope turns women into twits and Diller does that to men. She has always declined the mission of protecting males, endowing her work with a tart edge. "Fang," she says, referring to her ubiquitous husband. "He's so dumb he thinks reincarnation means you come back as a carnation. He's so dumb, when we were kids and played doctor, he was the optometrist."

Diller has been in comedy since 1955, longer than any other woman. I want to know what spurred her and what she feels about the scene now. I wonder why she still obscures her sexuality, even though she's expended so much effort improving her appearance through plastic surgery and even though she works the stage with aplomb. The morning after her appearance, we meet in her suite. She's decked out in a drop-waist print dress and high heels. Her platinum wig is styled in a soft bouffant. And there is her face. Her makeup is a bit uneven. There are little creases beneath her eyes, and her cheeks are soft. But she's beautiful in a fabricated, theatrical way. "I'm seventy-two," she proudly answers when I ask her age.

In a flash we talk surgery, and she gives me a chart listing: the dates of her operations, where they were performed, and the names of her doctors. She's undergone thirteen surgeries on her face, including a complete lift, eyeliner tattoos, cheek implants, and a procedure in which fat suctioned from her stomach was injected into the deep vertical wrinkles around her mouth. (She's also had breast reduction and a tummy tuck.) She holds "before" and "after" pictures, and while studying her younger, plainer image, shakes her head. "Look at the bags under the eyes, the nose, the teeth." She looks up, beaming. "I've never been happier.

"I'm in complete control. The work, the money. My mother taught me to take care of myself. She wanted to be an actress, but she was practical. She used to answer the phone: 'State your business.' I was thirty-seven when I started in stand-up. There were no models. I looked to people like Sophie Tucker. I had five kids and a husband who *could* not hold a job. But he was the most handsome guy in the world, and I wanted children who would look like him. Milton Berle had just signed a ten-million-dollar contract with NBC, and my husband said, 'You look funnier in a dress than he does.' "

She delivers this line as if she's said it a thousand times, but it doesn't square with something she reveals later: She used to look terrific in dresses. We are on a couch. I ask about the origin of her sexless costumes, and she leans her head close. "I had a beautiful figure, like Miss America. I never had the face, no, but the shape, yes. I wanted to make body jokes. So I had to hide it."

"Why did you want to make body jokes?"

She looks shocked. "Comedy is about being a loser. It's a hostile act."

"But why attack yourself?"

"It got laughs. All those feathers, beads, the fright wigs." She pauses. "It didn't work in New York." She's referring to her recent gig at the Rainbow Room. "I had to get rid of the freak number." She smiles. "It was exciting playing for a sophisticated crowd. I found it hard last night switching back."

"Why did you?"

She sits up straight, the posture of a pianist—as a young woman she'd had dreams of being a concert performer. "That audience expected what I've always done. That's what they came to see. When I wear my old costumes I feel comfy, secure. My act is like an airplane flight. I don't want to risk losing altitude." She narrows her eyes. "I know what works. My instincts are one hundred percent sure."

"Where did the laugh come from?"

"It was a virgin giggle, out of terror. It stuck."

"Is there more freedom in comedy now?"

"In terms of sex jokes, yes, what you can get away with."

"Has the women's movement made a difference?"

"Not to my work." She looks at me directly, all artifice gone. "I hate this thing about abortion, turning back the clock. I remember it all."

I invite her to march on Washington in the fall.

"I'm booked," she says, not missing a beat. "My fans would think I was in favor of killing babies." She doesn't smile. "I hate it."

Rodney Dangerfield: Satisfying Sadness

February 1988

Sadness rises from Rodney Dangerfield, surrounds him, wafts across the footlights of the Mark Hellinger Theater. He's sad because he's clumsy and fat. He feels isolated and inept. No joke. And because the sadness is real—

because the tie-touching and squirming come from his gut—the comedy he spins from it is rich and conscious. His machine-gun delivery and dancer's timing share much with Henny Youngman's, but Youngman's manner is typically Borscht Belt: sunny and masked. You don't have a clue what drives him to tell jokes. Dangerfield's material grows from inside, and it's no wonder so many young, confessional comics credit his influence.

He's tan, and, since his last film—the hit *Back to School*—he sports a sandy brush cut, like Sting's. Otherwise, he's in regulation gear: black suit meant to slim the bulging belly, with white shirt and red tie—samples of which hang in the Smithsonian. His head is a filing cabinet, stuffed with jokes about failure and humiliation. They're rattled off, in his gruff baritone, according to themes.

About Rodney's father. "He worked in a bank. They caught him stealing pens." About Rodney's childhood. "I was an ugly kid. My father never took me to the zoo. He said, 'If they want you, they'll come get you.'" His dentist cleans his teeth and they're still yellow. "The dentist says, 'Wear a brown tie.'" Old Rodney walks into a sperm bank. "They thought it was a holdup." Finally, he gets a dog, hoping it'll help him meet girls. "It turns out the dog is using me to meet other dogs."

It's opening night, and the house is packed, mostly with people under thirty, who know the comedian from TV and his movies. It's doubtful they've seen him live, because he mostly does stand-up in Vegas and Atlantic City, and this crowd doesn't know from gambling. He does a few jokes on the subject, and they die. He takes a poll. "How many don't give a fuck about gambling?" Cheers come back, and he smiles, amused. He's not worried, because so many people are there.

He doesn't bet entirely on their love, however, not for his Broadway premiere. He's used to people with drinks. He likes the reassurance of flushed faces as well as the bridge alcohol forges between the audience's memories and his shtick. Beer is flowing in the theater, and patrons are allowed to take drinks to their seats. The audience is juiced by the time the star appears, and the laughter rips.

They love Dangerfield's vulgarity, which is often winning. His shlub persona, refreshingly, isn't based on being Jewish (he is), but on being low-class. The name Rodney Dangerfield (he used Jack Roy when he started) is a WASP tease, and the inclusion of the word "danger" tweaks his victim role. But he's not just a loser. He doesn't get respect, but neither does he fawn to fanciness. He looks around the sprightly theater. "Mark Hellinger. Big deal. What do you say we bust up this place?" He hates moralists, won't say no to drugs. He joined AA but still drinks—"I use another name." And, ineffectual though he is at getting dates, he's still dying to screw.

As in *Back to School,* he makes fun of snobs without trashing knowledge; he's proud of what he knows—performing. While there's nothing unusual about his view of life, there's something special about his candor and vulnerability. It lifts him from sap status and compels us to laugh at the shlub in us.

Mostly Dangerfield makes fun of his ineptness with women, ceding them appetite and savoir faire. "My kids are good-looking. Thank God my wife cheats on me." "I told my wife, 'You never tell me when you have an orgasm.' She said, 'You're never there.'" Even some dumb-wife jokes are funny, because they turn on class issues or get surreal. "My wife can't do anything right. I took her to the ballet. She forgot the sandwiches." "My wife is so dumb, I told her to get on top, she climbed on my shoulders."

Dangerfield is more vivid on stage than in the movies—but he can also be more repellent. His material gathers no vision, not even a thematic shape. Many jokes about sex—where rejection is viewed as the most terrible consequence—are remote from AIDS. The act just loops back on itself, with subjects and attitudes repeating. The audience stayed with it, but this comedian is too intelligent not to know he's cheating.

That knowledge, or some other frustration, grips him. His fame and the audience's affection aren't enough, and the angry, flip side of his vulgarity surfaces. He's spent too much time feeling women's power over him not to feel rage at them also, and when he caves in to anxiety his femme fatale becomes a slut. He tells fat-girl jokes and makes fun of gays, too. At the low point of the evening, he offers to trade his necktie for a kiss. A beautiful woman comes on stage, thinking she'll get a benign peck. Instead he grabs her, plants his mouth on hers, twists her back to the audience, and roughly squeezes her ass.

The response is shock more than amusement. When the woman is released, she doesn't protest. She's forced to worry about his vulnerability at the same time he's sliming her. Before the end of the set, he regains his balance, quipping that he could never go to bed with a man. Pause. A look at the ceiling. "Well, maybe Tom Cruise." But the moment when deprivation and loneliness got the upper hand can't be erased. Coming back for an encore, he stares out and quietly says, "Now I'm gonna tell you how fuckin' unhappy I am."

Mort Sahl: Long in the Tooth

October 1987

People I know who saw Mort Sahl in the fifties—when he played the hungry i and the Village Gate—say he had sharp teeth. He sunk those teeth into Eisenhower, Dulles, J. Edgar Hoover, and McCarthy's goons, coming on reckless, an intellectual Lenny Bruce, saying the needed, forbidden thing. "He was incredibly exciting," one male friend told me. "Of course he was a pig about women, but then everyone was, so no one noticed."

In the mid-sixties, when I saw Sahl live, he was already a crank, looming over the *Times* he carried, as if he were the only person who could decipher it. His upper lip was rising too quickly into a sneer, and he was flashing those pronounced teeth of his, grinning at his own cleverness before anyone else had a chance. But he was still gnashing at Nixon, Roy Cohn, and the Bay of Pigs goons. He was also still a pig about women.

In the late sixties and early seventies, Sahl cried "cover-up" about the Warren Report on John Kennedy's assassination, warming up our conspiracy consciousness for Watergate and Iran-contragate.

Then he kinda disappeared.

In his Broadway concert—running for an intermissionless hour and forty-five minutes—he tells us that, for the past seventeen years, he's been raking in the dough, living in L.A., writing screenplays on contract that don't get produced. Ha, ha. That laugh. How to describe it? A foghorn that *wants* you to hit the rocks. He says he has three topics: women, movies, politics.

He starts with women. "I was watching *Geraldo!*, and four women came on who didn't want to get married." Ha, ha. "By the looks of them, they were in no danger of that happening." Many teeth. Several hisses. This is what comes from a man who, even when he was young, had a mouth and chin that could politely be described as piranha, and who now, at sixty, his midsection far wider than his shoulders, looks like a pear in a V-neck sweater. Mort's hearing seems good, however, so he lays off the women jokes for the most part, although he can't resist explaining that "the new woman," who wants to screw her male secretary and doesn't want commitments, is just like "the old man." No laughs.

Many other jokes serve only to pinpoint when the comedian lost touch with the times. He does a pallid riff about "asexual" movie critics finding "existential rage" in *Popeye* and another bit about ridding the neighborhood of Unitarians: "Burn question marks on their lawns." It's a lame religion joke and more descriptive of agnostics than believers.

Sahl does inspire a few chuckles when he moves to politics and Hollywood. "Donald Trump is building a high-rise prison for friends of the mayor," he quips. Mohamed Hamadi, who has to hip-hop the plane he's hijacked all over the Middle East, is said to be toting up "frequent-flyer points." And when David Begelman, a dyed-in-the-wool liberal, complains that his children are conservative Republicans, Sahl asks, "Do you think all the recreational drugs you took in the sixties created mutants?"

Mort tells Charlton Heston that his dream of a military-run America has already come true, and for a moment the old, trenchant Sahl flickers into view. He disappears just as quickly. Sahl knows that the Pentagon and the CIA make foreign policy, but he's not unhappy about it. He admits to voting for Nixon and to forming a friendship with Alexander Haig. He makes fun of these people and also Reagan, but the humor is affectionate, less nip than lick. Haig is pecked at for smoking Cuban cigars, then given a plucky line: "I don't think of smoking Castro's cigars, I think of burning his crops to the ground." Reagan is applauded for telling jokes, for being a charmer. A barb by Sahl is comparing Ronnie to "a maître d' at a bad restaurant." Ha, ha.

Sahl spends the last half hour explaining how, maverick that he is, he resisted the pressure of the Hollywood liberal establishment and went to a dinner at the White House for Yitzhak Shamir. Names drop from his mouth like gold coins: Newman, Fonda, Redford, Redgrave. You can hear them tinkling under his feet, then more names cascade forth: Malcolm Forbes, Weinberger, Shultz, Bush, and Nancy—dear, party-loving Nancy. Sahl can't believe these eminences are talking to him, but, more important, are eating with him, *sharing* with him. Shamir implores him to tell his audience not to arm the Saudis. Sahl gets Reagan off the dance floor to break up a mushrooming tiff between Weinberger and Shamir. Ooh, what fun to mingle. Sahl doesn't go to the White House to make trouble but to hang out. And you know how it is when you eat someone's food, and drink their wine, and then dance to their Marine Corps band. You can't turn around and bite them without looking like a *schnorrer.* The worst has happened to someone in his line who's abandoned the work but still wants to collect his check: He's become irrelevant.

Bill Cosby: Race Track

December 1988

There aren't a lot of black faces among the fancy-dress audience at last week's benefit for the Carnegie Hall Society. Orchestra tickets cost $100, and the cheapest seats are $35. Most of the ushers, wearing short red jackets, are black—and hip-looking, with stylish hairdos. Bill Cosby, there to entertain, looks great, wearing a beautifully tailored tan suit, beige shirt, and brand-new caramel loafers—when, during a bit, he lifts his feet, you can see that the soles haven't been walked on. At fifty-one, Cosby looks healthy, no longer jockish and certainly not cutting edge (he never was, although he acted slick and wry on *I Spy*), but vigorous, prosperous.

Still, there stands a black performer before a sea of rich, mostly white faces, attended by a service staff that is largely black. What are the options? Richard Pryor would plunge into the race study, fangs first, taking the skinny-boy license to draw blood and plead puniness. He'd be vicious, hilarious, tilting the minstrel format of race humor to his advantage. The pain of being made to feel insignificant because of color continues to burn in him. Eddie Murphy wouldn't expose that vulnerability even if he felt it. He'd use the occasion to show off his shrewdness, display his amusement about white anxieties, demonstrate who's in control and who's being entertained.

Cosby doesn't say a word about race. Can you think of another black comedian who takes this tack? There was a time when Jewish comedians didn't comment on their backgrounds. Jack Benny acted like a WASP bank executive—although the joke about his being cheap was redolent, even if unconsciously, of his ethnicity. When George Burns talks roots he means vaudeville, not chopped liver. When a later generation of Borscht Belters came up, it was a sign of liberation to flaunt ghetto origins, but now for a comedian like Jackie Mason the once-freeing urgency to define the self has turned into formula piousness about being outside.

But a black person who looks black can't elude ethnicity, and Cosby knows this. Racial humor has never been his thing. Maybe that's because he grew up middle class and went to college, and, like most Americans in that position, felt more defined by the larger culture toward which he was swimming than by the tribe to which his parents and grandparents, partly due to racism, had cleaved. In any case, whenever Cosby appears, he presents an image of blackness, wealth, and professional success, a combination that adds up to racial pride and is given weight by his $20 million bequest to the women's school Spellman College, and by his conscientious hiring of minorities for his show. On stage at Carnegie Hall, Cosby signaled to the audience and to the ushers that some blacks have made it so successfully they don't have to call attention to race. He pulled it off.

Ever wonder where baby types Bob Goldthwaite and Howie Mandel picked up their whines? Listen to Cosby's tight braying, those gasped fragments that sound like they're being squeezed out against his will. Cosby uses his brat voice to tease himself. He milks charm and wit from the oldest business in the book: wife jokes and toilet humor.

After twenty-five years of marriage, things have changed. "The love didn't go anywhere, but it grew, sort of like a squash," he says, setting the tone for his mixture of satisfaction and rue. "I don't know whether it happened in the fifth year or the fifteenth year," he keeps repeating, chronicling his wife's growing intolerance with his overbearingness. "Hey, hey, hey," she protests, when, in bed, he slings his leg over her hips. "Am I a pack mule? Wanna ride me to sleep?" In the past, he'd go for walks when he was gassy, but one day he just "cut one." "Oh Bill, shut up," his wife said. Like Rodney Dangerfield, who puts wise barbs in the mouths of contemptuous women, Cosby lets his wife name his defining persona: a tyrant who wants to come off cute.

Cosby has a funny bit about kids feigning dyslexia to disguise they're just dumb. And he's as insouciant as ever—and sometimes poignant—speaking for body parts that increasingly break down. "When you're asleep in your twenties and the body says you gotta piss, you can say, 'I'll do it first thing in the morning.' 'Okay,' the body says, 'we'll put a lock on the bladder, let it fill up and spill over. We'll even mop up.'" Cosby's mouth becomes a thin, sad line. "At fifty-one, you better go or you'll be dreaming about a warm fountain."

When Cosby's motives are honest, he's funny—and not merely about himself but about human behavior. Too often, though, the observant part of him isn't after change, just buying time to go on being what he is.

Groucho Marx: Marxmanship

November 1991

These two pieces about Groucho—one on an HBO documentary, the other on a theater bio—complement each other, portraying the comedian as an original and offering behind-the-scenes material that illuminates his persona. Groucho remains a great outsider voice, but like so many men of his generation, he targeted women for abuse because he felt vulnerable to them.

■ ■ ■

There are lines, at once aggressive and Dada, that are pure Groucho. "I'd horsewhip you if I had a horse," he spouts to an obtuse straight man in one movie. In another, a prig asks him, "Are you a man or a mouse?" Groucho throws a glance at the camera—"Put a piece of cheese down there, and you'll find out." Most bio-docs come off like chicken dinner testimonials, the film clips random, the commentary lending only praise. *Here he is . . . The one, the only . . . Groucho* has the edge, wit, and melancholy due its subject.

In his movies, books, and TV shows, Groucho skillfully transforms the sorrows that plague his private life. His mother liked him the least of her five sons, and Groucho vented his anger at women by marrying those he could dominate—all three wives were many years younger, passive, and ultimately alcoholic. But as a performer, when Groucho letches at women, he plays the fool, the ineffectual.

For a long time he was poor, discriminated against as a Jew. Rather than distancing himself from these experiences, he plumbs them. His humor is assaultive, targeting the pompous, powerful, and rich. Informed that the Santa Monica Country Club doesn't admit Jews, he asks if his daughter, who is half-Jewish, can go into the pool up to her waist. His aim is to disrupt order. There's a doubleness to his comedy, an expression of discontent packaged in disarming silliness. His dignity resides in holding on to his sense of irony.

Groucho's daughter Miriam speaks of growing up with a man who adored her but devalued her sex. Everyone who knew him conveys the bittersweetness of his nature, and we see it in interview segments as he's aging. Invariably, from eyes washed with sadness erupts some lunatic flash. He nonchalantly lays his legs across Dinah Shore's lap. A woman on his quiz show asks if he's ever made love to a French man, and he takes a long pause, then answers in a quiet, breathy voice, "Not that I remember." He sings "Lydia," breaking into his noodle-legged, minstrel-inspired dance, hands flapping, head bobbing. Commenting on his chronic depressions, Dick Cavett astutely concludes, "He needed a Groucho to cheer him up. He was the only person who couldn't have one."

October 1986

The dedication of the makers of *Groucho: A Life in Revue* is intense. Frank Ferrante, who plays Groucho, has been doing a one-man show about the comedian since his undergraduate days and played him in *Minnie's Boys*. Les Marsden, who doubles as Harpo and Chico, has performed a solo show, *A Night at Harpo's*, since 1978. Playwright/director Arthur Marx is Groucho's son. He cowrote *Minnie's Boys* (with Robert Fisher, coauthor of this piece), and among his other credits are *Life with Groucho*, a biography of his father, and *Son of Groucho*, an autobiography. It's like a fever.

Marsden is convincing in his parts, but they're small and familiar— Chico-the-man as womanizer, gambler, and finagler. Harpo is even shadowier and appears only in his stage persona. There was one bit of news to me: Groucho was nearly ruined in the '29 crash, but Chico bailed him out with $50,000 in cash, won the night before shooting craps with Al Capone. Ferrante's Groucho quips, "Now why didn't I think of a safe investment like that?" and discloses that when Bugsy Siegel was found shot, he was carrying one of Chico's checks.

The evening is principally Ferrante's, as he chronicles Groucho's life and delivers a spookily vivid impersonation, finding the right voice and posture for each period, knowing when to cast his eyes heavenward in the classic faux-swoon, or stare deadpan, neck slightly bent, or dip into the bullet-headed, cockroachfast crouch. He shapes and sharpens Groucho's humor, a blend of self-mockery, Dada lunacy, and subversive observation. "We were so poor, even Mama and Papa had to sleep in the same bed." "I was the serious student; I wanted to be a doctor, so I stayed in school till the sixth grade." Ferrante can sing in Groucho's ineffable falsetto-to-bass voice and dance in his style. His "Captain Spaulding" number bubbles like a glass of seltzer; his suitably cool version of the nonsensical "Show Me a Rose (or Leave Me Alone)" is champagne.

The narrative progresses from the Marx Brothers's tenement origins to their vaudeville tours, to their plays on Broadway, to Hollywood, to Groucho's fourteen-year run on *You Bet Your Life* and his later role as comedy éminence grise. The Marx Brothers were free; they weren't trying to protect anything. Part of the delight in seeing people impersonate them is imagining that everyone, disguised behind a mop of blond curls or grease-paint eyebrows and mustache, can lose themselves in wildness.

From his early days, Groucho worried about money, work, and his lack of success with women, and joked ironically against the grain of his anxieties. He was whole in this way, and, from all accounts and indications, he never changed. His class insecurities made him see society funny; his insecurities about women, though, made him wish to degrade them. With the upper-crust Margaret Dumont as foil, the two hatreds rode up and down in seesaw fashion, and mostly Groucho was hilarious with her because his own style of physical comedy—the effeminate sways and loose limbs—undercut any scent of macho bravura. But without the diluting issue of class, Groucho's sense of grievance against women leaped out bald and ugly: in the routine insults on his TV show, in the dirty-old-man leering at young girls which was part of his persona, in the cracks he made about his marriages failing because his wives didn't think he was funny.

Groucho was great when he nailed his own absurdity. "I'm eighty-five and called a living legend," he says to a reporter. "Who first called you that?" the reporter asks. "I think I just did," he flips. If he had seen inside his anger at women, what a weapon that mouth could have made against sexist folly.

CHAPTER TWO

Modern Wild Cards: High-Wire Iconoclasts, Risk-Surfing Hipsters, and Political Provocateurs

Sandra Bernhard

The comedians in this chapter are the spiritual spawn of Lenny Bruce. Bruce predates some of the comics in the previous chapter and influenced several of them, but he has had more impact on a later generation that produced Robert Klein, David Steinberg, Woody Allen, George Carlin, and most significantly Richard Pryor. Bruce is a modern jester, an unrepressed voice hooking hypocrisy. Burlesque wafts off him, but he's more redolent of the nightclub—of darkened spaces where ice cubes clink and people fondle each other under tables, where jazz alternates with stand-up, and the races mix. Bruce added a lived, autobiographical element to stand-up, his stage persona presented as one with his life off stage, his commentary ripped from his experience with the courts, drugs, the street, strip joints.

The comedians profiled here have made a tradition of Bruce's style without turning reverential. They are rude, uncharming, demystifying, politically radical, outrageous on stage. They turn stand-up from lighthearted amusement to surreal, political theater, with some—Sandra Bernhard, Jimmy Tingle, Reno, and Bill Hicks among them—moving into the kinds of evening-length theater pieces presented by performance artists such as Spalding Gray and Holly Hughes.

■ ■ ■

A personal anecdote: I first saw Sandra Bernhard live at Caroline's in 1986. We chatted, and I wrote admiringly. I saw her a year later at Dance Theater Workshop, where she did a work-in-progress version of the solo performance that would become *Without You I'm Nothing.* I had reservations but afterward, speaking hurriedly, offered only encouragement. The piece was in flux, and I didn't want to be dampening.

A year later *Without You* opened at the Orpheum Theater, and this time I expressed my disappointment, along with praise, in print. She was angry and said so on stage, making the slam a running routine in her show. She dissed not only me but everyone who was critical. I heard from mutual friends that she was especially pissed at me, felt I'd betrayed her: been in her camp and then attacked. I was told she thought I hated her. I felt a little guilty for being less than honest at the earlier version. I called her, wanting to make peace and to say I didn't hate her, to the contrary believed in her talent, but instead of making that simple statement I gushed into her answering machine. I said I loved her, meaning her work, that I was her supporter, on and on, tangling myself in nervous declarations. I asked her to call so we could talk. Instead she played the tape on stage every night thereafter, and when she next did *Letterman,* played it on the air.

A reporter from the *National Enquirer* called wanting to know if Bernhard and I had been lovers. I dashed his hopes. When the film of *Without You* was being made, I was asked to appear in it, as a talking head who would sound off angrily at Bernhard. I said no thanks to the opportunity to present myself as a disingenuous idiot. And that was the end of my personal dealings with Bernhard.

Looking back at the first piece I wrote, I find myself revising the critique of her sexual shenanigans. I said she looked like she was trying to shock. Now she strikes me as staging a clever role reversal, Bernhard coming off as a terrorist lap dancer. Or at least she's playing with the ambivalence built into sex work: the hooker believing he/she is in control, while creating a scenario in which the john is made to feel powerful—unless he's paying for the opposite thrill.

The cavil ending my review of *Without You* now sounds self-important, though my predictions mostly materialized. In Bernhard's next show, *Giving Till It Hurts* (1992), she was wonderful, jettisoning the diva-worship that was amassing into a comforting blanket. With big wig and dark glasses, she teetered on stage, a Peggy Lee nearly comatose from self-abuse and crowd adulation, and lovingly, scathingly sent up star-fucking and fucked stars. At the end of the first number she outed herself, tweaking her own past coyness and claiming a freedom not merely to be outrageous but pointedly so. As her courage expanded, so did her acting and musical talent. Never had her tongue been more silvery or more firmly embedded in cheek.

My article on Reno was her first substantial media coverage, and it helped her get work. A piece in the *Voice* can do that for unknowns. Five minutes later, she was booked at Caroline's and courted by agents. HBO taped her first evening-length solo, *Reno in Rage and Rehab*. Peroxided tendrils danced as she erupted onto the stage and jabbed the air in a dizzying whirl of movement—a guerrilla fighter in the gender wars and a hostage to urban surrealism. She thanked Mayor Koch for purging midtown of knish salesmen—"I for one was having a very difficult time locating my crack dealer."

She's gone on to other solos, to acting at the Public Theater, and to playing the shrink in Lily Tomlin's animated series about Edith Ann. I write about Reno again in the section on queer comedy, covering a performance of her evolving political monologue, *Citizen Reno*.

Denis Leary needs no introduction these days. Ten minutes after I wrote the piece that appears here, he was catapulted into national prominence, doing spots for MTV. A minute later he was landing movie roles. In 1990 he toured with the solo *No Cure for Cancer*, coming off sexy and savage, but his film work has yet to approach the power of his stand-up.

Robert Schimmel is an interesting companion to Leary, both trained on mortality, though in different ways: Leary-the-beauty actively damaging his flesh; fearful Schimmel outing deviant desires. Schimmel remains committed to dark subjects, unconcerned about being marginalized. He works clubs, records albums, lands the occasional shot on late-night TV, but it's doubtful that anytime soon he'll be telling the beads-up-the-ass joke on network.

Richard Belzer remains mesmerizing on stage, his combination of brains and flow unmatched, and, over the years, he's quit bashing gays and women. Now a lead on *Homicide,* his deadpan delivery infuses his character, Munch, with melancholy and sexual longing.

I get on Damon Wayans's case for homophobia, too. My critique here is more complex than of Belzer, spinning from Wayans's once having been disabled. I write about John Epperson in other chapters, but his approach to gender anxiety, being the opposite of Wayans's, offers an arresting counterpoint. I happened to see them the same week, and the coincidence paid off. With his brother Keenen Ivory, Wayans of course went on to appear on *In Living Color* and to commit some groundbreaking irreverence, though there was no originality in the old boy atmosphere that ruled on that show.

I saw Calvin Trillin and Jackie Mason the same week, too, and their acts wound up commenting on each other. Though best known as a *New Yorker* writer, chronicling the folkways of American crime and eating styles, Trillin gives such economical, unsmiling talk-show panel he's gained a performance persona as well.

Jackie Mason's cracks against David Dinkins, then New York's mayor, have some history. Mason campaigned strenuously for Dinkins's opponent, Rudolph Giuliani, who would beat Dinkins in the next election, but in '89 Mason caught flak for using the slur *shvartzers.* Comedians had a field day with the flap and with Mason's stillborn, soon-canceled sitcom *Chicken Soup.* Harry Shearer quipped, "If Jackie Mason is the Jews' Louis Farrakhan, then where's Farrakhan's sitcom?"

I've included a review of Paul Krassner-the-stand-up and a larger analysis of his contribution in my piece on his memoir *Confessions of a Raving, Unconfined Nut*—the title lifted from a description in his FBI file. Krassner is another lynchpin to the humor that erodes repression. In his political activism and writing—he's been editor of *The Realist* since 1958—he comprises a history of subversive comedy, including personal relationships with Lenny Bruce and Groucho. Krassner is on to the sexiness of conspiracy theory, the way it hooks up with the early secret of what Mommy and

Daddy do in their bedroom. The secret is always imagined to be big, juicy, and hot—even if it isn't.

The boy with his ear pressed against the locked door remains alive in Krassner, and it's part of his sweetness, too. His comedy is generous, tolerant of folly, resistant to resolution for the sake of coherence that isn't real. Answers aren't always forthcoming, even solutions to conspiracies. Incongruity rules. When Krassner tells his mother he takes acid, she says, "It could lead to marijuana."

Sandra Bernhard: Pretty Poison

October 1983

When Sandra Bernhard was five years old, people were already staring at her odd features. She has wavy red hair; her eyes are lovely, smoky slits. But these are not the parts that arouse comment. A large, wide nose greets an expansive, flexible smile. The body is tall and knife thin. In Arizona, her high school classmates called her "nigger lips." According to Bernhard, Joan Rivers said she wouldn't get anywhere in "the business" without a nose job.

Not so. Bernhard, twenty-eight, has been widely acclaimed for playing Masha, the crazed kidnapper in Martin Scorsese's *King of Comedy*, and she is now performing her club act before responsive audiences throughout the country. During the seven years she worked developing her material— she earned a living as an L.A. manicurist for five of them—her performance has grown shapely and her presence authoritative. Bernhard does not tell jokes. She unravels herself in her own measured time. The result is an autobiographical rampage, during which Bernhard also sings, sometimes in a rock style, sometimes in a jazzy soprano.

Bernhard's looks have given her a subject and a vantage point. She is obsessed by her appearance, but even more so by the meaning of beauty in the world. She knows how important glamour is and also how vicious and stupid. Her piece is fueled by the rage of the ridiculed and the wit of the observer. Woody Allen and Elaine May, to name two comedians with similar stories, also use humor as a defensive weapon, but they stand in life as wimps and their comedy is the revenge of the repressed. Bernhard's posture is openly aggressive. She will not be wimpified. Why the hell should she be? What makes her tone special is that neurotic acting out is balanced with irony. Unlike assaulters Jerry Lewis and Don Rickles, Bernhard teases herself without falling into self-pity. She doesn't beg for approval, although she plays with whining and special pleading. She doesn't want us to love her. She wants our eyes glued to her.

One minute, she is musing about the ages of people in the theater: "Hume Cronyn and Jessica Tandy are ten minutes older than dirt." In a lash flutter, she is talking like a southern girl in a Calvin Klein ad and sweetly reminiscing about idling into a Scottsdale bar, playing Tammy Wynette on the jukebox, cracking off the top of a beer bottle with her teeth, and getting her lips all bloody because she loves life. At another point, she becomes Marilyn Monroe, singing happy birthday Mr. President and squeezing her whole body into cleavage. Then she is Mary Tyler Moore as Laura Petrie, hiccupping her tale of catastrophes in black Capri pants; and then Tina Turner, insisting on antiphonal responses, her nose and mouth aligned like an exclamation point. Bernhard is a wonderful mimic, but the impressions aren't about her subjects; they signal her own mood swings: the vulnerable exhibitionist, the suburban princess, the sexual terrorist.

When playing Tina Turner, Bernhard's sexual aggression is funny, but it works less well when she is taunting and flirting with the audience. She tells us she wants to show us her breasts. "They're so big tonight. . . . I never dreamed they could be so big, so dangerous." She focuses on a man, smiles warmly and says, "I really like you. I'm really attracted to you." Then the face goes mask hard. "And yet, there's something about you. I'd like to hurt you. I'd really like to smash your face." Some feminists have attacked Bernhard's style as pandering and antiwoman. I don't find it so: The seriousness with which she takes her work and the trust she has in her own vision are measures of her evaluation of femaleness. My objection is that the sex games shock less than proclaim her eagerness to shock.

She's most devastating in the role of female road warrior surveying a landscape of pop culture debris. There are no books in this world; the images come from TV, movies, and magazines. There are no stated politics, either—the arena beyond fashion and celebrity barely exists. Bernhard's most partisan riff is a dream about fucking Reagan so long he dies. She love/hates this narrow context, but it is what she knows.

The photographs in *Vogue* are of deep concern. "Two girls in leather are watching a third getting examined by a doctor. What does it mean?

They're waiting for a clean bill of health before they beat her up again?" She deadpans. Pauses. "I want to be soft," she purrs, confiding she is having fun in New York "kicking the shoulder pads off Norma Kamali dresses." She sizes up a woman in the audience. "I'll bet you're the type that wears Nikes with five-hundred-dollar designer suits. If you are I'll kill you. Get those Charles Jourdans on this minute. I don't care if you break your ankles."

She is back to herself a second later. She has never left herself. "Next year, I'm going to do my first one-woman show: *Sandra Bernhard is Abraham Lincoln.*" Perhaps so, but not, she rails, Mick Jagger or David Bowie. "I'm not androgynous, goddammit. I'm a woman. I waited on line to see Judy Chicago's *Dinner Party.*" And if that isn't proof enough, she announces that Hanna Schygulla is her new favorite actress. Bernhard went up to Hanna at Cannes and said, "I'm so majorly blown away I'm meeting you." Pause, innocent face: "Do you think that was the right thing to say to her?" Bernhard primps about the stage, ringed fingers in hair, elegant arms poised at stunning angles, cheekbones catching the light so that she looks beautiful in flashes. She knows the moves. She has practiced them every day of her life. When she says, in mock Jane Fonda, she feels good about herself and then explains that she has taken to sleeping on a full-length mirror, it isn't difficult to imagine her really doing it.

The night I saw the show, two stoned women harassed Bernhard so badly they interrupted her flow. They were quieted and she went on, handling the scene with tact. Then she did a most marvelous thing; she transformed the experience right before our eyes. At the end of the set, she mimed typing a letter to Hanna Schygulla. She told Hanna about her adventures in New York, painting a picture of an up-and-coming star. A moment later, she stopped and confessed to feeling blue: "Tonight I almost cried on stage. I bit my lip. It will probably be swollen tomorrow."

It probably was. But only a dumb girl would care more about her looks than holding on to herself.

Nothing Ventured

April 1988

Sandra Bernhard stands on stage in her club act and on TV, her body a hanger, her fingers styling moussed tresses, and exposes the length and breadth of her absorption with ordinariness: rock-star gossip, TV celebs, her own urge to run ahead of the pack. Her frankness strips anyone veiling their solipsism and love of banality. Every time she's on *Letterman,* he becomes her creature. She terrifies and excites him. Responses escape his control. Argh, back vampire. Not feelings! Juiced by her power, she becomes truly spontaneous, his vulnerability pumping her confidence, sharpening her understanding of repression. This is premium Punch and Judy.

Bernhard plays so well on TV because she isn't afraid of it. But knowing the medium doesn't save her from its pitfalls. She's wired like a TV, her antennae trained on circuits of power, celebrity. She wants the sort of fame that is TV's special product: becoming a household name. She complains on TV that she isn't famous enough, and she gripes to print reporters, too. She expected movie offers to pour in after *King of Comedy.* They didn't. She hoped to become a rock icon after cutting the album *I'm Your Woman.* The wish remains unfulfilled. Although she has a substantial role in Nicholas Roeg's forthcoming film *Track 29,* and although, in July, Harper & Row will publish her book *Confessions of a Pretty Lady,* the fame she believes her due eludes her.

In the past, she'd lace the longing with irony: I mean this, but if I come off looking like an asshole I'll pretend I'm making fun of fame-seeking. Of late, though, the complaining has lost even the illusion of detachment. In an article she wrote for *Spin,* she self-righteously lambasted Hollywood execs, sounding oblivious of the fact that bureaucrats in *every* job market grind down the less powerful. She recently told *Newsday,* "My problem is that I've never been a phony." The trouble with the world is it won't let her be famous.

Bernhard's drive to find a venue that will catapult her career the way solo evenings boosted Whoopi Goldberg and Jackie Mason fuels and clogs *Without You I'm Nothing,* the theater piece she spent two years developing, along with writer/director John Boskovich. Her desire to develop her act is admirable, but this show isn't a step forward. A collection of autobiographical monologues, fantasy riffs, and musical numbers, it's often inert. It doesn't know what it's trying to say, except notice Sandra and take her seriously.

To be sure, there are evocative details, funny bits, and some well-aimed satire. Bernhard remembers New York in '65 when Streisand was "simply Barbra." She conjures a Jewish kid's Gentile fantasy of having an older brother named Chip—"You're so cute, I wish you weren't my brother so I could fuck you." She raps photographer Bruce Weber for using women as accessories in his Calvin Klein ads and, in his layouts for Ralph Lauren, for fetishizing white, upper-class America. And she blasts Joni Mitchell for singing about Ethiopia and not budging from "the Malibu colony in ten years."

But these moments aren't frequent enough. Instead of, as she used to, showing off her clothes and being advertising's plaything—a happy consumer—Bernhard mentions brand names in italics, as if diction constituted a critique of media. And she justifies the incoherence in her writing by claiming it dramatizes our fragmented times.

Her stories trail off, or wind into private associations, or devolve to pettiness and bile. She hates her father's second wife because the woman talks nasal. She loathes a famous fashion photographer just as much for being homosexual as for being a snob. A whole number is devoted to Bernhard's ex-manager, who's accused of obstructing her path to fame and who gets attacked for being fat. Skinny Sandra, dumping on this woman for eating deep-fried food and at the same time begging us to see her as a victim—it doesn't wash.

Bernhard's performance quickens when she sings. A sensuous rendition of "Me and Mrs. Jones" opens a door on her sexual ambiguity and, in a nervy version of "Little Red Corvette," she reveals her awe of and ambivalence about sex. But the erotic energy usually flowing between her and the audience gets short-circuited here, because the show is so rehearsed. When she does kibitz, she's unpredictable, open. And at the end of the evening, cavorting in black panties and bra, there's heat and wildness again. It points up what too often has been missing.

Sandra: Someone is going to give you the TV talk show you deserve. You're going to turn people upside down, and we're going to hear their pretensions and terrors clatter to the floor like loose change. In the meantime, don't hand out the excuse for mediocrity you gave *Newsweek*—"This is a stale age, and it's impossible to be fresh today." That statement is the fashion equivalent of wearing Reeboks with an Ungaro.

Dark Victory

July 1992

For a spell, on stage and in print, Bernhard whined about not being famous enough, but self-pity has since washed out of her voice. She's back on TV, this time with her own show on HBO, *Sandra After Dark*, and her sense of the absurd is again balanced with neurotic acting out.

Remember *Playboy After Dark*—booby bunnies ferrying drinks, gold chains glinting on Vegas chest hair, cameras winking at hot tub gropes? Bernhard's lair, too, is studded with climbers, arrivés, and has-beens, but she sends up fake bonhomie and ego massaging by celebrating rather than sneering. This show creates a dreamy new standard for joyous vulgarity. It's a Warhol movie without the pimples.

Isn't that Ricki Lake? My God, it's Theresa Russell comparing eyebrows with Debi Mazar. On that couch over there, Roseanne and Tom Arnold! Sandra, wearing a bra and G-string under a sheer lace peignoir, sidles up to Roseanne: "If you looked any hotter I'd sleep with you, bitch." To the couple: "Do you swing?" Tom: "I wish." Timothy Leary predicts that orgasms will get better in the nineties. Lypsinka mouths bites from one of her greatest psychotic breakdown tapes. And Tom Jones, looking a bit Elvoid around the gut, sings EMF's "Unbelievable" as everybody gathers and sways. Sandra safe-sasses him—"You want to touch my pussy, you want to taste my jam, you got to be usin' a dental dam."

Bernhard has always craved attention more than love, and it has freed her to be ridiculous. Getting ready for the show, she nags her hairdresser, "Grab that root and work it. Are you scared of my hair?" To her makeup artist: "I don't want that red lipstick anywhere near my mouth. I am not Paloma Picasso."

Not every flight lands her safely. She can look desperate writhing on the floor using a mike as a faux dildo or miming sucking off men. But her exhibitionism makes voyeurs of us all. Even the longueurs on her show are fun, because you don't know what she'll do next.

Regarding Reno

December 1987

Reno erupts onto the stage, a voice in her head saying, "You can't do it," her body answering, "Oh, yeah?" She grabs the mike by the balls and scans the audience for attack dogs. Last Saturday at the Duplex, we'd just been pummeled by a twenty-minute whine act—"I'm lonely/I'm neurotic/I'm fat"—and Reno's explosive edge and punkoid style were a wake-up call.

She looks like Robert Taylor with Madonna's hair, four weeks after the roots started growing. She favors cotton pants and loose-fitting shirts but doesn't like bras, she confides—or underwear at all. "I have to go to court next week, and I figured I should get some—in case the judge makes me go down on all fours."* In the old days, she only wore a bra so she could burn it. "I'm still pissed, though. Nobody told me to take it off." Face in pain. "Yeah, the good old days. I burned my bra so some twenty-four-year-old could trade futures on Wall Street." Groucho slouch. "I'd like to trade futures."

Reno's mind is quick, dark, and free-ranging, and her body cuts graceful as well as slapstick figures. The content of her sets varies, depending on the venue and her mood, but their form suggests free-association, with real improvisation—sometimes flying, sometimes flopping—woven in.

"I looked up vagina one time." Stare. "One time, sure. The dictionary said, 'A sheath of skin to receive the penis.' Uh-huh. How about pussy? Something that can be tossed over the telephone wires and land on its feet." She has a Liza/Judy moment and does a few bars of "The Night Is Bitter." A Billy Crystal Jewish crank materializes. "Have you ever walked down the street and gotten a little night in your mouth? Feh, like the skin of a plum." A confessional interlude. "I'm a nervous type, you may have noticed. My friends told me, 'Get a massage.' I did. But halfway through I realized he was never gonna get to my favorite part. Why beat around the bush?" She gets a part as a man in a play, and the director tells her to wear a dildo in her panties. "Sort of a cocksimile." Baboom. "At first it was embarrassing." Long stare. "Then I got into the power. I'm a dick junkie. Men were letting me get a whole sentence in."

Between performances, we had a meal. Offstage conversations start the way onstage ones do: edgy, forceful. But soon she's open. Thirtysomething years ago—she won't give her exact age—she started out Karen in the usual suburban nightmare childhood. Her mystique of being an outcast, however, was fed by the fact that she really had been adopted. "I was born in Lenox Hill Hospital and abandoned there."

---

*She's referring to a notoriously abusive Brooklyn judge who had the female plaintiff in a sexual assault case abase herself this way.

Her natural parents were Hispanic, her adopted ones kind but fearful Swiss Protestants—Reno was originally Reneaud. Early, she escaped into sex and flamboyance. "I was the kid who made up the party lists, but then I wasn't allowed to go because the mothers banned me." After high school, she vagabonded her way to California, found theater, got trained in acting at NYU, and in the late seventies worked with a Cockettes offshoot and toured the country with Lilith Women's Theater. In '83, she started working solo at WOW and learned to turn the self-dramatizing rebel in herself into a wry critic of the world.

She thinks her act needs developing, and she's right. Not every bit lands on its feet, pussy-style. But she's disadvantaged less by the roughness in her performance than by the male locker-room atmosphere of stand-up. Even Silver Friedman, owner of the Improvisation, busies herself vetoing Reno's dildo bit. The night I saw Reno at this club, she followed a guy who directed everyone in the room to yell "asshole" when he repeated an audience member's name. The crowd went along, and then out marched Reno. Why not learn tightrope walking over a pit full of alligators? She returned with her body parts intact and even got some laughs.

Lewis Black: Black Humor

July 1988

Lewis Black has been doing stand-up in small clubs for twenty years, but if you haven't heard of him you're not alone. His relative obscurity isn't a reflection of his skill, though. For the past five years, Black, who's also a playwright, has been sharpening his performances in the midnight shows at the West Bank Café, a theater space he cofounded and runs with musical director Rusty Magee and artistic director Rand Foerster. On a couple of occasions, I saw Black warming up the audience for other entertainers. Most of the time he was funnier than they were, and when he scheduled a series of hour-long evenings, I caught one.

His look is sixties—still with the wire-rimmed glasses and longish hair. The red tie gives the impression someone said, Lew, you need color. The suit looks as if he thought, I have to make like I'm going to work. His head is sixties, too. New Left, the sex wars—although the night I saw him he

omitted his personal life and stuck to the world. He places newspaper clip-
pings on a stool and reads from them, the way Mort Sahl used to.

Sometimes, to get a laugh, all Black has to do is read a headline. "Bush
Gets Endorsement From Qaddafi." Quick riff, "I'd love to see him sing at
the convention." Black's disbelief at the Reagan years chokes him. He
chain-smokes and sips Rolling Rock to keep from flailing his arms at the
ruling powers. From time to time he does just that, turning his back on the
audience, seeking consolation from the wall, a Job who doesn't want the job
but has a talent for complaint.

He asks us to contemplate Howard Baker. "The last vestige in the
White House of anything to do with right and wrong. Gained four hundred
pounds. When he left he looked like Pokey the dog, his tongue searching for
moisture." "*Meese,*" Black's voice rises. "He questioned whether the people
who stood on line for food were really poor." Reagan. "He said it was a mistake to give Indians reservations. A lot made money in oil. He called shooting down the Iranian Airbus 'an understandable accident.' I've never heard
those two words used together. If it's an accident, it can't be understandable." Bush. "He wanted Jeane Kirkpatrick for vice president. Waldheim
wasn't available. If you know anyone planning to vote for Bush, tell them,
'You will go to hell. You will wind up in a room with Kissinger for twelve decades. He will tell you about his sex life.'" Donald Trump. "He can have
the yacht and the tower, but then he doesn't get the mansion in Florida.
He's like a crack addict. There comes a time when you have to say, 'Stop.
You need help.'"

A few days after the show, Black and I had lunch, and I found him as
voluble off stage as on but free of complaint about his life. This guy who almost never smiles when holding a mike is contented. Growing up in the
suburbs of Washington, D.C., he learned about politics, dissent, and theater. His father worked for the military designing sea mines. "He could
stand making defensive weapons, but when Haiphong Harbor was mined
he quit and became an apprentice to a stained-glass maker. As a poor kid in
New York, plays were my father's way into the world. Seeing Paul Robeson
take Uta Hagen in his arms in *Othello* showed him a way the races could live
that had not existed for him before. We used to follow theater reviews like
baseball box scores."

Playwriting and stand-up started when Black was at the University of
North Carolina. "Two secure fields." He also acts. "I'm an actor the way

Lassie's an actor. I come when they call for the modern American Jew." After college, he worked at regional theaters, taking productions to schools, army bases, and prisons. "I wrote a musical, which I thought was about the joys of male bonding. It was good for about forty-five minutes, but then it turned, and I couldn't figure out what was wrong. The weird thing was, people didn't leave. Guys especially kept watching. I read it a few years ago, and I cringed. Every neurotic male tendency was in there. I was abusive to women, abusive to my parents, abusive to myself."

In the early seventies, he worked as a secretary for two women in the Appalachian Regional Commission. "I was the only male asked to join the women's group. I had exactly the same hatred of those guys in suits." Marriage to an actress in the mid-seventies lasted a year. Following that were three years at Yale Drama School, then New York and the writing/producing/performing life he's led ever since.

"I finally have control over what I do. Of course, no one is saying, 'Here's five hundred thousand dollars. We want you to work with the seals.' " Steven Olson, who owns the West Bank Café, gets the bar tab. Magee, Foerster, and Black split the $6. "I have a cheap apartment on the Lower East Side. My parents aren't hocking me to get married and have kids. Mornings, I read as many magazines and newspapers as I can. I'm on stage five or six nights a week, so I can be watching the six o'clock news and get up at eight-thirty and do shtick on it that night. The majority of my material each week is new. I'm going to be forty in August, and I'm ready."

Denis Leary: Dead On

October 1990

Denis Leary looks like an angel on a drunk. Lithe and long-haired, with flashing blue eyes and one of those Peter Weller sculpted jaws, he stalks the stage and chain-smokes, waiting for death. Mortality is always with him. At Stand-Up N.Y., he whips up applause for the comic who's preceded him. "Come on, she's got cancer." Disease is poked at, stared down. "Tumors are better than moles; there's no hair on them."

Leary's pain—"We're all gonna be dead in five years; we broke the sky"—makes him tense. He puffs loud into the mike, in and out, still alive.

He's melancholy, savagely sober, a bloodhound scenting out piety and sentimentality. "Keith Richards is on TV telling people not to do drugs. We can't *do* drugs, Keith, you did them all." Leary doesn't smoke to prove he's macho or to deny the habit's dangers. He just won't lie about its pleasures. "I love cigarettes. I'm going to get a tracheotomy, so I can inhale two butts at the same time."

He has a soft spot for open addicts. He swigs some beer. "Here's to Kitty Dukakis." Her consumption of hair spray and deodorant impresses him. "*There's* a woman who knows how to party." James Garner's meat-eating inspires similar sympathy. "That's great, Jim. Two coronaries. They opened him up and found a flank steak glued to his heart."

To Leary, the problem isn't toxic food and drugs but that the wrong people are being wasted by them. "The ones you want to overdose never do." He's incited to a poison spray at musicians who adulterate rock's dissonance with reassuring sentiments and sounds. He points to his wrist. "See that scar? I heard the Bee Gees were getting back together. Stevie Ray Vaughn is dead, but we can't get Milli Vanilli even near a helicopter. Here's ten dollars," he says to a young guy up front, "bring me the head of Barry Manilow. You write the songs, we'll drink the beer out of your skull."

Leary focuses on this fellow, whose name is Ivan; he's twenty-one and doesn't smoke or use drugs. Leary turns avuncular, wheedling, a recruiting officer from hell. "I want you to go home and get a rifle and listen to a Judas Priest album." Leary reflects on the criminal suit brought against this band. "Does that mean I can sue Dan Fogelberg and James Taylor for making me wear hiking boots during the seventies? I didn't have sex until I was thirty-one. Where's my money?" Returning to Ivan, he implores, "Promise me you'll at least try a speedball. In your neck."

Ivan's readiness to engage keeps the banter sporting. Leary isn't sneering or smug in this set, nor at Caroline's, where he plays a few nights later. His landscape is nightmarish, yet his act is exuberant, partly because of his rock-drive delivery and because he examines decay while enjoying its stink. No carcass is exempt. He thinks it was a good thing that Jesus died when he did, because, with his sycophantish disciples, "he would have ended up like Elvis. They were the equivalent of the Memphis Mafia." Considering plane crashes in the Andes, he advises, "Feed your friends. You don't want to be stuck in the snow with your anorexic pal, Freddy." And Leary's position on Ted Kennedy: "Good senator, bad fuckin' date."

Leary acknowledges that some acts exhilarate because they can cause harm. Sobriety may be a practical choice, he says, but it doesn't ensure salvation, not while corporations and governments have the power to desecrate the water, the earth, the food.

Off stage, Leary, thirty-three, who really does smoke four packs a day, can refrain. During lunch, he doesn't light up, and he eats fruit salad instead of meat. "I've *got* to quit cigarettes one of these days," he says. It matters that his father, who smoked five packs a day, dropped dead at age sixty of a massive heart attack. It matters that, six months ago, Leary became a first-time father to son Jack. It matters that he's beginning to feel winded during the ice hockey workouts on which the Boston-born performer is also dependent. But he's not ready to wean himself. In his act, he confesses he'd prefer sucking breasts if he could carry them around. "There's too much going on right now," he says, admitting that having so much to live for is scary. He looks at me squarely, and I notice a tiny triangular shape below the iris in his left eye. "It's from my mother's side. They live to be a hundred. It's a crap shoot, the genes, the luck."

Leary's parents moved to the United States from Ireland. His father worked as a mechanic, his mother as a hospital aide. He grew up—under the protection of a tough-kid older brother—in a world where "the police and the priests and the nuns all knew your family." He first saw through bogus authority when he was an altar boy. "I drank some holy wine, and the priest told my father it would cost two hundred dollars to have me reinstated. My father said, 'No thanks.'" Leary decided to become an actor when, at thirteen, he was cast as young Patrick in a high school production of *Auntie Mame*. "You were allowed to live for wanting to perform if you could also do sports. I had a problem with the kind of authority that doesn't talk to you but just tells you what to think and do. I turned it into an act."

Robert Schimmel: Orifice Hours

October 1989

Robert Schimmel is always getting caught in some humiliating mess. A woman promises seismographic orgasms, and, although dubious, he allows her to shove beads up his ass. The next thing he knows, he's in the emergency room, a doctor is yanking out the beads, and he's coming like a house on fire. He pauses and lifts his eyes from their usual oblique angle. "I only wish my parents weren't there." Schimmel's mother and father have uncanny radar for their son's degradation. At another juncture, a cop shows them Robert's corpse, accidentally electrocuted by a sex toy. Then there's the time that Schimmel calls his dad and says, "I just took a shit and it's black." "Bob," his father responds, "you're not going to believe this, but I'm in a business meeting, and you're on the speaker phone."

Schimmel—who played Caroline's last week and appears regularly in New York clubs—evokes farts, diarrhea, semen, and contraceptive gel. No effluvium is taboo as he ricochets between delight and disgust. Sometimes, he likes nature straight up. Scented douches are a turn-off. "Pine, right, natural. I think I'll finish the fence. Vinegar, water, and mesquite—what are we doing here, fucking or barbecuing?" At other times, he prefers his fantasies to the truth. Anal sex excites him if he thinks he's initiating the woman into a deviant act, but just let her lift her ass and suggest they do it, and his dick, he admits, shrivels.

Because Schimmel details sex acts, he's been compared to the expletive-spouting Andrew "Dice" Clay and Sam Kinison. But while these comics see themselves as victims and slash women, gays, and minorities, Schimmel exposes himself. I can't think of another straight male comic who plays openly with homosexual yearnings.* He tries to evade the army by telling the examining officer he's gay. "Fine," says the man, "blow me and I'll give you a deferment." Schimmel stops and stares out. "He lied." To Schimmel, the body—with its frail flesh and parts that fly out of control—is a disaster site from which he cannot pry his eyes, a map of inevitable decay. Though short and balding, he's powerful, charged by curiosity. With his modulated delivery and resonant announcer's voice, he's an adult fixated on arrest, no more a stooge than was Kafka imagining himself a filthy beetle.

I saw Schimmel on a rainy Thursday. The house was only half full, but he kept the laughs coming. The day after, we talked in his hotel room. Off stage, he's just as intense and self-revealing as on. He sat cross-legged atop his bed, jumping up every so often for a cigarette. He said that playing

*I hadn't yet seen Jon Stewart, who is equally unguarded.

the Montreal comedy festival last year had given him courage. "This is my ninth year in the business, and I'm finally getting my voice."

Comedy came relatively late—Schimmel will be forty in January—and as something of a surprise. He was living in Scottsdale, Arizona, with his wife and daughter, managing an electronics store, when he went to L.A. to visit his sister and she took him to the Improv. "She looks at me and says, 'You're funny. You could do that.' We go to amateur night and she puts my name in the bucket without telling me. Suddenly, I hear 'Robert Schimmel,' and people are applauding, and I go up. I have no material. I say the first thing that comes: 'I'm into humiliation. The best thing you can do is not laugh.' They crack up, and I go on about my fantasies, and [Improv owner] Budd Friedman comes over and says, 'I want you to work for me.' I fly home immediately and tell my wife I've got a job. I actually believe he's going to hire me and I'm going to be a comedian. We sell the house, pack up everything, and drive to L.A. I get off the freeway to show my wife the club, and it's burned down the day before. It smells like a campfire."

Schimmel doesn't regret the move. "My illusions were dashed, and I started slowly like everyone else." Days, he installed stereos for Steve Martin and Mel Brooks. "I told them I was a comedian, and they said, 'Wire the speakers.' I don't blame them, that's what everyone tells them." Five years later, Rodney Dangerfield spotted Schimmel and invited him to appear on one of his HBO specials. The break led to steady work, but by then his son had been born and, at age three, been diagnosed with brain cancer.

"He was given only a twenty percent chance of surviving," Schimmel says, "but he's made it to eight." The boy's health, however, remains unstable and is always on Schimmel's mind. "Now that I'm getting somewhere, my agent and manager want me to drop the sex. They say, 'You'll never get on *Letterman*. You'll never get a sitcom.' They're right. But when I'm on stage, for those forty-five minutes, that's the only place in my life where I have control. I have no control whatsoever over my son's cancer. If I get to guest host on Carson, no one is going to say, 'Now your son is going into remission.' No one is ever going to say that. When I work, I want to be myself, and sex and guilt are what I think about.

"I was always preoccupied by sex. It makes people edgy and embarrassed. It controls their whole lives. My parents are Hungarian and were old-fashioned. I didn't have sex until I was twenty-one. When people laugh, I feel I'm not the only one who thinks like me. I'm not a freak. When they don't laugh, it makes me wonder if I've missed my time, because of AIDS. On the other hand, that's what we can do now, talk about sex."

Will Durst and Richard Belzer: Flex and Reflex

May 1988

On Will Durst's first and only *Letterman* shot, he ignored instructions to tell lifestyle jokes and went for his strength, political comedy. A Reagan dig was bleeped: "The president is on the radio saying, 'The bombing starts in five minutes.' That's his idea of a joke. My idea of a joke is to give Hinckley a bigger gun." Durst hasn't been asked back on *Letterman,* and he considers himself banned. According to the show, he just wasn't funny.

A few weeks ago, at Caroline's, Durst juiced a crowd hungry for thinking comedy. He wheels on stage, long hair flying, a cigarette balancing on his lower lip. At thirty-four, he has the face of a hound dog in need of a good night's sleep. He likes acting the part of a no-mush guy. A kid annoys him on a plane. The kid's mother says, "Watsamatter, mister, don't you like children?" Durst: "Yeah, with lemon and capers."

But Durst has plenty of heart—plus a point of view. Growing up in Milwaukee and working as a third-generation machinist for Alyce Chalmers—his father drove a forklift, and he did a factory stint until comedy paid off—Durst evolved into a populist suspicious of hierarchies and alive to blue-collar angst. Nothing piques him so much as preachers and pols. The Catholic Church. "Some of its clergy have AIDS. Yeah, they finally have to admit some priests are drug addicts." Pat Robertson. "God told him to run for president. God should sue for slander."

Durst likes Jesse. He'd be pleased to see an ethnic candidate in office—say Cuomo. But as for getting votes in "the heartland," well, based on Durst's experience, "Mario is not the name of the president, Mario is the man who runs the tilt-a-wheel." That job might be just the ticket for dizzy Ronnie. "Reagan didn't know he was shot. That scared me. Call me silly, but I like a president with a central nervous system." Reagan gets cancer every six months. "Nose, colon, nose . . . you figure it out." Reagan vetoed the Clean Water Act—"What was going through his mind?" Durst is amused by our government's hard line on dictators. "Duvalier is in the south of France, Marcos is in Hawaii, I bet Noriega is having nightmares about Tahiti." But Durst doesn't think we're exactly in the catbird seat where crooks are concerned. "The only way Reagan is going to remember his cabinet is if Nancy keeps a scrapbook of their mug shots. 'What's Ed doing these days?' 'Oh, eight to ten.' "*

A large crowd turned out at Caroline's last week for Richard Belzer, and the comedian stuck his fingers in the sore spots of the nation. Tall and rock 'n' roll skinny, he looks like all the Rolling Stones mixed together. He slinks across the stage or spars with the mike stand, his body controlled as a dancer's. And his impressions are perfectly pitched, whether playing a strutting Noriega, bargaining with Reagan for "a case of Oxy-10," or the president, his tongue sliding along his lower lip like a big pink slug.

MCing for five years at Catch A Rising Star, Belzer developed one fast mouth. Much of his work is improvisational, a collage of exchanges with the audience—flashes of wit and jangling angles, like the movements of his body. He looks for conversation, not punching bags, then he pushes, snooping into briefcases and handbags. At the same time flows a continuous stream of consciousness. "I used to be a Jew until I saw some guy break a girl's arm with a rock."** "Springsteen's so rich God borrows money from him. 'I need three million. I wanna do another earthquake in Mexico.' "

Belzer's politics rise off his don't-fuck-with-me stand. He hates, he loves. Basic. Most of the time, identifying with potential fuckees, he sprays a democratic vitriol that's bracing. On the other hand, part of being a tough guy for Belzer is bashing women and gays. The worst thing he can think to call Poindexter and North is "dick-smokers." Likewise Margaret Thatcher is a "dyke." To a woman in the audience he chirps, "Speak your mind, young lady. Contradiction in terms." The audience hisses. And how does Belzer come back? "Yeah, *this* is a crime. People sleeping on grates. Yeah, America, land of priorities."

Belzer's old-lefty line about the rights of the poor being worthier than the sissy causes of women and gays is dust. So is the idea that real men hate anyone who would suck a dick.

---

*Ed is Ed Meese.
**He's speaking about Israeli attacks on Palestinians.

Bill Hicks

March 1994

Bill Hicks was the stand-up to keep your eyes on. He didn't take the mike to get a sitcom but to master the art of disruption. He would wear black and pull his fingers through slicked-back hair. His features were puffy from too little sleep, too many cigarettes, and too many days spent drinking and doing drugs. It was a face at once impish and melancholy, the lower lip jutting to a tease or a pout. "I have the kind of face," he would quip, "where people who don't even know me come up and say, 'What's wrong?' " He quit drinking and drugs, because they hurt his work, but he didn't pretend that excess wasn't fun. Railing against antidrug pieties, he complained, "I quit, but—*big but*—I never murdered, beat, or raped anyone. I never lost a job. I laughed my ass off and had a great time. Where's my commercial?"

Last October, he made news when a set he did on *Letterman* was censored. As usual, he was pulling the underpants off incongruity, musing on the less-than-cheerful iconography of the crucifix—"Do you think when Jesus comes back he's really going to want to look at a cross?" And he suggested that Right-to-Lifers illustrate their love of life by linking arms not around abortion clinics, but cemeteries. Though the taping went smoothly, the segment was later axed for having "too many hot spots." Hicks was flabbergasted but agreed to another appearance. Then he got sick.

Last week he died of pancreatic cancer at age thirty-two, which is a shame for the obvious, miserable reasons but also because he'd honed an original voice and had the equipment to work it. He read. He wrote all his stuff. He learned to play a room and to score a set, intensifying themes and building tension. He would have become great.

He never got to grow up entirely, but who does? At a memorial last week at Caroline's, a childhood friend of Hicks's pointed to the circularity of Bill's experience in a markedly Hicksian way: "The end of his life with cancer was like the time I knew him back then: the real skinny Bill, who slept all day and fought with his father."

I hung out with Hicks three years ago in Montreal, just as he was hitting it big. Off stage, he was as gentle as he could be ferocious under the lights; the day after I saw his performance, we had coffee, and he asked me to speak openly and include my reservations. I said that instead of targeting prudery wherever it surfaced, he'd depicted women as priggish, and soon we were launched on a discussion of pornography's pleasures. I realized how free I felt, how uncensored and unworried, and I remember thinking that this was the lesson Bill radiated to his audiences—to go where the juice is and to know it is trust.

Damon Wayans and John Epperson: A Man's Got to Do What a Man's Gotta Do

April 1989

Twenty-seven years ago, Damon Wayans was born into a poor Harlem family as one of ten kids. He also arrived with a clubfoot, and he had to wear a thick-soled, boxy shoe. Outside of Harlem maybe people noticed his skin color first, but in his neighborhood it was always the shoe. These days Wayans is tall, sleek, good-looking, and solvent enough—from club gigs and roles in *Hollywood Shuffle* and the blaxploitation spoof *I'm Gonna Git You Sucka*—to have quit his job in Paramount's mailroom. But his splenetic comedy still springs from the perspective of the shoe.

It saved him from street brawling, he noted recently at Caroline's. "You don't find too many handicapped bullies." The notion spins into a fantasy of menacing "crips." Wiggling his limbs spastically and slurring his speech, he warns, "Don't make me get up."

In gimphood, which froze the able-bodied in shameful feelings of superiority, Wayans could get away with anything. And flying with that freedom, he unclosets a riot of vengefulness at the toughs who once made him feel puny. Playing scowling, leather-capped heavies, he gets to impersonate and also punish his former idols. His race humor is wildly mean, a tonic for pious depictions of blacks. Detailed and felt, it doesn't reduce its targets to racist stereotypes. "When I want to see the people I grew up with," Wayans says ruefully, "most of the time I just go to the morgue." In a sustained routine—redolent of Gleason's grandiose, defeated Ralph Kramden—he becomes a once-reigning slick fresh out of jail: "I'm gonna get me a job at McDonald's, become manager, then have my boys come in and rob the place. My lady works as a bank teller. I'll get her to forge checks and have her prostitute a little on the side. Can't have no full-time ho in the house. I'm Muslim—no pork, no hos."

Wayans sees the way black men, made impotent in society, feel feminized and infantilized and react by striving to prove their masculinity with violent acts and hardened hearts. The trouble with Wayans is that he isn't always in control of this knowledge. Sometimes, the pain of being black and once disabled wells up as pure rage—and gets directed at gay men. Gays obsess him. All are flaming queens who hold limp wrists to their chests, screech in high voices, and run from danger with spaghetti legs. These figures seem to embody his secret fears about himself—and some reveal self-loathing. Wayans hates his flesh; nothing horrifies him more than the thought of a man incorporating his cock. And, reporting the flack he's received from gay rights groups, he huffs, "If you can take a dick, you can take a joke." At another point, riffing off Michael Jackson's surgery, he quips, "If I had a hundred million dollars, I'd have the crack on my ass removed."

By becoming the kind of bully he first dissects, Wayans tries to rescind the vulnerability he's shown, but that's only one motivation. Playing queens—with his limbs flailing out of control and his face suffused with joy—he recovers the freedom he had wearing the shoe. While his mouth insists he's a real man, his body says he's dying for a vacation from boot-camp masculinity.

■ ■ ■

Drag entertainer John Epperson, a.k.a. Lypsinka, made that escape and never looked back. In his one-man show, *I Could Go on Lip-Synching* (Theater Off Park), he mouths lyrics, dances, flounces, and vogues to numbers by showbiz belters like Connie Francis, Nanette Fabray, Ann-Margret, Pearl Bailey, and Mimi Hines. Every note is choreographed, sometimes with Epperson's entire body, sometimes with merely the flick of his eyelashes—long enough to be seen in the last row.

Numbers flow into one another, and costumes are changed, with a maximum of tease, on stage. Epperson's makeup—huge red lips and eyebrows that zig up, then arrow toward the floor—is part clown face, part showgirl mask. His mouth is complex; outlined in black, it conjures the race drag of minstrel shows and the gender frolic of Little Richard's pencil mustache. Bean-pole thin, Epperson's body skirts gender differences; his form is a hanger on which he drapes ideas, a series of lines he animates into cartoons. The breast portions of his strapless gowns move in one direction while his flat chest twists in another, just as breasts, cast as objects of fantasy, have lives of their own.

Epperson impersonates bawdy, fame-obsessed divas, because their appetites are naked. Reveling in trash, he re-creates the tantalizing state before taste developed: a polymorphism in which all books are intriguing because they're intelligible, all brands of ice cream delicious because they are sweet, all movies thrilling because they eclipse reality. In this period, boy emotions and girl emotions aren't distinct. Epperson's drag is purposely crude; kicks are extended without pointed toes, his body is always unpadded. As a man, he resurrects the bliss of dancing in front of the mirror in underwear, a time when anything that feels good can be embraced without moral or aesthetic rationales.

After indulging in the pleasures of the shoe, Wayans cringes back in shame and becomes hateful. Making a spectacle of himself, Epperson is lovely loving freedom.

Calvin Trillin and Jackie Mason: Mensch and Minstrel

October 1990

Two Jews get on a bus. No, two Jews are walking down the street, and one says . . . No, two Jews debut comedy shows in the same week: Jackie Mason and Calvin Trillin. What, you didn't know Mason was Jewish? Oh, you mean Trillin. The name fooled you. Don't quote me on this, because I don't know it for an actual fact (as Mason would say), but once upon a time *Trillin* was probably *Trillinski*, and the Jew part fell off when the family made its way to Kansas City—nothing intentional, but you know how easy it is to lose things when you're traveling.

Not that Trillin is trying to mask his ethnicity. In his wry performance *Words, No Music*, at American Place Theatre, Trillin mentions that his grandparents argued about Yiddish pronunciation, and he recalls his father's rueful philosophy, "You might as well be a mensch." That is what he became—a curious man who strode from home into the world. He feels free to tap society on the shoulder and state his opinions, because *he is free.*

Trillin's comedy is founded on his entitlement, one that asks for no special status for himself or anyone else. For eighty minutes, he talks about words, politics, and pleasure. He's dry. No smiles, no truckling. He's a Kabuki basset hound who can flay a piece of pomposity or piety with one pitiless stare.

About the Reagans's decision to change the address on their house from 666 to 668, because three sixes are associated with the devil, Trillin says, "Fine, but now where's the devil supposed to live?" Trillin imagines Bush's first private words to Gorbachev: "Where'd you prep?" And the humorist is sponsoring a constitutional amendment making a C average a requirement for the presidency.

Ambling with amiable aimlessness from podium to armchair, he slips into silly mode. Learning that whales can communicate across a span of three hundred miles, he wonders what they say to each other. Hands to mouth. "Can you still hear me?" His daughter introduces him to the word *dweeb*, and he goes to England to find out what the British call nerds. Jack Benny pause. "Of course that's not what I told the immigration officer." He proudly declares his claim to *Guinness Book of World Records* fame: He is the first person on national TV to say "deer penis." He was on a talk show, chatting about exotic food, when he recalled a menu that offered "double-boiled deer penis." Reports Trillin, "I thought about ordering it, but I was afraid I'd say to the waiter, 'Why don't you take it back to the kitchen and boil it one more time.'"

Trillin wobbles in one area. He mentions his wife, Alice, several times, always showing her concerned about appearances—worried that he sounds crude and dresses shabbily. He thinks he's saying that she has standards. He thinks he's telling us that he's a slob. Really, though, he's bragging that he's anarchic and showing up Alice as a prude. This isn't too far from take-my-wife humor.

■ ■ ■

The coy conceit that stresses Mason's spiel in *Brand New*, at the Neil Simon Theatre, winds up swamping it. The issue isn't about being a man but a Jew. Since he was charged with racism during the Giuliani campaign, Mason has toned down his stand-up. He doesn't go after the weak as often, though he can't resist insisting that the denigrating word *schwartze* simply means black. He booms *schwartze* about a dozen times. It mounts to a taunt.

Like Trillin, though, Mason has a nose for piquant ironies: "How come a grandchild never shows you a picture of a grandfather?" He can nail political hypocrisy, noting, "It took Dinkins eight months to buy a piece of fruit in a Korean market. Now, if they were selling designer jackets . . . " Dusting off the mayor, he adds, "Dinkins has a tough job. He has to look for the criminals. Koch appointed them." And the comedian lays open Souter's surly waffling. "If you hired a plumber and said to him, 'Did you ever see a toilet?' and the man answered, 'None of your business,' would you hire him?"

Unfortunately, through most of his hundred-minute set, Mason slinks away from the world and hunkers in a concocted ghetto. First, there's his thick, old-world accent. Maybe, just maybe there is a guy 104 years old sitting on some boardwalk who talks this way. But Mason is what, fifty-five, sixty? He compulsively asks people in the audience if they are Jews or gentiles, then paints gentiles as bland, inscrutable rubes. Jewishness is conjured as the most delightful, zany condition possible, a club of clubs, but guess what, you can't get in unless you're born there. To top it off, the smugness is packaged as defense for an excluded minority.

This is minstrelsy—Mason sustaining an ancient stereotype and portraying nostalgia as present reality. Sure, there's anti-Semitism in the United States, but Jews are no longer systematically barred from power. Insisting they *are* still ghettoized is an insult to groups now struggling for the opportunities Jews have won. Mason slimes Jews who don't see gentiles as the dreaded/exotic Other. He slimes gentiles by depicting them as ineluctably phobic about Jews. He has a talent for sniffing out social predators who fatten by exploiting people's vanities. When he becomes that creature, he slimes himself.

Paul Krassner: Comedy Left

September 1988

Paul Krassner—wearing baggy pants, purple shoes, and a satin jacket that says "Margo's Dance Parlor" on the back—shambles onto a dark stage while his recorded voice mumbles, "Dan Quayle." He turns off the tape machine and switches on a TV. It doesn't work. He smiles, confessing it's supposed to. And that smile—sheepish, ironic, prepared for all incalculables—redeems the gaffe. It keeps rescuing him, through times he gets tangled, catlike, in unraveled threads of thought. Drugs? Age? (He's fifty-seven, but his curly mop of hair is dark, and despite thick acne scars on his face and a limp caused by back surgery, he looks ten years younger.) Sometimes the meandering is intentional; themes left dangling are wittily looped back into the monologue. Krassner's been doing stand-up since 1980, mostly in southern California, and I caught him at L.A.'s intimate Odyssey Theater.

His voice is conversational and sincere. He doesn't mention the *Realist*, the underground paper he's been writing and publishing off and on since 1958. He doesn't remind us he cofounded the Yippies with Abbie Hoffman. His focus is on surreal politics. "John Hinckley came out for gun control; Reagan was against it." "Reagan promised to revoke the inheritance tax, 'for rich and poor alike.'" On Bush. "When Jessica McClure fell down the well, he said she was rescued by 'the American spirit.' What, a Third World country would have left her there?"

Sifting through media, Krassner finds similar disjunctions. A doctor opposed to abortion but forced to perform one on a rape victim reports to the conservative magazine *Free Inquiry* that during the operation God made the fetus disappear. "An immaculate abortion," Krassner terms it. He turns on the TV (it eventually works) and finds no-comment comedy. A commercial announcer says, "All you can eat is not enough." Increasingly, Krassner can't tell if he's dreaming. "Did Koop really take a pipe away from Mr. Potato Head? Did Nancy really sit on the lap of Mr. T, who was dressed like Santa, and plant a smacker on his cheek?"

Most engagingly, Krassner tells stories about political activism and family life, tales that reveal the ways public and private events inform one another. He hasn't mellowed. He's ripened. He's in Chicago with Hoffman and Jerry Rubin, and they make friends with the cops sent to trail them. They give the guys Yippie buttons. Hoping to vomit in court during the conspiracy trial, Krassner drops acid, but when he's asked to swear on the Bible, he gets the crazy idea to refuse, electing instead his right to affirm his testimony. Then he can't throw up. "Violating one taboo short-circuited the other."

He remembers when his daughter was sixteen, called him on the phone, and played Carly Simon's "Daddy, I'm Not a Virgin Anymore." "I was torn between pleasure in her showing this creative way of sharing a new stage in her life and jealousy that I didn't get any at her age." Near the end of the set, all of his themes converge in a tale about power and autonomy. He's in his late forties, and his father not only buys him a parka but shows him how to put up the hood. There, in this scene at once ordinary and trying, Krassner encounters a supreme high in pure form: the option to deliberate. "I'm standing in the jacket, and suddenly I know something has changed, because for the first time in this house I can make a decision. I can either point out to my father that he's frozen me in childhood." Krassner pauses, and his palms go out. "Or I can practice putting up the hood."

Confessions of a Raving, Unconfined Nut: Misadventures in the Counterculture

March 1994

It starts with the bris. The moyl is unlicensed, a butcher by trade and, as luck would have it, a bungling surgeon. He accidentally leaves an extra flap of foreskin clinging to the underside of Paul Krassner's "pippy," and said flap has the discomfiting tendency to stick to his balls. The boy, trying to separate flesh from flesh, is judged a flagrant masturbator. To distract him, Krassner's parents tender a violin, in hopes that he will substitute a musical instrument for the anatomical one. Young K is aroused to compete; his older brother is already taking lessons. And by age six, the prodigious stroker is at Carnegie Hall, the youngest performer ever to solo on that stage.

It is 1939. He is dressed in a Little Lord Fauntleroy suit and a white, puffy-sleeved shirt. He is in the middle of Vivaldi's *Concerto in A Minor* when his leg begins to itch. Should he use the bow to scratch it? Impossible. The performance must go on. But the itch taunts, and darts its tongue. K balances on one leg and uses the other foot to scratch it, thereby inspiring laughter from the audience. The boy feels truly alive at that moment, becoming aware that he has been asleep—passive before his desires, uncertain even of what they are. Now he can transform them into action.

This, in condensed form, is the Krassner scenario. The rumpled foreskin representing everything imposed on K: the pressure to reap glory for the family, to press his nose to the grindstone, to leave his dick alone. Forever more, the rumpled foreskin will be a reminder that he was good: a nice boychik, a droid in unsafe hands. Standing on one leg, he balances between impulse and action, but, once awake, impulse can seldom be denied. Each itch feels like an imperative, each scratch a break for freedom—a move that is always defiant, releasing tension with great, quaking force. The pattern hardly deviates in the sixty years Krassner chronicles in his uproarious and mostly delightful memoir. He makes compulsion work for him much of the time.

He tells three interwoven tales about the development of his personality, the period from which it sprang, and the rise of the counterculture—an awakening en masse. Most of the time the elements are craftily meshed, Krassner glorifying his own rebelliousness less than the benefits of license and dissent. He is a traveler with the news, his voice at once ironic and free of scorn—spinning a stand-up spiel. His focus is on incongruity: the source of laughter and the truths we're not supposed to know.

In training to be an artist of disruption, young K plays Mendelssohn in the subway, using the money he collects for junk food. But one day he finds a way to harness irreverence to a larger good. At the Steeplechase in Coney Island, a dwarf is paid to zap unsuspecting passersby with a cattle prod, and he targets with special vigor the rumps of women. Seizing his opportunity, K gets hold of the prod, chases the dwarf, and earns cheers from the crowd.

But how to make this guerrilla theater into a life's work? By the time he reaches his mid-twenties, Krassner still lives with his parents and is a virgin. He's at risk of becoming an anarchic nerd—an overeducated cabbie, maybe. Then he meets Lyle Stuart, publisher of the alternative magazine the *Independent*. He lands a job with Stuart, working in the building where Bill Gaines produces *Mad* magazine, and after proving his talent, at age twenty-six, Krassner is appointed editor of his own iconoclastic publication, the *Realist*.

It is 1958, and taboos sit like juicy blackheads on the body politic. It's a time when "father knows best" is said without quotes, when police hunt down and arrest anyone involved with abortion, when Lenny Bruce is persecuted for obscenity on stage and other comedians fail to rally to his cause. Krassner publishes an interview with atheist Madalyn Murray, who speaks of the Virgin Mary's orgasmic potential. He publishes early interviews—still funny and trenchant—with Bruce, Norman Mailer, and Albert Ellis, who suggests that angry people say, "Unfuck you," so as not to demean the pleasures of sex.

The magazine puts its muscle and money where its progressive mouth is. After the *Realist* publishes an anonymous interview with underground abortionist Dr. Robert Spencer, Krassner becomes an abortion referral service, channeling hundreds of women who call his office to safe medical care. He helps fund William Baird's free birth-control clinic, and the *Realist* helps launch and finance a domestic Peace Corps called People. The organization establishes neighborhood reading programs, a day-care center, a bail fund, and a children's camp inspired by Summerhill.

The *Realist* is the perfect conduit for Krassner's urge to make trouble. He's opposed to hypocrisy, prudery, and repression, sure, but he's also wild, brimming with a need to shock. He flashes a macho absorption in grunge, orifices, effluvia—unleashing the goosh usually contained by skin and sphincters. He concocts a character called the *Realist* Nun, played by future hooker-activist Margo St. James. Dressed in full nun regalia, she and Krassner tongue kiss at the airport and, one afternoon, she wanks him off in a porno theater. The magazine becomes "a clearinghouse for bizarre news items . . . and unusual material from medical journals." Krassner publishes reports on "fracture of the penis," "the caloric content of semen," and "objects found in the rectum," including "a tennis ball" and "a frozen pig's tail." An offended reader cancels his subscriptions with the kiss-off: "I trust that you know what you can do with your magazine."

But no stunt proves as notorious as "The Parts Left Out of the Kennedy Book" (1967), a chapter supposedly censored from William Manchester's account of the assassination, *The Death of a President*. Krassner has Lyndon Johnson fucking Kennedy's neck wound—not, mind you, merely for necrophiliac gratification but as part of the cover-up. Johnson's cock is making an entrance wound, from a bullet fired from the grassy knoll, look like an exit wound, from a bullet supposedly fired from the book depository.

Krassner immerses himself in conspiracy theory as well as every other deep and shallow outpouring of the counterculture—the *Realist* helping to set a tone of skepticism as well as chronicling the movement's course. Krassner is late to drop acid, but Timothy Leary is his guru. Passing along his expertise, Krassner inducts Groucho Marx into the drug's mysteries, the two of them tripping through one night. Krassner hangs with prankster Ken Kesey and with Ed Sanders of the Fugs. Passionate about Vietnam, he joins with Abbie Hoffman and Jerry Rubin to form the Yippies and stage the 1968 antiwar protest at the Democratic Convention in Chicago. Their candidate for president is a pig, named—what else?—Pigasus.

Drugs seem not to have dimmed Krassner's memory, for he captures the youthful solidarity and street-power politics of these times in all their tie-dyed, hormonal splendor. His Abbie, Jerry, and Paul are rivalrous siblings as well as revolutionaries, each personality in place: Jerry the media operator, Abbie the visionary leader, Paul the irrepressible gadfly. FBI agents and police are swarming, carrying real guns and ammo. Rumor has spread that the Yippies plan to spike Chicago's water with LSD, and a pair of cops is assigned to tail the trio. After a while, the boys see they are being followed and confront the officers, and suddenly they hit Krassner warp—threat dissolving into improbability, time stopping so they can thrill to the variousness of the human beast. The cops accept Yippie buttons, in case they get separated from their quarry in a crowd. The cops are hungry and propose a restaurant. "How do we get there?" ask the out-of-towners. "Follow us," say the cops, and they do.

The Yippies—self-promotion and delusions of grandeur notwithstanding—represent the lighter side of Krassner. Inside the shadows lurks Charles Manson, who slashes his way into the zeitgeist in 1969, sending his cult minions to slaughter Sharon Tate and her guests. Manson first writes to Krassner from prison, complaining about a piece in the *Realist*. The magazine, upon learning that Manson had spent time in Boys Town, published an apocryphal account, "Charles Manson Was My Bunkmate," by Richard Meltzer. Manson is pissed off, protesting he was only there for two days. But the link is forged, and as the sixties give way to the seventies and Krassner finds himself in the middle of his life—a bit stuck and doing a lot of acid and dope—he feels more pressed than ever to be bad.

What could avenge the rumpled foreskin—the Jewish kid with the violin—more than trying on the devil's hooves? At the beginning, Krassner is fascinated by the straight media's distortion of Manson, which he astutely corrects in his memoir: "Manson was portrayed by the media as a hippie cult leader, and the counterculture became a dangerous enemy. Hitchhikers were shunned. Communes were raided. In the public's mind, flower children had grown poisonous thorns. But Manson was never really a hippie. He had grown up behind bars. His *real* family included con artists, pimps, drug dealers, thieves, muggers, rapists, and murderers."

Krassner, already a hound after cover-ups, finds evidence that the Los

Angeles Police Department unwittingly facilitated Manson's carnage. Manson, while on federal parole, was arrested twice for statutory rape and yet was left on the streets. Krassner interviews Preston Guillony, a former deputy sheriff in L.A., who contends that the department believed and hoped that Manson, an avowed racist, "meant to launch an attack on the Black Panthers."

But Krassner is just as attracted to the man as to the case—to Manson's utter outsideness, aloneness, abjectness, and bloody recklessness. Like Krassner, Manson strives to sabotage decency and violate respectability. How can the journalist not look at the unprincipled, vicious version of these impulses? He meets and befriends Manson-cultist Squeaky Fromme (yet to attempt her assassination of Gerald Ford). "Squeaky Fromme," Krassner recalls, "resembled a typical redheaded, freckle-faced waitress who sneaks a few tokes of pot in the lavatory, a regular girl-next-door except perhaps for the unusually challenging nature of her personality plus the scar of an X that she had gouged and burned into her forehead as a visual reminder of her commitment to Charlie."

Krassner sees Fromme a few times in San Francisco, where he is living, and one bizarre day, laced with acid and who knows what, he plays erotic games not only with Fromme but with two other Manson women, Sandy Good and Brenda McCann. He feels perversely complimented when they compare his aura to Manson's, and at one point slips on Charlie's corduroy vest, "a solid inch thick with embroidery—snakes and dragons and devilish designs including human hair that had been woven into the multicolored patterns."

You have to credit Krassner for refusing to categorize Manson as nonhuman and seeking connections to knowable behavior. At the same time, his Manson gambit is a comedy sketch. His own, real nastiness involves little murders, a pattern of betrayal that repeats and repeats. He screws people to show them up or to get his way, rationalizing the slam as protecting free speech or another noble cover. Exposing hypocrisy in government and rubbing the inconsistencies of friends in their faces seem to him equally pressing.

Lyle Stuart, Norman Mailer, his wife Jeanne, Abbie Hoffman, and quite a few others are either publicly humiliated or defied. Krassner earns someone's trust, and then pick, pick, pick, a tendency that resonates to a peculiar habit he once developed. Before facing the draft board, he tells us, he opened sores on his face, etching a disfiguring map of scars. The ploy succeeded in getting him off, but he couldn't stop the lacerations. Later, we come to observe, when loved ones present a strong need, Krassner hears a command. He views compliance as surrender, and he can't not pick.

But none of this is analyzed; it's just set forth. We don't know what Krassner thinks spurs him, and after a while the confessions are more self-important than self-revealing. A similar lack of perspective thins the last few chapters, which aren't shaped, as are earlier sections, around pivotal social events and magnetic figures such as Lenny Bruce. They come off like scrapbooks of Paul's greatest stunts and quips. He drops names as if trying to convince us he's worthy of an autobiography, when this has been made clear by his rich sentences.

But even at his most self-advertising and New Age foggy, Krassner retains pert antennae for incongruity, pointed apocrypha, and cosmic jokes. When he is tripping with Groucho, the elder comedian says, "Do you realize that irreverence and reverence are the *same thing*?" It's a druggy perception, but it's also the satirist's code: not to sneer at folly but to plumb its depths. There is so much soulful humor and precious daffiness in this book. One of the Yippie leaders, Super-Joel, was the grandson of Mafia boss Sam Giancana, and when the Yippies are in Chicago, the cops warn Giancana that Krassner is a bad influence. In the seventies, Krassner writes to Manson, asking what he thinks of his public persona, and the prisoner replies, "I've always run poker games and whores and crime. . . . I just ride and play the cards that were pushed on me to play. Mass killer, it's a job, what can I say."

Krassner's daughter Holly is grown, and he has remarried. He's again publishing the *Realist*, now a quarterly, and damn if it doesn't hit the old lurid and ridiculous highs. (Recent lampoons featured J. Edgar Hoover caricatured as Jaye Davidson in *The Crying Game*, and Howard Stern, whose balls are revealed to be Beavis and Butt-head). His is the sort of life—so improvised and alert to serendipity—that could make you wonder each day if you were building something or riding a runaway train. It is most definitely a life, thread by thread, groping for consciousness, laughing.

CHAPTER THREE

Lunatic Fringe:
Clowns and Character Assassins
Who Detonate from Inside a
Persona or a Series of Alters

Emo Philips

What distinguishes this batch of comics from the previous assortment is that they are almost never themselves while performing. It's as if, in order to enter the world, they need to become dummy heads in their own ventriloquism act. Like Harpo. Like Cliff Arquette, who was perpetually Charlie Weaver, or Mae West and W. C. Fields, who, in movies and plays, portrayed characters with other names but acted them as their stock figures: West the wise bawd; Fields the graceful bumbler. Among early soloists and sketch performers who specialized in an array of types, Bea Lily, Ruth Draper, and Fanny Brice come to mind.

TV in the fifties and sixties pulsed on character comedy—Milton Berle, Sid Caesar, Red Skelton, Jackie Gleason, Carol Burnett. Of them all, Gleason's Ralph Kramden is the strongest touchstone for the disturbing comedy that would follow—informing, for example, the best of John Belushi and Bill Murray during their stints on *Saturday Night Live*. Gleason's powerful, psychologically freighted performance in *The Hustler* came as a revelation to many, because he'd shown so little of that side in his comedy, which was typically one-note, or sentimental, or flashy. *Except* for Kramden. Kramden's fat encased him in a helplessness from which not even his aggression could free him, firing comedy as painful as it was hell-bent.

The most enduring contribution of the sixties collage *Rowan and Martin's Laugh-In*—more gently satiric than knife-edged—was that of propelling Lily Tomlin onto a world stage. The troupsters in *Beyond the Fringe* and *Monty Python* were bolder models for spiked sketch comedy, serving as smart older brothers to North America's lampoon factories of the seventies and eighties: *SNL* and *SCTV*. (Speaking of Brits, has anyone equaled the chameleon genius of Peter Sellers in *Dr. Strangelove?*) Even in its brief heyday of irreverence, *SNL* never achieved the ingenuity and intelligence of Canada's media satire *SCTV*, a nest that hatched ace character channelers: Catherine O'Hara, Martin Short, Dave Thomas, Joe Flaherty, Rick Moranis, and Eugene Levy. (John Candy was an alum, too, but, like Chris Farley and unlike Gleason, he came across less a puppetmaster of his heft than a sacrifice to audience sadism.)

Most of the comedians spawned on these shows have done their best work on TV. Whether hosting *SNL* or clowning on talk shows, Steve Martin is usually brilliant—preening under the guise of being gawky, one-upping while appearing dim, planning meticulously while seeming to improvise. He successfully transferred his stand-up persona to the films *The Jerk, All of Me*, and *The Man With Two Brains*, and he's agilely inhabited twisted brothers as the salesman in *Pennies from Heaven* and the sadistic dentist in *Little Shop of Horrors*. In most of his recent movies—*Leap of Faith* and *Sgt. Bilko*—though, he's looked stymied and inert.

No one has known what to do with Martin Short since the hilarious sci-fi spoof *Innerspace*. (Rent it, you'll thank me.) Bill Murray has fared better, especially in *Groundhog Day*, which may well be the most original comedy of the last decade. Directed by Harold Ramis, the film riffs on repetition:

on how a neurotic comes to see his compulsions, and how, through a series of refining revisions, art emerges from life.

The pieces in this chapter move from comedians whose personas are close to their identities to performers who are more radically disguised. It was a toss-up whether some comics belonged here or in the previous chapter—Whoopi Goldberg, or Robin Williams, since their work is political. Whoopi can get down as herself—on her talk show and hosting award ceremonies. But she came to prominence doing characters, and her alter Fontaine endows her with special candor. The categories in this book are somewhat arbitrary for all the performers, since most mix politics, social observation, and personal confession, and yet in almost every case, some element is most defining.

Robin Williams is suffering from his success, becoming wildly rich and popular in family-friendly dreck like *Mrs. Doubtfire* (pepped up by the drag collage with Harvey Firestein). In most of the other movies he's made this past decade, he's either saintly or emotionally arrested, in all cases sexless. What happened to the canny grown-up he played in *Moscow on the Hudson*?

Steven Wright is as still and solemn as Williams is fluid and hysterical. Wright is verbal, but his comedy resembles Buster Keaton's mimed resignation and passivity. Reporting from his menacing dreamscape, he dubs himself "a peripheral visionary," who can "see into the future but just way off to the side." He says he knew he wasn't his mother's first child, even before he was born. "There was graffiti in the womb. 'Bob was here.' " The sex wars inspire him. His girlfriend asks, "If you could know how and when you were going to die, would you want to know?" "No," he responds. "Forget it, then," she comes back.

If you've caught Emo Philips on television, you've seen only his shadow. You need to behold him in his emaciated flesh, hear the trademark wheeze that is half phone-sex breather, half patient on a respirator. In a typically sly piece for Showtime, a cop directs him to jog in a park, not a graveyard, and Emo deduces, "He's obviously not a hurdle man." Emo's girlfriend is miffed because he tells her she looks sexy with black fingernails—"And now she thinks I slammed the car door on her on purpose." In addition to his usual *Silence of the Lambs*–style grisliness, over the years Emo has struck a few new notes. Like counsel for the young: "The way to teach kids not to be afraid of the dark is to fill their daylight hours with as much horror as possible, so they'll *pray* for the darkness to come."

Father Guido Sarducci is as capacious to Don Novello as was the Little Tramp to Chaplin. Novello has been tweaking orthodoxy since the early days of *SNL*, and he still kills, dreaming up new irreverence—not so much antichurch as antiauthority—for stints on *Letterman* and Leno. What makes the work enduring is that Sarducci isn't just a mouthpiece for jokes but a fleshed character with dreams and anxieties. We've watched him scouting the stations of life, progressing from hippy scam artist to hood ornament on the tank of hierarchy. It's a life story.

The alter Pee-wee Herman, on the other hand, got a choke hold on Paul Reubens, and word was he was ready to do in the emotionally arrested case before the intercession of fate in the form of his police arrest. In my piece, I nail the hypocrisy of Reubens's critics and the double standard of sex scandal when it's white male het versus anything else, especially gay. The ruckus surrounding the arrest of Hugh Grant for procuring a blow job on a Hollywood street is a case in point. Instead of owning his act as a caprice between consenting adults and telling the media to bugger off in its judgment of him as vile and ignoble, Grant stuttered apologies, debasing himself more than any sex act could have. But, hey, his career didn't suffer. Bottom line: He was a guy doing a guy thing, something expected if chastised. Reubens was made to feel he'd be unemployable, although that's no longer the case. For the last few seasons, he's been the brightest note on the otherwise depleted *Murphy Brown*.

It's sometimes incalculable the way an entertainer will click into focus, then sink—for reasons other than scandal. In the eighties Dennis Blair did musical impersonations and shtick. He asserted that Keith Richards was in the Rolling Stones to make Mick Jagger look healthy and reported that the Ethiopians were raising money to get Bob Dylan off the *We Are the World* record. Where is Blair now? Another inspired loony, Jim Turner, didn't carve a career fitting his talent. In the piece here, he comes off a prodigy at turning self-loathing into hilarity.

In his pointed editorials and uncanny impressions of Reagan and Bush, Jim Morris was so dead-on he harked back to David Fry, the peerless Nixon impersonator, who could furrow his brow and seem spontaneously to grow a five o'clock shadow. Morris did Clinton and Perot during the '92 election: "Bill Clinton wants to amend his stand on Sister Souljah—'If the week for blacks killing whites is in Houston during the Republican convention, I'd have no problem with that.'" But Morris couldn't find enough to dislike in Clinton, so this portrait was never as blistering as his portrayals of Reagan and Bush.

Louise DuArt speaks about the "cannibalism" of impressions—the invasiveness of doing other people, the appropriation and plundering of identities, and how much more difficult this is for women, trained to curb their aggression, than for men. She raises issues about the messiness of physical comedy, with women traditionally feeling inhibited from appearing out of control and dirty.

Harry Shearer should be cast in bronze just for playing/creating Derek Smalls in *This is Spinal Tap* (1984)—one of the comic gems of any era, teasing everyone's wish to be an inane British rocker. The movie remains a high point for director Rob Reiner, who went on to make *When Harry Met Sally,* a film that reveres male vanity as lavishly as *Spinal Tap* lampoons it. Shearer is a rare bird in showbiz: acting since he was a kid and appearing on *The Jack Benny Show,* yet remaining independent. Shearer cowrote *Real Life* with Albert Brooks, worked with Martin Mull on *Fernwood 2 Night,* piped up with a chorus of voices on *The Simpsons,* and created his own long-running radio program *Le Show,* featuring his biting Reagan soap opera, *Hellcats of the White House.*

Whether Jim Carrey's comedy will evolve remains to be seen, but there's no denying his spectacular physical skills. The word *elastic* doesn't convey his seamless morphing and flip-book inventory of gargoyles. I liked *The Cable Guy,* though its grosses were disappointing. Fans wanted a sunnier Carrey, though his strength lies in his darkness. Manic and uncontained, he's a walking aneurysm.

The last piece in this chapter chronicles a week in the life, where I catch performances in a mix of venues and mull on their different atmospheres. Cream rises in the form of character actor Jeffrey Essmann and surreal tummler Gilbert Gottfried. At his best in piercing literary satires, Essmann fires stand-up bits, too, flashing his own mordant chops: "In first grade my teacher asked what I expected of life. I said, 'You color for a while and then you die.' " Essmann, whose composed, equine face veils a rude disrupter, teases out the poisons tamped down by surface decorum. Hostility keeps erupting from a nail-chewing aerobics coach—"Imagine that you've got this invisible grappling hook through your chest, lifting you through the ceiling . . . okay, nice and relaxed." An embittered, boozy Barbie, wobbling on feet frozen in high-heel position, runs a nightclub for wasted former playthings: "Pinocchio came to audition. I said, 'You want to do an act? Kneel down and lie to me.' "

On sitcoms, Gottfried plays the punishment date, and he gained peculiar celebrity as the parrot's voice in *Aladdin*. His club work is genius lunacy, based on an improbability only he can devise. Gilbert: "A grasshopper takes a seat at a bar, and the bartender says, 'We have a drink named after you.' The grasshopper chirps with disbelief: 'You have a drink named Schlomo?' " In another bit, aliens hover menacingly and finally exit their spacecraft. Their first, eagerly anticipated words: "Ben Gazzara is a good actor, how come he can't get a series?"

Whoopi Goldberg: Goldberg Variations

January 1989

New Year's Eve, the Felt Forum. Near the end of Whoopi Goldberg's set, she tells a Hollywood story. Opening her mail, she finds an invitation to Liz Taylor's birthday party, which catapults her to the Gap for the tightest, baddest black Levi's. At Taylor's front door, she's told to carry her delivery to the back, and when she gets inside she hears Bette Davis croaking, "Who is Whoopi? She's been in the business for two minutes." Later, Goldberg is seated beside Taylor. To reach the hostess, women with faces tight as drums and bodies liposucked of cellulite dangle jeweled pendants on Goldberg's forehead and, as she says aloud, "hang old, wrinkly white-woman titties" in her face.

Goldberg imitates Taylor taking a crap like a diva, and she serves up a dead-eye impression of bellowing Davis, mowing down bystanders with her frustration and disability. On Carson, Davis once blithely reported that to commemorate her seventieth birthday she wore blackface and dressed in black to signify death—toward which her thoughts were then inclining. I don't know if this Rorschach stoked Goldberg's pitilessness, but whatever did, it was cheering. So, too, Goldberg never loses sight of her own arriviste absurdity. After hearing Davis's derision, she gets ready to "kick some old-lady ass," but just then Davis turns and says, "Hello, Whoopi." Goldberg clutches her heart and in an awestruck tone responds, "Hello, Miss Davis."

Mainly, Goldberg performs as Fontaine, a black male ex-junkie. Fontaine observes that while Reagan sent a congratulatory telegram to Jessica

McClure, the little girl who slipped into the well, he extended not a word of condolence to the Ray brothers, the hemophiliac kids with AIDS who got burned out of their home. Fontaine, who recently quit drugs, Negrifies his sponsor by calling her Bet*tay* Ford. But, most of the set lacks the tooth of these riffs.

Ever since Goldberg burst on the national scene, she's been searching for contexts that could embrace her acting talent, politics, and unusual persona. In the series of monologues that launched her, she proved she could portray an array of characters. Her writing, however, tended to wax pious or slide into clichés.

She's fared somewhat better in the action movies she's mostly shot; they're formula, but a brash, original persona is emergent. The Whoopi figure, who's grown up feeling like an ugly duckling, has transformed herself into an eagle. She has style: leather and scarves, dark glasses and Reeboks, perky dreads that curtain her cheeks. Her voice is melodiously deep, and she doesn't care if she's thought androgynous.

Playing spies and cops, she gets shot at and beaten more than any woman I can think of; she also defends herself and goes on the attack more. But the movies themselves are inadequate to her gifts. This includes *The Color Purple,* Spielberg's Disney-literal melodrama, where she is touching as Celie, a woman scorned for her looks and physically abused by men. In a sense, Goldberg's Whoopi persona is a vindication of the Celie in her and in every female. The women who see her live, myself included, applaud Goldberg's success in gaining mass appeal for her manner and aesthetic— as have Barbra Streisand and Bette Midler. But these performers have also discovered means to develop their talents.

Goldberg, who cuts a far more deviant figure and must have a harder time finding the right exercise equipment, doesn't yet know her strength. She accepts potboiler roles. Her confidence wavers on stage; in a peculiar lapse, she tells the audience in the $50 seats she wouldn't have paid that much for her show. She is trying to sound like the girl she once was, the girl who grew up in the Chelsea projects, but she comes across apologetic. Her juices don't flow unstintingly until she takes us to where she lives now: Hollywood, with its seductiveness and contradictions, the land where she exults in the bounty of stars and finds herself alternately snubbed and reaping her comeuppance. Like any immersion, the subject deepens her social comedy, stimulates her intelligence, motivates her acting.

Robin Williams: The World According to Mork

August 1986

"In the presidential debates, Reagan called military uniforms 'costumes,'" Robin Williams noted Saturday night at the Met. "Not a good sign," he added, instantly becoming a movie-besotted Reagan. Imaginary barroom doors swung behind him as he entered Congress. The faces of politicians melted into those of actors: Weinberger, advising nighttime raids into Nicaragua, slipped into Bela Lugosi; Kissinger—"the phantom of Congress"—slid into Peter Lorre, purring, "I'm your only real friend." Reaching a crescendo of alarm over the president's feeble grip on reality, Williams concluded, "Reagan is Disney's last wish." Becoming Disney, he boomed, "Make me a president!" Switching to Dopey addressing the other dwarfs: "You heard what he said."

Satirizing the arms buildup on both the domestic and international fronts, Williams became a suburban crank: "I'll bet this Cruise missile will stop those kids from playing ZZ Top." In another bit, he was Lester Maddox conferring with South African President Botha: "There are fourteen million blacks and three million whites; does the name Custer mean anything to you?"

But Williams's intelligent takes on the larger world weren't in sufficient supply. The show was strained. Every comedian has hot and cold nights, and clearly Williams was nervous, his timing off. The Met appearance—produced and taped by HBO—capped a three-month tour, and part of the problem is that the material is no longer fresh to him. One of the reasons he's so electrifying on TV talk shows is that he wreaks havoc on their routinized formats. He has a true improvisational wit; thoughts he's never formed before come flying out of his mouth—I've also seen him invent in this dazzling way on small club stages.

But his work Saturday suffered from endemic troubles, too. In his films—*Moscow on the Hudson, The World According to Garp*—he comes across as sexually eager and sensual, a man who delights in and admires female flesh. In his stage act, this attractive, feeling man is almost entirely eclipsed by a creature raging with fear that his penis is too small and that his grace and physical vanity signify he's less than fully male. Whether impersonating Sly Stallone or simply displaying a tic, he grabbed his crotch an average of once a minute. His routines were studded with unfunny cracks about gay men—always depicted as swish—who were ridiculed precisely because they're *not* ambivalent about their vanity. Black men got swept up into his sexual insecurities, too; they were always well hung and menacing to white men—especially to their genitals. Williams has a feminist line (as well as an antiracist one), but when his sexual terrors were driving the performance, he was bent on stressing how women's hormones overwhelm them and how innately frightened and disgusted they are by male sexual desire.

Again and again, he demanded we see him not as the man he is—with a nice body, an expressive face, and stylish clothes—but rather as putrid and crude. A bit where he goes on about "the Titty Fairy," which arrives soon after his wife gets pregnant, was adolescent. Williams kept searching the audience for confirmation of his views. The gay-baiting got plenty of response, partly because he milked it with vaudeville prancing. But the stereotypes about men and women mostly laid there. No one has Williams's combination of intelligence, curiosity, gift for mimicry, and ability to stir emotions. But the movie and TV deals as well as the adoring crowds say, "You don't need to think about what you're saying; whatever comes out is fine."

Steven Wright: Wright in Time

May 1984

What beloved comedian has most influenced conceptual art? That's right, Henny Youngman. Steven Wright, a Youngman scion (except for the absence of props: there's no violin, no nothing), stands on the stage for fifty minutes and tells jokes lacking in narrative connection but hinged together by point of view. He looks like a combination of Simon and Garfunkel, with the former's pitiless gaze, the latter's receding frizz halo, and the skinny-kid body of both. Wright's voice is flattened, often a choked sob. His persona, it appears, was born depressed; he has no memory of a harmonious time before the fall—or fallout. Where other comics stoke their performances with leashed violence, Wright relies on language.

His landscape is a dream he can't shake, in which everything is unfamiliar yet menacing. The ice-cream truck in his neighborhood plays

"Helter Skelter." One time, he went camping and accidentally borrowed a circus tent. The people around complained; they couldn't see the lake. Another time, he lived in a house that ran on static electricity: "Whenever I wanted to cook something, I had to take off my sweater real fast; to use the blender, I had to rub a balloon on my head." Apropos of nothing discernible, he mentions that six thousand ants dressed up as rice and robbed a Chinese restaurant. Blank face. "I don't think they did it. I know some of them."

Wright is fascinated by light, by time/space connections, and by gadgets. When the electricity in his house (this one made of balsa wood) went off, he got around using a flash camera. He had to take sixty pictures of his kitchen to make a sandwich. "The neighbors called the police. They thought there was lightning in my house." Pause, stare. In the middle of a job interview, he interrupted his prospective employer and asked, "If you were driving in a car at the speed of light and turned off the headlights, would anything happen?" The guy didn't know. Wright said, in that case, he didn't want to work for him. Back home again: "I put instant coffee in my microwave oven. I almost went back in time."

Little nervous breakdowns punctuate the monologue, functioning like rest periods between musical movements. He leans against the wall: "Don't look at me; I have to do something," he whines, then stands there. He can be deadly with one-liners, but his best pieces work like small movies, the visual jokes expanding with skillful timing. Hitching from Seattle to L.A., he's picked up by a trailer truck hauling twenty automobiles. The cab's too crowded, the driver tells him, directing him to one of the cars. Then the man picks up nineteen other hikers. They ride down the coast, in separate cars. When the driver does ninety and a cop pulls him over, they all get speeding tickets.

Emo Philips: Emotional Rescue

June 1987

Emo Philips, of the stork limbs and Minnie Pearl voice, got famous about a year and a half ago—after nine years scrabbling on the road. His HBO special, *Live from the Hasty Pudding Theater*, ran in April, and an album with the same name has just been released. He was in town last week at Caroline's.

His trademarks are odd: the asthmatic wheezing, the "kick-me" stare, the willowy, anorexic body, suggesting a long, limp penis. But his is not a trademark oddness. It's thorough. Like Ray Bolger and Danny Kaye, Emo is sexually dislocated, but while Bolger and Kaye made audiences squirm with embarrassment for their gelding personas, Emo explores sexual terror. He is the humiliated child we have all been. His look is pure arrest, but it's only a memento, which heightens the smartness of the mouth, the vengefulness of a battered but unembittered psyche. He never seems dumb, castrated, or used. Emo is Kafka's sly, irreverent hunger artist made skinny flesh. He's not starving for lofty reasons; he just can't find anything tempting to eat.

"I heard my parents arguing in the other room," he confides. "You know how parents will argue . . . 'Oh, I told you he'd live.' " Pause, twirling of hair. "Dad was a kidder. Whenever I misbehaved, he'd bury me in the backyard." A finger jabs the air. "Only up to my waist, but you get *dizzy* with all the blood rushing to your head." When kids would come by the backyard and tease Emo, he'd attack. "Lucky for them, the chain would snap my neck back and they would escape." Mom, who was intrusive, once caught Emo in bed with a chicken. "Boy was there egg on my face."

The boy dotes on puns and homonyms, although they sometimes trip him up. In Jerusalem, he felt like an idiot. "You know." Toss of Prince Valiant mop. "Standing at the Wailing Wall with my harpoon." Mostly, though, he wields ambiguity cunningly. At school the principal once scolded, "I can expel you," and Emo sassed, "First you'll have to catch me and eat me." He was having trouble dividing fractions in math class. "Now, Emo, what's our common denominator?" the teacher asked. "A fondness for little girls?" In a bar, Emo picked up a woman who said, "Do you have cable?" Heavy breathing into the mike. "Oh, I think the ropes I have will be strong enough to hold you." A confessional note enters. "I caught my girlfriend in bed with another guy, and I was crushed. I said, 'Get off me, you two.' " Confiding he's handy with the ladies, Emo shoots lewd eyebeams at a woman in the audience—"You prob-a-by think you're superior to my girlfriend. . . . Just because you're real." Then he sweetly inquires of two men sitting at a table: "Are you friends?" Voice even. "So who would be the dominant one?"

Kids used to call Emo "neo-Calvinist." Not for nothing. The comedian is metaphysically bent. "I'm not a fatalist, but even if I were, what could I do about it?" In a dream he went to heaven, and after God got on Albert Schweitzer's case for "upsetting the ecosystem in Africa," he asked Emo to describe his most selfless act. "I once filled a rental car with premium," was his answer, which inspired hosannas and God's cry, "We have a winner!" Waxing nostalgic, the lad recalls grammar school. "So many things I didn't appreciate, like being spanked by a middle-aged woman." Pause, underbreath. "Something you pay good money for later in life." Waxing avuncular, he cautions, "Stay away from cocaine. Oh, it might seem glamorous at first." Steady stare. "But one day, one day . . . it will be your turn to buy." And lest we think his concerns are all personal, Emo tenders a view of the capital. "There're a lot of rip-offs. I mean the Washington Monument." Pained expression. "Do you think that *looks* like him?"

Emo's set lasts an hour, plus there's an encore. The laughs don't flag. Alternating with the stream-of-consciousness murmurings are longer stories, which are among his best work. Walking by the Golden Gate Bridge, Emo meets a man about to jump. He turns, revealing he has the head of a horse. "Oh, why the long face," Emo asks, and tries to show him that life has meaning. "Do you really think some random collection of atoms in the universe had the sense of humor to give you that head?"

Has success spoiled Emo? "No," he told a reporter recently. "I just haven't been able to do the laundry. That's what you're smelling."

Don Novello: Altar Ego

March 1991

Chaplin's Little Tramp, Cliff Arquette's Charlie Weaver, Reubens's Pee-wee Herman—these doppelgängers are innocents or feign naïveté. They aren't cynical enough to crack the social codes that could win them status, and they aren't bold enough—or else feel too physically insubstantial—to defy corruption openly. So they disrupt by being wily, devious, anarchic.

Foremost among these subtle subversives is Don Novello's Father Guido Sarducci, gossip columnist for the Vatican newspaper *L'Osservatore Romano,* as well as *Saturday Night Live* regular and frequent talk-show guest.

With his droopy mustache, floppy hat, and rose sunglasses, the father is stuck in a Sergeant Pepper warp, but, otherwise, he's a power maven for the ages, piercing pomposity, weaseling around rules that are too mighty and dangerous to break. Novello's ostensible target is Big Church, but he's no simple clergy-basher. The church is *all* entrenched, masked authority. Our man in the pulpit could be a factory worker under Stalinist siege. Sarducci—part commedia dell'arte buffoon, part Shakespearean fool sucking up to and making end runs around authority—reveals that the system is run by people with clay feet. Novello loves the church because it's home, familiar, the smell of his armpits and crotch. He hates the church because it won't admit it has a stink.

Sarducci, always looking for angles and passing them on, discovers the check for the last supper (really the last brunch). He sees that one guy had only a soft-boiled egg and tea while everyone else stuffed themselves, and he notes that the bill was divided equally. His moral: "In groups, always order most expensive thing." He does an exposé on "the missing commandments": "Moses was an old guy, grumpy. He had chip on his shoulder from the cow incident. After he broke the tablets, he could only remember the negative ones. 'Don't do this. Don't do that.' But most of them were more like advice. Twelfth commandment: 'Whistle while you work.' You thought it was from Disney. Stole it from God."

On a Carson show, Sarducci hawks an ant farm in the shape of Vatican City. "This is the Vatican nuclear plant, Enrico Fermi/Pius XII facility. There's a little leak, but I don't want to say too much about it, upsets people." In another bit, the father explains, "Life is a job. You get $14.50 a day, but after you die, you have to pay for your sins. Stealing hubcap is, say, $100. Masturbation is 35 cents, or three for a dollar, but to get discount you have to do it three times in a row. If there's any money left, you can go to heaven. If not you have to go back to work. Born again. Most nuns are Mafia guys working it off."

Novello, who lives in northern California, was recently in New York as a guest writer for *SNL*, and I seized the chance to talk with the father's father. Out of costume and character, he shares traits with his persona. Although he was born in Ohio, Italian cadences bob on his English. He's soft-spoken, gentle. His humor doesn't jump up and lick your face, but rather, like a canary you might not have noticed, suddenly starts to sing.

For twenty years, he's produced fine work that doesn't sound like anyone else's. During the heyday of *SNL*, he created bits like John Belushi's

Greek who serves only cheeseburgers and Pepsis. During Watergate, as right-wing fanatic Lazlo Toth (another figure inside the system), he wrote to government officials and corporation heads, zinging them with critiques couched in endorsements. To Agnew, he oozed, "You were the best Vice President this country ever had and they go treat you like some ordinary crook!" To the president of the R. J. Reynolds Co., he wrote, "Tobacco is eternal! Like our flag!"

Novello/Toth received replies from almost all his targets, including Nixon (always addressed as "the best"), Ferdinand Marcos, and Chung Hee Park, former president of South Korea, to whom Lazlo wrote, "I'm glad to see that you are cracking down on literary men." Says Novello, "You could write, 'I like your coffee. I like Adolf Hiter.' And you'd get back, 'Thank you for liking our coffee.' " The correspondence was published as *The Lazlo Letters,* and is still in print. Also available from the Novello archives are the videos *Father Guido Sarducci Goes to College* and *Gilda Live,* in which he costars, as well as the album *Breakfast in Heaven.* And Novello has become a member of Francis Ford Coppola's stock company (they met when Coppola guest-hosted *SNL*), appearing in *Tucker, New York Stories,* and the current *Godfather III,* in which he plays Don Corleone's publicist.

But Sarducci remains his most capacious invention, one inspired, Novello says, by a Jesuit priest he met while studying in Rome. "He was a real wheeler-dealer. Even after he married a student, the school still kept him as director." Since 1973, when Sarducci's voice first sounded in Novello's head, it's lost none of its playfulness or bite. His solution for the Gulf War? "Turn Kuwait into a Palestinian homeland, and send the Kuwaitis to Graceland." There could be problems, he admits. "The Kuwaitis might find Graceland too dull. They're party animals. And the U.S. probably wouldn't go for it, because we own Kuwait. It's rich. I'm still going to talk to Priscilla. She could be heroine of world peace."

Pee-wee Agonistes

August 1991

What did Paul Reubens do? Went to visit his folks in Sarasota. Trauma, of course; regression, naturally. Memories of the childhood bedroom where sex first slid from the brain to the hand to the crotch. Private and scary, because parents could barge in, find out, and smirk, or worse. So Reubens goes out for a little air, a little space, a little wank. That's what people do in all those porno theaters across the country that replaced the last picture show. Reubens says he didn't even take out his pud.

He hasn't been found guilty of any crime, and yet CBS canceled reruns of his Saturday morning kid show, Disney yanked a Pee-wee video from its tour attraction in Florida, Toys "Я" Us and Kiddie City removed Pee-wee dolls from their shelves, the tabloids and TV news have trumpeted the story for days, and talk shows have buzzed with snide jokes. Newspapers and broadcasters have enlisted psychologists to advise parents on how to explain Pee-wee's actions to their children. Last Tuesday, *Entertainment Tonight* invited Soupy Sales to comment. Sales was introduced as a former kid-show host, although it wasn't disclosed that the entertainer had himself been tossed off the air for instructing his audience to mail him dollar bills. About Pee-wee, Sales raved, "It's over, it's over, it's over. He signed his own death warrant. Where else is he gonna work? Television will never give him another chance."

With the scorn and reprisals heaped on Reubens, you'd think he'd joined in a gang sexual assault. If that were the case—especially if the target were black and female—he, like the men cleared of charges in the St. John's case, might well expect to be exonerated. There's a whip-cracking tradition in this country of ruining public figures with sex scandals. It's so much easier to savage a contender not yet ensconced, someone like Gary Hart, for betraying the public trust through private acts than to tackle the profound, damaging hypocrisy of powerful officials, men who trade arms for hostages and conjure up Hitlers whenever warfare is craved. But not everyone accused of sexual misconduct is crushed. Until the rape charge against William Kennedy Smith, Kennedy cocksmanship lent glamour to the males in the clan. They were guys being hormonal. When videotapes of Rob Lowe screwing female minors surfaced, he was teased, yet, in no time, was on an Academy Awards show singing a treacly duet with Snow White and making a far more socially approved move to sabotage his career.

Driving the panic about Reubens is his connection to children and the belief that he touched himself; he expressed libido and manifested it, supposedly, in the form of masturbation, as children mostly do. The proximity of sex to children stokes visions of molestation, although in this case there's no suggestion of pedophilia. The mention of masturbation is enough to undermine the conviction that children aren't sexual and reinforce the drive to isolate them from anything erotic. In Pee-wee's orbit, however, children were never in that vanilla ether. The name *Pee-wee* is so close to the word *wee-wee*. There he cavorts, this flaccid noodle in slicked hair and lipstick, okay as long as he stays limp. The kid hosts that reassure parents are eunuchs—Mr. Rogers and Captain Kangaroo, the Muppets because they're not fleshly.

Reubens doesn't look like a eunuch in the mug shots released by Sarasota's vice squad, his hair grown biker-long, his face shaded by a goatee. But even the Pee-wee persona is less a eunuch than a peculiarly sexed guy. Libido is always erupting out of him in the form of campy flounces, risqué asides, and hip wisecracks. He is resolutely deviant and accepting of other oddball types who light on planet Playhouse.

Pee-wee impersonates the child deemed precocious by adults but who feels estranged within the world of other children. He's comfortable in fantasy, a realm where inanimate objects possess personality, sensibility, and where he is the ringmaster. His quirks—spaghetti limbs, a wobbly voice, an amorphous sexual identity—become a style esteemed and imitated by his fans. He makes a virtue of what, outside, can leave him prey to humiliation. It's no wonder that children adore his freakishness: all kids feel dislocation amid grown-ups—steering through perilous, Brobdingnagian landscapes, jealously beholding adult coordination, examining marked sexual difference, deciphering code-filled speech.

Pee-wee has always been a wanker-figure, exulting in solitary, imaginative pleasure. The charges brought against Reubens have only made this association inescapable. Solo sex isn't just a hot potato when it comes to children. The narrator of Martin Amis's novel *London Fields* points out that masturbation, a lifelong preoccupation, is almost never described in fiction. The narrator doesn't speculate why, but one thought is that the subject is too painful. Masturbation evokes ambivalence not only about sensual pleasure but aloneness. We're told that solitude is a deprivation, often the punishment for antisocial actions. We're supposed to feel lonely in that state, not enjoy separateness. Companionship, comfort, and protection are said to flow unremittingly from connection—from families and familylike groups. But masturbation, an encapsulating activity, declares that some experience needn't be shared, reminds us that some experience *can't* be shared—most crucially, death. Like fantasy and art, masturbation can prove a consolation in being apart.

Last week, in a statement quoted in *Newsday*, Joan Rivers said that Reubens's situation was "terribly, terribly sad," adding that if he was convicted she was "sure" he was "going to go for help." Find someone else to do the wanking? Seek guidance in choosing porno theaters? Bill Cosby faulted CBS and Disney/MGM Studios for diving into hysteria and trouncing due process. Indeed, those companies have set sterling examples for children. Cyndi Lauper offered the summation of the event as a "petty, victimless occurrence." And in homage to Reubens, Dave Herman, host of WNEW's *The Rock & Roll Morning Show*, played "Tequila" and encouraged parents to let their kids play with Pee-wee dolls. Herman, in a phone conversation, said his show had elicited thirty fax messages supporting Reubens and none attacking him. He reported a caller's evocative detail: Reubens, who, before the arrest, had declined a CBS offer to do a sixth season of *Pee-wee's Playhouse*, has been saying he'd like "to kill off this character." He was an actor. He wanted to play other roles.

This may be the time to go for it.

Jim Turner: Hurt So Good

February 1990

Wherever Jim Turner appears, you can bet there'll be some acrylic fur from hell, the kind of acid-colored shag a guy would use to line his '57 Chevy—his love grotto. In *Walk a Mile in My Head*, a series of edgy, shrewd character sketches Turner is performing at Steve McGraw's, the shag is fashioned into a hood worn by puppeteer Tom E. Dell. Tom has one of those overly bright voices that arrested adults adopt when talking to children, but his turbulent inner life roils up among his damaged and dyspeptic puppets. They include the Candide figure Mr. Jeff (a rubber doll head stuck in a plastic milk jug); Mr. Hammer (a snarling, unadorned carpenter's tool); Mr. Menudo (his head is as big as his body); and Mr. Bubble Wrap (he suffers from an appalling skin condition). The creatures seek out a wizard to whom they put the question: "When do we start feeling better about ourselves?" Their ineffectual, blunt guru declares there is no cure for their pain.

Turner, thirty-seven, a tall, rangy performer with a mop of yellow hair and a resonant voice, is known to MTV audiences as the brain-scrambled hippy relic Randee of the Redwoods—he wears an old baseball stirrup as a headband. Turner has been a member of the San Francisco–based comedy troupe Duck's Breath Mystery Theater for fourteen years, and the quick-change training lends grace to his solo work, as he glides among his incarnations, shedding layers of pants, adjusting his face from gee-whiz innocent to armored con man. His landscape is strewn with pizza crusts and gin flasks; it's a world of stubble and unsettling smells on the fingers that, the next morning, can't quite be placed. He peoples the stage with depressives on the fringe of showbiz and the vain, cynical windbags to whom the despairing are ineluctably drawn.

Big Bugs bills himself as "The Happiest Clown Alive," though his life is a desert of failed inspiration. The freckles on his face look like a measles rash. When he tries mining his dreams for ideas, he's ultimately forced to admit he's faking sleep. His one claim to fame is having been a suspect in the murder of Troodles, "the self-proclaimed *real* happiest clown alive," whose material he stole.

Choam Underhill, on the other hand, is never at a loss for words. Decked out in spandex pants and a wig of flowing curls, he leads women in a training session designed to purge the "mascu-femme facade"—as well as sell vitamins. "Ladies," he intones, "I'm not here to be your friend. I'm a scientist, a jogger, and an ex-lawyer. The truth is sometimes a frown it hurts to wear. I will be that hurting frown." In other sequences, Turner blooms into dark flower Gary Lewis, Jerry's son and a burned-out Vietnam vet; B-movie queen Tammy, star of *Tough Girls on Lonely Street* (she plays the leader of an all-girl immigrant gang); and Grudge Hanson, a lounge lizard/poet, whose most recent performance piece is driving south on Interstate 80—on the wrong side of the highway.

Walk a Mile in My Head grows funnier as it unfurls, each study enriching Turner's clowning, which, like the most compelling foolery, arouses as much anxiety as it tames. Tom E. Dell crudely handles and sometimes drops his puppets; his set evokes the nightmarishness of childhood, of being at the mercy of adult control, at the same time it offers the horror-show thrill of watching others suffer. (It's a frisson lost to kids served only Muppets, who move independent of manipulating hands and cavort unthreatened by sadism. Talk about perverting a child's sense of reality.)

Turner's goofs are post-Beckett beings, as grandiose and subjugated as Gogo and Didi, but lacking their valor. Mere survival is the most exalted condition Turner holds out. He stays clear of poignance, preferring thwacks in the gut, but his work remains human and funny because he fleshes his creations, contriving comedy of manners as well as of impulses and drives. Grudge Hanson, perennial wanderer and car-culture maven, recites a jarring pseudobeat poem called "My Love Is a Slow-Moving Vehicle." Sycophantish Tom E. Dell interrupts his show to recall a visit to Liberace's house, during which he pored over the pianist's "solid gold Bible, which had Jesus's words in red velour." As MC of a rock revival concert, Gary Lewis (leader of the sixties group the Playboys) quits ingratiating himself and bursts out, "Did Brian Wilson go to Vietnam? No." Turner doesn't mistake damage for courage or accomplishment. He inhabits his characters. There's no translating, no smirking, no patronizing. His hucksters, deadbeats, and failures at love and work aren't someone else.

We had coffee a few days after I saw his performance, and the relaxed, fluent Turner I met described the attraction of his repertoire. "I like people without skills trying their damnedest to pull off something creative. I feel this half repulsion, half fascination with disaster cases, and I love characters who are always on the road, their cars piled up with stuff in the front seat, stuff in the back, racks on the roof, and they're in this little cocoon world, driving—they can't stay still because they always think it's going to be better somewhere else. When I was a kid, my dad was in the air force, and we moved a lot. I developed a very sarcastic voice. As a traveling child, you had to be funny to trick the new people into liking you. I was awful in school. I couldn't concentrate on my own. In Duck's Breath there was always someone to say, 'Uh, Jim, we have that sketch due tomorrow, don't you think we should *write* it.' To this day, I wing material the first time on stage. I get a click, and I see the possibilities, and then I calm down."

Jim Morris: Bushwhacking

January 1989

For several weeks last year, Jim Morris impersonated Reagan on *The Hollywood Squares*. His eyebrows arrowed heavenward. His mouth searched fruit-lessly for a resting place on his face. His tongue peeked from his lips like an anxious actor parting curtains. Morris, who is thirty-two, seemed to grow wattles and wrinkles. And there was aptness to his appearance as a "square"; the show, inflating has-beens as it's wont to do, is the sort of gig for which Reagan, had he not been elected to office, would have been grateful. Maybe he still will. In sly one-liners, Morris jabbed Reagan's policies—he said in a phone conversation that the producers of *Squares* are more freewheeling than the powers steering Carson, where his material on Central America has been excised. All in all, his politics are muted on TV; his befuddled Reagan comes across more cuddly than dangerous.

But on Inauguration Day, at the packed Village Gate, he improvised so nimbly and editorialized so pointedly, he became a live political cartoon. As George and Dan were grinding out gaffes, Morris, almost instantaneously, was mulching them into his act.

To play Bush, Morris dons wire-rimmed glasses and arranges his features so that his forehead searches for his chin and his tongue crawls, snail-like, across his mouth. The nasal whine and fragmented diction —"ed-*jew*-cation"—are dead on. Laughter is evoked by Dada excess. The president is sworn in as "George Herbert Walker Griffith Joyner Kersee Cougar Mellencamp Bush." Malapropisms and memory lapses become Rorschachs. Bush welcomes "Hispaniels" and wonders why he should send Quayle to "that Hirohito thing." Taking the oath of office, he promises to "preserve, defect, and pretend the Constitution." Silliness tickles out the paranoia and ignorance of our chief executives. Bush confides Ronnie's advice on Gorbachev: "Whatever you do, don't stare at the whatsis on his forehead. That's what they *want,* make you see strange shapes, confuse you."

In the second part of the set, Morris does Reagan at his final press conference, drifting on wayward streams of consciousness, coming aground on pitiless ideology. Rehearsed Grouchoisms are woven into fielded questions—"My colon? Part of it was removed, now I've got a semicolon." Asked to decode "a thousand points of light," he submits, "I thought it was a thousand pints of lite." Rejoinders spring from this week's news: "Why did I pardon George Steinbrenner? Because we have to guard against the first strike."

Morris doesn't scant the venality in Reagan's seeming triviality. Musing on an album of his greatest hits, his Reagan recalls the radio test, "We'll be bombing in five minutes." He declares that the homeless choose to live in the streets while he prefers the White House. His mission to "overturn Roe" is trumpeted in an antisushi riff. And when, in Spanish, a man in the audience decries military terrorism in Guatemala and the CIA's subversion of leftism in Central America, Morris grows as steamed as his original, praising Somoza, claiming he "never mined" regions, trailing off, " . . . never mind . . . "

Sometimes Morris's targets are unclear. As Bush, he jokes that while Barbara has fewer dresses than Nancy, her clothes take up as much room. Women in the audience hiss, because here, instead of setting up Bush as a man who publicly exalts family values while, among his fishing buddies, he brags about secretarial conquests and bashes his frumpy, unsexy wife, Morris himself exploits fat-lady humor.

But he gets points for bucking the trend of making Barbara—you should excuse the expression—a sacred cow. For the moment, Barbara is protected by the fact that lambasting her weight is being equated with endorsing Nancy's skinny, controlling gestalt. Nancy's anorexic body has long been fair game because her hard little form is in concert with her mean narrow mind, but Barbara's vulnerable body oughtn't to obscure the unsavoriness of her views.

Last Friday, she and George were interviewed by Barbara Walters. Watching the inauguration, Walters was seized by patriotism; she would red-carpet Attila the Hun if he got elected and came on her show. George's tongue deported itself with the maladroitness for which it was justly famed before being Atwaterized. Admitting there were far more homeless people now than eight years ago, he refused to finger Reagan, saying the problem "is too acute to apply blame," and adding, with disconnection worthy of his predecessor, "some of the homeless are not competent to judge what is best for society." Barbara Bush anted up in bluster and insincerity, claiming her interest in literacy was "very loose, I mean very broad."

She smiled tolerantly as George patronizingly named her worthiest quality preserving the family, and when Walters questioned her about abortion, she played footsie, saying she'd remain silent because she wasn't an elected official. To Betty Ford and Rosalynn Carter, the role of first lady didn't cancel citizenship. The problem with Barbara Bush is that her thinking is fat, gray, and wrinkled.

Comedians are hard-pressed to exaggerate the fatuousness of our current heads of state, but Morris's scorn for callousness—typically, the $30 million spent on the inauguration in view of D.C.'s homeless—is incisive. Friday night, when Morris was sworn into office, he took a stand beside Harry Shearer, Will Durst, and Richard Belzer to pressure, pierce, and depreciate all puffed-up bodies politic.

Louise DuArt: Objet DuArt

April 1990

First the face is long and sultry. Next the cheeks are sucked in and an air of strained gentility is conjured. Then the tongue juts out and a finger is thrust down the throat. Louise DuArt is doing Cher, Barbara Walters, and Joan Rivers in rapid succession. Cher, her tongue working her lips, slips a long hair out of her mouth and stares at it, enchanted by her vulgarity. Barbara, abandoning her usual ramrod posture, hitches her chin and narrows her eyes, going in for the question with razor blades. "Tell me," she says to Katharine Hepburn, uncorking her own prurience to snare this priggish prey, "when you were doing those love scenes with Spencer Tracy, did he ever slip you a little tongue?"

Like other inspired impressionists—Martin Short, Catherine O'Hara, Billy Crystal—DuArt isn't a mimic but a caricaturist, drawing psychological portraits and satirizing manners. She's done all the female, and some of the male, voices for the life-sized puppets on TV's *D.C. Follies.* Her first Showtime special debuted in January; another airs this fall. But mostly DuArt plays clubs, rotating between small venues like the Backlot in L.A. and glitz-barns in Vegas and Atlantic City.

There is something ineffable about her ability to change voice, face— a gorgeous oddness, something in the bones and lineaments that comes along once in a blue moon. DuArt channels Barbra Streisand, Roseanne Barr, Jane Fonda, Liza Minnelli, Whoopi Goldberg, and Tammy Faye Bakker. She does men, some in full drag, including George Burns, Woody Allen, Willie Nelson, Henry Fonda, and Popeye. And she sings in character as accurately as she speaks. When her imagination rips—when she free associates and sends her incarnations ricocheting off one another—there's anarchic madness in her work.

DuArt's malice is exuberant; her subjects are her alter egos. On stage, she spews a stream of Joan Rivers venom: "I don't want to say the Queen Mother is top-heavy, but her brassiere has curb feelers." DuArt looks up. "You don't know how *good* it feels to do Joan."

Each of DuArt's impersonations expresses a drive. Streisand is narcissism, Cher exhibitionism, Hepburn self-importance. In a tour de force sequence, she plays both George and Gracie, swiftly changing voice, mannerisms, and moods. Sometimes, she fractures gender altogether. On stage, she becomes a wizened, inching George Burns while still wearing high heels and flashing long red fingernails.

Incorporating, appropriating, is the charge that fuels DuArt, and she parades this in two of her wildest turns. For her Showtime special, she introduces Rita Mapp, an idiot savant modeled on Dustin Hoffman's character in *Rain Man*. Rita is a crack impressionist, and as a talk-show panel screams out cues, she snaps from bit to bit, balking at Elvis. "I don't do dead people, definitely not dead people." Between impersonations, Rita repeats herself and breaks a vase in frustration; she's only someone when she's someone else.

A taped piece DuArt screens in her live act is equally self-revealing, a gloss on the impressionist's disposition to seize, possess. She plays Shelley Winters during a police interrogation. We see only Shelley, tires of fat bulging between the ropes that bind her, confusion contorting her face. An offscreen man demands, "What did you do with Zsa Zsa Gabor's former husbands?"

"I . . . I ate 'em." Her voice quavers.

"All *eight* of them?"

"I ate seven."

"What did you do with the eighth?"

"Froze him."

■ ■ ■

A few weeks ago, DuArt and I met for lunch at the Plaza—her choice—and as the pianist played a Muzak version of Beethoven's Fifth Symphony, DuArt did Barbara Walters interviewing Ivana Trump. "Ivana, Ivana, Ivana, when did you first feel Donald slipping away?" Then she's Louise, a thirty-nine-year-old woman with straight dark hair, large eyes, a full mouth, and an open, friendly manner. She shifts in and out of character, right before my eyes, and it's intensely pleasurable, this private performance staged in public.

Her skill with voices came in childhood. She'd get her friends out of class by calling school and pretending to be their parents. Later, she worked in an employment office with six phone lines; to make the operation seem larger, she'd answer calls as different people. In her early twenties, she slipped into showbiz, her true desire, and worked as a sketch comic in a series of venues. Ten years later, she stopped performing and raised two sons with her husband, Barry, who now manages her act. Barry encouraged her to audition for *Star Search* six years ago; the appearances launched her solo career.

"I'd love to work with other comedians—Steve Martin, Harry Shearer, Billy Crystal, Martin Short. I'd love to do a special with another woman. Catherine O'Hara would be a dream. Also a sitcom, me as a female Walter Mitty. That's what I'm like. I have trouble confronting people in authority. My characters speak for me. I send out the proper person to do the dirty work. Then the responsibility isn't on me."

She smiles, admitting that this is a fantasy, that the characters express her ambitions, feelings about which she was taught to be ashamed. "I come from a background where children were supposed to be seen and not heard. I wanted to go to college and study theater. My mother wanted me to be a stenographer. I became a stenographer. I had this boyfriend she hated because I loved him so much. She was afraid his dominating would compete with her dominating. She'd go through my purse, balance my checkbook. She'd get upset if I locked a door. To this day, I hear her speaking in my head, thinking for me."

DuArt's voice betrays no anger. She's enjoying explaining herself. But despite her understanding, insecurity sometimes gets the upper hand. On stage, she's occasionally self-effacing. At Harrah's in Atlantic City, where I saw her live, she depicted herself as a housewife who *happened* to have a talent. She spoke of "hauling my butt on stage," as if she were trade rather than a skilled performer.

She says it frightens her to acknowledge the gist of her Shelley Winters routine: that the impressionist is predatory. But this thought also thrills her. She leans forward. "I'm ready to try a sexual male. I'm going to do Dustin Hoffman in my next special. I love dressing up and becoming that other gender. I love exposing Woody's self-righteousness and the shark in Barbara

Walters. You can see her get the tears, and then her mind clicks and she's thinking, 'Now the camera goes in for the kill.'" In front of an audience, DuArt gets to be the puppet master as well as the puppets. She gets to be shameless, bitchy, erotic, flamboyant, intrusive, and egotistical. "I love it," she says in a voice that's her own.

Julie Brown: Brown Knows

August 1994

Julie Brown craves nothing so juicy as a big, femmed-up diehard, a monster who is always right, embattled, a killer lest she *be overlooked*. Madonna. Tonya. Evita. Imelda. Leona. A woman whose vanity absorbs the air where irony might breathe, a diva exactly the opposite of Julie Brown, who plunges so confidently into clownishness she never looks the fool. Lucille Ball and Carol Burnett—anxious about being girls and doing messy things—strained for decorum when not taking pies. Brown, like Tracey Ullman and Janeane Garofalo, is part of a new breed of female physical comedians, emboldened by Gilda Radner's slobbering rocker, Candy Slice, and testing the envelope of unselfconsciousness as boldly as male peers John Belushi and Steve Martin.

Brown's new pastiche, *National Lampoon's Attack of the 5ft2" Women* on Showtime, doesn't reach the delirium of her Madonna spoof, *Medusa: Dare to Be Truthful*, because in the second half she takes on Lorena Bobbitt (renamed Lenora Babbitt), who, despite her extravagant mayhem, is more pathetic than venal. But Brown is inspired in "Tonya: The Battle of Wounded Knee," which she also directed. Scrappy, hungry Tonya is satire gold, because she's irrepressible. Flatten her with a steamroller, and she pops back up.

You might think her story too ludicrous for parody, but Brown does the old *Mad* magazine shtick of playing the obvious deadpan and spiking with over-the-top flourishes. Tonya cuts a pizza with her skate blade. Jeff Googooly devises an elaborate mime routine to divert attention from Tonya. Hitmeister Sean refers to 'Nam, and Tonya needles, "You're twenty-four, you went there in kindergarten?" Nancy Kerrigan, here Cardigan, is dispatched with equal relish. She gobbles cupcakes and chirps that she never gains weight. She glides up to the camera in a pork commercial, holds a slab of meat, and intones, "Just make sure you cook it." Brown gets so inside Tonya's resentment of her rival, we can't help sharing it. Especially when Nancy whispers to Oksana Bayoul, "You may have the gold medal, but I have parents."

Tracey Ullman: Top Girl

October 1993

If Tracey Ullman were a guy, she'd have a career like Steve Martin's, or Robin Williams's, or Marty Short's, because she's that good—butter. Ullman is a junkie for abandon, losing herself in every portrayal. She is a satire scanner, her senses absorbing in a beat details of gesture and speech that etch not only the look of someone but their motives, longings, nursery dreams. And her power is combined with a total lack of vanity. Ullman, who is thirty-three, endures baggy eyes, padding, and bad hair to win points.

Because she isn't a raving beauty—though she can look fetching— she's mostly landed film roles as doormats. Kevin Kline was her cheating husband in *I Love You to Death*. She languished under gobs of makeup as a horny witch in Mel Brooks's *Men in Tights* (don't ask). And in *Household Saints*, she is passively handed from father to husband after the former loses a round of pinochle.

But now she and producer husband Allan McKeown have gathered crack actors, writers, and production staff—some from her innovative Fox show—for two brainy comedy specials on HBO: the first, *Tracey Ullman Takes on New York*, the second, *A Class Act*. Both shows anatomize class: sorting out the different ways that Brits and Americans conceive of status.

In the first show, Ullman is Janey Pillsworth, a magazine czarina with a Tina Brown résumé and Anna Wintour bob. Off her feed, she can still force down "squid and shiitake lasagna." Anxious about her looks, she forbids spray in case of "tense hair." While "inventing herself," she has killed off her working-class parents in a ski-lift accident in Aspen, but, courtesy of a jealous coworker, they materialize while she is on camera with a Barbara Walters-esque viperette.

"Mummy! Daddy! You're alive! Why didn't you call?" Janey hiccups. Taking them aside, she hisses, "When you came to my graduation in your cut-price shoes and mothball clothes, I thought it was the most embarrassing day of my life. I was wrong." "Is it the hat?" gently inquires Mum—Ullman in gray makeup and a Mamie Eisenhower wig.

The second show documents the early Pillsworth years. Father Frank (Michael Palin) sells a kidney to send little Janey to Hetherington Hall; mother Jackie forgoes Christmas turkey and roasts the pet hamster instead. When, after five years, the couple see that their daughter despises them, Frank beams, "It's everything we ever dreamed of."

In another piece, Ullman and Palin spin off Michael Apted's *35 Up*. Palin, playing upper-class Tim, is first seen at seven. With bare knees jutting at the camera like enormous fists, he predicts, "I will become a conservative MP, have to resign because of a sex scandal, and die of cirrhosis of something." Ullman is Cockney Kelly. At twenty-eight, sporting a high-rise platinum mohawk, she reports a divorce, remarriage, and some adjustment—"I had to have my tattoo changed from 'This Is Steve's Bitch' to 'This Is David's Bitch.' Didn't mind, really, David's a classier name."

Within the two shows, Ullman plays more than a dozen parts, a gamut stretching from Jackie, who won't lower the air-conditioning in her hotel room (the temperature having been set by the authorities), to Fern, the quintessential insecure Long Island Jewish matron, who *must* complain to be seen. Ullman is not just spinning pie plates. She's fascinated by how, in different cultures, social anxiety may be reflected in complete inhibition or a total absence of control.

I talked with her the other day from her home in London. She was chewing on Britain's class obsession, explaining that the tabs incorrectly pin her as "cor blimey Tracey," meaning bottom-rung working class, when, in fact, her background is suburban. "My husband is the true Cockney." It's quickly apparent how all the nuances of accent and manners that hounded her early on have been transformed into art.

She plans to do more shows for HBO but would like, as well, to have a late-night program, "a *That Was the Week That Was*–type review, where you could make some comment." She yearns to do a multicharacter comedy with the scope of *Dr. Strangelove*, Peter Sellers being her "idol." Woody Allen has cast her in his next film, and she has a part in a future Robert Altman movie. "Most people don't know what to do with me, don't even know what I look like," she says. "Women are expected to be glamorous. It's hard to find a makeup person who will make me look the way I want. Good thing I own seventy wigs. I never dreamed of being Cinderella. I like to be the person with the problems."

Comic Chameleon

February 1996

"He's got a wanger like a King Kangaroo," confides Australian stunt-woman Rayleen Gibson about her husband, Mitch, a dwarf. Fern Rosenthal has organized an "all-Kosher wild-west spectacular" to benefit "diseased tots," but when a cure is suddenly found, she cries, "Oh my God, my event is in the toilet!" Watching a guy in a coffee bar hold his finger over a lit match, college student Hope dreamily concludes, "He's probably an art major." These are but three chameleon takes in *Tracey Takes On . . .*, Tracey Ullman's new ten-part series on HBO, spun around such open-ended themes as "romance" and "charity."

Working with producer-husband Allan McKeown, director Thomas Schlamme, writers Jenji Kohan and Allen Zipper, and actors Michael Tucker and Julie Kavner, Ullman weaves satiric flashes with longer tales and reprises characters from earlier shows. Back is Tina Brown-esque Janey Pillsworth, who feeds a homeless man leftovers—"Dungeness crab salad, warm goat cheese, and wild mushrooms on crostini"—then uses his poems as copy for her photo spreads. Ullman dons full beard as lothario cabbie Chick, who buys his rubbers at "the big and tall shop." And Ullman is the quintessential sport wife playing the lesbian lover of Kavner's golf pro Midge Dexter—veteran of the Nancy Kulp Invitational. When the women kiss on TV, Fern, who is watching, is aghast, but her husband Harry comes back, "Two women, two turtles, what's the difference?"

Harry Shearer: Shearer Brilliance

November 1987

"It's a widespread misconception—or it would be if more people believed it—that the bass guitar is not a melodious instrument," says Derek Smalls, the British rocker Harry Shearer played in *This is Spinal Tap*. Smalls—his Sonny Bono mustache, scraggly mop, and heavy metal stupor still intact—is doing a solo since the band's breakup. He comes on stage, bare-chested and clad in scarlet spandex pants, and launches into a two-song medley, "Stairway to Pennies from Heaven." It's heavy, metallic. He says he's doing

Christian rock now but doesn't see it as a real departure from his previous stand. "We weren't Satanists per se, but I've always believed a man's relationship with the supreme evil one is a very private matter."

When Shearer does Blackwell, the L.A. talk-show host, he's smarm incarnate, complete with snake-oil salesman leisure suit. He leans his head back, searching for his next wild hype, or stares into the camera, piercing the boundaries of the TV screen with evangelist bravura, promoting his religion of trivia. His guest is Bobby Bouché, who's been doing *Irma La Douce* for twenty-five years and now has a gig at the James Franciscus Dinner Theater in LaMarada. Bobby, played by Tom Leopold, becomes increasingly pained as his pathetic circumstances are dissected. "Very good, a *scaled down* version, out in an hour. Yes folks, and *directed* by Robert Clary who gave you the great *Hogan's Heroes*. Oh, you work with someone who worked *with* Clary. *Okay*, let's talk menu. I can feel the quality of the food just by looking at it. A Leading Man/Leading Lady—that's the steak and lobster. $14.95. Can anybody top that? Seriously?"

Shearer wears a Juilliard quietness on his intelligent face, but he transforms himself in every bit. A part of him identifies with the salesmen and egoists he especially enjoys lampooning, and the affinity deepens his takes. This satire of recognition is quintessential Bob and Ray. You see it, too, in Paul Shaffer's Vegas smoothies and Billy Crystal's old Jewish cranks.

Shearer's humor is grounded in news and media. He studied political science at UCLA, did graduate work at Harvard in urban government, worked in the state legislature at Sacramento, and had a brief stint as a freelance journalist, covering Watts for *Newsweek*. While selling radio ads for a rock club, he met a group of burned-out newscasters hooked on the AP wires, and together they formed a comedy group, the Credibility Gap. In the seventies and eighties, Shearer worked with Martin Mull and Rob Reiner, and spent an unhappy period on *SNL* (the stuff he wrote was consistently killed). Now, in addition to performing, he does a weekly hour-long show on KCRW-FM in L.A.—for free.

Shearer's Reagan is a rambler whose ignorance doesn't eclipse his perniciousness. Before going on the air for an address, Ronnie clowns, "My fellow Americans, I've signed legislation ordering all the Jews to live on farms." Later, while actually broadcasting, he observes. "If this country had a few more Ollie Norths and a lot fewer Arthur Limans, there'd be a lot less seeds in our rye bread." He confesses that he discovered racism working in the movies, but now that he knows about it, he calls the attack on Bork "a lynch mob." Forever dependent on film for his sense of reality, he huffs, "The Sandinistas have no more respect for the contras than Darth Vader has for Obi-Wan Kenobi."

Some of Shearer's sharpest work rips open TV—that great traveling salesman in the skies. Five monitors sit on stage behind him, sometimes showing different images, sometimes the same one, and he's collected amazing footage from a satellite dish in his backyard. In a piece called "The Great Silence," the presidential candidates sit passively, staring into space or nodding off, looking like glassy-eyed fish on a cook's table. In another bit, Shearer summons the network anchors. "Dan," he says to Rather, "I'd fire you in a minute for that *Children of the Damned* stare." He likes "Pete" Jennings but not the man's salary. "We're watching the wrong border. Guys come from Mexico to do work no American would touch, while Jennings waltzes in from Canada and makes two million a year. He should at least have to ride in the trunk of a car."

In one deft video, Shearer impersonates Laurie Anderson—voice distortions, white tux, and all—doing a maxipad commercial. Another segment comes from the PR department of a cosmetics company— "Fifty-three percent of North Vietnamese *would* use the lip gloss even if it caused small liver cancers." But for a boy like Shearer, few experiences can outpeak the Iran-contra hearings. His funniest and most ingenious piece is the video *Shredding Party*, which zaps the media's penchant for choreographing history as well as our appetite for this entertainment. Three black marines boogie across the desks of the Senate hearing room singing the zippy "shredding party" refrain. And while a giant shredder churns out reams of confetti, Arthur Liman, in perfect rhythm, keeps asking, "What did he tell you about a shredding party?" and McFarlane keeps replying, "Well, just that there had to be one."

Jim Carrey: *The Cable Guy*

June 1996

In his new film, Jim Carrey plays a rogue cable installer, a guy who can burrow through any circuit to get under people's skin. When he was little, his mom used the tube as a baby-sitter while she barhopped, and he grew up media's creature, his mind wired with infomercials and Oprah babble, his fingers working the remote with Zen wizardry. He wants connection to other people so badly he has become pure nerve ending, a frayed, crackling ganglion of need. Carrey, with his liquid body, pugnacious jaw, and morphing face that can compose a brooding, Neanderthal brow, is a perfect id puppet, knowing no boundaries. When newly single guy Steven (Matthew Broderick) offers him $50 to provide free service, the cable guy sees an opening.

The movie, written by Lou Holtz, Jr., and directed by Ben Stiller, lacks the razor tooth of such media satires as *Videodrome* and *Robocop*. It isn't as dark—it's too much like television—and Carrey's performance isn't modulated; it's clever but not reflective. Still, there is startling clowning, foremost Carrey doing a karaoke version of "(Don't You Want) Somebody to Love?," ratcheting up Grace Slick's vibrato into a howl of yearning. Steven is suavely mugged on the electronic superhighway when Carrey's character, enraged at being rebuffed, secretly videotapes him bad-mouthing his boss, then beams the scenes into the mainframe computer at work. But the slyest comedy is the film's take on character in the screen age. Everyone *but* the cable guy is larval, without opinions, supremely passive, ripe for invasion. The cable guy may be TV's demon spawn, but he is his own invention, and his energy makes even his most craven hungers understandably riveting.

Jeffrey Essmann and Gilbert Gottfried: Getting Hip to Humor

February 1988

John Waters discovered corruption at the *Howdy Doody* show. "It was all lies. There were five puppets, and Buffalo Bob was mean to you." The experience was painful but liberating. Before that he'd been wide-eyed, trusting. He'd even had freckles. Afterward, there were no more romantic illusions, no more pretty pictures masking funky-bunky impulses. The kid got into sleaze. At least it was honest—you could even say clean. But he didn't embrace sleaze to crusade. No, it felt good. And it wasn't long before the freckles faded and a thin, cheesy mustache—a David Niven/Little Richard thing—sprouted above his lip.

John Waters, the director of *Pink Flamingos* and *Polyester*, was at Caroline's two weeks ago for a one-night gig. As he says, he's "a human trailer" for his new movie, *Hairspray*—a satire of "the teen flick and the message film," his two favorite genres. He leans against a small table, his pencil-narrow body dressed in garish chic, including a black tie with white and green diamonds. He speaks about his taste, how he got into movies, and how he makes them. And for seventy-five minutes he's the most charming, amusing talk-show guest imaginable.

He savors the damaged, the low, the incomprehensible. He'd like to do the Diane Linkletter Story and of course cast Joey Heatherton, except she scares him. So he'll settle for an Alice Crimmins bio or one on Squeaky Fromme—he passes around a Xerox of Squeaky's cheery-looking yearbook picture. Waters has the highest regard for emotional arrest, his and anyone else's. He thought he'd get himself to quit smoking by eating all the butts in his ashtray. He did. But decided they didn't taste all that bad. Of course this is a man who's seen far viler things sucked. This is the man who directed Divine to eat dog shit. Waters is generous with movie dish. His biggest thrill making *Hairspray*? "Waking up every day and knowing the joy of having Sonny Bono in your life." How to make censors happy? Give them a vomit scene to cut—"Just get a can of creamed corn." Favorite porno film title? *Sperms of Endearment.* And just when Waters convinces you he's completely shallow, he comes up with a social vision. *Hairspray*'s motto: "Her hair was perfect, but the world was a mess."

Waters has lectured at colleges, and the practice shows. He has sharp timing and quick ad-libs. Someone in the audience says he looks young. "Are you kidding? I look like Lillian Hellman the day before she died." Caroline's didn't bill Waters as a comic. He was booked for an experimental Monday night "lecture" series, which has included Timothy Leary and Sydney Biddle Barrows and in the future will present Tom Wolfe. Waters is in the tradition of the raconteur, a mantle that could slip as easily on Will Rogers and Mark Twain as on Charlie Weaver and Bea Lilly.

If Dickens were alive, Caroline's would no doubt schedule his road show. This club and several other New York nightspots—the Duplex, La MaMa's "The Club," The Bottom Line, Wah Wah Hut—are these days ignoring the labels "stand-up comedian," "performance artist," and "actor"—terms that traditionally boxed performers into the discrete venues "nightclub," "performance space," and "theater"—and instead are scouting talented acts, period.

Smashed boundaries and adventurous bookings are a boon for audiences, luring them to mix up their scenes. The crowd who came to the Seaport to see Waters was a new, artsy one for the club: charcoal clothes, platinum spiked hair, jewelry looking like blacksmith equipment. We're talking denizens of P.S. 122 and Dance Theater Workshop. Of course DTW has gotten hip to humor in the last few years and showcased comics—comics, that is, trying to move from comedy clubs to theaters. Whoopi Goldberg made her first New York appearance there. Last fall, Sandra Bernhard and Margaret Smith tried out new work, and attending their shows were the same downtowners who schlepped to see Waters at Caroline's.

But people don't act the same in every venue, or make the same demand for pleasure and stimulation from all performers. In the last two weeks, in addition to seeing Waters at Caroline's, I watched two other acts: the stand-up comic Gilbert Gottfried and "Mike's Big TV Show," a "new vaudeville" lineup hosted by Mike Smith and featuring a roster of performance artists, videos, and comedians. I also saw Karen Finley at P.S. 122 and Jeffrey Essmann at La MaMa's "The Club." Smith and Finley attracted the same kind of crowd that came to see Waters. Essmann, who does characters à la Danitra Vance and Lily Tomlin, drew a frumpier theater audience, and Gottfried netted one of several typical comedy club assemblies: thirtyish couples on dates.

Everywhere, people appreciated material that made them laugh and/or satirized society, but they felt most entitled to these pleasures from comedians and most free to demand them in comedy clubs. On the other hand, while watching performance artists and sitting in performance spaces and theaters, they respectfully suffered tedium and trivia. These reactions were most graphic at Finley's performance, *A Suggestion of Madness*, and at "Mike's Big TV Show."

Finley begins with a play. The set, including a shabby Xmas tree and a model of Michelangelo's David, looks like the log cabin of a born-again Christian enrolled in art classes at the New School. Finley, wearing a limp forties dress and a disheveled hairdo, stares boldly at the audience and declares she's a discontented Middle American housewife. Andy Soma is her loutish husband and Monisha Lundquist their teenage daughter. Finley says she's leaving. Soma says he's trapped in his life and doesn't want to have feelings, then turns on *Wheel of Fortune*. At the end we learn father and daughter have an incestuous relationship, and Soma does a riff in which he describes shitting on taco chips, topping the mess with cheese, and serving it to guests.

In the second part of the evening, Finley, wearing the same clothes and expression, holds a mike and does fifteen minutes of her more customary ranting/testifying. She complains about visiting parents who don't see her as an artist and who have the power to reduce her to a yowling maw.

This was not one of Finley's better nights. A hissing radiator distracted her. But even under optimal conditions, this work would not have cohered.

While Finley fumes about banality, performance artist Mike Smith pops it like a Quaalude. He's the ultimate couch potato, arriving home from his job, turning on the microwave, and settling down before the TV's beacon light. In a video, a voice intones, "Mike makes the ordinary extraordinary." In his dreams. Smith is bland rather than pompous, but like Finley he offers untransformed representation as social commentary. He shares Waters's absorption with trivia, but whereas Waters is witty and makes no demand that we see him as anything but a sleaze junkie, Smith, with his superstupefied manner and arch videos, presses us to distinguish him from a real couch potato and to take him seriously.

In performance spaces and theaters, audiences accept this treatment, perhaps feeling edified for not feeding low tastes. At Caroline's, however, the crowd got restless. They were in a nightclub, with dim lights and drinks in their hands. They were seated at tables, able to see one another's faces, whisper in each other's ears. They did not indulge tedium, and when stand-ups Margaret Smith and Reno came on, they went wild.

Smith's rattlesnake orneriness contrasts amusingly with her scrubbed looks. She goes out with a marine who says he can kill her in seven seconds. "Okay," she growls, "then I'll just have the toast." Openhearted Reno goes to the Odeon and sees celebs, fancy food, and million-dollar clothes. "Suddenly I want everything I've trained myself to despise."

Jeffrey Essmann calls himself a character comedian and plays clubs as well as theaters. Though much of his material has the surface flash and pointlessness of minimalist fiction, his best sketches build to sly satires. His St. Paul's good looks and unemotional expression mask a loon within; he's as convincing playing a fire-and-brimstone nun as a solipsistic exercise instructor. "Relax," the instructor commands his class, biting his nails. "Imagine you're in a glade with fresh foliage. Now imagine a herd of deer approach. The deer lick you. That's right. Now let hunters jump up and shoot the deer. Your tension's gone."

In another funny bit, he's a New Age convert, complaining about his past lives guide. "He made me boring in every incarnation. I was an accountant during the French Revolution." And in the most sustained piece—a parody of every mythicizing one-woman show ever done—Essmann is Patsy, a Croatian poet who falls in love with the future assassin of Archduke Ferdinand. She's lionized for her lyrics: "Death pulled me over/I didn't know he had a car." The day her lover fires the gun, she tells her diary: "Gavrillo did it. Elana just gloating."

You may have seen Gilbert Gottfried on Letterman or in *Beverly Hills Cop II*. He's in his mid-thirties, a small, rumpled guy with a mop of dark hair. He faces the audience, twisting the mike like a pickle jar that won't open. His eyes quaint to slits, his neck recedes like a turtle's, and when he opens his mouth, out comes an old Jewish crank.

There are plenty of actual Jewish guys doing old Jewish guys, principally, these days, Jackie Mason. Billy Crystal, too, has perfected the heartburn and wheezing. But Crystal's view is often sentimental. And although Mason merrily makes the world Jewish, endowing everyone—including Reagan, Nixon, and Falwell—with the uninhibited emotionalism and social crudeness of immigrants fresh off the boat, he addresses a strictly Jewish audience and invites them to sink into their ethnocentrism. Gottfried does something different. Like Mason, he makes the world into an old Jew, and like Crystal, he identifies with the vulnerability and anxiety of being outside but he also shows the poison of ethnocentrism. His act dissects not only Jewish racism but the impulses driving all bullies, including bully performers.

He achieves his effects by letting everything in the Jew hang out while carefully picking his targets, so the shtick doesn't boomerang into anti-Semitism. The Jew has been to Africa. "It's all black," he screeches. "They got in! They got in! You can't go there anymore." The Jew's tour de force stretch is burrowing beneath the black man he fears. Near the end of the set, Gottfried brings the bit full circle. Breaking into a natural voice, he says, "Just once I'd like to hear about a black man getting on an elevator and seeing a Jew." Becoming the old Jew again, he shrieks, "I was never so scared. I don't even think he lived in the building. Give 'em anything they want. It's not worth it." In the space where a black man who talks like a Jew fears a Jew who looks like a black man, ethnocentrism can't breathe.

CHAPTER FOUR

Performance Trance Channelers and Puppet-Masters of the Character Gallery

Danny Hoch

The Lower East Side—as in downtown, Loisaida, and Alphabet City—rises off the performers in this chapter. Showbiz may beckon or ricochet in their nervous systems, but it isn't their reference point. The street is. The street that smells of cat piss and human piss and opens onto an abandoned lot planted with giant asters looking like moonflowers. The street where Euro-nomads, junk peddlers, and drug dealers mingle, the street that harks back, in its spray of ethnic eateries and social clubs, to immigrants who thronged this quarter in the past. The street where panglobal *luftmenschen* mix with the stigmatized and exiled. AIDS, homelessness, drug dead ends and drug ecstasies, black sheep, baa, baa, baaing, sex with strangers, ethnic border crossings, gender drag. The downtown that isn't just a neighbor-hood but a planet.

The performers here—among them Eric Bogosian and Danny Hoch—are homesteaders, not daytrippers looking for a thrill or a cab ride out. And their art is an act of retrieval: of turning found experience into subjects, marginality into a new, glamorous tag. There is wonderful energy in these works of reclamation, capturing the vagabonding of young bo-hemians, the morning-after feel of the stubbly face and cottony mouth, the midlife awakening to limits and time's arrow. Personal fantasies scroll into social visions, the body dancing to the music of precariousness. There is no safety, security, or credible tradition amid this flux, which offers freedom and instills a state of longing, though not a ready solution to loneliness. The only reliable power, perhaps, lies in language, the Beckettian consolation of the human voice—the self reconstituting itself in reflection and love calls.

Brit transplant David Cale specializes in the dream rants of self-navi-gators. Fellow character tripper John Kelly ghosts in figures diverse as Joni Mitchell and legendary tightrope walker Barbette. Rose English is a romp with a rump. Her bare, magnificent posterior is flashed with mesmerizing aplomb during her monologue *My Mathematics*, named for a stallion. And with her raw, excremental vision, Karen Finley throws Swiftian shit tantrums—pouring Hershey syrup over her body while outing the human love for squish and sniff, her tongue licking the squeezed butt hole of offi-cial authority. Though it's past the time to lose her tortured-artist pose, she's winning in stand-up, shaggy-dog yarns, knitting together diary en-tries, TV dish, and pet peeves.

The chapter opens with a Q & A between me and Mark Russell, artistic di-rection of P.S. 122, the venue where many of the performers here were first presented and nurtured.

Eric Bogosian is captured starting out, before he became known for his solos *Sex, Drugs and Rock and Roll* and *Driving Nails in the Floor with My Head*, his play *Talk Radio*, and myriad TV and film performances. He recently per-formed a retrospective of his work at a benefit for P.S. 122, and the newer monologues hurtled forth with great directness. In some of the older char-acter sketches, Bogosian looks down on the subway panhandlers, drug dealers, and Hollywood agents he plays. Speaking from his gut, he whips out fears and failed hopes, edged with irony but still in love with his gallery of macho styles.

Bogosian's world is vacant of women. He doesn't play women; his male characters don't even relate to them, except in fantasy. This is the locker room, where the penis speaks. Bogosian is at once grappling with the discontents of maleness and submerged in his sexual braggarts and escape artists. His men can never get enough edge play, drugs, oblivion. Because dissatisfaction is his subject, Bogosian does not wholly embody characters like himself: an artist with a career that is cooking.

In their politico-sexy solo evenings, Argentine Benito Gutmacher and Brazilian Denise Stoklos clown in the language of Planet Downtown, working with few props and costumes, evoking the world with their bodies and voices.

The late Danitra Vance was ineffable, hard at work, wired like no one else. At dinner one night, she explained why she quit the British drama school she attended for a year in the late seventies: "They wanted a nigger in the woodpile, not a militant colored girl from Chicago." In addition to stints at Second City, *SNL*, and the Public Theater, she mounted solo evenings—part showbiz extravaganzas, part personal diaries, all grounded in spontaneous comedy and risk. After her mastectomy, playing Harriet Hetero the Feminist Stripper, she whipped off her shirt and bared her torso, creating an erotic, cathartic moment. "This wasn't something I wanted to do. But I had to show, for other women, that this body is still okay. I think my scar is beautiful."

The next three performers—John Leguizamo, Dael Orlandersmith, and Danny Hoch—are street kids who anchored themselves with art and whose work is juiced by the knowledge of what lies beyond rescue. I was lucky to see them when they were beginning, and what glared out in all was not raw talent but concentration and theater craft that had already been honed.

What lifts the portraits of John Leguizamo above photorealism and stereotyping is his willingness to let ambivalent feelings simmer. In his first solo evening, *Mambo Mouth*, he served a tapas table of Latino characters, their ambition trained on social power, their idiom spiced with the longings of the marginalized. Leguizamo caught some flak from the tribe for opening the ethnic closet to reveal clown costumes and for gratifying voyeurism by unbuttoning the ethnic fly. But he wasn't looking to be reassuring.

HBO taped a fluid version of his next solo, *Spic-O-Rama,* a series of dramatic monologues that again survey hyphenated existence, this time in a single, frazzled family. In *Mambo Mouth,* one of his characters is a transvestite. In the next show, he plays a woman. Here, as well as in the '96 movie *To Wong Foo, Thanks for Everything, Julie Newmar,* where Leguizamo plays a drag queen, he dodges gender-policing machos and goes AWOL in androgyny. Elsewhere in his portraits, though, machismo is fondled as much as resisted, cocksmanship portrayed as the only surviving romance in lives bereft of other dreams.

Dael Orlandersmith is a hardy trekker who could easily have stretched out under the avalanche of her childhood. Instead she learned to see her experience in three dimensions. Her people teeter on the edge of action, wanting to penetrate fantasy and get real, but Orlandersmith knows, too, how life leaves them unequipped to move. A poet as well as a performer these days, in addition to performing her new solo, *Monster,* she competes in poetry slams, touring with the Nuyorican Poet's Café.

Danny Hoch makes you gasp with his powers of mimicry, this slender white kid scoping people with accents, lousy apartments, and full-frontal body language. Leaping class and race borders, many performers contort themselves to translate, or they go native in grunge drag, getting off on lives in peril. Hoch doesn't patronize or translate—hell, one of his pieces rolls on entirely in Spanish. His respect radiates from his absorption, and how astutely he has observed! Half of his characters are motormouths whose inner lives he reveals. The others scrabble for words—a street rapper, nearly drowning in *yos* and glottal stops, flows only when rhyming. Hoch's comedy doesn't dilute the darkness in his characters' lives, and difficulty doesn't squash their spirits.

Hoch won an Obie Award for his show *Some People,* and after touring for many months took to globe surfing. "I was in Cambodia, India, and Croatia," he said when he returned, "interviewing young people who had been through war. I talked to Tibetans living in India and to kids who'd survived the Khmer Rouge. I'm working on a hip-hop show, set in 1983, about hybrid language and being a minstrel, wearing other people's skin. I'm something between a Baptist preacher and a Jewish cantor."

Mark Russell

1996

Mark Russell, who is forty-two, has been artistic director of P.S. 122 since 1983, and has cheered thousands of performers. He loves to laugh and dance, with his ponytail flying. He has a genius for making others feel seen—even if he doesn't always get what they're up to. Almost every performance artist named in this book has trod the boards of P.S. 122, the lumbering red-brick building on the corner of Ninth Street and First Avenue that in one incarnation actually was a public school—though the initials now stand for performance space. Russell has championed performance art and his generation of actors and dancers, following the tradition of avant-garde promoters Ellen Stewart, impresaria of LaMaMa; Crystal Field and George Bartenieff, founders of Theater for a New City; and Joseph Papp, founder of the Public Theater. Russell's collection of performance texts, *Out of Character,* has recently been published by Bantam Books. We spoke in the spring of '96.

L S : What are the origins of P.S. 122 as a performing venue?
M R : The city had abandoned it in '76 for official use and after that, community groups occupied it. If you could pay rent on a room, you could keep it. There was a Polish day-care center in one space. Some painters came in who could pay and got to use some of the classrooms. In '78 Sally Eckoff invited Charlie Moulton to see what he could do with a space. He started tearing up the tile, found a great floor, and wanted to turn it into a dance space. He had been working with Merce Cunningham and was beginning to do his own pieces. Charlie Moulton, Tim Miller, Peter Rose, and Charles Dennis founded it as an artistic center, wanting to turn it into a kind of Westbeth, where dancers could rehearse and painters could set up studios. At this time the city still owned the building, and at this point, too, the movie *Fame* was being filmed and the production got kicked out of the High School of Performing Arts, where they were shooting. The movie production took over P.S. 122 and gave the resident artists alternative spaces for three months. Charlie moved to Warren Street and started throwing great big parties that turned into Avant Garde Arama. Molissa Fenley, Carol Ar-

mitage, Charles Dennis, and Eric Bogosian performed, generating a great amount of energy, and that energy moved back into P.S. 122 when the film crew left. They also refinished the floor.

LS: How did you enter the scene?

MR: It was '79, and I was part of this event that is still going on and was one of the roots for the transformation of the space. It was called Open House. Robert Wilson started having these weekly parties in his storefront on Spring Street. The Wooster Group got ideas from the parties. They'd play records and do improvs, and the event moved from loft to loft. It was held together by Charles Dennis, who also settled down at P.S. 122 and created Open Movement, a kind of happening influenced by Peter Rose, who had been to Poland and worked with Grotowski. So did I. So when I came to New York, I gravitated toward these experiments.

LS: What was your life like before New York?

MR: I grew up in the Midwest, in Wisconsin, Minnesota, and Ohio, then later Texas. My dad was a bonus baby for a high school ring company. We moved often. I had a kind of Army brat upbringing, where it wasn't possible to form long-term friendships. I lived in a fantasy world until I was sixteen. I told stories to myself, actually to a stick I carried around. I had all sorts of imaginary friends. It started when I was five or six, part of moving so much and having to keep to yourself. I would enter a trance. My hero was Smoke, who later became Jimmy. Sometimes I would tell people the stories I made up, and that would make me incredibly happy. They were adventures, without resolutions or conflicts, more like travelogues. I would create utopias. I feel that P.S. 122 is a sort of utopia that I hold court over. I'm the gatekeeper, but once you're inside you can do whatever you want. I want to be just as surprised as everyone else by the outcome. I would have a harder time doing my job if I had more specific ideas. I try to create a playground for the artist and audience. My stories were playgrounds. There wasn't much about death and dying.

LS: What happened at sixteen?

MR: I discovered girls, and the fantasy world evaporated. We'd moved to Texas the year after the sniper shootings from the tower in Austin. It was '67. I was thirteen and going into eighth grade. I would go out into the hills. I smoked dope for the first time at the legion hall and got turned on to ZZ Top. I had cousins who were doing community theater, and I got involved with it. I kept acting in high school, and people said I was good, so I was able to take acting courses in the college while I was still in high school. There was a teacher, Minnie Field, who staged avant-garde student productions. She was very intense. We did *Antigone, Mother Courage,* and *Mary of Scotland.* The kids in the drama club got to grow their hair long. We were special within the school. It was another secluded, magical world, and it provided some insulation from the brutality of the Texas environment. There was a raging cultural war. Cowboys would pull you off the road if they saw long hair and cut it off. I was dodging bottles, being called a dirty hippy.

LS: But you were part of a group at this point, not isolated.

MR: That was important, and my parents were encouraging, too. I went to the University of Texas in Austin and did a directing major. I studied with Francis Hodge, who wrote an important book on directing. Everyone had total fear of him and loved him. My parents also got me a subscription to the English magazine *Plays and Players,* and I discovered Robert Wilson, Sam Shepard, and Robert Patrick. We did our own production of *Kennedy's Children* before it was done in New York.

LS: Why did you switch from acting to directing?

MR: Actually, I started out as a visual artist, but I thought I could do more in theater. My problem as an actor was that I knew how everyone else should do their roles, except for me. By directing, I became a better actor. I worked with a teacher who had been exiled from Poland, and he set up a project for me, so I could take a course there. It was a wonderful trip. I took a year off and hitchhiked around the country, getting a VIP tour of Polish theater. I worked with Shiner, Kantor, and Grotowski. I lived in a castle, while doing these paratheatrical projects. On my way back I stopped off in New York to visit a cousin, who had a small place and a job. While I was there, I directed Harvey Perr's play *Afternoon Tea* in his loft. I went back to Austin, finished my degree, and in '78 I came back to New York for good. I was twenty-four.

LS: What were your early experiences in New York?

MR: I met people in a contact improv class taught by Danny Lepkoff and David Woodbury. They were second-generation dancers, like Trisha Brown, coming out of the Judson Church movement. The idea was to construct movement from the gravity between two dancers' bodies, to go with the motion. It was a movement language, which was really fun to do and sometimes fun to watch. Stephanie Skira and Ishmael Houston-Jones were also working stuff out at Open Movement nights at P.S. 122, every Tuesday. That's how I first came to the place, as a participant. I would pay my two dollars and dance. There was no music, no leaders, whatever happened in the room for three hours happened. Plumbers and ballet people were moving together. It was the cheapest aerobics workout in the city.

LS: How did you support yourself?

MR: I worked at a yogurt shop and at a custom-made shirt shop. I did phone sales, sold coffee to office workers, and delivered Baby Watson cheesecakes, driving to all the Mafia restaurants in midtown between eleven and noon. I worked for *Other Stages,* selling advertising. I was the only full-time employee. I started freelancing and working for *Alive* magazine, a glossy that focused on performance. Performance art got its American art definition out of happenings in the seventies, and there was a feminist action art linkup. *Alive* thought it would be the Soho *High Performance* but even cooler. John Howell and Jed Wheeler ran it. Philip Glass and Karen Finley were in it. It was beautiful, but it only lasted for five issues. I was still going back to Poland, whenever I could, for my Grotowski studies. I was a Grotowski guinea pig in "The Tree of People Project." I used to think of Poland as an extension of Long Island. It took seven hours to get there, and I could never afford to stop off and see England. It was one of those really cheap flights or nothing.

LS: But *Other Stages* was still your chief means of support?

MR: Yes. I stayed for three years, and it went bankrupt three weeks after I left. Danitra Vance came to me to place the first ad for her show. Because of *Alive* magazine, I got to know all the downtown players: David White, Tim Miller, Charles Moulton, and Charles Dennis. Now their careers were taking off and P.S. 122 was becoming a larger monster to handle. They hired me. It was '83, and I was twenty-nine.

LS: What was your official job?

MR: I came on as managing director. When I arrived, the place didn't have not-for-profit status and it wasn't incorporated. There were no books. I started all that. People paid rent for rehearsal space and to put on performances. That was our income, in addition to a few grants, one from the Beard Foundation. I was paid seven thousand dollars a year, but part of that money included what I could get from unemployment. I would work, and then fire myself, claim unemployment, and hire myself again. At the time, I was still going to the Open Movement nights. People would be rolling all over me and saying, "Did you get my phone call?" I looked at it like this: The unemployment scam was my first government grant.

LS: Explain how the space went from being a rentable venue to a presenting institution.

MR: After the books and nonprofit status were set up, I began applying for grants and tried to formalize how people got into the space. We needed to take more responsibility for what we showed audiences. I didn't want it to seem like a vanity house. I began to create a season. I was lucky. There was a general feeling around that good people performed here, but I still wanted to weed out the poseurs. I began to book shows and to create a general audience that wanted adventure, instead of each artist hustling their own attendance. We charged artists less money and took on more risk, but we were also more involved with the finished show. In the old days, P.S. 122 would get five hundred dollars for the space. We switched to sharing the box office fifty-fifty. The upstairs house holds a hundred and fifty people, downstairs seats sixty to eighty. With tickets eight or twelve dollars, you can see the economics.

LS: What were you looking for when booking artists?

MR: I used the place to expand my own aesthetic. If something scares me or I can't decide if it's art, I can put it in here, and it might be more powerful than me, and I can see it and decide why I don't like it, or I might change my opinion. I don't mind if work disturbs me in a negative way. The main thing is not to be bored. Reno made me uncomfortable. I didn't know if she belonged in the stand-up world, whether she would work here. She did well. I'm not particularly fond of loud women, but I seem to have booked a lot of them . . . Karen Finley, Penney Arcade. I did it so I could see how I would feel.

LS: Explain what you mean by negative disturbance.

MR: Ron Athey was a watershed event for me. It was lucky we met up when I was at a point in my development when I could be open to him. I'm not down with urban primitives. Ron is HIV positive. Daryl is not HIV positive. Ron takes a razor and cuts Daryl, then he makes prints by blotting the blood with paper towels. Here is this modern black man involving himself with a body modification related to his former African culture. What does it mean to him? I don't know. I didn't ask a lot of questions of them. I tried to set it up for them to speak for themselves. Athey puts on a spectacle. These are passion plays. Lighting is very important, and the event takes place in theater time. At the Clit Club Athey did a performance that had people in the audience fainting. I saw Pain Boy there, hanging things off his tits. I thought it was sideshow stuff. Athey takes the circusy stuff and touches different tones. Booking him is going into one of the deepest, scariest parts of my world and making a justification for it. Since he appeared, I've received many requests that go, "I cut myself. I heard you like that." To me that's been there, done that. When Ron bleeds, people want to touch him, and you can't. He's HIV positive. He has a new piece he's not sure I'll be able to deal with. It involves rimming and dildos. Ron thinks I'll be too grossed out. I don't know. I've seen a lot. He does something when he talks about being a junkie and puts twenty-five hypodermic needles in his arm. He looks like a porcupine.

L S : Within a two-month period in 1988, all of the NEA four performed at P.S. 122, the year before Jesse Helms lit into performance art. Did you feel repercussions?

M R : We were spared. We looked like a school. It messed up the sound bite.

L S : Still, the general climate of arts funding is chilly. How have you been coping with the cutbacks?

M R : We quickly began to wean ourselves from NEA funds and earn more from producing, like the Field Trips we send out across the country. The tours were inaugurated in '86, after noticing that young performers who went on the road came back more mature and less in the ghetto of downtown. The aim has been to build up recognition for these artists and have them bring back complete works. Blue Man Group created a lot of material touring. Presenters who can't fill a house with one artist can sell out with a lineup. This year John Kelly joins the tour in April, but for most of the fifteen-city gig, the troupe consists of Molissa Fenley, who's returning to dance after radical knee surgery, Tiye Giraud, a singer/storyteller who's collaborated with Urban Bush Women, James Godwin, who does a character called "Antler Man," plus Reno and Danny Hoch. Each performer gets twenty minutes, but the shows aren't a strict lineup. Part of the sport is to weave the artists together. This year, for the first time, the tour is going out without federal funding, though with twenty-five thousand dollars from Philip Morris.

L S : What are some other developments?

M R : We've been commissioning work. I give artists a sum of money that they can do whatever they want with, but I will get a new piece of work when they perform here. Danny Hoch will perform next fall. We've given him five thousand dollars for the project. With producing, we also get a piece of future action. We gave Danny twenty-five hundred for *Some People*. We do about ten to twenty commissions a year, including Ron Brown, Dave Rousseve, and Blue Man Group. There are frustrations. I wanted to do the final part of Eric Bogosian's piece at P.S. 122. He turned me down. Nothing frustrates me more than someone not wanting to be in my space, because it's too high profile or not high profile enough. I've been doing this a long time, and I sometimes wonder if I should get out. I don't want to turn into a bag person with a theater. We've got a small deficit, too, at the moment. Working with Dominic Balletta, who is the current managing director, we're racing to erase it. It's dealable. We've decided to do more instead of less. If this organization is going to die, I want it to die fighting.

Eric Bogosian: High Protean

July 1983

"Ever wonder about the skid marks on the road? Ever wonder what happened? I don't, I think about the rubber," Eric Bogosian growls into a mike, which he practically devours. He is seated at an oak desk, circa 1930. On it is a telephone and a green-shaded gooseneck lamp. The look is film-noir sinister, and in keeping with the achromatic decor, Bogosian wears a white shirt, black jeans, and black Velcro droid shoes. He's small and tight. The short curls on his head are tight. Only his slightly protruding eyes aren't held in check. They probe the audience, tense and insinuating, all during his hour-long performance, a collection of characterizations bound together by the actor's will.

On occasion, Bogosian tries too hard to be dangerous, and the effect backfires; he comes off young. Some pieces go on too long, and in several— a Richard Simmons exercise tyrant, a Hispanic chick hassler, a gospel con man named Reverend Tim—the impersonations don't add surprises. Still, there is funny, edgy writing in even meandering monologues. A drunk, panhandling a commuter, asks his mark why he's "in such a hurry to get home and mow the lawn." A slick salesman gives a lecture on the latest in torture devices: "Some people like to work with telephone books and broken fingers, but hey, we're not in the dark ages, we have electricity." In a trice, slight Bogosian becomes an overfed mafioso, gasping with heartburn from fried scungili, chasing away intimations of mortality by cataloguing his friends' ailments: "Joe went in for gallstones. It's nothin'. They just cut him open and throw 'em in the garbage. Cancer comes from the food, but ya gotta eat, right, or else ya get the anorexia."

The strongest sequence is a long, Lenny Bruce–inspired complaint, consisting of clichés reinvested with irony. The ranter is an old man, and at the end of his tirade, he lifts a stick against modernity's assaultive sights and sounds, in particular the acid rock of street radios; then suddenly, Bogosian becomes that rocker and the stick becomes his guitar. While the voice of Bon Scott of AC/DC screeches "If You Want Blood You Got It," Bogosian snakes across the stage, his rigid parts becoming rubber and his tongue darting lizardlike. It's a marvelous transformation, and the mean, joyous music is an anthem for the best in this spitting, sweating performance.

Bogosian gives himself a workout, using the theater as a gym and a confessional. His is a particularly naked form of acting—gallant, exciting to watch, and rewarding when it works. In *Funhouse*, Bogosian is all dark, aggressive energy. I'd like to see him do some women.

Premium Bob: American Style

July 1996

Painful laughter is the arrow sharpened by the duo Premium Bob, consisting of Paul Boocock, the tall one with the fake-looking mustache, and David Latham, who is short and bespectacled and writes the shows. They've been together for years, and practice glints from their liquid timing and choreographic ease with each other's bodies. Like the Kipper Kids, they embody a single character, Bob, a creature dressed in UPS browns, a cyborg with enough plastic to grieve for the rapid obsolescence of synthetic culture and enough humanity to groove on other people's unhappiness.

Having eaten the history of comedy, the team references the Marx Brothers one minute, Lypsinka the next, in an original way that intentionally frustrates description. They torture language, juggle it, pity it for its remove from sensation. Their latest lunatic image-rant, *American Style* (1996), wryly directed by Gary Schwartz, is a loop on a sound track, a stream-of-paranoia/vanity/sadism, with inserted commentary and gestures. The guys morph agilely, musing on "plastic yearning," on wearing "linen that says I'm sipping cappuccino," on the difference between "having it all and having it all ladled into your mouth."

American Style is "not a low-end mutual fund for beige people playing it safe." It's about packaging and coming unwrapped. These droids, implanted with home-shopping microchips, have grown up in a suburban noir, beside a pop debris waste site. Is it any wonder their conversation is net nattering, their angst recorded by the Talking Heads, their capacity for delayed gratification reserved for extending the process of injuring each other? They hawk "aromatherapy necklaces redolent of success," champion "really hurting and really healing for profit and notoriety on the late-night network." Though demented, these mutants are passionate rather than cynical, mongrel but not random or vacant. More than any other sign they flash, these guys love being on stage together, forging connection. To them modernity doesn't suck, it bleeds, and their comedy leaves you in stitches.

Benito Gutmacher: Traveling Light

June 1990

Benito Gutmacher—the name alone tells a story of uprooting. "My parents were Polish Jews who escaped to Russia, then Buenos Aires. My mother wanted to call me after her father—Benjamin would have been his name in English. She was offered a menu of Latin equivalents, and she chose Benito."

He smiles, as he frequently does, at quirks of fate. His white teeth, shining against his olive complexion, lend his face a South American cast, and his English is gently accented with Spanish slides. He's making his New York debut at La MaMa, in *The Cry of the Body*, one of five solo pieces he has performed throughout Europe and South America. We're having lunch a few days after opening night, and he's unfolding his life with the same uninhibitedness with which he performs, nearly nude—except for a pair of skimpy briefs.

The Cry of the Body is a nonnarrative collage divided into ten scenes exploring themes like "violence" and "work." With his Jesus body and Barrymore profile, he leaps around the floor like a possessed toad. He's a gorilla baby, fingers in mouth, gurgles and squeals erupting. Gestures and sounds crop up like tics—at once robotic and impulsive—through his joyous tour of Artaud's synthetic suffering and Reich's traumatic politics. Jabbering in French, English, Spanish, German, and Italian, he takes himself seriously in no language. He shows the silliness that being mortal imposes; storming around with a sword, he suddenly needs to pick his teeth.

Taped music—a Romantic aria, a martial snatch—erupts unpredictably, but most of the sound comes from Gutmacher's body, as he springs gymnastically, takes deep breaths, and strikes various surfaces. Though his theatrics are basic, Gutmacher's evening is fresh and invigorating. For a guy who flashes so much flesh, he's unvain. He's playful, puncturing suffering and estrangement with yelps and tongue jabs. His work comes across as autobiography without a text.

"I'm interested in the price people pay for denying death. So much vitality is lost in the effort of pushing away this reality. From the time I was six, I knew I wanted to be an actor. I wanted to be Brando, Alain Delon, Gene Kelly. When I was seventeen, I read Artaud, and saw I could show the futility of denial on stage. In Argentina, my parents said they felt safe. They wanted to forget the past, but they spoke only Yiddish to me and of course passed on their fears and nightmares. To escape, I went to Paris."

Gutmacher became a practicing Jew in the mid-seventies, not long after a severe case of pancreatitis—contracted, his doctors theorized, from acrobatic flips—brought him near death. "I was in San Francisco, kept alive with a then experimental procedure of tube feeding. For two months, I was like a chicken, attached to hoses. America is a good place to have pancreatitis." He is grateful to, but not religious about, Judaism. "I'm aware that religions divide people, but mine gives me order."

So does the discipline of acting, though the work sends him ricocheting across the planet. The term "international" understates his personal life. His oldest child lives in Paris with his first wife, and he and his second wife live in West Germany. Their three children speak French to their father and German to their mother, and Gutmacher and his wife speak to each other in English. "We never fight. We're not emotionally involved in English. I'd have to rant in Spanish, but it wouldn't mean anything to her."

He speaks jokingly, but, in his accessible fantasies for the open way he talks about his life, Gutmacher projects a brilliance—his parents' compelled dislocation turned into willed non.

Denise Stoklos: Cant Opener

January 1989

When Brazilian performer Denise Stoklos strides on stage—black jumpsuit clinging, blond punk-crest flying—you think *she's* the eponymous orgasm in Dario Fo and Franca Rame's *Adult Orgasm Escapes from the Zoo*. She vamps, showing off her slender form. Bare feet slink, hands embrace an invisible lover; her appendages are so spirited, they're like possessed animals. The exhibitionism might grow exasperating were it not leavened with clowning. Stoklos—evoking Chaplin and Giulietta Masina, Peter Sellers and Gilda Radner—is ludicrous and lewd, and joy derives from her intentionally silly English.

She is at her wildest in "We All Have the Same Story." A woman imagines giving birth to a daughter, then telling the child a story: A girl has a doll, who talks dirty and enjoys the beatings of her lover, a cat. The cat is killed by the poisonous, phosphorescent "pee-pee" of a dwarf, who in turn is vaporized by the deadly fart of a computer-programmer prince. In time the girl is widowed and winds up amid women, all of whom have the same story. Here metaphor subsumes rhetoric, and Stoklos is lyrical: in a trice acting a mother giving birth and becoming her own baby, in a wink leaning over, toes devilishly splayed, to impersonate the gaseous, ill-fated hero.

She is inventive in two slighter monologues that follow. In "A Woman Alone," she plays a housewife who's had an affair and, as punishment, is imprisoned in her apartment by her husband. Stoklos, her face and body jerking like a marionette, embodies strain, as the woman, compelled to put a sunny complexion on everything, lets desperation leak. Smiling manically, she confides, "If I'm alone and don't have the radio on loud in every room, I get this desire to kill myself."

In "Waking Up," a woman factory worker takes us through another daily round. Trying to figure out where she's left her keys, she becomes a Lucille Ball who has permanently misplaced her bearings. Discovering she's mixed up sugar and bicarbonate of soda, she stares into space, lips parted, as current lights her bulb: "For how long have I bathed the baby in sugar? That must be why at nursery school the teachers say, 'We can't put your son outside, the bees are all over him.' "

Danitra Vance, 1959–1994

September 1994

We were at dinner the night before Danitra left for Sundance "to be a glamorous celebrity starlet diva." A movie she'd made, *Jumpin' at the Boneyard*, was being screened. She said it was serious, about a homeless, drug-addicted couple, but she couldn't help clowning and lambasting the typing of blacks—"I'm speaking for all those crackhead women out there." That was Danitra: her delivery as caffeinated off stage as on, her ambition traipsing through minefields of power, her wit set on fearless.

She'd burst onto the performance scene at La MaMa in 1985, channeling alter egos and rocking out, backed by her trio, the Mell-O White Boys. Aquanetta Feinstein was a Bronx kid, zoning into the avant-garde. Jill Brazeale, a buppie, didn't know she was black. Hired for the 1985–86 season of *Saturday Night Live*—the first black female cast member—Vance felt shabbily treated and was underused, but, smartie that she was, she didn't sniff at being recognized, thank you.

The Public Theater was a sturdier perch—especially collaborating with George C. Wolfe. In *The Colored Museum*, playing a slave-ship stewardess, her body twitched with bad faith as she lullingly sang "Summertime" by George Gershwin—"who comes from another oppressed people, so he understands." She won an Obie Award for her performance in Wolfe's *Spunk*, adapted from short stories by Zora Neale Hurston, and during the summer of '92 debuted a new performance piece as part of the Public's festival of new voices. Her bout with breast cancer wasn't a secret, but when she stripped, baring her gorgeous body and revealing one round breast and a taped X over the space where her other breast had been, she was deliriously brave, theatrical, and sexy. The show was a smash, and a fall run was planned.

At the veggie restaurant she'd chosen, dubbing herself "a third-generation vegetarian," she told stories about her hometown, "racist old Chicago." When Vance was at Chicago's Roosevelt University, an anthropology teacher suggested she go to Haiti and dig her own latrine; she said, "I want to study cultures like Los Angeles." In London, where she studied at the Webber-Douglas Academy of Dramatic Art, she wasn't served in restaurants but learned *Under Milk Wood* with a Welsh accent. "I thought if they ever do the Shirley Bassey story, I'm it."

She described the surgery performed two years earlier, when her right breast and several lymph nodes were removed. "I became a baby, reduced to basic needs. I wanted to show everybody my scar. I think it's beautiful. I was so immersed in my body. I turned on the TV and Peter Jennings was talking about China, and I thought, 'China! I have *cancer.*'" Now she felt she'd advanced to being a child—wanting to get "everything at once and as soon as possible." The boldness of children had inspired her piece, "The Radical Girl's Guide to Radical Mastectomy." "I was desperate to get back to the antic little girl in me, who didn't have breasts. There's a lot of information in those years. Seeing my shirt fly off felt like an out-of-body experience. I had to show that this body is okay."

At some point during dinner, she mentioned that her arm had started hurting her and that she was having trouble lifting it. Her tone was breezy, uncomplaining. I chewed the inside of my cheek, and she promised to see her doctor before leaving for Colorado. A few weeks later she learned that the cancer had recurred. We spoke when she was in the hospital and after she'd endured a grueling, experimental treatment. She knew where she stood but was hopeful, admiring her doctors for working hard to save her. In May '93 she opened at the Public again, playing a streetwise angel with no illusions about God in *Marisol,* José Rivera's apocalyptic parable. She was still mannequin svelte, still vibrating with hyperkinetic energy, still enchantingly sly and confidential in conversation. She hoped to mount her solo again, where she could vamp, terrorize, confess, and fantasize as no one else.

She died at thirty-five, on August 21, at the home of her grandfather, Clarence Edwards, in Markham, Illinois. She wasn't averse to the blaming business but preferred conjuring delight. She didn't know the whereabouts of her father. "If I ever go crazy, it's his fault," she said, but imagined him "an American in Paris." Once she dissed Pinocchio for wishing to be a little boy—"Why would anyone want to be real if they could be magical?"

John Leguizamo: Border Crossing

December 1990

In Amsterdam last summer, I met two young men with progressive views on women's rights and national health and just about everything but the large migration of Turkish people into the Netherlands. It was okay for Turks to live in Holland but irksome that they didn't jettison their language and clothing styles. "For the sake of their kids," the young men contended, "they should try to become Dutch." I offered, "In time, the Dutch will become more Turkish." The men shook their heads in disbelief. "Twenty years ago," I said, "if New Yorkers had been told they would one day take for granted that Latin culture was part and parcel of the fabric of their city, that they would crave Latin food and adopt Latin street fashions, they'd have said, 'That's crazy.' But it happened."

Mainstream interest in Latin culture has gathered gradually, inevitably. With this shift—as has been the case with every other minority lifted from the margin to the spotlight—boldness follows, courage spurred by public attention, curiosity, focus that feels like a handshake, a pat on the shoulder, a set of fingers on the shirt buttons and fly. "Let's see," the majority chants, shivering. "Okay," coos the alien, titillated and seductive, "I'll show you my closet. I'll strip."

This momentum powers actor/writer John Leguizamo, who was born in Bogotá twenty-six years ago to a Colombian mother and a Puerto Rican father and whose solo show *Mambo Mouth*—in an open-ended run at American Place Theatre—bristles with the energy of secrets unleashed at last. Leguizamo has dark curly hair, Incan eyes and cheekbones, and the grace and quick moves of a lightweight boxer. He radiates intelligence and drive. His hunger makes him notice every bit of humiliation. His empathy allows him to place brutality in the context of defeat and pain. The tension between his sadistic glee in unmasking weakness and his willingness to portray vulnerability produces satire that is supple as well as raw. He's fresh-faced, brimming with exuberance and promise.

Among his seven Latin characters is Yakimoto, who formerly made the streets his office but, in an attempt to attain clean, straight security, has bypassed becoming American and turned Japanese. Yakimoto conducts crossover seminars to fellow Latinosans, instructing them how to walk without bopping to internal salsa music and how to color their hair shades "found in nature." Leguizamo also plays Agamemnon, the Cuban host of a public access call-in show whose machismo salves an ego battered by lost dreams. In his dazzling white suit and pencil mustache, Agamemnon explains "The Goldilocks Syndrome": "It's when a blonde sexy mami comes into your life, eats your food, sits on your fine upholstery, and gives you nothing." We glimpse the wound, too, under the peacock's feathers. "I was a lot of comfort to my popi," Agamemnon confides. "He said, 'I can't believe that out of a hundred thousand sperms, you were the quickest.'"

He counsels men, "Don't fall in love with beautiful women, so when they leave you it don't mean nothin'"; then he rails against Raul Julia and other Latin successes for plotting to keep all available parts for themselves.

Leguizamo loves the humor, born from hard-won survival, of the marginalized—their voices and accents, their verbal inventions that arch toward poetry. One of his rogues, a punk arrested for beating up his girlfriend, feels momentarily sorry and, inching as close as he can to tenderness, explains, "I wanted to breed with her." Manny, a snap-queen hustler, sasses to a trick, "Don't you hear me? What do I look like, a hologram?" Another incarnation, a stoned street seller, cajoles a passerby, "Can you spare some change? I promise I won't buy nothin' to eat"; then he plies the woman with rare Shakespeare manuscripts—"This, here, is from *The Merchant of Venezuela*." Loco Louie, a fourteen-year-old describing his debut sexual experience, is at first fearful and observes that his "red-helmeted warrior is in a coma." After completing his mission, though, Louie crows, "I'm the Sperminator."

Leguizamo and I had lunch on the Upper West Side, and, one-on-one, he is as playful and undefended as he is on stage. Between bites of grilled salmon and salad, he riffs through Latin accents: Cuban, Mexican, Queens homeboy, Loisaida girlfriend, furnishing hand gestures—forefinger and pinky jabs, crotch holds, crucifix moves from chin to groin and across the chest, flamenco flourishes around the face and head. When he isn't doing accents, he doesn't have one.

Filling in his background, he explains he lived in Colombia until he was five, then his family moved to Jackson Heights. His father, who could speak Italian, worked in expensive restaurants, his mother in a doll factory. His father spent his earnings buying electrical appliances, planning to ship them to Colombia and sell them for a large profit, but the plan went bust when the goods were stolen. "He had high standards, but he was disappointed and abusive, especially to my mother." When John was thirteen and his brother eleven, his mother ran away from home with her sons.

"I used my mother for Manny, the transvestite who stands up for herself. Agamemnon is based on my father. He sees himself as a dethroned king. My father felt highly humiliated by his experiences in New York. I felt the shame in him. And Yakimoto was inspired by my brother, who is studying to be an opera singer. He tried so hard to assimilate and get rid of his street mannerisms. I was totally the opposite. I went through a serious homeboy period, and when I was fourteen I became a maniac, cruel. Hormones, the streets, my home life all came crashing down. Louie is me at that age. Sex was the thing that made you a man. To us it was so goddamn important. You have fewer things. The things that were available—sex and fighting—made you something."

Even early on, though, Leguizamo's wildness had a theatrical bent. Once, he and a friend commandeered the mike on a subway train and did shtick for the passengers. The prank resulted in a police arrest. "I was handcuffed to a chair." At school, he got into so much trouble that, in order to continue attending classes, he was forced to see a therapist. "But I liked it. It made my sense of deprivation and ostracism into a feeling of specialness. I learned where my anger came from and how my parents had been uncared for themselves." His therapist suggested he try acting. "I looked in the yellow pages and picked out Sylvia Lee's Showcase Theater. I liked the idea of being in a showcase."

It didn't take long before a film student from NYU spotted him and cast him in a movie. Suddenly, he believed he had talent. "I got serious for the first time. I took classes at Strasberg and at HB." He joined the improv group First Amendment, did comedy for a while, and began to write. "It always came out dark. I got too many problems to be light." His efforts have paid off not only in *Mambo Mouth* but in a series of stage and screen roles. He played one of the young marines in Brian De Palma's *Casualties of War* and was the lead in *La Puta Vida* at the Public Theatre.

But much of the film work he's offered frustrates him. "I played a blacksmith in one movie and a drug dealer in another, scuzzy parts. Directors call and say, 'I'd like to use you, but you're too ethnic.' I have mixed feelings about this. I don't want to be not ethnic, but it's horrible to me that white actors are playing Hispanics. De Niro was a Cuban in *Teddy Bear*.

Robby Benson played an Indian. Kevin Kline has been cast as Cesar in the movie *Mambo Kings*. Hollywood is saying, 'You people are interesting enough to make films about but you aren't good enough to portray yourselves.'

"The only way to change things is to write and get control of productions. When I was growing up I felt completely excluded from white culture. Latin kids still feel this way. Last summer, I shot the movie *Hanging Out with the Homeboys* in the South Bronx. Kids came up to me and said, 'You're really Latin? Wow. You're doin' so well. It's so amazing. Can you come to my house and talk to my mother?' "

Leguizamo has the drive and talent to get his views across. "I want to do the kind of work for my people that Woody Allen and Spike Lee have done for theirs," he says, "no apologies, no holds barred."

Dael Orlandersmith: Stronger Than Fiction

July 1995

"Functional madness" is how Dael Orlandersmith describes her childhood. She isn't exaggerating. Nor are the nine speakers in her fierce autobiographical solo *Liar, Liar*—whose run at Manhattan Class Company heralded a nimble new actor-writer. A revised version of the piece called *Beauty's Daughter*, directed by Peter Askin, was presented at American Place Theater. Orlandersmith's characters measure out their guts, saying just enough to conjure hell. The usual childhood trek through razor blades is compounded in their cases and in hers.

Orlandersmith, thirty-four, was born in East Harlem, named Donna Brown, and raised, an only child, by her mother, who was thirty-nine when she gave birth. Orlandersmith's father died at fifty-seven of stomach cancer when his daughter was three and a half. "The streets were wild," she says at lunch, "drunks and addicts everywhere, doing heroin and glue. I would walk in the door of the house and see a prostitute giving some man head. Kids would call up to me from the street, 'Can I come up and put my dick up your ass?' People fought with flying lye—petty jealous crap. They would mix urine and lye with honey, to make it stick when they threw it in someone's face."

Orlandersmith was sent to Catholic school, which she calls a "deranged structure." Nuns beat her with a yardstick. Orlandersmith's mother, Beulah, owned the house they lived in. "She worked for the phone company and considered herself better than the people in the neighborhood, because they drank on the street, while she did it indoors." Orlandersmith was forced to sleep with her mother. "She didn't molest me, but it was a highly sexualized environment. Every weekend she would go on a bender, filling up the house with drunks. I would put fingers in my ears to drown out the slurred voices." Orlandersmith had no privacy: Her room lacked a door. Her mother's friends groped her. Male relatives began molesting her at age eight. "I remember thinking, 'I'm on my own in this.' " She was raped at sixteen, and at nineteen another man attempted rape, but, says Orlandersmith, "I beat the shit out of him. I had to learn to fight."

She orders eggs and fruit salad, careful about what she consumes. Her body is large and imposing: nearly six feet tall and padded with worked, muscular flesh. It is an actor's tool, so pliant that, without makeup and with minimal costume changes, she can play males as well as females, old people as well as young, whites as well as people of color. A curtain of gold braids opens onto a handsome, smooth-skinned face that one moment looks guarded, the next girlish and sunny. She loves the attention that *Liar, Liar* earned: appreciations in the *Voice* and in the *Times,* with apt comparisons to Eric Bogosian, John Leguizamo, and Danny Hoch. But Orlandersmith is free of illusions about success.

She has a bedrock solidity, similar to the irony that grounds her characters, each brought to life in a distinct idiom. Hector, a Latino boy, dreams of college but sells dope. Reading Dostoyevsky is the way he blocks out his father's brutality. Dianne escapes Harlem's chaos, fleeing to East Village bohemia, but she still fears intimate connection. Aging boozer Beauty knows that she has leaned too heavily on her daughter but can't stop blaming the girl for rescuing herself.

The depression and abuse Orlandersmith has known aren't overt subjects but shades of paint. Most of her characters don't overcome their entrapment. This artist is trained on passivity and on the impulse to talk away life in dreams and justifications. She weighs the difficulty of uprooting and the allure of revisiting pain, but there is nothing pious or reductive about her portrayals: Each of her characters shows the poet, or comedian, or blues singer who could have gotten out.

Orlandersmith's mother died of heart failure five years ago, and the house they shared is no longer standing. A year ago Orlandersmith relocated to the East Village, which does feel like sanctuary to her. "I tried to leave while my mother was alive, but she kept threatening suicide. Reading was what kept me going. As a kid I read anything I could get my hands on. My mother encouraged it, also my acting. I used to come home from school and watch the four-thirty movie. Once they had Brando week, and I was blown away. I identified with him. And James Dean, his emotional expressiveness. I liked the aggression that guys have."

She made it to Hunter College and then studied at the American Academy of Dramatic Arts and at HB Studio. For brief stints, she worked with Miguel Piñero and at the Actors Studio, and after jobs helping runaway kids and modeling for artists at Cooper Union, she hooked up with poet Diane Burns and with Bob Holman, impresario of the Nuyorican Poets Café. That space became a base, from which, in the early nineties, she read her poetry and began building characters.

"A lot of my life I was depressed. I got myself into therapy for the first time when I was fourteen. I couldn't sleep. I had terrible dreams about incest. I radiated so much misery that once a man on a bus came up and said, 'It can't be that bad.' I still fear winding up back there, but I know I don't have to fail." Sorting through childhood legacies, she is perhaps least ambivalent about her jabs and hooks. "I was writing at the Oak Bar and this drunk started hassling me and wouldn't stop. When he reached for my notebook, I clocked him." She leaks a smile. "He got all bloody, but he just wouldn't listen when I was nice."

Danny Hoch: Out of Hoch

November 1993

Remember the first time you saw Whoopi Goldberg, Danitra Vance, or Sandra Bernhard, the way they got up in your face and bet the bank that you would want more? Now it's Danny Hoch's turn. He is only twenty-three, and has so much talent and such a clear sense of direction that it's doubtful he'll be rocked by the attention bound his way. Hoch was at P.S. 122 a couple of weeks ago, and the small downstairs theater was only half full on a Friday night. The stage was bare, except for a rough box, a folding chair, and a clothesline strung with shabby jackets. The lights went down and in the dark a voice started drumming, lilting, caressing, calling himself the Caribbean Tiger—"Well I tell you people livin' upya inna New York City is like a jungle and anything can happen, just like a tiger walkin' by on your radio waves."

He wanted to know who was out there, and soon there were other voices. "Disya i Sluggy." The islands came awake: Guyana, Trinidad, Tobago, St. Lucia, Grenada, Jamaica, "all Caribbean Massive." The calypso, soca, and reggae throbbed, and we could do nothing but listen—absorbing the social fabric in these cadences—because the lights never did come up. By the time they did, we knew we had stumbled on that rarity: the bold artist's voice that sounds like it couldn't come out any other way.

Hoch's show, *Some People*, features eleven characters, and is played without intermission. Every figure is desperate to speak, language a soulprint and a way of bursting through isolation. It can also be a stamp of dislocation, as throats choke on alien words. Yet even the most constricted keep up a natter, like the Polish immigrant, Kazmierczack, who has been sent on a plumbing job in the apartment of a teacher.

"Eh, you brok? You something brok? Something break? Something broki? Something breakin'? Ah I fix. What broki?" His strain is as valiant as it is absurd, Hoch capturing his bent-head shame but also his bright-eyed search for a bridge. The teacher has a cat, he has a cat. Ah! And thus ensues a series of anecdotes—one about a cat vomiting in his shoe—that so exhausts his vocabulary he's reduced to groans and sputters, a cat language that is weirdly pliant.

Blanca befriends a gay neighbor and yet denies that AIDS could touch her: "I was like, yo, you ain't sticking no fucking rubber shit up inside me, you might as well put on a rubber glove and do some Spic and Span in that shit. So we started kissing, and I was like, you know, I was like . . . You seen this on Channel Thirteen?"

Then there is Bill, who feels the space for white men shrinking perilously—"The Moroccans bought up all the real estate from the Jews. You didn't hear? You don't read the papers, that's your problem. No, I know because they bought up all the Baskin-Robbins. I know because I was in a Baskin-Robbins last week, and when I went to pay for the thing I'm standing there with this guy and I asked him his name, and he says to me, 'Mohammed.' " Bill is the only nonminority in the cast, and yes he's a racist and an easy target, but Hoch doesn't leave it there. His minorities have grievances against women, gays, and other ethnics, and Bill is a wreck, an agonizer.

Nothing can go right for this guy, racism emanating like the bad breath he probably also huffs (despite the mouthwash he no doubt guzzles). He's poignant in his worminess, and Hoch likes him because he keeps talking.

Hoch is a junkie for the way we reveal ourselves when we don't know it. Silence is the spoiler, the emptiness in which violence can flare. Tall and slim, with a bumpy nose drawn by George Grosz, Hoch has an agile body and a superpowered ear. The ear stalks streets and take-out joints, leaning toward poetry not ordinarily included in theater. His mimicry doesn't condescend, because it signals no arduous leap. He can slip into otherness, because it's not *so* other. Hoch is in love with strange tables and strange beds.

We have lunch the week after I see his show, at a diner on the Upper West Side. He has no accent, though he was brought up in Queens, a Jewish kid and only child, living with his divorced mom. He is eating carefully these days, no dairy to protect his vocal cords. He orders fish and veggies, and then, in a what-the-hell burst, a second portion of fries. He tells his own story with the same pounce on details that pumps his writing.

And a story it is. It's about New York, and the heads of kids with spray cans and street-corner raps—about the cultural smarts and confusion inside b-boy suits. Hoch's voices come from his neighborhood, which bordered four distinct sections: Forest Hills ("middle-class, white, and Jewish"); Corona ("Italian, Dominican, Puerto Rican, and Cuban"); Rego Park ("totally mixed, everyone from Sierra Leonese to Madagascans to West Indians"); and Lefrak City ("predominantly black"). His ear comes from his mother, a speech pathologist.

He was loved by both parents, encouraged to do what he wanted, and magic, mime, and impersonating took hold. By junior high, he could channel Indira Gandhi, Billy Graham, and Mae West with spooky aplomb. He was entertaining at parties and bar mitzvahs, but that was only one side of his creative life. The other was homeboy culture. "I thought I was black or Puerto Rican. Our cliques weren't determined by color. There were black JAPs and white homeboys, but I didn't see anything creative about being a JAP. I didn't understand the social aspects of race until I went to high school. I was writing graffiti, rapping, break-dancing in Washington Square, drinking malt liquor, doing drugs. I used the money I got selling drugs to buy magic equipment. I got arrested a few weeks after my bar mitzvah." He laughs. "Of course, I had become a man."

This arrest and others weren't for drugs but graffiti. "Drugs were something I did to be part of the group," he says, but by high school he'd grown dependent on being stoned. He was attending the High School of Performing Arts and becoming a star. "It felt good, and I knew I had to quit drugs. There was a teacher who used to call us *kinder*. He said, 'Suffer for the right reasons.' "

By the time Hoch graduated, he had become so focused, intense, and disciplined about acting that later training at the North Carolina School of the Arts felt redundant. Not so his scholarship at the British American Drama Academy in London, where he studied with teachers from RADA and Central and through which he appeared in a Middleton play at the Royal Court Theater.

Back in New York, shoehorned into a "ten-foot-by-four-foot box" in the East Village, he waited tables at a barbecue restaurant. "I was studying the way people react to difference, how they express fascination and revulsion with little moves. It's so exciting being a voyeur into people's thought processes." He was developing his first solo show, *Pot Melting,* which he would mount with the Next Stage Company in 1991. But he wanted to do theater not only about the disincluded but *for* them. In 1990 he landed a job with the Creative Arts Team, a theater group at NYU that reaches out to at-risk adolescents in prisons, detention centers, and schools. "We do structured improvs about AIDS, racism, and abuse. The things kids reveal are harrowing! I continually wind up in tears."

Presently, he's working on a musical with Elizabeth Swados. "I guess it's about my youth," he says, somewhat wary about portraying himself, yet aware of the challenge of unwrapping the whole package. He's planning a piece on minstrelsy. "Maybe 'Daddy' Rice meeting Vanilla Ice. What I do now is almost minstrelsy. I'd like to try blackface." But other roots, streets, and tongues are tickling as well. "I had a grandfather who died when I was one. He was poor, but he'd entertain the neighborhood with characters—a woman with a shawl on her head, a peddler. He was called the King of Orchard Street. I'm told I take after him."

An Interview with Danny Hoch

Hoch's success has been swift. The sort of rush that would dizzy anyone, and I wondered how he was coping with it and what his impressions were of his generation. We talked in the spring of '96. He was twenty-five.

LS: You started making your own shows at such an early age. What inspired that independence?

DH: I trained as an actor at the High School of Performing Arts. We went out for auditions, and I would feel wrong about being there. We were going up for parts in sitcoms, movies, plays, and I didn't like the lines I was supposed to say. Some of them were blatantly racist. I needed to find a way to be an actor in a different way. I found myself at North Carolina School of the Arts, and I studied in England, getting very disciplined about acting, but the real turning point was being hired to do theater in jails. That job answered my question about why I wanted to do theater. It put the work in a social context.

LS: How did that job come about?

DH: For the audition, we were asked to bring in materials about being an urban youth. I said, "I am an urban youth." I was in a jail or a school doing high-impact theater for four years, five days a week, and it totally affirmed my decision to be an actor. I was nineteen, and I found myself in jail, and the prisoners could have been me. I was trained to leave my neighborhood and never come back. But in this context, I was researching social theater, political theater, and educational theater. My friends would say, "When are you going to do real theater?" And I would say, "This is the realest theater there is." At a point, funding for the project was cut. The remaining money came from the Department of Health and Human Services, so we could only do pieces about AIDS, not about abuse.

LS: How did this work influence your solo characters?

DH: I began to search for why I was an actor in a social context. I wanted to know about ancient theaters of indigenous cultures around the world. I went to the Shomberg Center in Harlem for two months, reading about ancient African theater and rituals. I could tell that no one had opened these books. I took courses in the Performance Studies Department at NYU, studying with Richard Schechner, who is interested in theater and rituals. I found great similarities in what I was doing in the jails and as a soloist, based on the idea of community, entertainment, religion, health. I learned about Asian theater, the solo griot. The idea of the griot was very exciting to me. Here we have minstrels, preachers, rabbis, politicians, stand-up comedians, magicians, mimes, puppeteers, storytellers, but we don't have solo actors as a tradition. The theaters I was studying seemed more effective in achieving spiritual strengthening and education, in terms of who the audience was, and how the audience would react and participate.

L S : What does the idea of community mean to you?

D H : My first experience with the word was the community center in Lefrak City, Queens, where I grew up, and where fights used to break out. I grew up in a community with no majority. This definitely informed my beliefs. Identity becomes a problem at a very early age. I began to ask myself, what is my community? Is it New York Jews? I don't feel at home there. I identify with black people and Latinos. That's where I feel at home. Who I am is based on my personal history, who I grew up with, who I identified with. My village was composed of all these people, including Jews and white people, so they're not excluded. That mix is what I identify as my community.

L S : What are your thoughts about solo work these days?

D H : It seems everybody's doing it, like it's the hip thing. When Eric Bogosian gained popularity, people didn't know what to call what he was doing. They couldn't call him a comic, because he made people nervous. People would walk out of his shows. They didn't want to call it theater, because you need scripts. So it was called performance art. I say I do solo theater. For a while I didn't want to be lumped with performance art or stand-up, because I thought stand-up was only about making people laugh. Things in the world were too grave, so we couldn't just do that. Laughter had to be moved to a discomfort zone. I thought performance artists had self-indulgent aims. But I've stopped caring about categories. People are looking for alternatives in their entertainment and their art, and if they come to my show and they like me, it blows my mind. Out of town, people were coming two and three times, bringing their friends, almost everyone was under twenty-five. You're not supposed to be able to get young people to go to the theater.

L S : You gained recognition so fast. What were the immediate effects of that?

D H : After I did *Some People* at P.S. 122, I got offers to commercialize my work. I turned down more than a dozen sitcoms in '93. I was offered roles in films to play a white black guy, someone who was young, cool, and hip and embodied hip-hop culture, but who wasn't black, because that would turn off middle America. I was offered these kinds of parts in *The Substance of Fire* and *Ransom*. Instead I did a three-month run at the Public Theater, and I got an NEA solo grant. I drew up a travel plan for a year.

L S : Where did you go?

D H : I went to Cuba for a month to research theater. There was so much to see, and everyone there knew what theater was and was going to see it in different forms. I saw social theater, experimental theater, avant-garde versions of the classics, religious theater, and ceremonies. A lot of it was incredible and some was bad, but what impressed me the most was the sense that this country, under so much hardship, had preserved a powerful sense of theater. I came back and began a tour of twenty cities in the U.S., everywhere from Minneapolis to Seattle, L.A., New Haven, Kansas City, Providence. Then I was in Chicago, and it was July, and it was confirmed that Migdalia Cruz, Yolanda King, and Larry Sacharow were going to interview children around the world who have lived through war, with the goal of making a theater project.

LS: Who was funding it?

DH: The Asian Cultural Council and the Endowment for Mutual Understanding. I signed on. We went to Cambodia and talked to kids who'd lived through the Khmer Rouge. In India we talked to the Dalai Lama. We met Tibetan refugees of the Chinese occupation, went to Bosnian refugee camps in Croatia and Austria. The conversations with the kids were very intense and moving, but the whole time I'm asking myself, If we want to talk to children of war, why don't we include the children of Brooklyn? I thought we were going to find out about their healing process, but I found it difficult to see how we were going to take these kids' stories and make a play out of them. I thought, Who are we to do this research and tell their stories? I didn't want it to become an example of Americans saying that the faults with humanity lay abroad, without thinking about what was wrong here.

LS: How did you work this out, and did the others agree?

DH: We spent a week in Italy with Jerzy Grotowski, reflecting on our trip and constantly arguing. Everyone was contentious. That's probably inevitable with such emotional material. I took off for Scotland for a month and performed at the Edinburgh festival. Then I returned to Cuba, this time to do my show at the International Theater Festival. I did half the piece in Spanish. Cubans don't get to hear the kinds of views I was expressing in their language. I was fresh off the plane from Cuba when my manager got this call from *Seinfeld*. They wanted me to guest star on an episode. They wanted me to get on a plane the next morning.

LS: Did this feel like returning to reality or fantasy?

DH: I couldn't tell. My gut said, "No," but I was so uprooted, so knocked off balance from being away. I wasn't sure I was right to be reluctant. I started thinking, I never watch *Seinfeld*, but the few times I've seen clips of it, or it was on at somebody's house, I never had a problem with it. Not like some of the other shows I've been asked to do—*In Living Color*, and *New York Undercover*. The voices started coming in my head. Do you know how many actors would kill to be in this position? The *Seinfeld* people didn't even want to audition me. They saw my HBO special. They said, "We'd love to have you do this role." I mean this is the number one sitcom on TV. Maybe I could go out there and just have a good time. I said, "Send me the script." I had to decide in one hour, because the plane was leaving in twelve hours. They faxed it. I read it, and I was laughing here and there. It was funny. I mean it's one of those *Seinfeld* episodes that doesn't really have a plot, it's just got subplots, and the main subplot is about the guy who takes care of the pool and collects towels at Jerry's health club. He wants to befriend Jerry. He's really enthusiastic in an almost psychotic way about spending time. Eventually the guy shows up at Jerry's apartment, wanting to hang out, and Jerry disses him, and the guy gets pissed off and ultimately puts dirty towels in Jerry's locker.

L S : Did reading the script relieve your anxiety?

D H : Yes, except for one thing, the character was called Ramon. So I was thinking, I wonder why his name is Ramon? I mean this is 1995. This is *Seinfeld*. I know this can't be the stereotypical, Spanish-speaking "pool guy," who is psychotic and funny, and that's the extent of him. So we called and asked. The casting guy or the producer said, "Oh no, No no no no. Not at all. They saw your tape, they love you, you can make him whatever you want. They just want you." I said, "Are you sure? I don't want to get on another plane just to get into an argument over some bullshit like that, and put everybody in an uncomfortable position." The guy said, "He can be whoever you want him to be." So I got to the airport before the sun rose. They flew me out on TWA, first class. I've never flown first class, not even business class. I got there, and we did a read-through, and I did the character as this sort of young, uptight, neurotic Brooklyn kid, kind of like me, but higher strung, and people were laughing, but I was feeling really hot and flushed, and I couldn't tell why. Then we did the walk-through, and my first scene came up, and Jerry and the director were talking to each other about something and they came up to me and the director said, "So, could you do this in a Spanish accent?" I said, "I'm sorry, I can't do that." And Jerry said, "Why not?" And I said, "Well, look, I don't want to waste your time getting into an argument about why not. Why don't we look for an alternative? Let's make him Shimon or Ray, let's keep him Ramon but not with a Spanish accent." And Jerry said, "But I don't get it. Is it derogatory? Aren't you an actor? Isn't your craft that you do accents?" I said yes to the questions, and I asked Jerry why he wanted Ramon to have a Spanish accent, and he said, "Because it's funnier that way. His name is Ramon." I said, "It's not funnier that way. A character shouldn't be funny because of an accent. It should be funny because the writing is funny and makes people laugh at themselves."

LS: I can imagine Seinfeld wasn't charmed.

DH: Believe me, this was not the conversation I wanted to get into with a group of Hollywood millionaire stars. I said it apologetically because they were making me feel bad about fucking up their project. So then Jerry got on his cellular phone and called the producer, who came down and gave me a whole guilt spiel like, "Why did you get on a plane at five in the morning and fly across the continent for this? It's a half-hour comedy show. What's the big deal?" So we wound up walking through the whole show, and I was doing it as some other character that I was comfortable with. But in between the scenes the jokes started coming. Jerry said, "So Danny, how about doing the next scene in blackface." And they were all looking at me like I was crazy. So we finished the scenes, and even though the director was laughing, I could see Jerry wasn't amused. That night I got a call from my agent telling me I was recast and I could get on a plane whenever I felt like it. So I did. They never paid me.

LS: What sort of TV situation do you think would work, in addition to having HBO shoot your shows?

DH: I'm negotiating a contract for a show I'm writing with Darnell Martin. The producers want me to sign a five-year acting contract. That's okay with me, as long as we remain executive producers.

LS: What are you working on in theater?

DH: My new show is about young people, my generation coming out of hip-hop culture. It deals with issues of language, and it's more overtly political than *Some People*. A character is in jail. He gets arrested on Fordham Road for selling O.J. Simpson and Bart Simpson T-shirts. After three weeks in jail, he gets into a fight, because all the inmates are watching Tonya Harding and Nancy Kerrigan, and he doesn't want to, so a guy tries to cut him. He's in jail not because he's a criminal but because he's poor. When the cop pulls him over and sees someone who appears to be not white, almost everything that happens next and in this guy's life in general is determined by that. This understanding of the difference between how you see yourself and how you're perceived is a culture, a way of life. It is a language, not in the sense of oral language but a social language. Hip-hop comes from when people used to b-boy, and that got called break-dancing. The hop was part of the dance, in which you move your hips. The term began to be associated with the life the kids were living, with graffiti art, break-dancing, b-boying, rap, and DJ-ing, the urban art of taking two turntables and a mixer and making art out of existing records. The clothing and the oral language come out of jail. People wear their pants hanging off their asses, because they give you extra-large sizes in jail. Kids put fat laces in their sneakers, because in jail they give you no laces, so you can't hang yourself, and you come up with novel alternatives to tie your sneakers. It's a culture of resource, revenge, and retrieval. The hip-hop piece is set in 1983, the time when I was formed by it. I'm also mulching a piece about what happened with *Seinfeld*. I'm thinking about hybrid languages and the feeling of wearing other people's skin.

CHAPTER FIVE

Comedy Confessors: Stand-up Analysands, Autobiographers, and Reporters from the Gut

Holly Hughes

Admit it: You're writing an autobiographical monologue. It looks simple: Cast out memories like Tarot cards, connect the themes, dance with shame, and hope your deviance hasn't become the kink du jour. On the plus side, autobiographical writing feels urgent; it's about you, and everybody is to some extent a solipsist. On the minus side, no one's experience is intrinsically interesting, no matter how fringe and exotic, and it's hard to shape autobiography into something more than a description of you. If that's all that is accomplished, the solo will sound like a bus talker, with tales of medical misfortune and greedy relatives.

Each of the performers here has found a key to transforming personal events into social commentary. Tone of voice is crucial, that mysterious cocktail of honesty that doesn't well into confession, bemusement that doesn't curdle into gloating, detachment that doesn't stiffen into sarcasm. These performers find in their experience stories about character, place, feeling.

I include three stand-ups—Angela Scott, Margaret Smith, and Richard Lewis—though the work in this chapter is predominantly performance. While most stand-ups thread some autobiography into their routines, the three profiled here work primarily from their life stories, their acts becoming a diary, a gloss on temperament. Roseanne, Ellen DeGeneres, and Paula Poundstone also work this attitude, as well as David Steinberg and Louie Anderson.

Margaret Smith radiates the dull gleam of happy malice. Her mother asks why she doesn't come home for the holidays, and Margaret explains, "I can't get Delta to wait in the yard while I run in."

Richard Lewis remains devoted to stand-up, but he's a working actor, and he was fine on the romantic comedy *Anything But Love*. He wasn't fine in two projects that followed: a non-written part in Mel Brooks's limp Robin Hood spoof *Men in Tights,* and a poisonous teaming with Don Rickles in the short-lived sitcom *Daddy Dearest.* Lewis has been our bard of melancholy, our DJ of the inner life, a man who bores into himself rather than hacking up other people. *Daddy Dearest* (1993) in which he played a buffoonish therapist, was a nightmare of bad judgment.

In solo performance, the proportion of women is greater than in stand-up, and women work in a range of forms, from burlesque and cabaret, to shaggy-dog sagas, to memory yarns, to imagistic reels. Male soloists perch along the same spectrum. Gayness is a subject for many soloists: a way to come out and also write your own out-of-closet parts, with AIDS, the policing of pleasure, and the throb of sex snaking through most of the texts. The next chapter chronicles queer theater, where lots of figures here also fit, though, of course, not every queer performer does autobiography. Those placed here are more distinguished by the autobiographical aspect of their work.

Even Mark Ameen's campiest moments are enlarged by his tender melancholy. In the solo covered here, *Seven Pillars of Wicca-Dick: A Triumph,* he eyeballs mortality in a series of monologues. Ameen's head shifts and vamp/rough-trade poses are visual equivalents of his metaphors. AIDS is the particular death he contemplates, but he's absorbed with how all of us pursue pleasure in the face of physical finiteness. He argues against puritans who use the illness to sanction sexual disgust and who proclaim, "The party's over." Returns Ameen, "What party? Weren't we just living our lives, and who declared them silly?"

Claudia Shear and Josh Kornbluth are alchemists, turning their sense of puniness into a subject. The triumph of their monologues is that they remain trained on failure and loss—rather than on freedom—without coming off as whiners.

Holly Hughes and Spalding Gray are at the peak of this genre. Hughes works collage style, narratives and anecdotes triggering metaphysical associations, until, all the pieces in place, the picture emerges. Gray works on-the-road style, the digressions and detours leading to a body of water, an amniotic vacation from consciousness.

Hughes navigates not only her own course from Middle America to Planet Downtown but the emergence of lesbian artists into mainstream culture and the sometimes awkward collision of the two. Reporting on her early attempts to find material on lesbianism, she recalls reading a sixties sex manual: "Dr. Reuben said that, like cancer, impending lesbianism had its warning signs. The most ominous of which was, and I quote: 'The enlarged clitoris of the lesbian which can be inserted into the vagina of her partner.' "

Grove Press has published *Clit Notes*, Hughes's first collection of plays, and in '96 she presented a new exploration of love and sorrow, *Cat O'Nine Tales*, which begins with an erotic clap of thunder at once graphic, poetic, and comical: "And now she is kissing me. And I mean SHE. The one I was telling you about, yes it's HER. She is kissing me and I mean KISSING and I mean ME. Kissing me right on the ol' kisser of all places. I am shocked! This is so unexpected. Not that I hadn't thought about it. Wished for it day in and day out like I once wished for a palomino. Or at least that's what I said I once wanted. What I was really looking for was a rider. I wanted to be a golden muscle beating between someone's legs. I needed somebody on top of me if I ever wanted to be fast. The weight of another body unlocking my gallop. And now she is kissing me and it is happening, here I go! I am rearing up on my hind legs, my body carrying us both into the new world."

Before the publication of *Clit Notes*, Hughes and I talked, and she summed up her career thus far. "In the early days, I was trying to develop a theatrical language to talk about lesbian desire. A lot was borrowed from gay male theater and from pulp fiction—titles like *No Blond Is an Island*—that we were supposed to hate but that was sexy to me. In *The Well of Horniness*, I had two tools: rage and silliness. I was criticized by straights for being gay and by lesbians for dramatizing sexual contradictions. The lesbians I knew thought penetration and getting on top of another person were controversial. I got this image of two salmon lying side by side, wiggling and rushing to release their eggs before the stream dried up.

"In searching my own confusions, I looked into the wounds that are at the core of sexuality, the scenes that console us for our original injuries and excite us by replaying them. There is an unresolvable longing for the rejecting parent, and it's painful and can't be assuaged. *Clit Notes* touches on the love I felt for my father, who was rejecting. In *Cat O' Nine Tales*, I'm probing the connection between my love/hate relationship to my father and my attraction to butch women—to masculinity mediated by a woman's body. The earlier work showed the escapades of an escape artist. Now I'm writing as an exile, who understands there is no complete escape from the original family."

When I met Spalding Gray for lunch in the summer of '96, he came in with a story. He'd been away from New York for six months, during which time he hadn't needed to write a letter, but now he did, and in the post office no one would tell him the price of a stamp. "They cowered back, as if I were imposing on them or a madman about to go off." He shouted into the room, eliciting a few tepid bleats, "Thirty-two cents." Had he become more wild-eyed, or had the city grown angrier? Who could tell? Of course this was the salient question, the one that has powered Gray's work: his endeavor to winnow out projection from what is actually going on.

He described the piece he'd been working on since *Gray's Anatomy*, called *It's a Slippery Slope*—about learning to ski at fifty-two. Of all his monologues, this one raised the most concern about the ethics of autobiography. Gray knew that, as an artist, he owned the materials of his life, but did he have the right to portray others who shared it with him? While he and Renée, his ex-wife, were together and collaborating, that question hadn't been as pressing, but he and Renée had broken up, and this piece involved their separation and the pain it caused her. Gray was troubled by the idea of profiting from something that depicted, and could exacerbate, her grief. Gray has a child now, too. How much of the child's life will he portray in subsequent work? He wasn't sure. Of course, the dilemma had become a new subject. The chapter concludes with a review of *Slope*.

Angela Scott: Scott Free

June 1988

I first saw Angela Scott a year and a half ago, opening for Margaret Smith at Caroline's. She did a funny riff about moving to Concord, Massachussetts, as a kid. "See any black people there? No? That's right, we're here now. Girls would come up and say, 'Oh, hi! Move.' In history, they'd turn to me whenever Africa came up and expect me to chant. I'd say, 'My spear's at home.' Then I'd make it rain." She put a taut wrap on male posturing, too. "Men touch themselves." Stare. "Then they want to shake hands with you. Women don't have to keep checking. They know where they leave things."

A couple of weeks ago, I caught her at Stand Up N.Y., and her manner was easy, cool. An apartment becomes available in her Chelsea building. She wants it for a friend, but the landlord says no, so when white gentry arrive she's out on the landing in slippers and curlers, a beer can and chicken leg in hand. "*Leroy*, don't start no shit. You put that knife down. Come on out here kids, all twenty of you." Her finale is a sultry ode to young flesh, sharpened with a kiss of incestuous longing for her twenty-year-old son—she's so youthful-looking, the news she has a kid this age surprises the audience. "The nice thing about a son who's six-four and gorgeous is the young, healthy friends who come by." Her voice gets smoky. "Sweaty boys lifting weights, boys who sleep over and trot to the bathroom. You know how boys are in the morning? 'Mrs. Scott, now don't look.' Of *course* not."

Scott and I had lunch a few days later, and long into the afternoon she talked about what it was like to be in the middle of her life, in the middle of her career, in the middle of New York. The Concord move was real and even more estranging than she makes it sound. She was also the first brown-skinned child on her mother's side—the side she grew up around—and relatives told her she was ugly. Her aunt used to lock her in a bedroom when friends came. "Isn't that a child I hear crying?" "I don't hear anything." Her grandfather called her monkey until she was seventeen.

Scott went to college in Cambridge. "It was the sixties, and there were quotas. I felt alone." When she saw white police shooting at black kids in Roxbury, the rage she'd sat on for a lifetime welled up. She became a Panther, got arrested, and then expelled. There were men and babies—son Peter and daughter Ericka, seventeen—a move to Manhattan in the early seventies, and soon after acting at the Negro Ensemble Actors Workshop. Robert Townsend was in the group, and the two became part of Kitchen Table, an all-black comedy troupe. "I didn't even know I was funny." When the company broke up, she had to solo.

She and Townsend stayed friends. "He encourages me to turn off the censors in my head. I want to bring out all that stuff about race—hair and skin and bodies." When Scott cooks, that's what she's able to do. She riffs on her grandfather's nickname for her. "A date would come to the door, and he'd yell, 'Mon*key, Mon*key, swing on out here girl.' " It's a dangerous moment, but Scott nets laughs that sympathize with the powerlessness of childhood. Standing on stage as the lean, wavy-haired, soignée woman she's become, most of the pain is past and there's vengeful gratification to be reaped.

Spontaneous malice has provided some finer moments. She goes on stage at the Improv in '82, and a drunk woman yells, "Where's Kunta Kinte?" "With your mother," Scott shoots back. But anger and fear of anger can trip her up. In the bit about her grandfather, what she doesn't divulge is that he's not a light-skinned black man, as we're led to believe, but Puerto Rican. "He thought he was better than Negroes," she tells me. She edits the detail because she's still too angry to discover the humor in the situation. I watched her work in two other clubs after her smooth performance at Stand Up N.Y., and the audiences—one boisterous, another skimpy—unnerved her. In both cases, she was afraid she'd show her disgust. When a college kid heckled her by assuming, ipso facto, she watched *The Cosby Show*, she turned gray and uttered a few faltering, protective phrases.

"I've replayed and replayed that moment. I wanted to murder him, and I knew I wasn't going to get anything funny out of that, so I shut up. It's no good. I don't want to feel the anger I felt in Cambridge, but it's like with Pryor, you've got to go into the craziness and weakness to bring back something worth saying. If I can't risk being misunderstood, I'll never get people to see things my way."

She never goes anywhere without her black-baby pin—a gift from Patrick Kelly, the dress designer who makes them. "My mother would say, 'Take that thing off.' She'd think it was racist." Shakes her head. "It's all those gorgeous chocolate women who used to dance at the Cotton Club."

Margaret Smith: Getting the Skinny

May 1990

"Do you really think I'm deadpan?" Margaret Smith asks. By deadpan I mean her slow, monotone delivery as she limps through family mayhem— bruised, pissed off, looking for a gun. A street kid from Chicago's South Side, she's hurting and getting her kicks.

Smith is in town for an appearance on *Letterman* and a gig at Caroline's, where I'd seen her the evening before. It was the first night of Passover, and the turnout was small, but she made the group laugh, evoking her father, a gambler and alcoholic who is also vain. He saves enough money for a hair transplant but one night gets drunk and on a $20 bet shaves his head. Smith stares out. "So I owe him twenty dollars."

I first caught her four years ago, with her cool delivery and hot candor. She etched her subversive aloneness, a refusal to belong or forgive. At the Montreal Comedy Festival in '88, she was strong: "I wore a neck brace for a year. I wasn't in an accident or nothin', I just got tired of holding my head up."

Now, as a headliner, she satirizes the impulse to suck on old injuries. Her mother asks when she's going to have kids, and Smith's eyes fill with dread. "Yeah, like I need a bunch of people running around my apartment, complaining because I broke their yolks." Growing up, the adults she knew were mostly angry—men like her Uncle Swanee. "On his gravestone he had carved, 'What are *you* lookin' at?'" Smith admits she isn't trusting. "I can't get a relationship to last longer than it takes to tape their albums." She's prone to sadistic traps. When she finally goes to a therapist, the woman spooks her. "I don't know, does your therapist have a balloon business on the side?"

In fact, Smith, thirty-five, is seeing a shrink and says she feels more unguarded. She auditioned for *A League of Their Own*, about women baseball players who toured during World War II. She went up for a tough part, but the casting director wisely had her read for a character seeking contact and warmth. Smith, having jettisoned some defenses, worries she's lost the ability to protect herself. "A friend said she'd come to this interview and kick me if I started spilling my guts."

Her need to conquer appetite came early, she explains. Her siblings—she's the third of six kids—were obese. "My mother loved with food. I remember her trying to stuff my face. I shut my mouth. She said I would be trouble. I felt guilty going on dates when my sisters wanted to. They made me feel left out. They were always going on diets together; being fat made them close. Whenever I'd buy food, I'd lock myself in the bathroom and eat real slow. They would bang on the door, saying they wanted to use the toilet. I wouldn't budge."

If her mother's medium was food, her father's was intimidation. A big guy, he drank heavily and frightened her. In her work, Smith jousts with violence, tapping a subject most women comics shun, for fear of compounding the butch role of stand-ups who wield mikes and stalk stages.

Comedy was Smith's escape: She would regulate the flow of food into her body and the stream of words out of it. "I was never funny in the family. I made my friends laugh. It was a way of feeling intimate. I didn't know people did comedy as a profession until I was fifteen. I wanted to be a surgeon. It was probably that I wanted to stab people, not make them well." She began appearing in clubs in 1982. "I have tapes labeled, 'Horrible Beginnings.' I should give them to people starting out." Most of the time now, she knows she has something to contribute. "I have a few stories to tell about the family. I want to get this stuff into comedy. I talk about all these negative things. But I feel hopeful."

There are still times when her confidence strays. "Last night someone said, 'Can I have your autograph?' I thought they were teasing me." She can't get over the fact that she, alone among her siblings, didn't re-create the domestic morass. At home in L.A., she lives alone, walking her dog, Molly Shapiro, and tooling around on her 450 Honda Custom. "Why did I get out?" she wonders, and looks at me. "If someone were interviewing you, would you be this revealing?" Perhaps she thinks the words have been coerced from her. Maybe they always are in interviews, where attention inspires quick trust. She smiles, realizing that no one can capture her true measure. "I'm five-foot-four, but when anyone asks how tall I am, I say six-foot-two."

Richard Lewis: A Fine Madness

December 1989

Richard Lewis is vaulting. His HBO special *I'm Exhausted* was nominated for an Emmy last year. *Anything But Love,* the sitcom in which he costars with Jamie Lee Curtis, is a hit. And on December 27, Lewis, forty-two, fulfills a lifelong dream to play Carnegie Hall.

Oddness warms him; it's his element. Little about him is in control; he's overwhelmed, stooped, anxious. On stage, he paces like a zoo animal, grievances and wordplay flying. His family was dislocated and phobic. "In December we had a tree. It wasn't Christmas, and it wasn't Chanukah. It was Chronica." Fingers flip to temples, and his neck inclines toward the floor. "I want to worry closer to the ground." The posture is secular davening, where self-disclosure substitutes for prayer. But the material doesn't play solipsistic; Lewis is too aware of his condition and his effect on other people. "I have so much on my mind but so little to say," he muses. "I had a great night's sleep and yet no rest."

He's frank about subjects males usually avoid: the disappointing shape of his body, hurt feelings that keep throbbing. He is nakedly melancholy, and this quality heats his shots on *Letterman,* where he gained national prominence. Letterman treats sincerity as a stupid human trick—Lewis's wacky self-awareness thing. But Lewis describes real hypochondria and his actual tendency to fall for rejecting women. Letterman tolerates the candor, because Lewis doesn't extract it from him.

Lewis's role on *Anything But Love* may yield his best work yet. Most comedians are bowdlerized on sitcoms. But Marty Gold, the Chicago journalist tailored for Lewis, offers a rich context, including a sharp supporting ensemble that features Downtown comic Ann Magnuson. She's editor-in-chief at the trendy weekly where Marty works, a chic-obsessed, hilariously opinionated Anna Wintour/Tina Brown sphinx. He parries her blows and pirouettes slyly; he doesn't have to take over to maintain his balance.

Lewis is cannier and sexier here than on the stand-up stage, and his romance with Jamie Lee Curtis, who plays fellow writer Hannah Miller, revs on the eroticism of camaraderie and androgynous pairing. Lewis, with his flowing tresses and plush wardrobe, is a soft-edged man; Curtis is angular and boyish, and they both have the same strong chin. Most importantly in romantic comedy—where funny equals powerful—they're both wits. The show exploits the sexual charge of a shared sense of irony; the couple's ability to act silly and admit similar, ancient fears generates grown-up humor. Characters speak about kinks and body functions—about handcuffs and sleep-drool. In one sequence, Hannah consoles Marty, who is guiltily fantasizing about an adolescent girl he helps support, by confessing that she once had sex with a young man she used to baby-sit. "Of course he never called me Mommy." Pause, quiet smile. "Well, just that one time."

It's Tuesday, and Lewis is in New York. His plane landed an hour ago, but he's on time for our meeting. He just played three concerts in Florida, boom, boom, boom. Before that he was in L.A., shooting *Anything But Love.* He'll do *Letterman* on Friday, and between now and then jet to Ohio for a concert, appear on the Howard Stern show as well as on the syndicated radio program *The Comedy Hour,* and visit an orthopedist for his bum knee. The appearances and medical exam are preparation for the Carnegie Hall gig. Every cell in his black-garbed, hunched-shouldered body is homing toward that date. Despite his move to TV and assumption of leading man status, live performance still matters most. "Out there, I'm in control of the material. I'm as completely myself as it gets."

Slumped in a leather chair within the tony, faux library environs of the Ritz Carlton Polo Club (his choice), he comes off unmasked—also zany and maniacal. A waitress dressed like Princess Anne approaches, and he jumps. "I thought you were Jack Ruby. Any shadow in late November." He rhapsodizes about Brando: "I like people who are purely instinctual, who act like animals." He becomes his idol making mincemeat of Connie Chung: "You're making me mad, Connie."

Mostly Lewis has a clear trace on the pain that made him a comic. The youngest of three, he was controlled by his fearful mother and ignored by his largely absent father. His mother constantly smelled danger, whether from unfamiliar food or the feet of Richard's dog, who was not permitted in the house and eventually—to Richard's lasting sorrow—ran away. His father, who died of a heart attack when Richard was twenty-three, was a partner in a catering business. When he *was* home, he habitually cut off his son in midsentence. "Truly," says Lewis, "the reason I went on stage is to have people listen to me talk about my feelings without someone saying pass the meatloaf."

Yet pride fills his voice when evoking his father's work. "He was the

Babe Ruth of caterers. He'd come into an empty room in the morning and by night turn it into a wonderland. He'd put lights under the tables. I admired a big callus he had on his thumb. It was from folding napkins into accordion pleats." Lewis doesn't exaggerate his wounds. He describes them, rightly, as ordinary.

Conjuring the shrinks he's loved and lost, he's grateful and mischievous. "I was going to two at the same time, and I had to make a decision. They were both women. One day, they talked about me on the phone. I'd give my bootleg Dylan tapes to hear that conversation." When he went to California, he maintained contact with his therapy group by listening to tapes of the sessions. "Suddenly I hear a voice tell a woman, 'Cry closer to the mike.' That was it. I quit. It seemed too unfair."

Although catalogued, his compulsions aren't tamed, he feels, and several trot out now. The waitress sets down a bowl of nuts, and Lewis whisks them to another table, out of my reach but within his. He does the same to a plate of fruit and cheese and every so often nibbles the food. Shades of his controlling mother and catering father? At another juncture, I propose there's sadistic pleasure in airing family laundry on stage, especially exposing his mother's antics: "You have all the power, and she has no way to get her side heard." He protests, claiming he's not cruel to his mother. I press for a while, then desist. He smiles. "We had a fight. Wasn't it exciting?"

His face relaxes. "I have been ambivalent about everything in my life except being a comedian." Reflecting on the field, he deplores Dice Clay/Kinison thuggery. "I imagine the girlfriend of one of these comics saying, 'It's my birthday. Could you not use *pussy* and *cunt* in the same sentence?' 'Okay, bitch.' " Lewis is hopeful about his sitcom, but he expresses reservations: "The flirting is coy. I want Marty and Hannah to be in love and have a real modern relationship. They should come to the office after having trouble in bed and have to repair the damage. Marty is much more self-confident than I am about his success. He doesn't have esteem problems. The relationship with Hannah should open him up to himself." He raises Groucho eyebrows. "I feel Jamie's body and my bad posture make quite a sexy curve."

Though doubts still shroud him like an overcoat he can't shed, he admits he's never been in better shape and proffers a bicep he and his recently hired trainer firmed. "I worry my work is narcissistic and self-indulgent, but every so often I see I'm touching chords. The other day, a bunch of rosy-

cheeked UCLA kids paraded by my car, the picture of health and content-
ment. They shouted, 'We're in pain, too,' and it made me very happy."

John Hockenberry: Nerve Center

February 1996

Twenty years ago, John Hockenberry was a nineteen-year-old kid, hitchhik-
ing with a college friend, when the car he was riding in went over an embank-
ment and for seconds held him suspended between the past, where he could
walk, and a future without use of his legs. The young woman driving the car
was killed. Hockenberry's friend emerged unscathed. Hockenberry's spinal
cord was severed, causing paralysis from below the nipples down.

He writes about the accident and its aftermath in his memoir *Moving
Violations*, which hurtles past victim-chronicle into thrilling honesty. He is
locked in a paradox, knowing that his life changed radically because of the
accident and knowing, too, that disability is not a dividing line but a contin-
uum enfolding everyone. We all age. We have genes. There is entropy. He is
both different and the same, but it is the denial of his sameness by the able-
bodied majority that juices his defiance. *Fuck your fantasies* is the mantra driving *Moving Violations* and the theater solo, *Spoke Man*, he's now performing.

He wheels himself up a ramp to the stage, his back angled, his hands
stroking with a rhythm that matches his breathing. While his book is intimate, sexy, and meditative, the theater piece projects more the public man,
the guy wheeling unstoppably on urban streets and reporting, during the
Gulf War, from Kurdish refugee camps. Though his voice is familiar from
years on NPR and his handsome, blond presence known from stints on *Day
One* and *Dateline*, acting is a leap, a free fall.

There are miscalculations. A long-sleeved shirt covers the massive
neck, shoulders, and arms we should see, for there, in his power to propel
himself, is where his joy resides. The piece's strength is its language, tacking
associatively, echoing images. He wants us to see beyond the chair; beyond
his anxieties about being an exceptional marginal and beyond our fears of
imperfection and loss of control. "Look carefully," he directs, rolling into
the audience, "any bags, any stains, any oozing."

We ride in his chair, feeling the earth's topography—"the teeth-rattling cobblestones of Hudson and Greenwich"—and seeing through the Hock-enberry-cam, as the fish on Chinatown's streets stare up at us. His body, with paralyzed limbs he cannot animate and spastic muscles he cannot stop from moving, is Hockenberry's metaphor for the dual states in life that cannot be resolved. Paralysis, he explains, is like trying to call Sting and never getting through. Spasticity is a guy shooting up a McDonald's because he cannot get Sting on the phone. "Bosnia is paralysis, Colin Furgeson is spasticity."

But there is beauty in these states as well as horror, for magic, too, is a form of spasticity. *Spoke Man* is both an elegy for "all those things that cannot be recaptured or reclaimed" and a celebration of flux. Hockenberry has fallen in love with accident and with the suspended sensation of mixed feelings. Anchored in his chair, he chugs up steep inclines, then flies down, snaking between pedestrians and outpacing bladers. In two beautifully crafted monologues, he identifies both with the exaltation of champion broad jumper Bob Beamon, and with the defeat of his uncle Charlie, who, through a genetic quirk, grew severely retarded and was locked inside an institution from childhood on.

One day doctors said they knew what Charlie was thinking and that he was thinking nothing. Hockenberry weeps for the uncle whose phone line to the world was severed. Later, amid Kurds dying of starvation, Hockenberry grieves for human disconnection, false assumptions, the helplessness that summons no aid. But on another day, out of the blue, Beamon jumped twenty-nine feet, two and a half inches, though neither he nor anyone else had ever jumped farther than twenty-seven feet. "Beamon, for that moment he was in the air," muses Hockenberry, "had stumbled into another frightening parallel world only to fall out of it again and back to earth, never to forget what he had glimpsed." He had been branded by unpredictability.

On the way to lunch a few days before his first performance, Hockenberry navigates ably through the snow. He gains weight during the winter, because his road work in the park is curtailed, but he eats steak and fries anyway. I ask to see his hands, which are large, leathery, and strong. The bottoms of his feet, he says, are soft as a baby's. After his accident, he considered a career as a pianist, going so far as to design a pedal contraption that could be controlled with breath. "I refused to see limitation. Everything was climbing Mt. Everest. I had to get over it, or I would have worn myself out."

He doesn't imagine the way his life might have developed without paralysis. His focus is on the double-edged ways that disability has shaped him: confining him to a condition that threatens to engulf his identity, while providing him with a mine of crip customs to out and deshame. Not wanting to use "his wheelchair as a crutch" (an accusation his father once made), he nonetheless cannot succeed, he knows, without scratching up the scent of tokenism. He had the most powerful and strangely ambivalent sensation of being wrongly construed when, arriving in Kurdistan, he was sneered at by a man. "He thought my crippled body was a symbol of Bush's bad faith: '*This* was what America is sending, no help at all.' He was wrong about me, but right about America. I felt permission to go: 'Okay, so this is how disability is meaningful.' "

No doubt the gonzo ferocity that rises off him preceded his accident but has, subsequently, been afforded a lasting structure. He got married in October, and he and his wife want to have a baby, so these days he's trekking not through the Middle East but amid penile docs. I press for details, and he says he's experimenting with shots that produce erections. With the sort of exactitude that detonates his writing, he explains that he injects the shaft, close to the base, "at two o'clock or ten o'clock." Dimples appear on his cheeks. "It doesn't hurt, luckily for me."

John O'Keefe: Brilliant Recovery

January 1989

John O'Keefe, a compact man in his mid-forties, has wide-set eyes that have known loss and street-fighter arms that have fended off aggression. Violence crackles on his skin, nodding to beatings he suffered and delivered—to the eroticized familiarity of pain. But he moves with the energy of a kid, and his voice, which can slide into a resonant baritone, is free of sarcasm.

The wisdom in his body marks his monologue *Shimmer*. O'Keefe grew up in Iowa, in a series of Catholic orphanages and state juvenile homes run like prisons. His father was a mean alcoholic, his mother an abused, scattered woman, deemed unfit to care for him. O'Keefe tells of meeting Gary Welsh, who arrives at the juvenile home when O'Keefe is nearly sixteen. O'Keefe is known as Spacey because he wants to be an astronaut, but until he meets Gary he has no ally in imaginative flight.

The other kids think Gary weird, and he is. A conspiracy theorist, he believes that incandescent, advanced societies exist amid stagnant life. Penguins and seals dive to a blue ice world and discover what humans have yet to learn. Radio static is really a secret language, "on the edge of things"—he calls it Shimmer—that most people aren't smart enough to decode. It doesn't matter to Spacey that Gary is preposterous. He can be loved, trusted, and for teaching Spacey about alternate realities he inspires his friend to devise an escape plan.

Shimmer, which lasts seventy-five minutes, is a story about caged adolescents—and the prison of adolescence—echoing *Oliver Twist, The 400 Blows, A Member of the Wedding.* The lyricism captures boyhood emotion. Alone in the dark, in a punishment cell, Spacey says, "I get this buzz that is specifically me." And O'Keefe's descriptive passages blend detail and feeling. He etches the horrors of the juvenile home with the intimate's matter-of-factness. Spacey's world is one of ham-fisted guards and brutal matrons, of rules and rituals designed to humiliate. Lights must be turned off at eight-thirty P.M. Five razor straps hang menacingly in the hall leading to the showers, and in the cafeteria, where children aren't permitted to speak, if boys and girls so much as make eye contact the penalty is a whack that makes mouths bleed and ears ring for a day.

The escape, when it is finally attempted, is thrilling: adrenalized Dada, with terror-time drawn out like liquid and barbed-wire boundaries heedlessly risked. As the boys taste freedom, O'Keefe becomes drunk on glee. A temporary rescuer, who provides a ride in a Bel Air convertible and plays Buddy Holly on the radio, brings them "out of captivity like a rock 'n' roll Moses."

On the page, *Shimmer* would have poignancy and power, but the conviction and concentration in O'Keefe's performance give it immediacy, wholeness. He works on a bare stage, save for a music stand with notes. Lighting by Jim Cave keys scenes, most dramatically when Spacey becomes his loutish father and the air turns red.

O'Keefe moves with a sensualist's awareness of gesture. Through shifts in his voice and posture, he becomes other characters, but the story is always channeled through Spacey or O'Keefe the man. In the figure on stage, we see the person made by the events. His sculpted haircut bespeaks an amour propre skirting vanity. His white T-shirt and jeans are both a state home uniform and garb showing that Spacey grew into an actor, not a suit.

He grew, as well, into a shaper of his own experience. He uses autobiography to reveal a world.

Mark Ameen: Man Alive

January 1992

"I always thought of myself as slightly tragic," says Mark Ameen, thirty-three, cracking a grin. Ameen wrote and performs *Seven Pillars of Wicca-Dick,* a luminous meditation on the dangers of childhood and the sorrows of AIDS. The piece, which was recently staged at Duality Playhouse and which Ameen plans to take on tour, is poetry made stageworthy, a series of dramatic monologues unified by the actor's seductive presence and deepened by his openness and wit. Ameen is a healthy-looking hunk, more rounded than cut. Dark eyebrows—a legacy of his Lebanese father—encircle melancholy eyes. In his piece, he quips, "I look sad and angry and ethnic," and because of that, "my people ask me to beat them into pleasure." *Seven Pillars* is the culmination of twelve years of writing and of building a persona in downtown clubs. Ameen surveys loss, yearning, and the excitement of recaptured pain—he's masterful, not reckless.

We're at lunch, and he's explaining the seeming anomaly of his dark subjects and his start in comedy groups. But while munching a chicken sandwich, he realizes that, even as a kid, humor kept rescuing him. His mother beat him repeatedly. She was overweight and over her head, her husband having left by the time Mark was nine. One of her rages is branded onto *Seven Pillars.* Mark is sledding near his home in Lowell, Massachusetts. A girl pushes him, and he careens over icy rocks, severely injuring himself. After he crawls home, his mother beats him "into the wall with a broomstick." Then, "when the color had completely cleared from my already pallid face and she saw my eyes roll under fluttering lids, she carried me to her bed and made me feel loved as we awaited the ambulance."

He's not sure how he survived. He thinks he was lucky—within the context of nightmare. At thirteen, "I suddenly got embraced by cool kids. I was shy, but they thought I was funny. I used to entertain my mother—comedy from hell—and I developed this really nasty sense of humor. I'd go out drinking, then hitchhike home. It was amazing, every time I put out my thumb there was a man and a sexual opportunity, and I got this double quality about life. All those anonymous people in cars were saying: 'There's a whole other world out there, and even though we're here and it's late at night, you're gonna find it.' "

Ameen's sense of perspective protected his sanity, and, early on, he felt an impulse to document his experience. "We were asked to write dreams in second grade. Mine was about a kangaroo who beat me up and left me bloody until I was picked up by an ambulance." He lifts his eyebrows. "I didn't know what I was revealing, you know, about mothers and pouches, but much was made over me having a sad, active imagination."

Solo performing developed out of poetry readings. "I used to be so nervous, I couldn't get my hand to stop shaking. Then I realized I didn't have to hold a manuscript. I could look at people. That's what makes you forget the fear." Childhood abuse—unfair, overpowering, and brutal—has been his training ground for the terror of AIDS. "I may be dying," he announces at the start of *Seven Pillars*. Well, we're all on that track, but Ameen takes us inside a head fastened on the clock. The proximity of death steadies him, keeps him honest. The need to know is swift and hard, like a sexy rush. No illusions, no cynicism—that's the desired balance. He has a taste for ecstasy but not denial or fantasy: "Shall I embrace my disease and claim it as 'the gift of love' like gonorrhea? Or consider it earthly penance for the sins of sleaze and beg further absolution of heaven above? No, no, no on both counts. I shall go out as I came in, breathless and alone."

The possibility that life may be cut short makes him love whatever is real, get serious and distill: "Let me breathe deeply and stop blinking within my death so as to stay alive enough to really record it." He roams the streets, Whitman in a muscle T-shirt, grooving on nature and its contradictions. "A handicapped woman" wants him to buy five-year light bulbs, but he declines: "I don't know what kind of light I'll be using in five years."

Pain is Ameen's medium, but he's not self-pitying. Pleasure is his drive, though he's frequently denied. Sex is his drug, comfort, mirror, and weapon; it's dangerous but so is being born—so is a Rorschach if you're disgusted by the inner life. A pickup leads Ameen to a cellar, ties lead pipes to his balls, then ruefully declines to kiss him. A dozen teenage boys waylay him, and he can't stop eroticizing one who splits from the group: "He folded and slowly rolled his body into my abdomen. It is still difficult for me to accept the fact that he wasn't trying to make love."

"I am a tender beast and I am tired of being punished," he sings, his freedom expanding so that even an elegy is safe from sentimentality. His lost father is cradled in his imagination: "I embrace a feeling father I don't even have to invent: We used to hold hands until I fell asleep dreaming of his fur. He's the one who touched me with the tingle only hidden fingertips possess." The emotion drums a consoling mantra, as well as the saving grace of irony. Crows Ameen, "Always remember, never forget, damage is the house from which we place out bet. The cause of your suffering is the source of your pride. Endure life on earth without thickening your hide. Clutch and release, gurgle and gawk, Oh, Daddy, Oh Daddy, I want your cock."

Ameen says that his father has never seen him on stage, and he doesn't urge it. "I think it would make him uncomfortable, the eroticism." Ameen has just completed an autobiographical novel, *Night Manager,* and he's floating on a sense of release. He wants to keep performing but hasn't a clue what he'll write next, except that it will reflect being "a mature gay man incorporating menace." Another smile opens his features, crinkling his eyes. "It's so sad, having to be afraid of the thing that gets you through. People in trouble, where would they be without sex?"

Claudia Shear: Blown Sideways Through Life

Summer 1995

Claudia Shear's voice drives every sentence of *Blown Sideways Through Life,* as steadfastly on the page as on stage, where for years she performed before packed houses. Finding that voice is her subject: how she mined humor and perspective under fat, depression, and sixty-five jobs that floated her above destitution while sucking her blood. Her misfit childhood, absent father, and succession of coglike gigs could easily have produced a murderous postal worker or an underground ranter, jagged on being ignored. But she scuttled away from silence and bitterness, living in her experience as an initiation rite, and she emerged with a shapely yarn.

Blown Sideways Through Life shoots a montage of the schlepper's cave, revealing how it looks and feels and how the bear eventually lumbers forth. Shear dramatizes all entrapment in which we conspire—the way we hunker down in passivity and armpit smell—but her specific morass is the service job, about which she is ingeniously panoramic.

Forget Roman comedy and Fran Drescher's wish-besotted update, *The Nanny,* where sly servants manipulate puppetlike masters. Shear is consigned to the kitchen/desk/counter/telephone reality of rubber gloves, filthy floor mats, fatigue, and insults. She admits when she spits in her own soup, overstating her skills or venting frustration right out of the chute, but mostly she is at the mercy of a marginalized existence that both reflects and magnifies her inner state.

Meant to sit mutely at a business meeting, she offers a comment and thereby mistakenly reminds the assembled that she is not a piece of furniture. Bartending in the basement of a Chinese restaurant, she's toxified by a jukebox that endlessly coughs out "Another One Bites the Dust"; to shield her face from public view, she has no recourse but to plunge her head into a storage cabinet. Proofreading legal documents on the graveyard shift, she resists rest because "(a) it isn't allowed, and (b) you will slide into a dream so fast that when you have to sit up, it is like getting stabbed in the head with a nail."

A Dickensian flood of details that might, in conversation, come across as overkill here strikes emotional keys that shift between throat-grabbing vehemence and ironic relief. "You always have to say yes to get a job," she explains. "Never have a personality, a life, a light, an opinion. And just yes isn't good enough. You have to *smile* at some cocksucker in a cheap suit engorged with the majestic power to hire and fire. And if you don't it means you have a bad attitude. . . . What I really want to do is grab him by his swirly tie and scream, 'I'd like to smack you so hard your whole fucking family would cry! I'd like to kick you to death in front of your dog!' Those are the times when you can't take it. When to smile and say yes makes you feel like your mouth is packed full of sand and shit. Still, it's *great,* that moment when you get the job."

With crisp compression, Shear evokes the inertia following getting fired. Books and food are her consolations. She gets so fat she refers to herself as "the human sofa," because she wears a gray skirt made of upholstery fabric—wears it every day. Riffing on obesity—Shear is at once invisible and conspicuous—she strips away larding sentiments. Things get so bad they gather a kind of negative luster: "Failure reflected back as danger. The shudder of black leather, of the East Village, of facial flesh pierced with rings. I felt proud. I felt cool. I could do this. I could live through this. Mine was the cocksure glance of the handcuffed as they're led to the van." Bottoming out, she takes a job booking johns in a whorehouse, a *Pulp Fiction* squalorscape sans John Travolta that she strips down with luxuriant exactitude, conjuring the lassitude, piles of sheets, donuts, and petty thugs.

Throughout it all, Shear struggles to shed the uniform, the blanketing flesh, the puny expectations, the lousy roll of the dice. She attends a college populated with tree stumps who grouse, "Do we *have* to read the whole book?" She discovers transcendence in Buster Keaton: "I was so afraid of being vulnerable or babyish or foolish and there was Keaton, continually thwarted and mocked by the world, sometimes looking sadder than I could bear, but holding fast to who he was, what he loved."

Shear is dying to laugh, not to cry. Humor does combat with bordello languor and greasy spare ribs. Humor preserves her dream of becoming an actor and writer, and humor is what teases out the knowledge that steers this generous, poised work: We are all blown sideways through life until we kick away the costume designed for us and fashion a new suit.

Josh Kornbluth: Sum Thing

May 1995

When Josh Kornbluth is nine, his father tells him that he will become the greatest mathematician who ever lived. The two are looking at the George Washington Bridge, and Papa K., who has just hauled a bookcase down six flights of stairs, explains how his son will one day possess that bridge: through geometry, algebra, and calculus—"the mathematics of change." Josh does not factor in that the prophecy is issued by the same man who stubbornly hauled the bookcase without removing the books. No, young Josh believes, and why not? It is better than being told that he is a roach. The only peril is in one day hitting "the wall," the limit of his mathematical powers and of his father's enlarging eyeball.

Josh hits the wall as a freshman, during his first calculus class at Princeton. And his eighty-minute monologue, *The Mathematics of Change*, zooms into that day, zigzagging through time to retrieve a spectrum of emotions. This is Kornbluth's third evening-length monologue, and each grows more assured. In *Haiku Tunnel* (1990), about his misadventures as a legal secretary, he honed the Josh persona, a guy with a doughy body and stringy hair, who turns his frustrations in love and work into wry narrative. His second piece, *Red Diaper Baby* (1992), chronicled his childhood amid Communist parents, especially his deceased father. Kornbluth meant to rescue his father from the failure of his life by showing, with the proof of his own achievement, that he'd emerged in one piece and that his father was thus a good parent, lovable. It's the one part of the story driven by nostalgia, for Papa K. is not made even likable.

With *The Mathematics of Change*, Kornbluth not only dramatizes his departure from his father but buries the ghost by creating a work that is as fanciful, faceted, and consummated as his father was doctrinaire and ineffectual. Formerly a math prodigy, Kornbluth becomes a metaphor juggler, illustrating his associations with blackboard and chalk.

As a child, numerals are corporeal. Curvaceous Three evokes tits and ass, Nine inspires awe—"with its huge brain looking down beneficently on all the smaller numerals." Later, math becomes a Rorschach of the inner life. Josh is X, the unknown of algebra. X is burdened, driven, tremulous, as eager for a clean slate as he is for transcendence. Every image in the monologue deepens Josh's ambivalence. One minute he's a child, entranced by his father's math tricks and politics. The next he's installed at Princeton, hub of WASP privilege and of an intricate intellectual food chain, where pure mathematicians reign over plebeian applied mathematicians and lumpen physicists. Josh, who has an unusually large head, aspires to the top of the intellectual heap, but because he is poor he must find a job, and because he has so neglected the rest of his body he must pass a dreaded swimming test—ordeals that relegate him to a series of Dantean sub-basements.

In one he accidentally injects himself with cancer targeted for a mouse, in another he's entrusted with the care of a pet catfish, creatures with whom fate forces him to identify. Having been lofted by numbers, he becomes impaled on a formula that equates an infinite series of almosts with the solid certainty of one. Failure is horrifying, but it is also a relief—for the first time he's not sweating to measure up. With his love of math and mastery of his family story, Kornbluth transforms the raw materials of his plump body and boy-comes-of-age tale into an entity that is at once a wave of possibilities and a point of contact.

Holly Hughes: Mother Lode

April 1989

When the lights come up in *World Without End,* Holly Hughes strikes a Balthus-like pose: Her legs are flung over the side of an armchair; a sleeve slips to expose a shoulder; her childish bob curtains a face that has never been innocent. Balthus's violence-in-the-nursery dovetails with Hughes's tawdriness. Here, as in *Dress Suits to Hire,* her language soars like skywriting; keen ironies, delivered in her tough-girl drawl, flare into lush poetic riffs. She maps an intimacy redolent of incest and the pair this time are mother and daughter: Holly and Mom.

Hughes spent her childhood in Saginaw, Michigan, an area so flat that a mound of landfill loomed magically mountainous. The locals discharged their fancy in naming fast-food emporia—like Riborama. Amid this predictability, the lustiness of Holly's mother crackled like a foreign language and filled her daughter's senses. Mom is evoked on her deathbed, hungering for the firm ass of one of the ambulance drivers. "I can't do anything, but you can," she whispers to Holly. Hughes portrays her mother naked in the bathroom, sliding her hand up herself, advising her child, "If you want to know something, just remember the answer's inside you."

Mother/daughter eroticism has been excavated by a few: Colette in reminiscences of Sido, Mona Simpson in *Anywhere But Here,* Vivian Gornick in *Fierce Attachments.* Hughes is similarly adrenalized. Describing a transcendent sport-fuck with a geeky computer programmer, she runs the clichéd image of the biblical apple through a pop culture Cuisinart, then, conjuring her parents' last feed on each other's flesh, she reconstitutes the apple's mythic loveliness.

Hughes's tabloid sensibility, effective in busting high-art pretensions, is sometimes an end in itself, and although she rails against the aestheticization of pain, she sometimes falls prey to it. Her tone, swinging between irony and romance, too seldom reveals her feelings. In the scene where her mother stands nude, Mom insists that Holly watch her excite herself. This violation is dodged with cute grimaces, and another disturbing sequence—in which Holly's mother slaughters a porcupine—is presented as Gothic funk.

Hughes resorts to jokiness and shock tactics. Bad-girlitis grips her, and too many anecdotes come across as ingredients for the creation of Holly, the adorably bent vixen. Lording it over male rapists who feel murderous if they don't come, she boasts, "I slept with fifty men before I was eighteen, I never came, and I didn't think of killing them." Are we supposed to believe that sexual terrorist Holly never even *thought* of mayhem?

Mama Mia

February 1993

Holly Hughes is laughing at her own play . . . well, maybe not at her words, exactly, but at the clowning of her cast. She is watching a rehearsal of *No Trace of the Blonde* in which, again, she brews lush poetry and sexual high jinks, mapping the brands that mothers and daughters leave on each other. The plot: Two high school girls, one black and one white, describe their science project at a Michigan Elks Club. But the setting is really inside Hughes's head. *Blonde* is a Dada dreamscape by turns rollicking and elegiac, a rumination on white bread and brown thighs, a debate about whether to save Mom or send her off on an ice floe—lest a girl's future becomes her mother's past.

Dominique Dibbell is arranging props on the body of Kate Bornstein, who plays the mother and represents, for the purposes of the scene, Ma Earth. Ma *Earthquake* is more like it, given the character's instability. She is a colonel in the patriarchy, upholding the old order that has confined her but also lent a feeling of safety. Bornstein—hair waving around her face, voluptuous curves adding weight to her convictions—has a knack for acting blowsy, lost, and bloodied. The fact that she is an out transsexual and that layers of maleness glint through her gender-change adds poignance to her searching and a comic gloss on Motherhood. Dibbell, darkhaired, lithe, and pretty, is veering as far from Mom as she can, adopting a k.d. lang/girl-as-gay-boy look. And completing the ensemble is Pamela Sneed, a strapping African-American, who sports a skinhead coif and plays Dibbell's lesbian sweetie. This is the kind of slam dance the boundary police find irresistible.

They have already answered the call, Hughes explains over dinner, filling in her escapades since being denied her NEA grant along with three other performance artists because of the sexual content of their work. "I received other NEA money for *Blonde,* but before I'd even written it, Donald Wildmon instigated a Justice Department investigation. He charged me with using tax dollars 'to force twelve-year-old girls of different races to have sex on stage.' The Senate took it seriously. I had to present a statement to a subcommittee, promising not to use actors under eighteen."

A cackle explodes from her. At thirty-seven, with her cropped hair and sloe eyes, she's still a Balthus temptress, a Lolita on the rampage. It is a measure of pride to be targeted by the proper witch-hunter, but becoming a household name, as a martyr to censorship, has left burn marks. "I was one of the anticensorship poster children. I felt a need to be engaged, especially to speak up for art that talks about the body and homophobia. Then I saw the homophobia in the anticensorship movement. I was repeatedly asked not to talk about gay issues, warned we would lose the larger cause. For some people on the left, the enemy shifted from Helms to artists. We were seen as *privileged*."

The charge hit a tender nerve, since Hughes has been striving to bring race and class into her work. "The world I grew up in was very white. I was raped when I was eighteen. The first thing I was asked was the man's race. The police would only show me mug shots of black men, even though I told them the rapist was white. I saw how racism and sexism are mixed together, and I tried to put this recognition into Chevy, the white girl. Genre, the black character, isn't the focus, because I wasn't confident I could represent her experience. The play is a prelude to their having a relationship."

Hughes relates her life to her writing, stopping when she hears complaint in her voice. She moves to analysis, echoing the seesaw rhythms—the shifts between emotional explosion and ironic detachment—that shape her plays. "I'm prone to depression," she admits. "During the NEA circus, I was filled with hopelessness and despair. I couldn't work." She grins. "It brought out my mother in me. She was so bitter."

Hughes warms to the subject of her mother, June—the combination romance and cautionary tale that inspires so much of her originality. It is a story she tells, with increasing insight, in everything she writes. Her point of view is always the daughter's, but leavening contempt for her mother's passivity is grief for the wasted talent, a dawning comprehension of why it was so often preferable for her mother, who died in 1987, to say no to life rather than yes.

"My mother always struggled to put her size-eleven foot into Cinderella's glass slipper, and she questioned her foot, not the shoe. Most of her life was lived before my sister and I were born. I look at pictures, and she's beautiful. I see power and intelligence. Then she became unhappy and looked old. What happened? She once gave me this bizarre advice: 'Stay a virgin, because the more sex you get, the pickier you become and a great lay is not necessarily a great meal ticket.' She felt unable to take care of herself in the world. She needed constant approval. My father was withholding on an emotional level. I remember thinking, A job might be easier than this. My mother couldn't stand the possibility that a daughter would escape."

She picks at her salad. "You have to get over your mother to get on with your life . . . and you never do." She laughs, acknowledging she has at least progressed from Mom's vision of mating. She whips out a picture of her current squeeze, a woman she's been with for two years, the singer Phranc. "She does a mean impersonation of Neil Diamond." In the snapshot, Phranc is lanky and butch enough to pass for a man. "I like 'em that way," Hughes vamps. "Her real name is Susie Gottlieb—a nice Jewish girl with a flattop."

Tongue Untied

Spring 1994

In *Clit Notes,* Holly Hughes once more hauls out her props: the geography of Michigan as a soulprint; her flirtatious mom; her withholding pop; Holly-the-baby-deviant taking her first fugitive steps. But these totems have been so boldly examined that their poetry and mystery are in her control. Blistering and poignant, *Clit Notes* is an apologia, a kind of letter to her dead father, chronicling how she came to be a lesbian and how sex, the out life, and solo performance merged into a calling.

Hughes means to seduce everything. In her clinging, ruby dress, she is the snaky temptresses Vivien and Lamia. She is all beguiling, anarchic, and hungry daughters. Eleanor Savage's lighting lends her skin a creamy vulnerability that plays against her tough mouth. And Hughes is newly mobile, under the direction of Dan Hurlin.

Clit Notes weaves back and forth in time, but its nervy heart is the central section, about loving her father. "I'm going home because there are parts of my body I can't feel," she confides when learning he has cancer. "A part of me is still asleep. Dreaming in my father's bed. Waiting for some kind of wake-up call. A sign. A word . . . okay, I'll say it: a kiss."

Knowing the transgressive power of this admission amid lesbian orthodoxy, she is emboldened, evoking a man whose body she adored, even as
he shrank from her and reviled her sexuality. Purged of complaint, her
voice is astonished, as she tries on her adversary's clothes and tells the story
of *two* unsatisfied souls.

Hughes can be triumphantly mordant. Learning that her father has
cancer, she tells herself that he can still have "a normal life," realizing that
this is how he reacted when discovering she was a lesbian: "He figured he
had two daughters. So he lost one. BIG DEAL! It wouldn't kill him." The
cancer also reminds her of the stoicism she admires, his saying he has "the
good kind of cancer." This, in turn, evokes the daddy who calmed her fears
by explaining that their property had only "the good kind of snakes."

She admits how much she savored his protection—still does. Later she
revels in the body of her lover, a woman who cultivates looking like a man.
"She pulls [out] a pair of Jockey shorts. Not Jockey for Her. And a pair of
secondhand jeans worn all white in places from the sweat and strain of
some stranger's body. A strange man's body. Men's clothes." Hughes is into
the drag and into being kissed in public, but she also thrills to her lover's
beautiful, large "tits."

Dad and mom in one? Nothing that reductive. Hughes spreads herself
out like a quilt, exposing square by square. In answer to her father's query,
"What made you a lesbian?" she of course has no answer. Instead she clues
him to the way she salvaged an identity, partly in defense and partly out of
affection for the materials at hand, reveling in the power of the imagination
to pluck erotic goodies from early defeat.

She closes with an image of two women, at once liberated and jettisoned from male protection. They still long for safety they know is impossible, for in treasuring each other they have grown more aware of the
precariousness of being alive.

Spalding Gray: Opening the Comic Vein

November 1990

Pauline Kael, reviewing the film *Swimming to Cambodia*, called Spalding
Gray, in essence, a solipsistic slime. He reduced war horrors, she felt, to a

sidebar in his inventory of personal anxieties. I remember thinking: Boy, Pauline probably hasn't seen a lot of performance art if she thinks this is narcissistic. I could understand what she meant about Gray's vanity, the way his preening doesn't leave much room for our admiration, but I thought his monologue was stirring, by turns trivial and large-minded, humorous and chilling.

Gray's next monologue, *Terrors of Pleasure*, chronicling his attempt to buy a weekend cabin from a crooked seller, sometimes shrank to fit Kael's puny estimation. Gray thought he was exploring the perverse, human preference for misery over gratification, but the piece didn't come off that way. He whined so fulsomely about being persecuted, there wasn't space for our sympathy: He scorned the house owner for his blue-collar diction and manners, even playing one of the man's crude phone messages on stage. Gray wanted approval for being a snob.

When press releases for his new piece, *Monster in a Box*, arrived, and I read that "the monster" was his novel-in-progress, I feared a cavil about writing as if it were victimization. Indeed there's some bragging. Gray, who feels hemmed in at MacDowell, the artists' colony, claims the place is too refined for him, when actually he's boasting he's too rollicking for the retreat. Gray uses a copy of his sixteen-hundred-page manuscript as a prop: He eyes it adoringly while referring to it as "the monster." It's like lovers' baby talk in public.

There's no irony in Gray's voice when he uses the term "girlfriend" to refer to Renée Shafransky, also credited as the piece's director. The forty-nine-year-old performer stares with a wide-eyed look that says: I can say girlfriend, because in my head it's the fifties, that era when men didn't have to worry about being patronizing, and besides, I had to take care of my depressed mother, so I'm entitled to vent as much hostility toward women, masked as dependence on them, as I want.

Overwhelmingly, though, *Monster in a Box* is ninety minutes of comic entertainment. Gray doesn't take himself as seriously as he has in the past, and this lightening up serves not to thin his work but to enrich it. He has found the true measure of his talent; his voracious eye for irony and incongruity, his capacity to show himself as vulnerable without undercutting the effect with aggression. Gray weaves story elements into charged arrangements, so that even details that at first seem mundane eventually become significant.

Told by his agent that he has a novel in him, Gray gets a contract and begins a book. It's autobiographical, tentatively dubbed *Impossible Vacation*, because he has never been able to enjoy *planned* pleasure. The monologue recounts what he discovered about himself while recalling the past. He can't vacation, he realizes, because during his first solo trip—a month-long trek to Mexico where he was unable to be reached—his mother embarked on the more radical journey of suicide.

The monologue also describes the myriad interruptions that seduced him away from the novel. Instead of a complaint against writing, *Monster in a Box* is part meditation on transmuting psychological pain and part celebration of wanderlust—the craving for the free trip disguised as "work," the willingness to go anywhere to see what will happen. The only impossible escapes are those baldly named *vacation*.

Owing to the success of *Swimming to Cambodia*, Gray is offered a series of gigs, including one to Nicaragua to serve as a witness to contra terrorism. Beseeched by the mothers of tortured children to appeal to Ronald Reagan's heart, Gray slips away from his feelings of helplessness and fixates on the paranoid ravings of a member of his group. Gray's entire personality, he reveals, is time-out from the tight-lipped, undemonstrative, alcoholic WASP nest in which he was raised. Gray is an openly prurient blabbermouth.

A riff on his farting, courtesy of a bean diet, is buoyantly low. A description of a child actor's projectile vomiting during a Broadway play is inspired clowning. Gray earns a prolonged belly laugh describing his police arrest, in the sweltering Hermitage museum, for rolling up his pants, and he evokes equal hilarity doing a scene from *Our Town* in the spirit of Frank Rich's savage criticism. Gray speaks about loss, depletion, and failure with confidence. This is a star turn, all eyes on him, just where he wants them.

Gray's Anatomy

December 1993

Serious trouble has made Spalding Gray funnier. He develops a retinal malady in his left eye: His vision is imperiled, the problem may be irreversible, and who knows about the other eye? The ray of light is that the plight is Spalding's, that it is, in a grisly way, a gift—an event with sufficient magnitude to enlarge his self-absorption and hypochondria. Like a discipline or a calling, the threat of blindness is focusing.

Gray's Anatomy, the monologuist's latest installment in his live-action autobiography, is hilarious, harrowing, and masterful for nearly all its ninety minutes. Gray, our hapless but intrepid guide, transports us to medical hell. The man who has spent a lifetime waiting for the other shoe to drop is conditioned for catastrophe, and all of his senses snap to attention. With his eyesight ablur, he sees surfaces and their underbellies more clearly than ever before.

After postponing an eye exam for four months, he arrives through a referral at the office of Dr. Mendel. Don't go to this man. He may be a crack diagnostician, but he is one of those tight-lipped technoids who have to be pumped for information. Gray isn't informed that his pupils are being dilated. "I'm sitting there reading and gradually I'm going blind. The whole place is turning into a fuzzball, just a big yellow fuzzball." He's shot up with a huge, dye-filled syringe and thrust into a confining contraption, unaware that torturous camera flashes await. "They finish and the doctor rushes off, his gown blowing in the nonexistent breeze. He doesn't say a word. He's madly taking notes on a little pad as he goes off to develop the pictures."

When the doctor returns, he phones a colleague and dictates medicalese into an answering machine. Gray begs for attention, and Mendel turns his back. Finally responding, the doctor addresses his patient as Gary Spalding and reports that he is suffering from a macular pucker, meaning that the vitreous humor has liquefied and pulled away from the retina, leaving behind a piece of Saran Wrap–type tissue. An operation is recommended, though success isn't guaranteed.

Thus begins Gray's chase for causes, treatments, and contingency plans for infirmity. Raised as a Christian Scientist, he's averse to invasive therapies, but nontraditional healing proves equally unsettling. His New Age friends pass such windy retorts as, "Well, what is it you *don't want to see?*" Consulting a "nutritional ophthalmologist," he enters a coven of practitioners who sniff over such information as the exact number of burritos, bowls of borscht, and servings of rabbit he's eaten in the past year.

These anecdotes and many more are bravura stand-up, and Gray's timing and delivery are honed to seem spontaneous. The bits progress chronologically but are arranged like movements in a musical score, terror alternating with relief.

When trained on his infirmity, Gray enters a space cleared of self-importance. He's naked and intimate, no membrane protecting him, so we're transported to his side of the eyeball. We feel him jumping for the bait of turning threat into a subject, plunging for dear life into storytelling, where he can temporarily escape lip chewing *and control something.* Art engages him with the world, lending him perspective. For in this age of AIDS and cancer, the threat of blindness to one eye has to be a comedy. This sufferer is aware that his ordeal is enormous and ordinary, and he juggles these irreconcilables without minimizing either.

We feel the aloneness of physical decline and of searching for remedies, but here Gray doesn't go far enough. Fear—of aloneness as well as illness—makes him passive, and in that state he agrees to marry his longtime lover, Renée. Once he comes through the operation, however, he wants to escape. This, too, could have been a subject: the way we make regrettable promises while feeling helpless. Instead the business with Renée remains a muddle. She figures more prominently in this piece than in others, but apart from being devoted and resourceful, she is always shadowy, instrumental to Spalding rather than defined in her own right, while other characters are so vividly conjured they can be whiffed. When Renée enters, the gallant clown becomes a kvetch, portraying himself in that singularly unattractive role, the reluctant bridegroom, and casting Renée as the old ball and chain.

Is this a case of emotional arrest on Gray's part? Of love drained of its oomph? Gray doesn't know, and the marriage that eventually takes place is as forced an ending as is the union itself. The refuge from random, stupid, shapeless reality isn't wedlock, this piece convinces, but sifting out the whopping tales.

Snow Business

November 1996

Spalding Gray's new piece, *It's a Slippery Slope,* is a scrapbook of his narcissism, and damned if he doesn't deepen the gaze—at least for the first sixty minutes. He is nearing fifty-two, the age at which his mother committed suicide, and he's tempted to meet her in Valhalla. Instead he takes up skiing, exchanging his anxious, New York, boho head trip for an in-the-moment flight from consciousness. On the mountain he's home, embracing his New England heritage, clambering up and slithering down the big mom tit in the sky he has longed to join ever since mooning out the window in his high school geometry class.

The monologue is stand-up, unreeled with grand minimalism, his acting honed to a Beckettian simplicity that ripples out levels of meaning from a sip of water or the slight rearrangement of his feet beneath the desk. His plaid shirt is as much clown garb as Bozo's red nose; his circumflex eyebrows shoot asides to the audience, like bubbles of thought above the head of a cartoon character. His writing is spare as a haiku and galumphing as a shaggy dog, as he embellishes his themes: the laws of triangles, emotional depression and geological elevation, acting instead of living, the evasion of consequences.

Between monologues he wonders (reasonably) if he creates crises for material. He feels his life is becoming one big memory and that he's lost touch with sensation. He questions why each day he forgets that you only live once, while white-knuckling through existence dreading mortality. There are hilarious set pieces, among them a ski lesson in which he unprotestingly permits himself to be called Sterling. Cast as a suicide in a Soderberg film, he strolls through his hotel with bloody makeup on his wrists and fails to get a rise off anyone, until, seized by a "diabolical eleven-year-old Halloween energy," he waves them before an astonished old woman and cries, "Have you got anything for my wounds?" Classically stalled conversations with his father are sporadic, but he reports one as the old man is nearing his end—a follow-up to their last chat, conducted on a golf course, when fourteen-year-old Spuddy was told the facts of life. Loosened by a couple of beers, Gray gropes for a Hallmark moment. "You had three sons, and I'm the middle. Why am I the only one who isn't circumcised?" Father: "You're not?"

There is more dick-waving here than in previous works, and this is where the piece goes slack (or, if you prefer, plows into a snowdrift). We've been on the road with Spuddy for years, but those were the days when he was with his "girlfriend"-and-later-wife Renée Shafransky, who was not only a character in his pieces but the director of several of them. He didn't confide, as he does now, that he used to have wild affairs on his tours. Unlike the "impingencies" of *Monster in a Box*, about a man who can't write a novel, and of *Gray's Anatomy*, about a man who may be going blind—both struggles with the self—the *crise* at the core of *Slippery Slope* is Gray's affair with a woman who bears him a son and the subsequent dashing of his bond with Renée.

Faced with the consequences of his impact on others, Gray loses his thread. He stops spinning tales of fear and loathing and psychobabbles: "Renée and I fused, she became very involved with my work. . . . I had to propose to Renée in front of my therapist who knew I was having an affair with Kathy. . . . Kathy was simple, she liked the outdoors. . . . Kathy had no leftover mothering energy." In *Slope*, we can see why the marriage to Renée in *Anatomy* comes off false—he was still fucking Kathy!

But spilling the beans doesn't turn him honest. Renée's suffering is mentioned but not taken in by the narrator or presented to the audience. Gray has no impulse to protect the women. He admits that, over both of them, he chooses the mirror of himself he sees in his offspring: "There is always another woman, but never another son." Instead of satirizing this peak act of narcissism, Gray squanders the best chance thus far of his career and waxes reverential, declaring his boy a "little Archimedes [who] had the geometry to split up me and Renée." It's not a crime to love your kid, even prefer him above others, but Gray speaks as if reproduction in itself is ennobling—redeems all that filthy stuff he was doing when it was just his dick and pleasure. Talk about returning to your Puritan roots.

CHAPTER SIX

Outstanding and Outwitting: Gay Stand-ups, Troupes, Soloists, and Drag Racers

Lois Weaver and Peggy Shaw

Among the theaters of gay life are the street and the closet. The first is of cruising and exhibition, the second of coded reference. The tension between the two theaters is theater, too. The queer comedy chronicled in this chapter, fueled by the street and the closet, has, during the past ten years, moved from the fringes to the mainstream with wondrous speed. Gay liberation greased the way, at the same time that queer entertainment goosed the movement. Of all forms of comedy, gay theater has been more influenced by politics than any other and has, in the past decade, had the greatest impact on the culture as a whole.

The change has been long in the making, and two books reveal the progress with insight and panache: Vito Russo's *The Celluloid Closet* (1981) and Julian Fleisher's *The Drag Queens of New York, An Illustrated Guide* (1996). Early American and European films, with their avant-garde origins, contain gay characters. Prewar Berlin, where sexual enlightenment flourished, was the scene of "the first gay liberation movement," writes Russo, "led by Doctor Magnus Hirschfeld, whose Institute for Sexual Science was the focal point of the battle against the antigay Paragraph 175, which outlawed homosexual acts between men." Hirschfeld's institute produced *Anders als die Anderen (Different from the Others)*, released in 1919, the first film to discuss homosexuality openly. Directed by Richard Oswald and starring Conrad Veidt, the movie "pleaded tolerance for what it termed the Third Sex."

American comedies of the thirties were more oblique, with stock sissy-comics like Edward Everett Horton and Franklin Pangborn playing endearing innocents and fops. By the forties, once it was clear these characters weren't merely zanies but coded homosexuals, they were cancelled, replaced with increasingly sinister representations, until there were only killer gays. (The same phenomenon smacked the new wave of feminism; at first assertive women were trivialized in media, but as their message gained support, feminists were for years depicted as ruthless, sex-hating bitches.)

Russo reports that gentle men choosing to love other men don't exist in American film up to the eighties, "except as slapstick comedy." He points to Stan Laurel and Oliver Hardy, who "had the perfect sissy-buddy relationship throughout their long career," and who, maintains Russo, consciously used that energy to deepen their comedy. In *Their First Mistake* (1932), produced by Hal Roach, Laurel and Hardy live literally as husband and wife—they are shown in bed together with a baby between them.

Other buddy pairings, with a childlike neuter, for the most part unintentionally gave off gay vibrations. In his movies with Bing Crosby, Bob Hope was soft and needy. Danny Kaye—sometimes paired with a virile twin of himself—played an array of sexual hysterics, and later Jerry Lewis was a slavish bottom to Dean Martin's aloof top.

The mass entertainment forms of film and TV remained rigidly homophobic in the forties and fifties—casting gays as psychopaths or suicides or, for the most part, denying their existence. As for gays themselves, Barbara Gittings, quoted by Russo, evokes the fear of being discovered, describing a meeting in 1950 that grew into the gay liberation movement. It was held "in someone's apartment in Los Angeles, and the door was locked and the blinds were drawn and there was a lookout posted because they thought it was illegal to talk about homosexuality."

By the sixties, with the advent of the sexual revolution, underground film and noncommercial theater were drawing inspiration from the streets and bars and beginning to propel gay life into the world. Downtown actor/visionary/filmmaker Jack Smith presented his polymorphous fantasia of sex and longing, the movie *Flaming Creatures*, in 1963. Andy Warhol was on his way to remaking the world: turning depravity into chic, spinning gold from commercial icons, transforming garbage into treasure. He combed the sidewalks for drag queens and dubbed them "superstars"— most articulate and stirring among them Jackie Curtis, Holly Woodlawn, and Candy Darling.

A couple of blocks from the factory, John Vaccaro and Charles Ludlam were making drag foolery in Vaccaro's Playhouse of the Ridiculous, until, in '67, Ludlam staged "a revolt," as Fleisher writes, frustrated by Vaccaro's self-censorship. Fearful of the police—following the arrests of people who had screened *Flaming Creatures*—Vaccaro wanted to eliminate homosexuality and nudity from his shows, and Ludlam walked, along with Ridiculous stalwarts Black Eyed Susan and Lola Pashalinski, founding his own inspired and radical troupe, the Ridiculous Theatrical Company.

Open gay defiance reared in the '69 Stonewall uprising: a combination of street theater, drag drama, and disruption inspired by feminist politics. A few days after the death of Judy Garland, police raided the Stonewall bar on Christopher Street. These were days in which laws still stood on the books forbidding a man from wearing more than three articles of women's clothing on the street. Instead of complying with police, several drag queens, led by Marsha P. Johnson and Sylvia (Ray) Rivera, with nerves raw from grieving, fought back with fists and bricks.

The next landmark in gay theater was the '71 appearance in New York of San Francisco's glitter queen troupe the Cockettes. Their performances proved loose and amateurish, but they emboldened New York queer theater pioneers, who coalesced under the camp counselorship of Jimmy Camicia. Camicia's troupe Hot Peaches included Minette, International Chrysis, sometimes Ethyl Eichelberger, and it specialized—the company still does—in literate genre parodies melded with gay mindscapes and trash environments. A group of dancers who'd worked with Ludlam formed the drag company Ballet Trocadero de Monte Carlo, and in '83 Ira Siff began singing female roles in public and founded La Gran Scena Opera.

Mostly artists and gays were the audiences for this work, but as it began to intersect with the mainstream, there were reverberations. Russo describes a '76 TV interview during which Geraldo Rivera tried to get under the skin of Holly Woodlawn. Rivera held himself as a white coat looking at a specimen. He wanted to peer under Holly's skirt, but instead of wondering about his own curiosity, he prodded her to hold forth—surrender her secrets, her platform, as if her life were a stunt. Woodlawn deflected his questions with flip rejoinders. Finally, in exasperation, Rivera begged, " 'Please answer me. What *are* you? Are you a woman trapped in a man's body? Are you a heterosexual? Are you a homosexual? A transvestite? A transsexual? *What* is the answer to the question?' Woodlawn . . . took a measured breath, looked at Rivera incredulously and dismissed his earnest concern with, 'But, darling, what difference does it make as long as you look fabulous?' "

Woodlawn's evasion of Rivera comes off as resistance in this context, for if the outsider isn't in control of the strip—determining the terms of self-revelation—disclosure can become a boxcar to cart off the undesirable. For the same reasons, in '93, k.d. lang toyed with Connie Chung, refusing to allow the almost-swooning femme interviewer to out her, while, a few months later, she spoke candidly about loving women to gay journalist Brendon Lemon, on assignment for *Out* magazine.

Warholian sass nonetheless began seeping into the movies, most especially *The Rocky Horror Picture Show* (1976), where deviants controlled the story, making their exploits look glamorous and frisky, conjuring a world not of killer fags but a place where gays have more fun. Writing in '81, Russo considered this movie "the gayest film yet made by a major studio," but chided Twentieth Century-Fox for failing to give it a proper release and relegating it to midnight cult status. "Tim Curry's performance," declares Russo, "especially in his rendition of 'Sweet Transvestite,' is the essence of what every parent in America fears will happen if our sexual standards are relaxed. It becomes the living horror of making deviant sexuality visible and tangible."

The next year, '77, a real gay figure—Quentin Crisp—spoke with clarity about his life in *The Naked Civil Servant* and in the film version, with John Hurt as Crisp, which captured the book's valor, poignancy, and guts. Crisp comes off a revolutionary, despite his lack of intention to be one, not because he shares a post-Stonewall agenda for liberation but because he remains true to his inner life. "Crisp may in fact have been one of the first gay activists in his own passive way," Russo says. "A man who dyed his hair, wore eye makeup and painted his lips and nails, a man who refused to deny his homosexuality, Crisp was a revolutionary soon after the turn of the century. . . . *The Naked Civil Servant* said that flamboyant, overt homosexuality was heroic and the struggle to remain different in a conformist world was admirable."

During the eighties, while movies and TV, for the most part, remained resistant to credible gays, queer theater flourished, most thrillingly with Ludlam's collages of classical literature, pop culture, autobiography, and entertainment history, in such plays as *The Mystery of Irma Vep, Bluebeard,* and *Camille.* Since Ludlam's death in '87, his lover and partner Everett Quinton has led the company and been its principal, dazzling star.

Ludlam scion Charles Busch founded Theater in Limbo, creating his own genre/gender-busting pastiches, but using as point of departure Hollywood B flicks instead of classical texts. Fleisher chronicles the rise of two competing drag showcases in the East Village: the Pyramid Club and Boy Bar, and their casts of performers, some—like John Kelly, Ethyl Eichelberger, John Epperson as Lypsinka, and RuPaul—honing talent that would catapult them far beyond these venues.

The first Wigstock combusted spontaneously in '84, when a flotilla of drag queens from the Pyramid put on a free lip-synching show in the decrepit band shell in Tompkins Square Park. And though now Wigstock is a cultural event attracting politicians and media coverage, Fleisher points to two events in '90 that thrust drag and queer theater from the margins to the mainstream: Madonna's video *Vogue* and Jennie Livingston's documentary about the drag balls of Harlem, *Paris Is Burning,* in which some of the performers in Madonna's video also appeared.

It didn't take long before drag queens were modeling in designer shows, a phenomenon with ambivalent signs. It suggested the arrival of drag and gay life into a new visibility. It declared what had always been true: that gay men—as clothing, hair, and makeup designers—had had enormous influence in concocting styles of femininity. It showed, too, that women, having gained more control over their lives, no longer felt described by established femininity—that, in essence, only drag queens of both sexes wanted to embrace it.

While boundaries were being shredded in performance clubs and the-aters, gay stand-up was far more ghettoized, for the reason that stand-up is showbiz, and showbiz is conservative, with straight, homophobic men—club owners, talent bookers, and TV producers—mostly controlling it. There are exceptions: the Duplex and Caroline's, which, early among com-edy clubs, booked out gay comedians. Cable TV, too, began offering air time, which was astounding when it happened, because gay comedians had long been discouraged from imagining access to the mainstream.

Not that the mainstream was entirely waiting with open arms—like the Christian right and reactionaries in government, who got excited by the explicit sexuality, much of it gay, in the work of Mapplethorpe and the NEA four. They went hunting for blood but in the long run only publicized the cultural changes that couldn't be stemmed.

Gay characters have become increasingly common in movies and on TV, and what's most heartening is that with many—Sandra Bernhard's character on *Roseanne*, Lisa Edelstein's role on *Relativity*—gayness is pre-sented matter-of-factly, not as sandpaper to arouse friction. For actors to come out is still fraught, though, and that question underscored the recent flap about whether Ellen DeGeneres's sitcom character would emerge as a lesbian.

Since DeGeneres is so identified with her character—a clone of her stand-up persona in the same way that Jerry Seinfeld's sitcom Jerry is—and since both DeGeneres and Ellen Morgan, the part she plays on her show, have been intentionally ambivalent about their sexuality, the real question was: Was DeGeneres outing herself? She went on a few talk shows to play footsy with the question, clowning that the rumor about her show was mis-heard and that her character would actually reveal she was Lebanese. Gay actors try to gauge the cost to their careers of coming out. Will they still be cast in straight roles? Will audiences reject them? For more and more per-formers, though, the freedom of being themselves outweighs the risks.

For the queer comedians who are out and do have access to the main-stream, the question becomes: What's the cost of visibility? If it's irrever-ence and edge, is it worth it? This is a problem for all artists who make a career dismantling propriety and then get invited to the big house: Will they censor themselves? For mass consumption, RuPaul has created a vanilla-friendly version of his character. Doing drag downtown, he used to mime being butt-fucked; on *Oprah,* his message is: Go after your dreams.

Fleisher notes John Waters's alarms about the "Disneyization" of drag. "I think drag queens should scare families and not make them feel good about themselves," Waters maintains, righteously protecting the sanctity of indecency. But it's up to every artist to struggle with the lure of money and acceptability. Once they are no longer marginalized, artists who've drawn their energy from being outside have to locate different sources.

In *On Edge*, C. Carr mourns the passing of Bohemias controlled by artists rather than mass culture, citing as the first example the Beats in the fifties, who were, almost as soon as they announced themselves, converted by the media into beatniks. She describes a "Bohemian diaspora," a flow of "energy that moved from Paris to New York, from West Village to East Village, from Old Bohemia (1830–1930) to New Bohemia (the sixties) to Faux Bohemia (the eighties)," claiming it has "atomized now into trails that can't be followed: the 'zine/cassette network, the livingroom performance spaces, the modem-accessed cybersalons, the flight into neighborhoods that will never be Soho."

There is truth to her outsider history. Mass media coarsen art by interpreting it to the mainstream. But Carr's perspective is tinged with negative classicism, the idea that the present is ineluctably a debased form of a golden age in the past. At least one part of her untrackable Bohemia—livingroom performance spaces—has gathered into a community which has, in turn, shot underground denizens into the unboundaried world. While in the past Bohemias may have been less subject to invasion and revision, we live in a culture that has never been as mongrel, never been as unpoliceable, never seen so many cultures and tribes jostling each other, misinterpreting each other, fearing each other, absorbing each other.

■ ■ ■

The performers in this chapter view gayness as a form of theater, because being out is a public expression: the individual stepping before the world and, depending on the path, feeling tension with the culture just by existing. These pieces—whose collective motto could be: Transgress, cross-dress, confess, and make a mess—suggest how small the community was and in some ways remains, how actor/writers are continually performing in each other's shows, working for peanuts, eating peanuts.

The same names crop up—members of Split Britches working with

Holly Hughes, the Five Lesbian Brothers performing in Carmelita Tropicana's plays, also Anne Iobst, who, with Lucy Sexton, make up the terror-
ist-clown partnership DANCENOISE. Peggy Shaw of Split Britches
started out in Hot Peaches. Shaw's lover/partner Lois Weaver worked with
Spiderwoman, and Shaw eventually did, too. I've arranged the pieces more
or less in chronological order, conveying a sense of the changes that swept
the genre during this time.

First I want to mention performers I didn't write about but whose
work juices the field. Jeff Weiss, genius deviant and musical-comedy
maven, is still concocting surreal noir epics—exuberant dreams salvaged
from the cutting-room floor of William Burroughs's imagination—these
days under the title *Hot Keys*. With his usual cast of what seems like thousands, a recent installment opens in a sleazy bar on the cusp of Chinatown.
Two lowlifes are planning to sting a gull who has a thing for soiled underpants. What's difficult to glean from reading about Weiss is the balance he
strikes between the luridness of his subject matter and the jolly, musical
sweep of his shows. Sleaze here isn't *Oprah* fodder, rather ordinary life,
Times Square ragtime.

I saw Randy Allen in a peculiar play called *Me and Jezebel* ('94), about a
month-long visit Bette Davis made in '85 to the home of a sycophantish
Connecticut couple. The piece was unremarkable except for Allen's extraordinary portrayal of the poststroke Bette Davis—a character he has
performed as a solo. In this period Davis's body was wraith-thin, her head
bewigged, her face like a pug's, with popping eyes and a skewed mouth. Allen so vividly embodied her, he transcended camp. Really, it's impossible to
exaggerate the poststroke Bette, with her chain-smoking and gasping delivery, but Allen, in a clinging red dress, established the actress's bemused detachment. You couldn't take your eyes off his mixture of frailty and drive,
drift and focus. His Davis wore grievance like a tatty stole but knew that
work was the only dependable nourishment; she valued it less as a fading
diva than as a hungry spirit.

The pleasure of drag for men isn't about the desire to be a woman so
much as a flight from being a man. The same can be said of women don-
ning male garb—the escape is from being female, but there is more to it.
For when a man wears women's clothes, he's always slumming in a way—
choosing to jettison male privilege on his terms, knowing he can reassume
his status. It's transgressive to abdicate male power, but it's riskier to seize it,

which is what women do when they impersonate men, complete with body hair and big walks.

A number of drag kings are not so much mincing masculinity as asserting, in the same way that drag queens do, that masculinity and femininity are constructions independent of sex. In *Drag Kings and Subjects,* Diane Torr says deadpan, "I'll show you how to make a penis. It's easy." In her wry, informative solo, she outs the secrets of female-to-male impersonation by becoming, before our eyes, macho maven Danny King, who counsels that it's more in the attitude than in the rolled sock: "Don't smile and stop apologizing."

In the spring of '96, Club Casanova in Alphabet City inaugurated the first weekly drag king night in the country, and what makes the scene especially lively is its freewheeling gender-fuck at every level. Though the place principally attracts a lesbian audience, men aren't reviled or rebuffed when they flirt with women who look like guys, and women who look like guys don't hold the pose unambivalently, enjoying the flash of bustiers and lingerie under macho leather gear. That same doubleness pumps male dragsters, too. Fleisher notes the pleasurable split in International Chrysis, who had "breast implants and a big dick," and Fleisher quotes drag queen Hapi Phace on Chrysis, "She would joke that her measurements were 34, 26, 9. She was very butch in bed."

■ ■ ■

It was a revelation walking into a weird little theater, attached to a hospital, and seeing Split Britches for the first time. The trio's oddness and energy leaped off the creaky stage. A few years later Deb Margolin left the group to create stand-up poetry in her solo pieces. Peggy Shaw and Lois Weaver continued to make theater, including their collaboration with Holly Hughes in *Dress Suits to Hire,* and they worked with Bloolips in *Belle Reprieve,* a pastiche of romance myths via *Streetcar.* For the past few years, Weaver has spent several months in London directing shows for the Gay Sweatshop. Shaw—who is capable of rubberbanding between Brando/Dean, vulnerable bad boys, and Rita Hayworth glams—performed her solo *You're Just Like My Father,* a moving, searching collage, exploring her identification with her father and her mother's desire for her. I include a Q & A with Shaw.

Sara Cytron and Funny Gay Males—Danny McWilliams, Jaffe Cohen, and Bob Smith—are pioneers of gay stand-up and are among the first to work mixed venues, clearing paths for comics like Suzanne Westenhoefer and Lea DeLaria. Thank Arsenio Hall for allowing DeLaria to hijack his show in March '93 and thrust queer comedy into the nation's face. DeLaria is unmuzzled, refusing to reassure hysterics that the fringe is like the center. "It's not that I don't like penises," she confides. "It's that I don't like them on men."

Bob Smith went solo in a '94 HBO special, packing his seeming ordinariness on a subversive cruise, queering the mainstream, retracing his steps as an infant deviant, and uncloseting the gayness camouflaged by apparent calm. He admits to experimenting with heterosexuality in college: "I slept with a straight guy." Sheepish face. "I was really drunk."

Bloolips, Pomo Afro Homos, and Julian Clary are originals, not without sources but without compare. It is the distance they've journeyed from their sources—remixing and reinventing them—that makes them extraordinary. Brits Bloolips and Clary play with music hall routines and pantos, and the Pomos with minstrelsy and political sketch comedy.

The final piece, a week of comedy inspired by the Gay Games in '94, is a smorgasbord of talent and styles and a testament to the postcloset age. New zinger from Lea DeLaria, on dating lesbians who run in a pack and are each other's ex-lovers: "Hey, girls, why not let me put some new blood in this family. All the kids are gonna be retarded."

Split Britches: Vixen Fire

April 1983

For about a dozen years during the 1930s and 1940s, Della Mae Gearheart, playwright Lois Weaver's aunt, took care of her backward younger sister, Cora Jane, and her aged spinster aunt, Emma Gay. The women lived in one room of a sprawling farmhouse, surrounded by acres of land in Virginia's Blue Ridge Mountains. Pigs, chickens, and a cow occupied some of the other rooms. Emma Gay, who had never lived in her own home, helped raise her brother's children. Cora Jane grew up and died without ever leaving the farm. Della Mae had once worked in town and lived in an apartment, but she came back to her father's house. The women were everything to each other, and *Split Britches* is an imagined re-creation of a day in their life—a lifetime in the day. There's no real plot, no climactic event. It's rather a mood piece, but one so deftly written and performed, it is full of surprising probes.

As Emma Gay, Deb Margolin is an arthritic gargoyle, frozen in her armchair, with bent head and twisted legs. To extinguish matches, she must wave her locked wrist back and forth, as if saluting a cruise ship with a hanky. She saves caught bugs in a bottle and marvels that the same flies buzz in each afternoon. "I recognize them."

Weaver's Cora Jane is an idiot savant, sipping tea from doll cups, spitting tobacco juice on the floor, replaying a fantasy about a mysterious lover at her window, and defying Della Mae. "The cow's sick," Della Mae complains. "It's not the cow" is Cora Jane's routine response, meaning it's her sister who is sick. "The cow's just moaning in the dark because she's having a good time," says Cora Jane.

Della Mae, played to perfection by Peggy Shaw, is the one who really knows about passion. She's got a fire in her pocket. Part commanding matriarch, part gallant swain, she waltzes with Cora Jane, pretending her sister is the fire whose pretty, dangerous face is smiling up at her. She's a lesbian in rural Virginia; with her hair slicked back and wearing her father's trousers and boots, she once held women close at the town social. Now she makes biscuit dough as if she were pounding away her desire and sorrow. Then she suddenly stops and dreams she's piloting a plane like soaring Amelia, who "never came down."

Split Britches builds power like a poem or a piece of chamber music, through repeated patterns and unexpected shifts. Sometimes, the characters burst into harmonious renditions of funky blues songs and hymns. Or they fly into fits. Della Mae and Cora Jane have a stamping, huffing stand-off, and their virginal orgasmic rages create great comic moments, with Della Mae finishing and turning away in exhaustion before Cora Jane is satisfied. At one point, the women pretend to change roles, recite each other's obsessional lines, and reveal how well they understand their condition. At another stage Della Mae, momentarily deserted by the others, cries out: "I'm the same woman if you're here or if you're not here. I'm a free woman. . . . Jesus don't care about you. I'm the one who cares about you."

The piece lasts for seventy-five minutes, during which we see not only the Gearhearts in their grim, flaky complexity but also the troupe's unsentimental attitude toward female character. Here is feminism without banners or goddesses. Split britches, by the way, the company's name as well as the play's title, are the leggings American agricultural women wore in the fields—to facilitate peeing while standing up. This work is as ingenious and peculiar as the eponymous gear.

On weekends, the company performs a second one-act play, *Beauty and the Beast*, a Dada burlesque of the fairy tale. Aside from a whispered homage to Cocteau, the mood is raucous, nothing like the lyrical first piece, and the actors display a new range of comic and musical talents. Margolin plays Beauty's father as a rabbi, complete with *talis, payes,* and pink toe shoes. "I look like a jerk, but I respect myself," Margolin says in one of her long, wonderfully inane monologues. This rabbi, named Hitchcock, always wanted to be Martin Buber. Beauty, played by Weaver as a Salvation Army accordionist/evangelist, confesses she always wanted to be Katharine Hepburn, explaining that in college she fell in love with a girl who thought she was Spencer Tracy. And Beast, played by Shaw, says she always wanted to be James Dean. True love could transform them, except these people don't believe in true love.

Beauty and the Beast is literate nonsense. "I eat out of loneliness, but I never eat the lonely," Beast tells Hitchcock, who is relieved for once that alienation has saved him. Shaw, lip-synching Perry Como's "It's Impossible" and trying to lower herself ever so slowly into a chair, is absurdness itself. Weaver, all smiles, does a Vegas-style "Do You Know the Way to San Jose?" to Margolin's upstaging accompaniment and delights in reporting that Pat Nixon had a stroke, then got up and redid her floors. The troupe's gritty sensibility is its sharpest piece of politics.

Dress Suits to Hire: Heartthrobs

January 1988

Peggy Shaw usually does James Dean/Gary Cooper numbers: eyes like slits, no smile, violence under the skin. In *Dress Suits to Hire*, written by Holly Hughes in collaboration with Shaw and Lois Weaver, Shaw dresses up like Rita Hayworth. The boys in her are still visible, scowling, hitching their hips awkwardly, but it's mostly Rita's show, and playing Hayworth unleashes a ribald hilarity and sexiness. Her character is called Deeluxe, she's the dumb, hunky one playing opposite Lois Weaver's Michigan, a savvy bitch-in-heat blonde. Their eighty-minute duel is a mellifluous ode to lesbian eros, an out-and-out hoot.

They live in the back of a costume rental shop. Michigan doesn't go out. Deeluxe doesn't, either, although she threatens to. They sip sherry, break into torch songs, and remind each other how they got there. Michigan evokes the freezing Detroit suburb where she grew up. Her birth was presaged with queer signs: "They ran out of Bird's Eye and plaid, people had to eat fresh vegetables and wear solid colors." Early she wanted sex and got it from her science teacher. He called her an animal. He said, "I bet you wish you had a father." "No," she answered, "but I wish I had his clothes."

Deeluxe hails from Ohio and was low-class. Sex was all around her, too, memorably embodied in Uncle Bert "porking his three-hundred-pound wife in a wood frame house, getting her after she'd served the ham, the mayonnaise still on her arms." Like Michigan, Deeluxe had a bad heart. "Not the kind that kills you, the kind that makes you wear too much eye makeup." But unlike Michigan, she has a man inside her, specifically in her right hand. His name is Little Peter, but he's tough and cool—he slaps her and even strangles her sometimes. "There I was, tryin' to decide whether to be a lesbian today or put it off until tomorrow." Tomorrow comes when she meets Michigan, who's pumping gas. Michigan fills her in on the deviant life, and then begins the struggle, the seduction. They make off for New York, where lots of people have bad hearts, but the struggle continues. They get off on it.

The play's distilled absurdity evokes Ionesco, the anchoring of high-flown images with pop references summons Orton, the fanciful geography lessons harken to Shepard, yet Hughes has concocted a pulp-laced idiom all her own. Images and themes recur—the moon, hearts, snakes—enlarging our sense of the erotic bond between the women and spotlighting the silly posturing of all romantic dances. Hughes depicts sex styles, not genders or sexualities, and the welding of word to image is especially powerful in Shaw's performance. With a flip of her red mane, she becomes a temptress in black garter belt and bustier, or a woman in female drag, or a male drag queen.

Weaver is a marvelous foil, the femme who calls all the shots, who's asking for it, like a cat on a hot tin roof—she even does a turn in a white full slip. Her direction is equally controlled. There isn't a flat moment in the piece, which is saying a lot for a work that lacks a plot and is more a poem than anything else. The songs are entertaining, especially Shaw's "Put the Blame on Mame" routine, complete with a glove-peeling bit. And the play's mood of romance/decoded romance is wittily enhanced by the production; from Joni Wong's moth-eaten closet of a set and dreamy lights, to Susan Young's attic-trunk costumes. We even get a marabou-fringed robe and a tux.

An Interview with Peggy Shaw

Fall 1996

Peggy Shaw and Lois Weaver have been a couple for eighteen years. Pillars of queer theater, they've worked in some of the most innovative troupes, from Hot Peaches, to Spiderwoman, to Split Britches, to WOW Café, which they founded and which has served as a lab and playground for some of the most adventurous lesbian performers, including Holly Hughes, Lisa Kron and Carmelita Tropicana. Shaw and Weaver created a body of plays, which have been published by Routledge as *Split Britches: Lesbian Practice, Lesbian Performance.* Shaw and Weaver have each created solo work, too, and now they are branching out into collaborations with other artists. Last year Shaw performed at American Place Theater in the play *Slow Drag,* in which she played Billy Tipton, a musician who passed as a man most of his/her life. I met with Shaw in the fall of '96 to talk about the snaking paths of her life on stage and off.

LS: How did you get into performing?
PS: I was crossing the street at Sheridan Square in 1971 when I saw Wilhelmina Ross, a drag queen, who was singing this song and inviting people to follow her for the second number. I was a social worker at the time, thirty-one. At that point, I had seen only one play in my life, *Bluebeard* in 1968, with Charles Ludlam and Lola Pashalinski. There were signs on the seats that said "shit" and "fuck." Charles leaped on Lola on the couch and dived into her crotch and picked pubic hair out of his mouth, and I thought, "Is this what theater is? Maybe I could get into it." But I didn't act on the

thought until that day in '71. A group followed Wilhelmina to the second act, which was at the Path Station. A bunch of people from Hot Peaches were singing about being gay. I couldn't believe it. The next act was at the Silver Dollar. They sang another song, wearing big red lips, and I started crying. From then on, I helped them, building sets, driving them around. I had a car.

L S : What was your life like before this?

P S : I grew up in Boston, one of seven kids, to poor Irish Protestant parents. When I came home and told my mother and father that my art teacher had said I was going to college, they said, "You're not going to college, you're going to work." But this teacher insisted. She took me by the hand and stuck with me, and got me enrolled. She changed my whole life. All through college, I worked forty-five hours a week waitressing to pay for school. After that I was with a woman. She got married and had a kid, so I got married and got pregnant. I married in 1967, wearing daisies in my hair and pants. The man I married looked like Lauren Bacall. We didn't have sex for four months, but the marriage lasted four years. By the time I started working with Hot Peaches, the marriage was over and my daughter, Shara, was two. I was living with a Polish woman. She used to beat me up. I thought it was wonderful. In those days we created reasons for jealousy in order to arouse passion.

L S : When did you start performing?

P S : In 1975. Jimmy Camicia, who was the leader of Hot Peaches, decided that we were all going to Europe. It was one of those moments in life when you know you just have to shake everything up. I still wasn't performing. Basically, I didn't talk. I drank a lot. I was all blocked up, fucked up. I sold everything I owned and gave away the rest. My girlfriend was so angry she burned my clothes and took my savings out of our joint account, the $6,000 I was saving to buy a building on the Lower East Side. The money was gone. We went to London, and the plan was to sleep in Hampstead Heath, the seven of us. And the first night we were there, a woman came by and asked what we were doing. We told her we were putting on a gay show, and it turned out she was involved with the People Show, a theater that is still producing plays, and she invited us to squat in the top floor of her mansion. We lived there for four months, sleeping on two mattresses, stealing food on the Finchley Road from the restaurant deliveries: strawberries, juice, bread, milk, eggs, avocados. We got booked into the Oval House, and we were opening in a few weeks, and Jimmy said to me, "Peggy, you're going to perform. We don't have any lesbian material so you're going to write it." They got me stoned on dope, and I wrote this piece called *Dyke*, and it was so angry and wild. I hadn't said anything for all those years, and when I finally opened my mouth, out came a freezing blast of air. It was about all the times people had walked up to me on the street and screamed in my face, "dyke," and "lezzie." In the old days, I would fight them.

L s : How did it feel finally to be on stage?

P s : It was a great release, and Shara was in the show. She did a number called "Yin and Yang." But the rage wasn't exactly conducive to comedy. I learned that from the drag queens. The whole style of drag queens is competitive. You have to be taller, use more glitter, be funnier. The life is combative, in-your-face theater. The drag queens in the company had high consciousness. They didn't wear tits. They were boys in dresses, but their look created instant humor, an instant clown persona. When I worked with Lois, I learned about subtlety and seduction.

L s : Where did you and Lois meet?

P s : Hot Peaches was in Amsterdam in 1977, and Spiderwoman was performing there. Shara and I went backstage to meet them. I said, "I'm Peggy, are any of you gay?" Two of the women said they were bisexual. Lois was one. We were all going to Berlin next. On the way, Spiderwoman's costumes were lost, and they had to perform, so we lent them a trunk of our stuff. They had performed in rags, and we had boas. They started putting on feathers and sequins, and they went bananas. They were never the same again. Their show was funny, "An Evening of Disgusting Songs About Pukey Romance." Afterward we went out for Chinese food. I leaned over to Lois and said, "I'll give you two years to come out." She did, but not with me.

L s : When did you join Spiderwoman?

P s : In 1978. They wanted to do cabaret and needed my expertise. I was with them for two and a half years. When Lois and I got together, we had to keep it a secret. The rule was don't shit where you eat, but that was easy for the straight women. Hiding was sexy, though. We had to make out in bushes and bathrooms, and it also established the basis of our relationship, that work was the center, and everything radiated off of that. Back in New York, we did *Medusa's Revenge* at the first Lesbian Theater started by Migaly Abalou and Ana Simo. We left Spiderwoman in 1980.

L s : Was the point to work independently?

PS: We wanted to do out lesbian theater, and we just about exploded with ideas and energy. We started dreaming together, and our dreams came true. Lois had a huge impact on me. I remember the moment I realized I hated women. It was in Berlin, and a woman came into a meeting, and I realized I knew nothing about this woman, and yet I hated her, thinking I hated her the way a man would. I saw I thought I was a guy, that I had taken on all that stuff. I had to tear it all down and build it back up. Lois and I started Split Britches and WOW. It was like coming out in a great public way. We just flew. We combusted together. We never slept. We began WOW as a festival, but it wasn't satisfying enough to put on women's theater two weeks a year, so we opened this place on East 11th Street to keep it going all the time. We were ravenous for this thing, and the Lower East Side was bursting with talent. Lois and I became major producers and established an aesthetic we had cultivated in Hot Peaches and Spiderwoman of vaudeville interludes, songs, genre-crunched stories, and flamboyant, ragtag sets and costumes. Holly wandered in as a visual artist, then got on stage. Carmelita walked in for a poetry reading and stayed. WOW was this beacon, and everyone fed off each other. We were people who never would have hung out together ordinarily. We were from totally different worlds, but the work bound us.

LS: What was the inspiration for the first Split Britches piece?

PS: Lois had these three female relatives in the mountains, whom she had always wanted to make a piece about. We asked Deb Margolin to be in it with us. She was a writer. This was the first time she acted, and she was brilliant. We did *Beauty and the Beast* in 1982 as a vaudeville and remix of Shakespeare. Everybody got to riff with their favorite toys. *Upwardly Mobile Home,* which we did in 1983, is still my favorite show. Stormy Brandenberger choreographed it for us.

LS: How did *Dress Suits to Hire* come about?

PS: We asked Holly to work with us instead of Deb, because it was great to all be lesbians. It was a two-year collaboration.

LS: What inspired you to try a solo?

PS: Hampshire College called and asked if I could do something for parents' weekend. I didn't have a solo but I said I did. This phrase had been kicking around in my head. When I was aggressive, people would say, "You're just like my father." That's what I called the piece, which explores being a butch. It was so exciting, working by myself for the first time. Lois developed a solo, too, *Faith and Dancing*, which is about being a femme from Virginia, which is also her mother's name. It's about leaving the state of Virginia and her mother. Working solo I started feeling my power and seeing I had a vision of my own. Before that Lois had always been the director, the brains. She was so happy I could meet her on a place where I was her equal and I was feeling my independence. It was better than having affairs. I started teaching and assuming business duties. Lois could take more time for herself as an actor, and she started doing amazing projects in London. She worked with the Gay Sweat Shop for years, but now she's branching off as a producer, presenting entertainers in gigs called Club Deviance and Club Bent, where people take big risks. She's attracting the most creative talent, MC-ing as Tammy Whynot, doing a striptease, in which she starts out naked and gradually puts on clothes.

L S : You talk about having affairs. How is that affecting you and Lois?

P S : We were monogamous for fourteen years, and we'd gotten so merged, we needed to shake things up. We were so merged, our first affairs were with the same woman. Now Lois is with a woman named James, and I'm having a relationship with a woman young enough to be my daughter. I'm fifty-two. She's twenty-six. One of the things that's great about this is that she has benefited from all the things we fought for and from having parents who wanted and loved her. She's not conflicted. She loves me in a way that's new. I suppose I have always been the one who did the adoring, but this woman makes me feel like the object of her desire, and it's wonderful.

L S : You and Lois seem amazingly accepting of each other.

P S : We feel like nothing can ultimately break us apart. That may not be true, but we are very close and committed. Which doesn't mean we haven't struggled and come to impasses. At the end of *Lust and Comfort*, we do a dance wearing identical flannel pajamas. I turn around and accidentally step on Lois's toe. She punches me in the stomach, and I flip her over backwards. She punches me in the face, and we go on like this for four minutes, dancing a choreographed fight to "The Ten Commandments of Love." At the end we're exhausted. Lois gets in one last punch, even though she looks like she's dead. It's like watching eighteen years of being together, and it always makes me cry.

L S : What are you planning to do next?

P S : With Lois possibly a version of *Who's Afraid of Virginia Woolf,* and I'm going to write a new thirty-minute solo. Lois is doing work on aging and femmes, on radical femininity. She's saying you don't have to perform the way you look, don't have to fuck in a certain way. Getting locked in roles, we weren't satisfying some parts of ourselves. No one is ever butch enough. In a way, everything is up for grabs, but Lois and I are dreaming of the millennium, planning a retreat in Hawaii for a year. We're still imagining the future. I get more jealous of people who dream together than who sleep together.

La Gran Scena

May 1984

The men in La Gran Scena Opera company play women's roles, but, more significantly, the performers really can sing. The emphasis is on parody, not drag, and the camping doesn't compete with opera, rather highlights it, like a brush of mascara. In the opening number, "The Ride of the Valkyries," a bevy of divas sings on key, at times even soars, and we're carried along with the romanticism, until two of the women notice they've struck Nazi salutes, quickly pretend to examine their fingernails, then draw back their hands and pat their coifs. All the selections gel around this savvy clowning. In the *La Traviata* sequence, the soon-to-be-ex Violetta riffs through her keepsakes and comes upon a ratty pair of Alfredo's jockey shorts. Holding them to her face and stroking them tenderly, she's Garbo with Robert Taylor's hankie.

Regardless of the silliness, the arias are musical. Philip Koch, who sings baritone as a man, is a controlled mezzo—and quite a sexy one, too, especially in the Seguidilla from *Carmen,* waving creamy shoulders and flashing Juliet Prowse legs. The accompanying trio of "cigarette girls" suggest girl-group backup singers without sacrificing their opera aplomb.

Koch isn't just Carmen, however, he's Philene Wannelle, a character in an opera company playing Carmen. *La Gran Scena* is as much a satire of the behind-the-scenes world—the feuds, love affairs, personal tragedies, etc.—as it is of the productions. The evening's hostess, Miss Sylvia Bills (Bruce Hopkins), "America's most beloved retired diva and General Director of an opera company," augments the program notes with lubricious commentary and a whipped-cream-wouldn't-melt-in-my-mouth smile.

Tenor Luis Russinyol (his real name), formerly the protégé of Miss Bills herself, "has learned to perform anywhere, any time, for anyone, any role desired." Maestro Francesco Folonari-Soave-Coglioni (Ross Barentyne) has, in his day, provided guidance for the mercurial Russinyol, as has the company's star, Vera Galupe-Borszkh (Ira Siff).

It's Vera, the still-singing soprano, whose story Miss Bills is most compelled to annotate. Born in obscure Chernomorskoye but destined for divahood, Vera had to swim to her music lessons in Odessa each day across a seven-mile bay, thus developing her renowned breath control. After a time, "weary of singing Aida in languages with no vowels," she came to Western Europe and secured a canto in opera legend with her brave, though controversial, underwater *Tosca* at the Baths of Caracalla. Since then, her allure has been fortified by a prodigious weight loss, her "Sutherland trill," "Tebaldi hair," and adamant refusal to record commercially.

None of this would mean a thing were it not for Vera's voice, and a marvel it is. At times it's a *shrei* that can shatter Memorex, at others a pussycat meow, at still others a combination of the two: Galupe-Borszkh has, without doubt, the best Doppler effect in grand opera. Siff remains on key and in tempo throughout his performance. He's a comic gem, as is the entire show. My favorite line comes in Vera's curtain speech, read in a croaking, barely audible, nonspecific foreign accent: "Please you will have to forgive me because I give too much."

Hot Peaches: Peach Corps

June 1988

This show, an anthology of Hot Peaches' greatest hits, is part frat party, part survival sermon, part primer on self-mythologizing. Between numbers, we're given a chronology of where Peaches-founder Jimmy Camicia lived, what he did for a living, and how, against all odds, he kept wacky, tacky, gay street theater breathing—for the cause, for the hell of it. The skits—boho trash in the Hamptons, the woes of addiction to antiaddiction meetings—are open mike night at the baths. And although there are three women in the cast, the show represents male experience. The women do feminist shtick, but they sing about gay male sexuality, not their own.

Camicia pulls off the gamit anyway. There he is, Mr. Phineas T. Chutzpah, with his cheesy mustache and showgirl eye makeup, his tux jacket and flowered kimono, conjuring the days following Stonewall when pride first wrestled shame. Sweetly, beguilingly he boosts his cast, whether, as in the case of living "gay archive" Marsha P. Johnson, they're talented at ridiculousness, or, as in the case of blues singer Amy Coleman, they're ridiculously talented. The song lyrics aren't much sharper than the sketches, but some are winningly silly—"Until I found androgyny I was lonesome," sung to the tune of *Bei Mir Bis Du Shane*. A set by International Chrysis is spellbinding gender-fuck. The voice is male, unless you're Mercedes McCambridge, but the creamy shoulders and fluffy hips are female (or I don't know my elbow from my ass). The headset is *all* drag queen. "You don't rip a drag queen's dress, and you never touch the face," Chrysis says, explaining why the Stonewall queens fought the cops.

The crowd whooped for every number, easing into Camicia's nostalgia and sparked by his hopeful sense of history. But they tore down the house whenever Coleman sang. She is a revelation, from her glamorous red hair and elegant aquiline nose, to her wry comic timing, to her voice, which touches like Janis Joplin's but has more range and control. Many of the lyrics she sings are blunt or coy, but she's so musical and ingeniously improvisational, the words register like abstract sounds.

Sand Blast

July 1987

Drag performer Danny LaRue's London theater is lined with pictures of the star out of costume; he appears as a butch male with his wife and kids. For LaRue, the transformation from male to female is a wondrous illusion, requiring gobs of makeup, intricate costumes, and much binding and padding. Femininity is achieved, like Mount Everest, and the audience is reassured that men and women are nothing alike.

Working in another tradition, Charles Pierce advertises his homosexuality by identifying with the divas he impersonates—Crawford, Davis, Garland, etc. He dresses up like them, but he doesn't like them. They represent his sissy, damaged self, for even if his subjects have strength, he plays up their egotism, loneliness, and self-abuse. This kind of drag is about slumming in femininity, a place like Lower East Bitch. And it's a day trip. Pierce's actual maleness, like Danny LaRue's, is never in doubt, and everyone is invited to share in the idea that femaleness is a bog.

Charles Busch is part of a third tradition, which includes Bloolips, Charles Ludlam, and La Gran Scena Opera. Busch likes to play feisty feminists, and his portrayals are affectionate. He not only enjoys the femme part of himself, he sees it as admirable: theatrical, emotionally expressive, and seductive. Unlike LaRue and Pierce, Busch's drag doesn't disguise that he's a man. His costumes, usually consisting of a wig, eye shadow, and a skimpy tog, don't soften his gawky boy's body, and he doesn't pad his chest—on occasion he even bares it. In Busch's art, to go from boy to girl or girl to boy is not an arduous climb or a decadent fall but a pass through a door inside the self.

Psycho Beach Party, starring Busch and his superb Theatre-in-Limbo company, is his funniest and wisest play so far. A spoof of early sixties surfing movies, it dismantles the *mishegas* of the age, while letting us enjoy our nostalgia for it. Remember *Gidget*? (Don't lie.) Busch plays Chicklet, a skinny girl who wants to surf. Best friend Berdine (Becky London) keeps her informed about existentialism—"Schopenhauer, Nietzsche, and dear, dear Jean-Paul." And sometime friend Marvel Ann (Michael Belanger), whose every bleached follicle and curvaceous falsie home toward marriageable flesh, makes Chicklet's head spin with awe and horror.

But that's not all that's whirring in the child's brain. Beneath the surface of this innocent creature and seemingly simple epoch lurk psychosexual beasts that can devour Cleveland. Chicklet's mom (Meghan Robinson) starts off talking like Donna Reed but soon reveals herself a full-clawed Faye Dunaway–as–Joan Crawford. Of course her kid's personality is shattered. And from the depths of Chicklet rises alter ego Ann Boman, dominatrix/empress of the world. Without giving all the delicious details away, suffice it to say she wreaks havoc on the denizens of Malibu, including the budding gays, Yo-Yo (Robert Carey) and Provoloney (Andy Halliday), and Bettina Barnes (Theresa Marlowe), a Marilyn Monroe-type iron butterfly, on the lam from her studio and heading for Lee Strasberg. At the end, Star Cat (Arnie Kolodner), a psychiatrist-in-training-turned-beach-bum, conducts a wham-bam five-minute psychoanalysis, and the parts of Chicklet are reunited.

Every aspect of the production, under Kenneth Elliott's direction, adds to its quick-wittedness. B. T. Whitehill's backdrop is at once a surfer girl and a Rorschach blot, suggesting a vagina flanked by two penises. (At least that's what I saw.) Costume designer John Glaser's bubble dresses and bouffant hairdos seem inflated with sexual hysteria, and choreographer Jeff Beazey's limbo number captures the klutziness of beer-guzzling white kids going Caribbean. None of the performers mugs or breaks character; all mesh within the controlling atmosphere of Busch's self-knowing persona.

This is a boy whose mother found him dressing in her clothes and said, "Darling, what a great Lucy. I'll be Ethel." Busch's art has passed through anxiety. He can say anything, imagine anything, and not despise himself for it. This unembittered acceptance is the key to his radicalism, allowing him to venture into his fantasies without minimizing their scariness.

He does miss a chance to stir our psyches, though, by not casting women as studs. Granted, to generate excitement, Western women can't just put on men's clothes, because, decades ago, they appropriated them for daily wear. Women have to wear facial hair, chest hair, and a stuffed jock—as Lily Tomlin does playing Tommy Velour. The sight of Tomlin smarmily ogling women and hitching up her pants is indeed exciting.

Still, so long as maleness is deemed superior to femaleness, the notion of a woman wishing to be a man will never seem as perverse as a man wishing to be a woman. There's evidence that men like to play with this fantasy in the fad of males wearing earrings, but the terror is defused by the macho act of piercing. Busch doesn't defuse it. He lets go of the masculine without fear of castration and takes pleasure in acts considered degrading and wimpy. "I like being girlish, womanly, and vixenish," his persona says. Who doesn't sometimes? His persona symbolizes the forbidden leap for everybody, whether it's a man wanting his female lover to stage all the parts of a sexual scene, or that woman enjoying taking control, or a butch lesbian vamping in high heels and a dress.

Funny Girls: An Interview

June 1988

"Why are so many lesbians doing comedy?" asked the editors of this gay rights issue. I said I'd find out, and invited stand-ups and comedy performers to a panel. All were free to use pseudonyms. Lisa Kron, Peggy Shaw, Sara Cytron, and Lois Weaver chose their real names. For professional reasons, one panelist chose to call herself Kay.

All the women are actors. Three do stand-up and solo performance, and many of their venues overlap. Kay isn't out in mainstream comedy clubs, but she and the others are out in downtown clubs and performance spaces like WOW, Dixon Place, and Café Bustelo. Increasingly, lesbian performers are capturing wider audiences in uptown theaters like Interart and crossover clubs like the Wah Wah Hut. The West Bank Café, a cabaret space on Theater Row, has just booked Cytron.

STONE: Why are lesbians in comedy?

KAY: It's fast.

KRON: Stand-up is something you can do on your own.

WEAVER: For me, comedy means breaking into new territory. In 1975, when I started, there wasn't much comedy in the women's movement. The dirty joke was a male prerogative.

STONE: Let's talk about the freedom comedy gives you to play with stereotypes.

WEAVER: I like being up there in lipstick and blond hair and high heels and a big badge that says, "Dyke." I want to sexualize lesbians, say, "We love women, we love to have sex." I love looking like something that's no one's idea of a lesbian.

KAY: Women are at the head of the laughs in my sets. This is real unusual in clubs. And I do a lot of stuff that's been the province of men. I flirt with women in the audience. I'm confrontational. I do a lot of physical stuff. I do dick jokes.

STONE: Are people becoming more receptive to lesbian material?

WEAVER: Yes and no. People are always looking for a line to cross, and lesbianism is one of the last lines.

KRON: The sexuality is a big hook. But just because straight people come, and just because they enjoy it, doesn't mean they get it. That we were all women didn't seem to penetrate.

SHAW: It's much easier for men to do drag. For a woman to be in male drag and claim that power, it's not funny. For boys to be girls is hysterical.

KRON: We come up against a lot of lesbianphobia—it's not homophobia, it's lesbianphobia.

STONE: Could you describe it?

KRON: We're angry and sick. We're cantankerous. We're just refusing to cooperate. There's an absolute horror that you can see when audiences get something they're not expecting, the outrage that is suddenly there, that you dare to bring this material to them. But it's not always anger. Sometimes they laugh *at* you. I remember one time we were doing *Cinderella*, and the show had gotten very popular, and all of a sudden there was a real outside audience with a lot of men. They were laughing at different things, or not laughing. Suddenly we felt like geeks on display.

SHAW: You take a big risk every time you go out there. But I think stand-up is the most terrifying thing, because you stand there and ask for acceptance, and when you ask that from the place of being an unacceptable person in the society, I just think that is terrifying.

KAY: Most of the trouble I've had as a lesbian in comedy is from club owners—me thinking they don't want me because they heard I was a lesbian. When I'm on stage and I feel the audience isn't with me, my insecurity is more tied up in sexuality, in the choice of sexuality, than in anything else. Hey, it's the way we all are, by the way.

WEAVER: This is what we're working on in our new piece—that theater is sex in the sense we're talking about. Performance is sex in that it comes from that place of desire, that real, deep-rooted desire to express yourself and to feel intimacy. Sometimes you make connection. You surprise audiences by creating a character that's a little ambiguous. People get to see they've been responding to a gay character. They like that person. They're surprised by their lack of prejudice.

SHAW: We performed at the University of Michigan, and there was a protest afterwards that men were in the audience. We defended the men's right: They paid. They stayed for a discussion. And the women on the panel were attacking them—my audience, who I had just worked with an hour and a half. Who I felt very close to. The guys were going, "Well, ya know, even though they're lesbians, I felt something. I felt lonely, I felt like, well, you know, my life has a little bit of this going on." And here was the greatest compliment: I was walking down the street and this jock comes running by in his sweatpants and slows down and says, "Good show."

KAY: I have that shit, too. I can't stand it in myself that once a bully says one little sensitive thing, I have the impulse to say, "Oh my God, I'll have your baby."

SHAW: Let me tell you why I said that. It's because you feel so much more successful in having been able to sway someone who was really hard to move.

CYTRON: I feel it's wonderful that there are people who would take on that responsibility, but for me, I refuse.

KAY: But you *are* taking it on, because you're performing in a public place, whether or not it's a mostly lesbian audience. You're saying, "I'm gay." And you get written up in the papers, and you show you don't care that people know. Anytime you show yourself as a real person, you force people to compare you to what's in their minds.

KRON: I'm out, but I've really had to weigh it. I've had to ask myself, what can you get out of it in terms of financial security, constant work, media acceptance, what are my venues?

CYTRON: I've made a choice to work only in places where I've been billed as a lesbian. I feel I'm whole. When I was doing straight clubs, there was such a feeling of being with another species. I think what we've been saying is that sexuality and self-esteem go together. You want the intimacy, and you feel it while it's happening. And if you feel the fear, the uncomfortableness, no matter how skilled you are at performing, you're not going to be as good as if the wave were there and you were riding it. There's a glorious, ecstatic feeling in being seen, in being out there, especially after so many years of hiding. This is me, come and take it.

KAY: I want to be accepted to the max. It's exciting forcing the issue, pushing against people's fears. I love having people know I'm a lesbian. I love walking down the street with my girlfriend, her arm around me. I love how we look. These are two fucking hot women.

CYTRON: I think so much of comedy is being able to take what was painful for you about being an outsider and turn it on its head, so it becomes the thing that gives you success.

KRON: Friends told me not to do out work. They said, "You'll limit yourself." Now they see that I'm getting all this media attention, and maybe even *because* I'm a lesbian.

Funny Gay Males: Gay in Every Way

May 1989

Danny McWilliams has tender eyes, the eyes of a boy bent on rescuing stray cats. His elastic clown's mouth is a ventriloquist's dummy that can't stop camping. At Catholic school, he had to choose a saint, so he picked Eva Marie. He goes to acting class; it turns out the teacher is "the Coronet mother." Bemoaning beached medical waste, he wonders why Bloomingdale's garbage never makes it to the shore.

McWilliams, thirty-three, is the lead act of Funny Gay Males, a stand-up trio including Bob Smith, thirty, and Jaffe Cohen, thirty-five. I caught them at the Duplex. The three work in different styles. For the most part, McWilliams does female characters—his drag a mere kerchief or pair of glasses—the high point of which is a version of *The Wizard of Oz* with Bette Davis as Dorothy: "To*to,* I'm afraid we're not in *Kaan*sas any*mooore.*"

Bob Smith, who is tall and buttoned-down, delivers in a deadpan calculated to raise anxiety: Does he know he's on stage and not in a Sears ad? Polite unemotionalism spars with bluntness in his persona. Smith's pet is half pit bull and half poodle: "Not a good attack dog but a vicious gossip." His suburban parents set strict limits; "If you were hounded by the Nazis, they wouldn't hide you, but they would offer to water your plants." Coming out to such people required delicacy, timing. "Mom," Smith said at Thanksgiving dinner, "could you please pass the gravy to the homosexual?"

Third up, Jaffe Cohen—a little guy with glasses and one turquoise earring—wanders a landscape mined with complaints. He sees Jesus as half God and half Jewish: "His father said, 'Walk on water'; his mother said, 'Don't track it in the house.' " Cohen's Aunt Miriam has just returned from a trip around the world: "She didn't care for it." True to family form, objections flare from Cohen as well, but they take a political form. "AIDS is a virus," he specifies, "*Bush* is a punishment from God."

Most of the gay men in stand-up are in the closet, which isn't surprising in a world where gay-bashing is standard material and MCs have been known to wipe off the mikes of men they know are gay. A few comics are out on stage, but Funny Gay Males is the only collective enterprise of its kind. One recent afternoon, I had drinks with the trio and learned how each came to comedy.

Cohen, who has been doing comedy for three years, was writing plays. "I kept reworking this one about a man trying to break away from his mother, but I didn't know how it ended, because I never broke away from my mother," he says in his half-clowning/half-sincere manner. "I grew up in a tough neighborhood, and getting people to laugh let me be a mascot instead of a punching bag."

Similarly, McWilliams used comedy to deflect the terrors of "an all-male jock Catholic high school," and he ventured into clubs when he was twenty-three. "I'd play Comedy U. and kill straight crowds. I was camping like crazy, but because I didn't do out material, I pretended to myself they didn't know I was gay. Sure." Smith, at eighteen, started working a comedy club in Buffalo, where he grew up, after his English teacher told him he could write satire. "I wasn't out, but I'm proud to say I never did girlfriend jokes." He went to college and stopped performing for a while. "AIDS inspired me to go back. I figured I better do what I want with my life."

The three were brought together by Sara Cytron. "We're all part of a writers' group that tries out new material," Cohen explains. "Sara is so bold about who she is on stage. She's given us courage." Smith adds, "Working as a trio has made us tougher. First of all, audiences know what they're getting, so it's not as scary to be out." The group gets booked mainly in New York clubs as well as at colleges and gay events, but they want a larger audience. "I hate hearing jokes that put down gays," says McWilliams, "and actually audiences are hissing at that stuff more, but there's something exhilarating about winning over a hostile crowd. You see them recoiling, and then you get them to laugh, and they're amazed." Smith comes back, "Yeah, but there's still a lot we don't do. We present ourselves as gay sons in families, but we're also adults with adult relationships. Putting sex in routines is another level of coming out. Of course, I've only just become involved with someone, so I'm in a position to push it."

An influential talent manager recently told Smith he could advance his career by dropping the gay material. He wasn't tempted. The others hold the same view. "There's no going back," says McWilliams, who earns his living by doing word processing. Cohen teaches English and speech at Manhattan Community College, and Smith waits tables at the Metropolitan Museum's staff dining room. Comedy earns them each an average of $3,000 a year, but they think it's only a matter of time before out gays get to mount pieces like *The Kathy and Mo Show* and sit across from Dave. In the meantime, they make comedy where they can. Smith served lunch to David Hockney recently, and as his contribution to the Met's employee art show, he glued Hockney's half-finished Heineken and an ashtrayful of butts to a pedestal, encased the mess under plexiglass, and augustly entitled it "Celebrity Leftovers."

Bloolips: Get Hur

February 1991

Camp is dead, thanks to Madonna. She has opened all the closets, turning deviance into a theme park. But if gender-tripping can't be subversive anymore, what's a drag company to do? If you are Bloolips, the veteran British comedy troupe, you wave good-bye to shock and stick to schlock. In these days of postmodern anxiety about indulging cheap tastes, Bloolips may be daring in just having fun.

The group's new show, *Get Hur* (at Theatre for the New City), is set in Roman Egypt during the reign of Hadrian. The plot, inasmuch as there is one, investigates the murder of the emperor's favorite, the lovely Antinous. Some creaky vaudeville bits are easily forgiven amid the inspired clowning and trash-compactor ingenuity. In the production number "Cleaners of Caesar's," palace gofers achieve an Egyptian look by sporting T-shirts and boxer shorts on their heads. Home from battle, Hadrian strips off his clanking armor (fashioned from industrial-sized soup cans) and bitches, "I hate war. So many accessories."

What shines through is less a romance with artifice than authentic stagecraft, especially in the performance, as Hadrian, of Bloolips' founder, Bette Bourne. As a man gotten up as a woman playing a gay man, he does a Tallulah (naturally), but inserts elegiac notes whose sincerity is piercing. Theater training grounds all the jesters, so the illusion of artlessness comes off without strain.

Pomo Afro Homos: Getting Under Our Skin

July 1993

Djola Branner becomes his mother. "Hand Mommy that black bra, would you. Is my strap showing? Tuck it in for me, baby. How do I look? Come on and dance with Mama." As himself, Branner muses, "Don't all little boys zip their mommy up? Fold their mommy's panties? Hand them a towel as they step out of the tub?"

Hello, Oedipus. Hello, Mom as big as the Ritz. A gay man and his sexual, self-dramatizing mother. But the monologue "Sweet Sadie" is no reductive case study. Branner is one-third of Pomo Afro Homos, the theater troupe that walks a tightrope above groupthink.

Branner's mother is forty-two when her surprise baby arrives, and she proves neglectful, barely notices the boy if he's not admiring, fetching. Now, in her seventies, she has Alzheimer's. Branner is angry at her narcissism, nostalgic for her church-lady piety and musky allure, proud of his transformation from fat kid to willowy dancer. What makes the story tender and tough is his willingness to open rooms locked in childhood, and this courage lends his performance its quiet authority.

All the pieces in *Dark Fruit*—arriving at Serious Fun! on Friday—and in the group's first collaboration, *Fierce Love,* flash secrets and codes. What could be more motivating than delivering news? What could be more titillating to hear? The company also includes Brian Freeman and Eric Gupton, who is presently on leave; Marvin White is appearing in New York.

Freeman, on the phone from the company's base, San Francisco, describes Pomo's birth in 1991. "We got tired of not seeing images of ourselves, except as absurdities, like the characters Antoine and Blaine on *In Living Color.*" For eight years, Freeman was a member of the San Francisco Mime Troupe. "It was hell at first. I got hired for being black and fired for being gay. They were Marxist and macho—'He can write, he can direct, he can act, but uh-oh, he's that way.' I said. 'Get a clue.' "

Freeman later joined Black Gay Men United. "There were about twenty of us. We did consciousness raising and raised money for Jesse Jackson. We wanted to build community, claim a space that was not a bar. We learned that we have our own humor with each other, and this synthesis was crucial to Pomo."

In another conversation, Branner laughs ruefully. "We think if we move out of the African-American community we'll experience less homophobia. And maybe we do, but in the gay world we get more racism. And not just from whites. A lot of black gays choose only white lovers. Black and white coupling has different weight for each group. Blacks are inundated by white culture. There's nothing we haven't read, seen, eaten, inhaled. With whites, blacks are in the risky position of being fetish objects."

The group's freedom to uncloset everything they know about race and sex makes them thrilling—that plus stopwatch timing, scalpel writing, and staging with shoestring ingenuity. Their black gay men are a world, hailing from diverse classes, a collection of types but with such rich interiors and pointed idioms they remain slippery, unpredictable.

Peaches, Popcorn, and Pepper are a trio of self-proclaimed PBUs— "poor, black and ugly" queens—who are tired of being "everybody's best girlfriend and nobody's dream date." The son of "an Adam Clayton Powell, Jr., wannabe" and "a Diahann Carroll wannabe" wins a scholarship to a Latin prep school but fears that his thralldom to Johnny Mathis and blossoming gayness will be viewed by the family as a social defeat. A married man sleeps with guys but denies he is gay and calls what he does "taking care of business."

In this theater, sincerity and wildness embrace. Whenever power is unequal, the Pomos show, the meaning of tripping into otherness varies: When a man dons female drag, or a white blackface, or a straight a gay persona, this may be a form of going native, but when blacks and gays pass or when blacks take white lovers, these may be acts of disloyalty and self-denial. And yet, who does not want to play dress-up, the Pomos insist and demonstrate, as they do comical race drag and play women as well as straights.

The Pomos show you can be swish one minute and militant the next, that you can alternate raucous hip-hop with the wrenching story of an AIDS funeral in which parents deny their son's gayness. Experience doesn't segregate moods, they illustrate, but rather seesaws between hilarity, melancholy, and rage. Rooted in the specifics of their lives—the way existence smells, tastes, and feels to them—their work speaks about the liquidness of identity and the artificiality of categories like gay and straight, butch and femme, passive and aggressive. On their stage, swishing by itself can be radical—a riposte to boot-camp masculinity.

You may not catch every reference (I didn't), but the Pomos make sizzling conversation. If they represent a model of anything, it is disinhibition.

Julian Clary: Seriously Silly

May 1991

Julian Clary is partial to dog collars, glitter lips, and costumes that could be parade floats. During his show—a concoction of musical numbers, anecdotes, and improvised banter, running at the Ballroom—he wears a black jumpsuit that, in places, consists of little more than rubber bands and reveals much of his slender, gawky, hairy-legged, six-foot-two-inch body. The shoulders on another getup soar like skyscrapers. When Clary calls a man on stage and briskly inquires whether, owing to his white pants and white T-shirt, the fellow works in a hospital, the critique doesn't seem savage coming from a man dressed as the Chrysler Building.

Clary, who is English and is making his American debut, has a large following in Britain. He used to perform in clubs with his dog Fanny, and the pair was billed as the Joan Collins Fan Club, until Collins's lawyers threatened a suit—which seems not only churlish but self-defeating, since she'd be lucky to look as good as Clary does.

He recently filled London's Aldwych Theatre for six weeks, and his game-show spoof *Sticky Moments* has toted up high ratings on Channel 4. Like the British troupe Bloolips, Clary's drag isn't about impersonating women; his made-up face is beautiful, but his maleness is always evident. His campy rejoinders, which he calls "smutty innuendo," hearken back to music hall shtick. He can lubricate questions as seemingly innocuous as, "What do you do with yourself?" At the Aldwych, he asked a man in the audience, "What's your name?" And when the fellow answered, "Neil," Clary cracked, "That won't be necessary."

He teases his piano player, Russell Churney—described as "the only heterosexual in show business"—by asking: "Have you ever found yourself waiting for the bus and seen some young slip of a boy and thought, 'I don't mind if I do'?" Counters Churney, "No, I haven't." Clary plays a version of *Sticky Moments* with members of the audience, who are asked to complete sentences. "Never judge a man by his . . . " says Clary. "Pockets," answers a woman with inscrutable flakiness. "I'm afraid not," Clary returns. "Testicles."

He retrieves bawdy relics—"I used to kiss him on the lips, but now it's all over"—paying homage to a time when sex practices were more closeted than they are now. But Clary's strength derives from being relaxed in his deviance; an originality rises from this solid source. He has no trace of self-pity turned to waspish spite. He likes what he is, celebrating the "strange and unnatural" wherever they reside. In his persona, effeminacy isn't linked to passivity or victimization. He is quietly authoritative, exerting, in his way, total control.

Some of his funniest work doesn't translate on the page, because it erupts from his delivery and timing. His voice is mellifluous, slow, unruffled; he's a tour guide who, with a ceaseless wave of words, incorporates (and drowns out) ambient hostility. Quickly, the audience is in his hands, willing to surrender to his pace and sense of fun. He tests, not only with creaky double entendres but with repetition that teases like foreplay.

In "Leader of the Pack," traditionally sung by a teenage girl, Clary is at his cheekiest; it's a piece of Pythonesque satire, by way of Fielding and Swift. Clary's accompanist inquires, "Is he picking you up after school?" and Clary returns, "No, I don't go to school anymore, Russell. I'm thirty-one." The leader's passing is painstakingly dissected: "He *was* the leader, but now he's gone. I don't know how else to put it to you. Sorry to be brutal. He was killed in that terrible accident with the lorry. There was *no* way he could have survived. The lorry was huge. I did manage to salvage a bit from a mud guard. Made an earring."

Composing himself, he delivers the report he's withheld. "What it means now is that *I'm* the leader. It was completely unexpected. I don't even have a motorcycle. I have got a Sierra Estate, and now all the boys can fit in the back."

Clary and I had lunch last week. Off stage, he isn't theatrical. He wears a black baseball cap and a bottle-nosed dolphin T-shirt. But he's just as spontaneous and droll, and his voice lopes musically. I mention the humor generated by his even, unflappable style, and he offers, "I am naturally slow. I walk slowly. I run the bath slowly." Flamboyance is reserved for performing—for dream time, the night.

Clary's father was a policeman, his mother a probation officer, professions he admits sound forbidding, although they were politically left-wing and personally accepting. "I always knew I was effeminate and homosexual. My father may have cared, me being his only son. He used to try and get me interested in cars, but there wasn't any open disapproval. There was never a time when I needed to say, 'I've got something to tell you.'" At school, some kids did bully him, but they weren't successful at making him hate himself. He agrees that his stage persona, where he gets to command, is in some measure a triumph over that abuse.

This year, he'll tour and develop a TV show with his writing partner, Paul Merton, about a straight, Cockney man sharing a flat with an out gay man who wears lipstick and eyeshadow. "I'll play the homosexual," says

Clary. But while British society cheers his humor, it's cracking down on gay rights. He describes Section 25, new legislation that, if passed, would make it a crime for individuals to allow two men to have sex in their homes. "It's particularly horrible, since it's linked to laws against rape and child abuse, and it plants the seed in the public's mind that victimless acts are equivalent to sex offenses. No one's yet been tried under Clause 28, but right now, if I do my act in a government-funded venue, I could be accused of promoting homosexuality. Of course, that's what I hope my work does."

Five Lesbian Brothers: Out of Their Minds

June 1993

We're in a Chinese restaurant on the Upper West Side, me and the Five Lesbian Brothers. *Brothers* is what they call themselves, even off stage. Dom and Mo have written a play called *Oh Darn!*, and in it Walt Whitman greets the heroine, Manhola, with: "Hello, strapping lad!" She says: "Well, I'm not a boy, actually, I'm a lesbian." Walt: "Oh, my mistake." Manhola: "Happens all the time." Lesbian Brothers is an homage to that confusion. To Peggy Healey, Lisa Kron, Babs Davy, Dominique Dibbell, and Maureen Angelos, confusion is a sandbox. Not that they look like guys. That would be less confusing.

These are crackling minds, no groupthink; the five having joined the collaboration with successful solo careers that they are continuing. But some kind of chemistry makes the team—their average age is thirty-two—larger than the sum of its parts, a fact they recognize with tipsy glee. They delight in outsider status, which they use as a watchtower, not a ghetto or exclusive club. They turn each other on and give each other courage to push lesbian theater beyond dramas of self-definition: the typical, WOW-produced sermons and therapy-sessions-got-up-as-fairy-tales on which they cut their teeth (vaginal, of course).

The Brothers toss together moods and styles, echoing the brothers Marx and Oscar Wilde. One minute they favor lewd, dizzy puns—a girls' school is called Pussenheimer Academy, a neighborly exchange of baked goods takes the form of "hair pie." The next minute mordant summaries trot froth—a "necklace of tears" is offered to an incipient lesbian with the instruction: "Add a tear every time a crushing disappointment comes your way." The Brothers acknowledge debts to Split Britches for their commando musical interludes, to Ethyl Eichelberger for his classical pastiches, and to Holly Hughes for her lyrical profanity. But in the team's full-length play *Brave Smiles* (playing at the New York Theater Workshop) they let loose a voice of their own, leaving rage and reassurance in the wings and achieving a nakedness at once exuberant and poignant.

Brave Smiles balances farce and melancholy, remixing tragic-lesbian types, with figures metamorphosing, Orlando-style, over seventy years. The cartoons are tweaked but also caressed for at least existing. *Voyage to Lesbos,* set in the fifties, chronicles lesbians Bonnie and Connie as they bash against marriage and a shrink's "cure." In one scene, the women masturbate side by side—Connie with a chair, Bonnie with a vacuum cleaner—and although Bonnie is wild for Connie, she cries out, "Fuck me. I want your dick." The sequence is funny and complex, revealing the dependency of lesbians, especially in the past, on het language. And the scene admits, too, that human beings are playthings of their imaginations, that stray longings and memories are too renegade to stay put, that the erotic house within contains many rooms, some of which may even include a taste for male flesh.

It is this freewheeling search, this psychological savvy, that distinguishes the group. These performers nail not only homophobic views of lesbians but fantasies lesbians harbor about themselves—a probe accomplished with particular cunning in a solo piece of Dom's, "Travels with Pecan." The speaker is a lesbian, but the story isn't about her exploits with women. She evokes a childhood memory of sending a dim-witted, shabby-looking pet dog to a premature death in the pound. Then she wonders if the estrangement she feels on account of her sexuality has made her heartless, unable to empathize with other beings. We know it has not, because she so touchingly faces the question, and because, it's made clear, her identification with the dog is what has stoked her cruelty.

Nibbling broccoli and tofu, the Brothers trace their meld of theatricality and sex, recalling how the public drama of coming out became, quite literally, a move across the footlights onto the stage. They rib each other, girls on the team bus. They camp and flirt—Lisa and Peggy are in fact a couple. They riff off one another's words, building rather than deflating, and there it is: collaboration in the flesh.

LISA: I studied acting at Kalamazoo College, and I was told, "We can't cast you in this role, because you aren't sexy." They meant, "You can't convey *heterosexuality*."

PEGGY: I assumed I was butch, because I didn't think I could be sexy. I knew in my head I was a lesbian from the time I was young. When Holly Hughes came along, she turned it around—she talked about cunts and pussies instead of blossoming orchids.

BABS: I didn't know I was a lesbian until I went to WOW. It was all jumbled together, the excitement of the women and doing theater. I ran lights for a show, and then got cast in a part. Finally, I could talk about things I'd swallowed my whole life.

PEGGY: Weren't you in a plastic bubble for a while?

MO: When I stumbled onto WOW, it was a little coming-out factory.

DOM: At Yale, the roles didn't appeal to me. Performance art was what did it, the emotionalism and uninhibitedness, and that you could write your own stuff.

MO: We got together in 1989. We already knew how to work with each other—where the stupid jokes should go. And there was so much sexual energy in the air, hot dreams and crushes.

BABS: We wrote *Voyage to Lesbos* at Peggy's parents' house. There were lots of rules.

LISA: When you woke up, before you even peed, you had to write for ten minutes. We had five notebooks, and each day we'd pass them around, and the next person would make comments on what had been written before.

MO: Boundaries were flying. The stuff we were writing was so personal, and it was scary, putting out your feelings like that. Each person was responsible for a character, and they were partly autobiographical. Everyone got paranoid. Who liked who better? Who was smarter? We were learning to trust each other.

DOM: By the time we wrote *Brave Smiles*, we could focus more on the work, less on ourselves under the microscope. We could be more critical of each other's ideas. We made lists of what we wanted to see in a play: a wedding, a funeral, uniforms, a girls' school, a fifties bar scene.

BABS: It's hard to keep coming up with five equally powerful parts for women, but so far we haven't played men. Male characters tend to take over, even when they are women in drag.

MO: When we started, we assumed everyone in our audience was lesbian, and they probably were. It was warm and fuzzy, but it can get easy, and we've become more demanding. Gay theater is getting big and sprawling. Five years ago, I knew all the gay performers. It felt like a community. Now I can't keep up. Like it's the thing to do, a career option.

PEGGY: Lesbianism is more threatening to the mainstream than gay men, because it shows women without men. Men without women isn't as big a deal—women are the ones missing, and they aren't as important.

BABS: We want to quit our day jobs and have an Off-Broadway run. Is that asking too much?

DOM: Our goal is to be commercially viable yet enchantingly homosexual.

Lesbian Bathhouse: Soaking It In

February 1995

A dominatrix sits on a stool flicking her whip, as "Love to Love You Baby" plays on the soundtrack. An innocent young woman walks by the cell door and the mistress directs her to enter. In a twinkling, the virgin is splayed over the mistress's lap, called a slut, and told to beg for forgiveness. The virgin apologizes for being bad but receives a smack, then another. But soon the mistress looks disappointed. She sighs. "I'm not getting enough from you. I never feel like I can count on you. I need to know where this relationship is going!" The virgin bleats, "I don't even know your name."

This is the essence of *Lesbian Bathhouse*, Helen Eisenbach's dry satire of moist emotionalism, concocted as a swift cabaret of sexy sketches. Devised on a shoestring, the piece is bracing and unapologetic—a mirror that catches every bulge.

When film director Rod—an off stage voice portrayed by Harry Shearer with campy lasciviousness—undergoes a sex change, he decides, as is the current chic among male-to-female trekkers, that he is really a lesbian. To pump his erotic education, he hires actresses to stage scenes from his pulp-fiction imagination. Out trot the handyman and the harried housewife, the hostage and the kidnapper, the ruler-wielding instructor, and the teacher's pet—with tools, boots, and tight bodices figuring prominently. Rubbing against the onstage porn is a backstage soap, involving lovelorn Grace, her stalker Renee, and the woman for whom Grace lusts, her ex-lover Caroline.

Rod wants the spirit of Genet—women with hard bodies and no hard feelings—while the realities of lesbian mating keep dousing the stage with messy emotions. Perplexed by her motivation as a horny forest ranger, one actress complains to Rod, "I just don't think a woman would order another woman to suck her dick." Turning to the other actress in the scene, she asks, "Would you?" only to receive the reply, "Depends on the woman." Lesbians are Eisenbach's subjects, but her satire grows yeasty on the disparity in all human hearts between the pleasures of stripping and the stickiness of being naked.

This is a first play by Eisenbach, thirty-six, author of the novel *Loon Glow,* and previously the executive editor of the weekly gay magazine *QW.* "Everything I write is about longing, improbably fulfilled desire, and every possible sexual permutation," she says over cappuccino. Eisenbach describes her piece as "a horny tribute to the perverse ways that women relate when sex is added to the mix. They go nuts in that grabby way. Women are trained to feel insecure about their worth and desirability, so when they are opened up in sex, they become excessively vulnerable. Love is the one area where women are free to be pathologically aggressive, so they are terrorists. If they could apply that energy to their work lives, they'd be unstoppable.

"Everyone has rules about who they're supposed to be, but what interests me is the unexpected common ground between people who are presumed to hate each other. In my novel, a woman is dumped by her female lover and becomes friends with a man who is also in love with this woman. Eventually the dumped woman and the man have an affair."

Eisenbach jabs her devil's tail at straightness—at the impulse to flatten contours—wherever it reigns. "When you've been a professional homosexual for many years, you can spend a lot of time talking about how much you hate gay people," she jokes. "It's considered suspect in some lesbian circles to hang around with men. One of my closest friends is this big slab of a straight man. I feel in tune with the way men can have sex and not immediately turn it into romance. I identify as a gay man," she says, curling her mouth and flicking hair off her cheek, "as a . . . oh God, my mother is going to read this . . . a pussy-munching gay man."

Outwit: A Week in the Life of Gay Comedy

July 1994

MC-ing a lineup of gay comedians at Town Hall, Sandra Bernhard raises a fist for aggression, bless her heart. A *Post* writer has dissed her aim to act in *Grease*, sniping, "Can a 36-year-old lesbian play Rizzo?" Shoots back Bernhard, "There's one in the role now." A couple of lug stagehands fear they'll sprout tails if they smile, and Bernhard needles them. And she cheers for the lesbian mom who won the first round of her custody suit—with one demur, "I wanted to give her a new haircut." As the subject of lesbian fashion floods her engines, her teasing turns to preening.

She has slinked out tousle-haired, sleek, and angled, but looking fabulous doesn't neutralize her acid. She huffs, "Can lesbians chill and get into a whole fashion moment?" She whines about having been outed, ordering the audience to visualize her licking dick: "I've sucked cocks, fucked men, and you're just going to have to digest that." Well, okay, but then she forbids us to turn her into an icon. "When you see me on the street, don't stare." Should we cover our eyes? And excuse me, but aren't divas the only species known to insert images of themselves into people's heads and to speak of themselves as icons? Bernhard preaches against gay separatism, chortling at the end of this and other rants, as if she were satirizing windbags. Nobody buys it.

Nobody has to. There are enough queer comedians for open hostility within the ranks! What a relief! Karen Williams appears last—the only black comic booked. She alone has the brass to call Bernhard a bitch for lashing lesbians with her designer clothes, and she snaps at Bernhard's sexual ambivalence with the authority of twenty years out of the closet. She looks hot in a clinging white suit and plays an endearing Candide, assuming that the pendants sported by young dykes are pacifiers instead of butt plugs.

No one on the bill exudes Bernhard's panache—how many terrorist strippers come along in a generation?—but the show is a menu of the next wave. Five minutes ago, only a handful of pioneers were out on stage, and already much of that work—comedy of the closet and of translation to straights—is finished. All ten performers are confident, skilled, and boosted by the responsive crowd. Their gayness is a given. It's still a subject, sure, but, increasingly, gayness emerges as a critical sensibility.

Suzy Berger plays a nice Jewish dyke: "My parents always said, 'No man will be good enough,' and for once I listened." On her answering machine is the message, "You've reached the home of Suzy Berger and Jodie Foster." Intent stare. "It could happen." Canadian Elvira Kurt is Jewish, too, but edgier, her nose trained on damage. Hers is comedy of disappointment—rueful and irresolvable. Slim-hipped, wiry, and butch, she is perceived by her parents as a sick joke. "Look at it from their perspective," she commiserates. "Two immigrants from war-torn countries come to Canada to make a good life. They give their daughter everything, and this is what they get." Satisfied grin.

Frank Maya isn't new to the monologue, but he's sharpened his stand-up, weighing in on the housing crunch: "New York really fucks you up. I was watching *The Diary of Anne Frank*, and I thought, what a great apartment . . . the skylight, the bookcase you can walk through." Maya prowls the stage looking studly. In general, the men in the show are easier flaunting their sexiness and are more graphic about bed tricks. Mark Davis, who has toured his solo *Faggot with a Gun*, counterpoints his explosive, dangerous air with the realities of solitude. Single too long, he's resorted to "a vibrating butt plug and the Clapper." Most ingenious, Scott Capurro transforms his index fingers into lovers joined at the hip, producing, with these minimal means, a sardonic send-up of smug couples and Punch-and-Judy porn.

■ ■ ■

While Bernhard sashays as a poster child for lesbian chic, Lea DeLaria pumps rowdy exuberance into the diesel dyke. With her big suits, slicked bob, and cannon mouth, she is the homophobe's worst nightmare of queerness run amok. Go figure, she's also the queer du jour, having appeared on *Arsenio* several times. Unlike Bernhard, who is confrontational and disruptive—an outlaw on medium cool—DeLaria is tube friendly. Embracing and demystifying, she encourages everyone to get laid.

She's less effective live at Irving Plaza. Maybe the problem is her show, which hasn't developed much from the version she was presenting several years ago. Though she is smart enough to take on the world, DeLaria is still introducing her persona. The evening of audience shtick, set pieces, and musical numbers only partially meshes. DeLaria has a bright jazz voice. It radiates a lyricism she doesn't permit to show at other times, and she makes no comment about her emotional shadings, as if she doesn't realize they exist.

She's most at home as the bawd: a top who is also a marshmallow, a kamikaze libido that gets off on talking about sex. A riff on lesbians and sex toys is deft comedy of manners. DeLaria wants a dildo that looks like a dick, but she's confounded at lesbian shops, because they are penis-free zones. She holds up a sample of what she finds: a small dildo in the shape of a dolphin. "Just what I want, to be fucked by Flipper." At a male sex boutique, she's offered a long, flexible dildo with two penis heads. She brandishes it, claiming to be stumped about its use. Call me literal-minded, but couldn't two women insert it into their twats simultaneously? Couldn't one woman use it for the front and back doors?

DeLaria is more imaginative demanding that the men in the audience stand and proclaim, "I am a lesbian." She teases, "No you're not. Your clit's too long." To latecomers, she sasses, "You don't get fisted." To a woman in the audience who asks to go home with her, DeLaria counters, "How big are your hands? I like girls who are well hung." Her response to Gabriela Sabatini: "She gives me a wide-on."

■ ■ ■

If DeLaria and Bernhard produced a demon spawn, it might be Reno: too flammable to be butch, too strident to be femme. These days Reno is unequivocally out, but, ironically, her latest show, the work-in-progress *Citizen Reno*, at the Westbeth Theater, is more detached from sex than previous pieces. She is hot and bothered by the body politic in this surreal rant about her inability to go outside and her fears for democracy. Just when she seems to be foundering on pieties, she pulls out limber pratfalls and oddball associations—like the quip that men wear neckties to keep their penises out of their faces.

About being ambushed by aging, she muses, "I figured since I wasn't doing anything all those years, they wouldn't count." On the possibility that people are born gay and that fetuses might be tested for it, she pounces, "All those right-to-lifers are going to decide that abortion isn't such a bad idea after all." And in a fantasy of rescuing Bill Clinton from his waffling, she asks in return that he fix her up with Hillary.

■ ■ ■

Whither drag? With gays entering the mainstream and the frontiers of transgression shifting, with straight boys wearing earrings and mall rats toting up piercings and tattoos—indeed, whither drag? Does anyone wear a dress now, other than ladies who lunch and queens? Charles Busch's *Dressing Up!* at Town Hall shows stress at the seams, with most of the performers—Ira Siff of La Gran Scena Opera company, Randy Allen as Marilyn Monroe, and Charles Pierce as Norma Desmond—reprising rather than extending themselves.

Busch is the exception. Put this boy in a gown and he becomes not a girl or even a queen but a channeler of his inner life, with Tallulah as medium. Dresses uncensor a rambunctious, playful sprite, and once unleashed, his voice is capacious and effervescently campy. Opening with a perfect Barbra, arms undulating like eels, he declares his dream: "to bring together all those who toil in the fields of female impersonation . . . and watch them scratch each other's eyes out." Aside: "The dressing room is like a women's prison movie." Busch identifies with neurotics, yes, but they aren't fragile or unhinged.

John Epperson, a.k.a. Lypsinka, likewise thrusts drag past a ghetto of damage. He has become an archaeologist of dinosaur femininity, at once protective and clinical. His *As I Lay Lipsynching*, presented at Irving Plaza, is a collage of crazed moms, every imaginable hard-boiled and softheaded type from the movies and suburbia who raised us, ensnared us, aroused pity, awe, tenderness, and a longing for the road away from home. His aim isn't to resurrect but to preserve, not to honor but to study.

Back are Lypsinka's divas and starlets, the overblown emotions, the vocal mannerisms, the self-abasing lounge acts, the Dada phone calls, the Arlene Dahl wig, the Vera-Ellen anorexic body that tries to elude gender by escaping from flesh altogether. It doesn't matter whether you've seen Epperson before. This piece is a free-associative marvel. Epperson has launched lip-synching into satire that admits infatuation, his features dancing through the Kabuki makeup. Who would have thought art could be wrought from such humble means?

CHAPTER SEVEN

Postmodern Clowning: Spiking Simple Pleasures

Members of the group "Slant": Richard Ebihara, Wayland Quintero, and Perry Yung

At the beginning of this chapter, I'm on the road in Montreal and Phila-delphia, at two kinds of comedy festivals that couldn't be farther apart in spirit. Montreal is the site of Just for Laughs, which books stand-ups and performance comedians from all over the world but isn't an arts festival—devoted to artists—the way, for example, Edinburgh's festival is or the events Mike Pedretti organized in Philadelphia for Movement Theater In-ternational. Where there are stand-ups there are entertainment sharks, and where there are sharks the tanks are designed for the predators—as well as the fish wanting to be caught. The Toyota Comedy Festival in New York and the Aspen Comedy Festival are business-tropic, too, although, in all, opportunities have expanded for minorities, gays, women, and edge surfers.

The four years I attended *Just for Laughs*—from 1988 to 1991—I had a great time, feeling like a kid at a bar mitzvah. Showbiz reminds me of the friendly, mustachioed uncles who breezed in and out of my childhood. Showbiz caters.

Movement Theater International, under the directorship of Mike Pedretti, was not without its retrograde decisions, but the atmosphere of its festivals—clown events alternating with mime gatherings—was art-centric, with workshops, panels, and studio performances unreeling continually, and deal makers, if they were even around, in the background. Sadly, due to a loss of funding and other management troubles, the festivals have been suspended. MTI's buffets weren't as sumptuous as Just for Laughs's, but the bodies were better—dancer-buffed and limber.

It's fun to look back and see how many original talents were showcased at the festivals. They're where I got my first looks at Tim Allen, Brett Butler, Kevin Meany, Jimmy Tingle, Julian Clary, and Bill Hicks, among others. Without MTI, I would not have been able to see live performances by clown innovators Ctibor Turba and Bolek Polivka. The greatest value of the festivals is their international scope, for there are few opportunities for performers to meet each other or for audiences to catch common threads as well as stark individuality. Just for Laughs, especially, has become a carnival of variant forms, welcoming everyone from antique shtick jockeys like Milton Berle to the uncategorizable juggling genius Michael Moschen.

The clowns in this chapter come the closest of any in this book to seltzer bottles and hat tricks. This is the Ed Sullivan portion, as imagined by postmodern collagists. Unlike the ahistorical reference cocktails some pomo artists stir, the performers celebrated here are archivists of ancient styles, paying tribute to tradition and extending the narratives in unprecedented ways. I'm transported by their physical skill: the body control of corporeal mimes, the hours of obsession flared by card handlers, the juggling of mortality in the unbroken flight of lofted balls.

The term *new vaudeville* was coined in the eighties to describe the work of artists blending their sideshow skills and love of circus with their experience of modernity—mixing physical purity with emotional sophistication. In *The Regard of Flight,* Bill Irwin set up a tension between his clown's helplessness and the extraordinary athletic mastery required to dramatize his slip-sliding and slo-mo falling.

I write about the unique clowning chronicler Geoff Hoyle, but I want to add some words about several performers—not included among the gathered pieces. I find puppets stuffy. Puppets are us in a way that seems even more literal than live fools; puppets are fetishes, voodoo dolls, dummy heads of the unrepressed. Even majestic, life-sized Bunraku figures, as arresting as they can be, often become wearying, with their physical limitations. But a number of artists—Paul Zaloom and Eric Bass among them—are challenging the conventions, creating prop mindscapes as dense as consciousness.

Zaloom, who trained with Bread & Puppet, invests his plain objects with hilarious importance. It's a metaphor for how humans feel under the heel of economic and political forces, not to mention aging and sexual confusion, which he does mention. In *Sick but True,* tiny objects are blown up on a projector, then there's a slide show, and last a sequence involving props. We're in the world of allegory, inspired nonsense, where a magnified tangle of barbershop hair gets passed off as the city's infrastructure. In the funniest section, Zaloom examines actual-but-insane artifacts: a course preparing journalists for covering nuclear disasters, a Desert Storm souvenir watch manufactured in the USSR. In Zaloomland, we're at the mercy of the expanding and contracting universe, secret governments, toxic terrorism.

Bass does ethnic autobiography with his weird grandma and grandpa miniatures. *Invitations to Heaven* is a valentine to ancestral traditions. Bass and his collaborators, composer Alan Bern and director Richard Edelman, embrace *Yiddishkeit*—klezmer music, steerage lore, religious observances— with the same abandon that new vaudevillians swoon over variety-show entertainment. The past comes equipped with historical meaning; the test is whether old forms can be reinvented. Bass goes a distance, with his mixture of fantasy and raw naturalism—à la Alechem and Singer—and with his skilled puppeteering.

Like the Klezmatics—a swinging, race-mixed klezmer band—two Yiddish theater classics are delightfully spit-polished with new vaudeville pizzazz. The pieces included here applaud *Kuni Leml* and *Schlemiel the First*.

Another element in this chapter is comedy teams and ensembles. Troupes have cropped up before—Pomo Afro Homos, for example, in the queer comedy section, and although the Pomos fit in this context, too, I feel their voice is most definitively gay. I want to mention a couple of sketch comedy groups not covered that have fired sparks. The members of Chuck-

202 ■ LAUGHING IN THE DARK

lehead cleverly puncture downtown pretensions and pop-cul icons—in a Letterman send-up, "Let's Humiliate a Recent Immigrant," an Asian butcher is interviewed about "lamp chops." Most ingenious are Michael Huston's turns, ranging from her terminally hipped-out, Paul Shaffer androgyne to her three-year-old blue stand-up. "What's the difference between a bugger and cauliflower? A kid won't eat cauliflower."

Fierce praise about Culture Clash—Richard Montoya, Ric Salinas, and Herbert Siguenza—has been wafting from the Bay Area for years. They are Chicanos, as in grapephobes, and theater sharks, ingesting Mexican *carpa*, vaudeville, El Teatro Campesino and San Francisco Mime Troupe agitprop, the Marx Brothers, Sid Caesar, and Robin Williams. In a sustained piece, Che Guevara is resurrected via Santería (actually a Whitney Houston doll) and hipped to the New World Order. He learns that though communism has run aground, he was a character in an Andrew Lloyd Webber musical and Converse sneakers copped the star on his beret for its logo. "I brought him back from the dead," boasts a Chicano to a kid delivering pizza, a hip-hopper whose grasp of history prompts the question, "Is that Jerry Garcia?" Culture Clash gives melting pot you can smoke, wire service from the global village, revolution that won't go away as long as have-nots have not.

Just for Laughs Festival 1988: Gut Laughter

September 1988

Bobby Slayton walks out, blond, boyish, but with a gravelly voice and cocked head that read Vegas. "Whenever you throw up, no matter what you eat, there's peas and carrots. Where do they come from?" It's my first night at the eleven-day Just for Laughs festival in Montreal. I'm in Club Soda, one of the festival's seven venues spread across the city. Brett Butler is next and riffs on womb envy. "Maybe that's why men declare war so often, they have this need to bleed on a regular basis."

Another woman on the eight-act lineup, a British comic named Jo Brand, goes by the name the Sea Monster because, as she says, she's fat. She harps on her weight. "As a kid I didn't have many friends, being the size of a small bungalow." She doesn't have to do this. In her punky hairdo and stylish clothes, she's not unattractive, and she shoots stinging observations in a funny singsong. About her black outfit: "It's so versatile. One day you might find yourself in a production of *Die Fledermaus,* cast as the head bat." About *Cosmopolitan*—"For the ever-so-slightly feminist woman, it shows you how to talk about quantum mechanics while giving a blowjob and asking the man to marry you, all at the same time."

Later comes Robert Schimmel, billed "X-rated." He looks like a deadbeat: short, balding, stubbly. He talks about sex. "Phone sex, my worst fantasy. 'You have your dick out?' 'Yeah.' 'You're thinking dirty thoughts?' 'Yeah.' 'Okay, your mother wants to talk to you.' " He has another funny line for friends his dog is humping. "He'll stop when he comes." Schimmel's insecurities are out there, helium we can get giddy on.

Three Canadian men, festival president Gilbert Rozon, thirty-three, Andy Nulman, twenty-eight, who books the acts, and Bruce Hills, twenty-six, who handles public relations, make all decisions concerning Just for Laughs. According to Glenn Schwartz, the festival's press agent, Just for Laughs, now in its sixth year, gathers performers from all over the world, acts chosen because they're the best and brightest available. Even before I arrive, I know this isn't true. Although the festival is nonprofit, supports a comedy school that pays and trains twelve students per year, and stages a number of free outdoor shows, its focus is commercial—it's the biggest supermarket for acts in the comedy circuit. HBO has paid $600,000 for the rights to shoot the galas—the main shows held each night at the St. Denis Theater—and HBO gets to determine the final night's lineup. HBO's money makes up a healthy portion of the budget—this year $6 million, collected from government grants, private sponsors, and ticket sales, in addition to TV rights.

Still, Just for Laughs has assembled a number of smart, unconventional comedians: Margaret Smith, Emo Philips, Gilbert Gottfried, and Judy Tenuta, who is slated for a bit on an outdoor stage. And while the festival is retrograde in terms of race and gender, it has expanded the definition of a comedy act to include variety entertainers and clowns.

Back at the Delta Hotel—a posh, comfy place in the middle of town that serves as festival headquarters—I go to the bar, where people are wolfing food from a buffet and schmoozing. Stork-thin Emo, whose clothes are held together with safety pins, says he's ravenous but doesn't eat. He's not sure the food is free. He wants to eat, but he decides he won't eat, free or not.

I plunk down beside Jeff Altman, a comedian who, in his act, pulls his belt to his nipples and does bits about his repressed, raging father. But before we can say much, Stevie "The Regurgitator" Starr, who is sitting near us, swallows two Canadian dollar pieces, and our heads spin like compass needles. Stevie is blond and blue-eyed, angel-faced and thin. He swallows four more coins. You can hear them tinkling in his stomach. Then he swallows the smoke from a cigarette.

"How many coins shall I bring up?" His brogue is thick, all showman. Bobby Slayton, the comic from Club Soda, plays straight man. "Three." "And a quarter of the smoke?"

Bobby nods. Stevie thumps his chest, and from his mouth fly three coins: a vision from a dream, a human slot machine. Behind the coins comes a ball of smoke, then more coins, then more smoke, the engines of commerce.

"I wish I had the goldfish." Stevie whets our appetites, while gobbling attention. In lieu of a fish, he pops a light bulb in his mouth, closes his eyes, and swallows. The room gasps. His mouth is open, and the bulb is gone. Chest thump. The light bulb shoots out. "This next one is dangerous." He produces a Rubik's cube, pointing out the position of the top row of squares, swallows the cube, does something with his stomach muscles, then regurgitates it, showing that the squares have moved. For his finale, he hands Bobby a closed lock and key and opens his mouth. Every time Stevie swallows something, Bobby squeals and sucks in a sympathetic gulp of air. Reluctantly, he places the lock in Stevie's mouth and watches him eat metal. Then the key. More stomach jiggling, as Stevie flashes his carny grin. Then he brings up the lock, open now, *with the key inside*! "It's different," he says.

"It's a trick," I hear people mutter. "It's gotta be."

I'm sure it isn't. I'm awed, horrified. I don't want to see him swallow another thing, but I want to know why he does it. Stevie isn't exactly funny, but he makes us edgy in a visceral way, and laughter, at once sadistic and empathetic, keeps escaping from us. I see a primal number developing: Emo using his anorexia to make us gawk, Schimmel tapping our fears with his sex rap. Stevie, the hunger artist, is all control.

■ ■ ■

The next morning, in the hotel restaurant, Lou Viola, the agent who handles Emo and Judy Tenuta, waves me to his table, and introduces me to

Budd Friedman, founder of the Improvs, and his wife, Alexandra, a pretty blond woman dressed in white. She says she helped Sandra Bernhard get her break. "She was doing my friends' nails. I told Budd to give her a try."

I ask Budd how he got started.

"I was too scared to be an actor, but I wanted in. My mother inherited five thousand dollars at the same time she turned sixty-two. She could receive social security, so she gave me the money, and I opened a hole-in-the-wall in 1963, a place where actors could get up and do shtick after their shows. It took off."

Several men come over. Lou identifies them as agents, managers, press reps. Deals hum in the air. I see Mike Malley, Stevie Starr's manager, and I make an appointment for that afternoon. Glenn Schwartz—he's a short, high-powered man with hair that floats down his neck—urges me to see Jango Edwards.

"What does he do?"

"He's a clown, a mime."

"I don't like mimes."

"You'll like him. He's unusual. Trust me."

I don't trust him but agree to go.

I wander to St. Denis Street, where the galas are held. Three blocks have been closed to traffic and several outdoor stages have been erected. Cafés and ice-cream parlors line the way, and the atmosphere is festive. Mimes and musicians perform. No one looks bored, and no one shoves.

When I get back to the hotel, Stevie is waiting in the bar. As he talks, he plays with a stack of Canadian dollar coins. He has the hands of a magician: steady, every gesture exact. Sometimes, seemingly without knowing it, he sucks his right index finger.

"I was brought up in an orphanage, although I'm not an orphan. I was taken there when I was four months old, and I stayed till I was eighteen. I know I have a brother and sister. My brother once came to the orphanage drunk, and they wouldn't let him in. He never came back. I don't remember when I first started swallowing coins. The matrons used to give us pocket money, but we were supposed to give some back, to save for holidays. I didn't want to, so I swallowed mine, then, when I was alone, I brought the coins back up. I got so I could swallow anything."

When he left the home, he took a job as a cook. A few months later, he entered a talent contest, won, and got signed by an agent who took him to

London. Three years later he met Mike—Mike, in his early forties, speaks with a music-hall lilt, flirts harmlessly, and has a parental rapport with his client. Stevie is twenty-five and lives in a house of his own in London, near Mike and his family. He works all the time, often in discos. He eats "a proper meal" about once every three days.

"Otherwise I'd throw up the food along with the coins. I survive on chips and candy." Smile. "I drink lots of water, so the acid in my stomach won't kill the fish."

He also drinks lighter fluid and liquid soap, in order to bring up bubbles of gas, which he ignites with a match. "What about the lighter fluid?"

"I get it all out. I can control every muscle in my body, a kind of yoga."

"You've gained a mastery the rest of us have only dreamed of."

"Needed to."

"Do you ever want to see your family?"

He shakes his head no, vigorously. "I'm doin' great on me own, why should I?"

"You might want to, on impulse. Someday, you might want to control the impulse to control your impulses."

He meets my eyes. "In four years, when I've enough money, I'll stop."

"You think you can?"

"I'm certain." He flashes a dollar piece. "Watch this." He places the coin in his ear, seeming to work it through his jaw, then he brings it out his mouth. He puts the coin back in his mouth, seeming to work it through his jaw again, and brings it out his ear. I know this is a trick, but, inches from him, I can't see how it's done. The night before, in the bar, he'd done extraordinary card maneuvers. I've heard he doesn't do them in his act, lest people take the regurgitating for a stunt. Now, I wonder if I've been swallowing everything myself. Maybe he doesn't really throw up. Maybe he eats three square meals a day. But he arrests these thoughts by popping four coins in his mouth. I hear them drop into his stomach, plink, plink, plink. He closes his eyes, preparing to tap his bile, and I imagine the combination of glee and loneliness he feels having such authority over his orifices. He thumps his chest.

"Do you have to do that?"

"Nah, it's for show. It would be too ordinary otherwise."

The coins pour out of his mouth, and he picks up the light bulb.

"Don't. It's painful."

He breaks into a wide grin, pops the bulb into his mouth, inhales it with a gasp, and convinces me everything that enters his mouth sails down his gullet.

■ ■ ■

For the next four days, I nibble buffets and take walks. In an abandoned lot, Stevie catches a bee, swallows it, bring it up, then lets it fly off his tongue. In a tent during the HBO taping, Stephen Schiff, a correspondent for *West 57th Street*, twists his arm behind his head and cranes his neck, doing an impression of Emo. I offer my version of Judy Tenuta, making her acceptance speech at this year's comedy awards show: "It's great, but what I *really* want is to be home with some *guy*, getting puffed up and making babies." Frank Gannon, a segment producer for David Letterman, says everybody has five minutes of material. Schiff and I look at each other, and that gleam comes into our eyes.

Sight-gagger Rich Hall comes on stage holding a rubber shower mat. "I'd like to say something about the senseless slaughter of squid." Eno Rosenn, an Israeli mime who uses sound effects, zooms around the stage on an imaginary motorcycle, then, with an insistence peculiarly sweet and implacable, draws people from the audience, directs them to ride behind his bike, to pilot their own vehicles, and even to race each other. The Reduced Shakespeare Company fractures the canon with vintage slapstick and California ingenuousness. "May the Bard be with you," intones Jess Borgeson. The group's ten-minute *Romeo and Juliet* captures the story's flavor, and as Juliet, Adam Long lets the gangly male in him concoct a willful, tomboyish heroine.

I go to see Jango Edwards, Glenn Schwartz's tip, and it turns out to be the wisest advice I get. "A mime, a clown" doesn't prepare me. Jango's show is at the Spectrum Theater, a cavernous hall that serves drinks. I take a seat near the front, and in a few minutes, without warning, a tall man, swathed in a plastic raincoat with leopard-skin swatches pinned to it, wobbles like a windup toy through the crowd. Hooked on the point of his umbrella is a water bottle, and as he passes, he spritzes. He wears bright red lipstick, a cloche hat, and glasses with one blackened pane. Drool threatens to slip from his lips and does.

When he reaches the stage, he looks out, his mouth working word-

lessly, his face registering lust, shame, vengeance—in waves. His expressiveness is transparent, gripping. Some of the shtick is ancient: paper that sticks
to one hand, then the other; cups with wills of their own. He crams potato
chips in his mouth, then coughs out a cloud of chip dust. He removes a gob
of chewed food from his mouth and offers it to a woman in the audience,
his face bright with hope and malice, his giant baby-brain calculating its
next lunge toward pleasure, reconciling itself to its inevitable defeats.

Suddenly he rips off the costume and hat, revealing a tight jumpsuit
and a flowing mane of black hair. He flicks the hair back and forth, the way
Cher used to when hers was long. He grabs a mike, the curtain comes up,
and a four-piece rock band blasts hot licks, while Jango does midair splits
and sings, growls. For the next two hours, musical numbers, including jazz
and swing, alternate with clowning pieces, but several motifs remain constant: a Strangelove hand that keeps grabbing for his "Bobo," terrorist for-
ays into the audience with spray cans of plastic confetti, love/hate high
jinks with the band.

Jango has a Dangerfield kvetch about his powerlessness, then shoots
the musicians with blanks. He sashays, Mae West–style. "Are you confused?
Are you thoroughly confused?" There's a corny sight gag: a huge pacifier,
made of plastic breasts, worn around his neck, and sucked from time to
time. A corny joke: "I'm bisexual. If I can't get it I buy it." He brings a
placid-looking man on stage, drops an Alka-Seltzer tablet into a glass of
water, pulls a condom over its rim, and hands it to the man, inspiring him to
giggle as the rubber grows erect.

In one routine, Jango does a devastating send-up of Marcel Marceau.
In another, he rolls out as a huge Elvis, his head nearly swallowed by the
costume's volume. "Where's my neck?" He extends it. "Oh." For his finale,
he enters nude, his genitals tucked between his legs, and he stands there,
swaying, a man/woman, all hostility, for the moment, purged. He shuffles
along, squeezing his parts, lest they escape, with his thighs. Then the imp
returns and he moons us, revealing the tip of his penis between his cheeks,
a hot dog between two buns.

Off stage, Jango is like a dog. If he doesn't know you or if he feels uncertain, he licks and sniffs. The morning after I see his show, I'm sitting in
the restaurant with the festival organizers, and Jango leaps over Gilbert Rozon and plants a kiss on the lips of Andy Nulman.

"Feh, back," Andy huffs. "You gave me a cold."

"I did not."

It takes forever to pin down Jango for an interview. Finally, at two A.M. one night, we retreat to a bench outside the bar, and instead of throwing his body on me or licking my hand, as he's done previously, he sits, becalmed. He's thirty-eight and comes from Detroit, but he's been in Europe for the past seventeen years. When he lived in the States, he owned a successful landscaping business but gave it up to study clowning in London. "I read a book, *The Fourth Way*, about self-development. Clowns know what they look like and show it."

He's now based in Amsterdam, where his wife, a performer, and their two children live, but he tours most of the time. He's organized the Festival of Fools since 1976, a clown/street-theater jamboree held annually in different countries. "My idea is to perform anywhere, for anyone, in any language." Last year, he and the band had an eight-month gig in Paris. He's opened for the Rolling Stones, made tapes for Russian clowns, and currently is at work on two projects with Fellini, one a movie about lunatics, also featuring Roberto Benigni, the comic pearl of Jim Jarmusch's film *Down by Law*.

"What's your real name?"

"Stanley. . . . You're laughing, see?"

"Where did Jango come from?"

"I was strapped for money in Morocco, so I started selling Bulova watches in the market. At the time, a series of Spanish, spaghetti-type westerns were popular. I used to wear boots and a hat like the main character, Jango, and the kids started calling me that. I kept it."

"What does it take to come out naked and hide your genitals?"

"Wanting to be silly more than wanting to be a man."

■ ■ ■

The last night, I wander to St. Denis Street. Earlier in the week, Jango's outdoor show had been rained out, and he's making up the date. The street is packed. I inch my way up a stoop, take a place behind boys slugging beer, and look out at Jango, who faces a sea of bodies. He prances before them, taunting and tempting, and his wildness, uncontained by a theater, now seems to summon the potential wildness of the crowd. He demands they raise their hands, and they do, in unison, and for a moment it's repellent, this scene of mesmerizer and mass.

The festival has laid a table for deals. Glenn Schwartz has signed Robert Schimmel as a client. Stevie has been on *Letterman* and is going to Vegas in the fall. (Who'll swallow whom?) But independent of HBO's interests, the festival has also brought Jango to North America. And now Jango, the master of ambivalence, is conducting his joyous, unnerving pageant. I look out again, and the tension has melted. The faces turned toward Jango—faces he says feed him like a drug—are hungry for response you don't deliberate: Just to laugh.

Just for Laughs Festival 1989: The Gag Trade

March 1989

Fun bubbles in meeting places throughout the Delta Hotel. One night in a bar, Stephen Saban, a columnist for *Details* magazine, teaches an assembly how to interview stars. Dispensing test questions, he says to me: "You have to sleep with either Tiny Tim or Mason Reese. Who would you choose?" "Mason Reese," I bleat. "Wrong," he shoots. "Always choose the more famous one in case you're discovered."

Comics do each other's bits. The routines are homages, but since stealing material is rife among comedians it's also a way to let off steam. In schmoozing, there is time to explore, probe. At a party, the comedian Kevin Meany (U.S.) relates how he translated pain into humor with unusual literalness. He was in a dark bar when a practical joker popped a bottle cap into his beer. Meany swallowed, felt a stabbing sensation in his neck, then in his stomach. The cap was too large to pass through his intestines, so he was forced to undergo major surgery. "I'm fine, except for the scars." He points to his plump abdomen and smiles ruefully. At the time, he was managing a restaurant and doing comedy part-time. He sued for damages and won a settlement large enough to support him for a year. "I quit the job and developed the act."

For several days, I've been enjoying Meany's improvisational shtick, gaining increasing respect for his comic gifts. At last year's festival, he was the newcomer who inspired the most buzz. I didn't fully respond then; he's something of an acquired taste, and he's sharpened his delivery. Now he shimmers, one of the event's high points.

Unlike comedians who continually audition and one-up, Meany doesn't come off compulsive—rather, ineluctable. He's been aptly compared to Jonathan Winters because they resemble one another physically and Meany shares Winters's ability to change personae with lightning speed. But Meany, always transmuting trauma into satire, seems more thoughtful.

His stage act is hard to describe: he doesn't tell jokes, and most of his lines aren't funny apart from his delivery. Often, he becomes his prim, Boston-accented parents. During his gala performance, he announces, in his own voice, that he's putting on weight for the summer, "so I can get a big tan." Becoming his mother, he heckles, "Look at the size of you, you look like Elvis on the beach." He segues back to his childhood and is again his mother, scrutinizing every lurch he takes toward independence, hipness: "You're not wearing those tight pants, mister. Go up to your room and put your big pants on." Later, he confides he has problems. Straight face. "I don't have a penis. I got circumcised every year for my birthday. I get special parking, though. My license has a penis with a line going through it."

Meany's penis joke, with its open lampooning of castration fear, washes like a tonic over the coded castration anxiety within stand-up's ubiquitous anal penetration routines. Meany doesn't skimp on his own humiliation, and he doesn't spare his parents. He casts the family matter-of-factly, as an anthropologist might. In his mad and ordinary world, we are all eunuchs, damaged by early cruelty and emotionally frozen. His irrepressible good humor is the boldest evidence, however, that the family failed to squelch him.

On another night, Jenny Lecoat (England) tells dry tales about sex. A man she isn't attracted to is pumping away. "Are you nearly there?" he asks. "It's hard to say," she returns. He: "If you imagine it as a journey from here to China, where would you be?" She: "The kitchen." Rick Ducommun (U.S.) says his one-year-old daughter has made her first movie. "It's with Rob Lowe. Roman Polanski's directing. It's called Fetal Attraction." Molasses-slow Michael Redmond (Ireland) hated when his grandfather came to visit. "It wasn't just that he was blind. It was that everyone said I had his eyes."

The most promising up-and-comer, Jimmy Tingle (U.S.), thirty-four, has been honing his material for several years, but at Just for Laughs he comes off self-possessed to an unprecedented degree. Short, dirty-blond hair juts up from his forehead. He has the open-faced good looks and contained energy James Cagney projected. At his gala performance, he does a routine about national defense. "Five hundred and thirty million for a Stealth plane that doesn't show up on radar. Why don't we just borrow planes from Noriega—they haven't shown up on screens for years." He leans his head forward. "What did the ayatollah fear the most? A book! We should be building bigger and better books." He strides the stage. "Czechoslovakia put a jazz band in jail, Poland fears unions. The U.S. should invade the East with pens, typewriters, a few Berkeley students, a couple of Teamsters, Lou Reed, and Edgar Allan Poe's greatest hits. The East could retaliate with national health and affordable housing." On to AIDS, he observes, "Here's this disease attacking Haitians, homosexuals, and drug addicts, and it has no cure. All the politicians are going, 'Yeah, what's the problem?' Then it turns out you can get AIDS from a prostitute. Now Congress is saying, 'Something should be done.'"

We talk the next afternoon, and he says he was raised in Cambridge, the oldest of four children. His father drove a cab; his mother worked in a medical lab. "When I was growing up, kids went into crime, or they went into sports, or they went to school. It wasn't hip to be smart."

Tingle still made it to college, then traveled to the West Coast and lived off odd jobs. In 1980, he saw Rodney Dangerfield for the first time. "I was back East. It was St. Patrick's Day, and a bunch of us went to New York. I'd been funny with the guys, drunken humor. I wanted to perform, but I didn't know any actors. Rodney blew me away."

Dangerfield's confessional style is closer to Meany's than Tingle's, but, for Tingle, Dangerfield's street-smart, pretension-busting persona was a fitting inspiration. Shortly after the New York trip, a club opened near where Tingle was living. The Ding Ho Comedy Club/Chinese Restaurant would soon launch Steven Wright, Steve Sweeney, Paula Poundstone, Jim Morris, Kevin Meany, and Barry Crimmins. "I worked as daytime bartender, doorman, janitor, and open mike performer. I was groping. I was around so many creative people who were using their brains and getting paid for it. At first, I worked with props and my material was blue, crowd-pleasing stuff. But two years ago, when I quit drinking, it was like my vision cleared. The struggle is hanging on to yourself while trying to get on TV."

Tingle appeared on Carson in December. He did political material and hasn't yet been asked back, though he's hopeful. Encouraged by performers like Reno and Sandra Bernhard, he's developing a one-man show—ironing the kinks at the Boston Comedy Club in Manhattan.

Meany's career surged after his success at last year's festival. Tingle deserves the same boost. The two are friends. Tingle contributes a bit to a video Meany is shooting for one of the new all-comedy channels. It's another stealing vignette: Meany does Tingle's material in his own persona, while Tingle looks on aghast.

Just for Laughs Festival 1990:
Killing and Dying in Montreal

August 1990

At the eighth annual Just for Laughs festival, bashing Andrew "Dice" Clay is required sport. Practically every comic takes a swipe at Clay, even men themselves known for sliming women and deviance. At one of the gala shows, Sam Kinison—who's rumored to have been paid $48,000 for his appearance—has the temerity to huff at Clay's crudeness, then blithely spray similar poison. He accuses Elton John of shoving gerbils up his ass and of needing a drawstring to keep his stretched sphincter muscle closed. Next Kinison whines about being misunderstood, becoming a Jerry Lewis clone, at once hostile and self-pitying. "I've taken so much shit from the gay community. I've tried to make friends with them. I'm a sensitive guy." To underscore the point, he waxes chivalrous, mistaking prudishness for respect. "I think it's rude to come in women's mouths. Don't do it," he preaches. "I love women. There's never been a penis close to my mouth."

At his press conference Bob Newhart is asked by a British journalist about the prevalence of "sexism, homophobia, and racism" in American comedy, and Newhart, his jowls drooping like a bloodhound's, edgily answers, "I work clean," as if the woman has said she was troubled by sex jokes and as if disliking bigotry was a function of priggishness. Later, another journalist, this time a man, raises the issue again, wondering what Newhart thinks of a routine he did twenty years ago about an incompetent woman driver—she does things like go sixty in the driveway. Newhart surprises the reporter by revealing he still performs the piece, adding, "If anyone's offended I do it as a Chinese driver, but most of the time audiences make me go back to the woman."

Introducing Newhart at the press conference, festival publicist Glenn

Schwartz unintentionally inspires one of the week's funniest interludes. "No individual will approach or touch him, or Newhart will leave," directs Schwartz. "We want to see his dick," pipes up British comedian Jeremy Hardy, but the assembled are laughing too hard at Schwartz's officiousness for many to hear.

■ ■ ■

Even offstage, Dave Thomas has the Bob Hope thing so bad, his lips keep twisting sideways, and his sentences roll out punctuated with growled "yeahs." Onstage, in makeup fashioned by Kevin Haney—the wizard responsible for Robert Morse's transformation into Truman Capote—Thomas-as-Hope is mesmerizing. His impression isn't a put-down. The portrait reveals the satirist's identification with his subject, his curiosity about the sour sauces cooked up by egotism.

In a riff at Club Soda, Thomas offers *his* version of Clay—a bit called Bob "Dice" Hope—and he nails the bluster brilliantly. Clay, the self-proclaimed dangerous renegade, is tweaked in the comparison to America's most predictable TV uncle, but a keener barb is injected into Hope. In massive leather jacket and black chinos, Dice Hope alternately plugs his upcoming appearances—"the big policemen's chili cookout"—and spews Clay-isms; he rhymes hickory dickory dock with entertaining "the troops at Xuan Loc" and Joey Heatherton grabbing his "cock."

Thomas taps the sexual disgust and fear of difference steering both acts. Hope, in his early films, was a sexual neuter; later, he became the strutting jingoist and cocky appraiser of female flesh. Just last winter, in a concert at Madison Square Garden, he slobbered over Miss Universe and made limp jokes at the expense of gays and Asians. Clay, with his chubby, unappealing body, has also created a stage persona meant to cloak his disability. Hope and Clay imagine that because females can reject them personally, women are powerful in the world. Both comedians victimize people whose offense, generally, is powerlessness.

Showtime has the wit to tape and broadcast Thomas's performance, and the network includes another appalled/attracted portrait by Tom Leopold. Leopold, primarily a writer who has worked with Paul Shaffer and Harry Shearer, plays Milt Wagonman, a no-talent TV writer, who lives to reminisce. The piece is taped at the Delta bar, where Wagonman sits, pouring out his drunken heart to the glib, natty Martin Mull. Their conversation—mostly Wagonman jabbers and Mull feigns sincerity—is Bob and Ray laced with sulfuric acid.

Wagonman's credits include *Meet Keeffe Braselle, Jerry Lester's Fun House,* and *My Mother the Chimp*—"starring Cara Williams and a fresh talent, Sid Melton, as Dink, her invisible neighbor." Wagonman goes on about George Gobel, divulging that the comedian has "a hairy ass": "When you visualize Gobel's ass, you think smooth, am I wrong?" Then suddenly he tells a story about Bing Crosby: the time the crooner, who was guesting on Gobel's show, invited Wagonman to his house.

"We're in Bing's limousine and as a courtesy to me, because he respected my work, he has a hooker there providing me with a little 'wind therapy,' if you follow my meaning. . . . I don't know if you know this, but Dixie, Crosby's first wife, was a terrible alcoholic. It was the great tragedy in his life and also something Bing thought was funny as hell. So we're shooting pool and Crosby's son Gary is there, the one he called Ol' Bucket Butt. He revered his kids. Now here's the cute part. Bing tells Ol' Bucket Butt to go upstairs and get Dixie, who's facedown in her own puke, to watch us shoot pool, which he does. We're playing and Bing drops his cue and tells Gary to pick it up for him. He does and Bing grabs my cue and whacks his son as hard as he can in the testicles. We all start laughing, even Gary, who's white as a sheet with tears running down his face. My point is about the power of humor and all that shit. Cute story."

The festival offers other celebrations of grunge. A hard-drinking friend of Dave Thomas's vomits on a Pekingese. He eyes the dog: "I don't remember eating that." John Mendoza, a branch from the Rodney Dangerfield tree, lampoons his resentment. "Ever hear the expression 'I'm glad I'm not him'? I'm him." He imagines himself a regretful transsexual who goes back to his surgeon. "You still got my dick? That's all right, I'll take the black one in the corner." A caller with the wrong number asks for Mary, and the comedian says, "She died this morning." The man asks if there's anything he can do, and Mendoza answers, "Yeah, send over a pizza."

Tim Allen wears a business suit and suspenders, but his material is pure burlesque, complete with vomit and spit jokes. He doesn't complain about women. He barely mentions them, except to claim crudeness as a male preserve; he insists, for example, that only men light farts. But his set is an ode to brute drives. He parodies the war between the sexes, rather than cherishing the differences.

"Men are pigs," he declares, grinning complacently. His eyes narrow, and his smile turns to a leer. "Too bad we own everything." His mother, who raised seven boys, thought her sons too primitive for words and insisted they grunt. Allen invents a grunt language, as suitable to the boardroom as the jungle. But sometimes description is essential. A towel drops off as he's exiting the shower, leaving "Big Jim and the twins staring at" his kids.

As a househusband, he's compelled to powerize the kitchen appliances. His forehead seems to protrude, and the grunts kick in as he transforms the garbage disposal into a wood chipper and rigs the sink sprayer so it can strip paint off his neighbor's siding. When Allen enters the tool department at Sears, his "nipples get hard."

Rich Hall, sporting a "world fashion jacket," opens it to reveal Albania, North Korea, and Cuba, "little pockets of communism." Rick Overton says that Bush treats the hole in the ozone layer like a bald spot. "He thinks he can comb over air from Canada. I don't think it works that way." Overton suggests that oil tankers wear big condoms and imagines the objections of a macho captain. "I can't feel the ocean. I'll only go halfway into your harbor."

The British contingent is the strongest block. Hardy, a slight fellow, wonders, "If AIDS is to punish people for homosexuality, what was the Black Death for? To penalize folk for wearing period costumes?" Jack Dee, who looks like Larry Hagman with an inner life, reports on the drought in southern England, the government's demand that people restrict toilet flushings, and the news that the Queen receives on average three turds a week in the mail. Admits Dee, "That's how I conserve water." He's stunned that Bjorn Borg attempted suicide: "He was always such a cheerful chap." Dee notes that Pete Best, the former Beatles drummer who quit the band in 1962, now works in a job center. "Imagine taking employment advice from Best." Dee hates people who think it's clever to take drugs—"like customs officers."

Chris Lynam becomes known at the festival for his finale: standing on stage naked with a Roman candle shooting sparks from his ass. As British journalist Carol Sarler remarks, "After you've seen it twenty or thirty times, you ask yourself, 'Why?'" I suppose you do. But Lynam, who is aptly described by one reporter as looking like "a cross between Keith Richards and

Eraserhead," is more inventive than the firecracker gambit might suggest. With his trained body and roster of physical tricks, he stalks the stage, a terrorist clown. He scowls at the huge audience at the St. Denis Theatre. "I'm gonna fuck you. *All*."

The festival's most novel departure is Julian Clary. Well-known in Britain, he's a stunning beauty who wears gobs of makeup but doesn't disguise he's male. Many of his jokes are camp staples and much of his repartee is directed at Russell Churney, his pianist. "There's a sort of umbilical cord between us. You could hang your wash on it." Churney is teased for being straight. "And you've got a girlfriend, as if to prove a point."

Just for Laughs Festival 1991: Northern Exposure

August 1991

At Just for Laughs, Bill Hicks declares his ambition to follow the Lenny Bruce trail and makes his move from the club scene to the stage by debuting *Relentless*, a ninety-minute piece at the Centaur Theater. The monologue displays more grit, energy, and courage than anything else around.

Hicks wears black, in classic thug style. He could use some sleep, some protein. He has to smoke, because he's inclined toward addictions, and cigarettes are legal. Pacing, running his hands through sweaty hair, he is passionate and vulnerable, rooting out hypocrisy rather than sneering.

He takes exception to calling the Kuwait rout a war: "A war is when *two* armies are fighting." About Patriot missile technology: "Couldn't we use that to shoot food at hungry people? Fly over Ethiopia. There's a guy who needs a banana. Zap him one." Hicks notes that in England, where handguns are outlawed, there were fourteen deaths from the weapon last year, while there were twenty-seven thousand such killings in the United States. "But you'd be a fool and a communist to see a connection between owning a gun and using it." Raised eyebrows. "Of course, there were twenty-seven thousand deaths per soccer game in England. No system is flawless."

About the public antidrug service announcement that compares brains to fried eggs: "I did a lot of stuff but *never* anything that made eggs look like brains. Did I quit too soon? The drug sounds neat. Probably CIA stash." What especially piques him is that "Just Say No" spots are followed by ads for Budweiser, et al. "The bad drugs are the ones that aren't taxed. Inherently evil. No profit.

Although he ferrets out double standards in foreign policy and in advertising, he hasn't examined his own biases against women. Instead of targeting prudery wherever it exists, he lumps women together and claims they hate giving blow jobs. It sets him up for the speculation that women don't want to blow *him*.

Hicks and I have a drink the day after his show. He urges me to say what I think, so I include reservations. He doesn't flinch, dragging on a cigarette. He's declared his ambition, and he's considering the responsibilities. He's expectant, scared. At twenty-nine, he's been doing stand-up nearly half his life.

"I grew up in Houston," he says. "My father worked for General Motors. By thirteen, I knew I wanted to do comedy. I used to stay up watching late movies, and one week I discovered Woody Allen: *What's Up Tiger Lily?*, *Casino Royale*. I cracked up. I identified with Allen, the two of us losers. I'd read anything I could find on him. In an interview, Allen said he liked Benchley and Chaplin, so I looked for their work.

"Houston's first comedy club opened in 1977. I wrote a set and killed. I was fifteen. When I was seventeen, my parents moved to Little Rock, Arkansas, leaving me at home with a car. It was a scene out of *Risky Business*, except I happen to be very responsible about property. Not about school. I barely graduated. Teachers couldn't compete with the excitement I was feeling in the club.

"After high school, I moved to L.A., but I was miserable, isolated. All I had was work. I started drinking and doing drugs. I had experiences on drugs that showed me life has many dimensions. That helped me, but I was out of control. I was going on stage drunk. It got so I wasn't funny, and that's when I had to stop. Comedy was more important."

Clown Festival: Jokers Wild

August 1991

A clown congress. It's a joke, right, like anarchists' convention? There are no delegates or plenaries, just 250 comedy artists gathered to perform, attend workshops, and schmooze while juggling Indian clubs and piloting unicycles. The event has been spawned by Movement Theatre International, a nonprofit organization based in Philadelphia and headed by Michael Pedretti. Over the past ten years, MTI has commissioned new pieces from, and produced work by scores of international theater troupes. Pedretti's nine-member planning committee includes the Czech innovators Ctibor Turba and Bolek Polivka as well as other luminaries, but it's solidly male, as are eight of the nine main stage performers. The one woman soloist, Joanna Sherman, is amateurish and makes a lamentable token.

I've been invited to speak on a panel about "clown criticism," for which I'm paid an honorarium. I'm scouting talent, floating amid actors who consider tightrope walking, mime, acrobatics, ballet, and music part of their basic vocabulary. Clowning here isn't kid-party shtick purged of politics, eroticism, and consciousness. These clowns mock authority, deflate the pressure to conform. Most are professionals with considerable physical skill. They're pursuing what is more elusive—a persona, a story.

Scruffy casualness dominates. A few good haircuts, from the dance world, punctuate the landscape, but, mostly, frizzy tendrils snake from ponytails. During panel discussions, the assembled stretch on carpeted landings and use railings for barre work. Athletic bodies, bike pants, and muscle T-shirts, or, alternatively, goofy character gear. A sticker on a prop case reads: "Juggling Is Catching." Patch Adams, a doctor who practices for free and considers clowning sound treatment, favors pantaloons he can hoist to his armpits and a baseball cap shaped like a dinosaur.

In a showcase performance, Canadian Paul Wildbaum is startling, his head encased in a Velcro hood, his black unitard outfitted with Velcro squares over his nipples, navel, and genitals. Slithering to New Age rock, he attaches organic-shaped Styrofoam forms to his body, switching genders and species.

On the main stage, in *My Civilization*, Paul Zaloom juggles props representing the S&L scandal, the real estate bust, the buildup of toxic waste, and Jesse Helms's attack on the arts—Keating is a cowboy hat, Seabrook a series of blenders, Philip Morris a huge cigarette, Helms a wooden leg. Turba, dressed in trademark overalls and wearing a thick fake mustache, splices video and film sequences into his act, then wrests back the stage by bursting through the paper screens. In *The Survivor*, Polivka, who spent time in a Czech mental hospital after refusing to serve in the military, is a Beckett figure stranded on a bed that feels like a life raft; his personal demons underscore the state's deprivations.

Ilkhom, an experimental theater company from the Soviet Union, based in Tashkent, is a revelation in *Clomadeus,* a two-hour phantasmagoria that treks through Stalinoid hysteria and the seductions of *perestroika.* Ilkhom means "inspiration" in Uzbek, a precious commodity to Mark Weil, who founded the group in 1976 when staging avant-garde performance was dangerously provocative. *Clomadeus* is by turns violent, pornographic, sorrowful, and exultant. The four players—part Fellini mummers, part escapees from the dreams of Polish impresario Thadeusz Kantor—include hulking Mikhail Kaminsky, who has the profile of a tyrant on a coin; Georgi Korshunov, a long-lost Marx Brother; Asian-eyed Bakhram Matchanov, slender and sinuous as a sylph; and babylike Ilya Limansky, a devil/angel with a curly mop. Using music and sound effects but scant speech, the work is visceral, available. Scenes pile up like cars at a wreck site, but patterns emerge.

In one sequence, the four sit on suitcases at a train station, drinking tea and sucking sugar cubes. They are saved, content, then one by one they depart, each separation inspiring effusive, painful farewells. Finally, only Ilya is left, naked and without possessions. He sobs for a while, but from his grief springs the new pleasure of solitude. In another scene, an unseen menace waits behind a fun-house mirror. Bakhram hefts a brick and leans toward it. Georgi is behind him, but even gripped by fear, he becomes distracted by Bakhram's ass and parts his coattails for a better view. Loss is continual, frustration numbing. The only solaces are sensation, invention, defiance. On a battlefield up pipes a tango, and Bakhram and Ilya devise a dance of resurrection and, later, become loose-limbed and drunk on the sound of tiny bells. Still later they vamp in gorgeous drag, swaying to Mikhail's crooning as a Vegas lounge lizard. Streamers descend from the ceiling and with them a banner that reads "Protest." But even this demand has a conformist smell. Ilya stares wantonly across the footlights and hisses, "Fuck you."

Mime Festival: Mime and Mime Again

August 1993

I am watching *The Man Who Preferred to Stand,* a reconstruction of the work of Etienne Decroux. Innovator of the movement technique, corporeal mime, Decroux was happier teaching than performing, so his repertoire isn't widely known. That's why Mike Pedretti, who heads Movement Theatre International and is ringmastering his twelfth festival—this one devoted to mime—commissioned a selection of Decroux pieces, painstakingly recreated by the French troupe L'Ange Fou.

The company serves a wedge of modernist history that is odd and often mesmerizing, studies performed by naked, dusted bodies that look sculpted by Rodin, work involving the precise articulation of jointed parts, a system of counterweights, and gauze-wrapped, silent heads. Some of the pieces register as living art, most notably *The Factory* (1946), in which eight figures, wearing black body suits and white masks, zoom around against a soundtrack of clanks and plinks. White piping on their costumes makes them look two-dimensional—like Gumby or forms from Leger. At times they become human sandwiches, swaying and pitching in unison, mechanized cogs from an assembly line.

I'm in Philadelphia for a week to speak on a panel about future trends in mime and to help judge thirteen showcase acts, three of which receive $1,000 and a booking on the main stage. The schedule is thick with master classes and symposia, but thanks to the warmth of Pedretti—who, with his beard and paunch, comes off more clown than mime—the festival plays like summer camp rather than boot camp. There is, nonetheless, an agenda: asserting the primacy of Decroux. All of the companies presenting evening shows are headed by performers who studied with the master. But a question keeps buzzing: Is Decroux, who died in 1991 at age ninety-two, a better source than goal?

On the downside, there's no sex and little humor in his approach. We get body parts but no orifices. No talking, fucking, goosing—no way to get under the skin. Decroux wrapped the face to focus attention on the body, but the gauze suggests a gag as much as a mask. Nothing escapes control; crotches are contained, lest pendulous appendages jiggle. Thomas Leabhardt, a festival organizer and author of *Modern & Post-Modern Mime*, emphasizes: "Decroux believed that mime was a serious art and only secondarily a comic one. For some reason mime is linked in the popular mind with comedy, while Decroux stressed the more sublime and noble aspects of the art."

Too bad he saw a dichotomy between humor and seriousness, rather than dramatic opportunities. Decroux called mime "an art of standing up," but it's sometimes hard to see what he was standing up for. Completely silent mime has subversive roots, developing as a protest in eighteenth and nineteenth century France against officially sanctioned productions, which, alone, could use speaking actors. In this context, silence, like deaf signing, can speak irreverent volumes—function, as pornography, to say the unutterable—at the same time, because symbolic rather than literal, remain hard to police.

Decroux's work doesn't contain much anarchic potential. His striving after universality could result in thin, overly general imagery. And by strictly dividing speech from movement, he overlooked the ways that verbal expression could be a physical activity, that wordplay could prompt feeling as well as thought.

The festival has its share of genre cops, intent on partitioning off corporeal mime from scruffier, less austere styles. Among the presenters, Daniel Stein comes closest to Decroux's focus—as well as to a grace and physical mastery absorbing on their own. Resurrecting his 1978 work *Timepiece*, he perfects rope tricks that limn line and curve, tautness and slackness.

But most of the artists are breathing the moment and striving for collage—not random appropriation but a celebration of boundary-busting, in our age of global toxicities and yearnings. The mimes are rattling their cages, using silent gesture as but one vocabulary, staging shows far noisier and queerer than Decroux's.

Mime underlies the work of many performance artists and new vaudevillians: Bill Irwin, Michael Moschen, Teller, Denise Stoklos, Culture Clash, and Geoff Hoyle, to name a few. Now mimes are heading for similarly dense terrain. You see the embrace in mime journals, including articles on performance artists Tim Miller, Rachel Rosenthal, and Guillermo Gomez-Peña. Ambitiousness juices the festival—a desire for the breadth, social immediacy, and mythic scope of total-theater, thinking headed toward Peter Brook, Martha Clarke, and Meredith Monk.

But can mimes make theater that doesn't reinvent the wheel? Performance artists, many starting out as painters and dancers, have been up against the challenge of learning stagecraft and playwriting. At the festival, there is more urbanity and insouciance off stage than on. Puppets, masks, and the standard mime shtick—underwear, brooms, poles, and guns—are an invitation to be coy, or pretentious and opaque. After many changes of stylish costumes and much violent emotion, *Sa Griffe*, a fragmented homage to Man Ray by the Dutch company Griftheater, summons up ads for Calvin Klein's Obsession. And when Stein chooses to open his mouth, out pours a self-important lecture.

Margolis Brown Adaptors rises most successfully to the theatrical challenge in its weird and witty, all-dancing (make that quaking), all-singing (make that vocalizing) *Koppelvision and Other Digital Deities.* Founders Kari Margolis and Tony Brown stress collaboration as a way of nailing movement and writing. They tease mime conventions, unreeling variations on their theme—the human addiction to authority—in increasingly gripping dreamscapes. In their most eye-popping sequence, characters poke their heads through a sea of undulating, sloping fabric, at once drowning and swimming, sealed off from one another but sharing a common fate. When, en masse, they sneeze, sensuality is restored as cascades of hair are released.

The most promising showcase work is similarly clear in its intentions, yet eerily evocative of states beyond speech. Taiwanese-American Shou-You Liu floats on stage as a Noh doll, all whiteface and sleeves, and is reborn as a butoh nude, body pulsing and ribs jutting like some infant pterodactyl. Drawing on another 'hood's idioms, Rennie Harris's street-dance company, Pure Movement, hot-wires the festival with electric boogie, martial arts, and robotic jerks. A brooding duet for two men is performed against live drumming. And in another piece, staged in dim light, Harris's muscled torso radiates longing and despair, as, in voiceover, a young boy evokes his only toy, "penis erectus," and remembers the day his brother smashed his sister for being a lesbian.

When, in an ensemble piece, the performers break into domino moves, their bodies piling up, doubling and tripling, Decroux's workers are suddenly there. It doesn't matter whether Harris is directly quoting the originator. The experience of being dehumanized, whether by an assembly line or urban poverty, has called up echoing responses that are written in the flesh: a mixture of ruefulness and rebellion, as droids commandeer the machinery for their own art and pleasure.

Geoff Hoyle: Fool Hardy

April 1990

Geoff Hoyle exploits the comedy of farts, dungballs, and sticky snot. His is the humor of the rampant unrepressed, of juggled jitters and prurient interests. In the first act of his solo evening, the absorbing entertainment *Feast of Fools* (Westside Arts Theatre), we're led on a historical tour of the fool figure. With a gargoyle mask covering his face and his moist tongue darting, Hoyle hunches, leers, and brandishes his rod as a vegetation deity from pagan Europe. Next he's a medieval court jester—ass ears adorn his hood—engaged in a battle of wills with his alter ego, a doll jester perched on his staff. He stages the elaborate "feast of fools," a French ritual in which, once a year, peasants traded places with bishops and performed mock masses. And he serves a portion of commedia dell'arte, playing the horny miser Pantalone—who confuses his codpiece with his money pouch—as well as his sly, fly-eating servant Arlecchino.

Four other pieces afford British-born, classically trained Hoyle arenas for stylish, inventive clowning. In "The Fundraiser," an intensely ill-at-ease public speaker grows hooked on humiliation. In another bizarre turn, Hoyle is a man with three legs inspired to dance a foxtrot. Masks, handkerchiefs, and sticks crop up in all the pieces. Gestures, too, recur: anarchic leaps, openmouthed grimaces, and anxious checks for pong. Yet each caricature is detailed. The fundraiser can't bring himself to scratch his head, only to place a finger on his scalp. Mr. Sniff, a clown with a huge phallic nose, categorizes audience members as either sweet-smelling or noxious by inhaling with his entire, jiggling body. Hoyle's silliness doesn't forget death and horror, but no new vaudeville self-consciousness competes with awe and laughter.

The fools Hoyle animates remind us our body parts inevitably escape control. They point out that power is circumstantial, that kings, priests, and politicians will someday feed worms. For Hoyle, life is a cartoon in which anxiety clings like molasses.

Over tea a few days ago, the comic actor—he's forty-four and always looks like he stayed up carousing the night before—maps his training with the French movement master Decroux and with British nontraditional theater groups. He charts his work with Dario Fo and the Pickle Family Circus. And he reflects on his fascination with tragic farce and physical theater, embellishing anecdotes with fine-tuned body gestures and rubber-faced takes.

Hoyle grew up working-class in Hull, a coastal town in northern Britain, and in childhood fell in love with the British variety comics who'd migrated from music halls to TV and films. "Tommy Cooper would recite 'Christmas Day in the Workhouse,' a terrible, maudlin poem. He'd play ten characters using ten hats and hurt himself on the props. He'd make me feel *so* sad, but he was also funny and extraordinarily skilled. I love sleaze and silly grotesque jokes," he confided. "I got the three-legged man from a book called *150 Comedy Props* by Patrick Page. The tone is 'amaze your friends.' It has bits like fake dentist drills and whoopie cushions.

"I spent my salad days in Paris, '68 and '69, working in the streets, honing movement skills. I was there when the riots erupted. It was the most incredible thing. We walked down one street, and there were barricades and cops, then another street, more cops, and then there was this enormous wall made of paving stones and boards, and at the top were students. For the moment everything in the streets was a theater of change. Decroux, on the other hand, was authoritarian. I found the discipline easy, though. I was raised a Catholic.

"The pleasure of doing a character like the Fundraiser, who's so dull and fidgety, is nailing and celebrating him at the same time. He's torturously tedious, so he has the audience in his control, but he's also trapped in his own humiliation. It's interesting to show a freak turning his disability into an element of beauty or power, also showing the pain of people in awful situations. The humor has an element of compassion, a sense that we're all in this together, all victims because we're going to die.

"Physical theater reminds us of mortality, that things are falling apart, tending toward decay. No one acknowledges the sense of smell. We talk about touch, sight, sound, and taste. But smell is more revelatory of our innermost functions. Body odor, assholes, pricks, feet, cunts. Thoughts of death remind us that life is brief. We better have fun while we can. For a clown now, the landscape is extraordinarily grotesque. We've caught up with Breughel, beaches with pieces of stomach and hypodermic needles sticking out of them.

"For me, Beckett is still the most eloquent. 'I can't go on. He goes on.' I'd like to do a film of *Beckett's Last Crap*, no, that's *Krapp's Last Tape*."

Michael Moschen: Air Apparent

December 1988

Although juggler Michael Moschen and clown Bill Irwin have often collaborated—and both have been dubbed "new vaudevillians"—their recent work strides in opposite directions. Irwin's latest piece, presented at City

Center last spring, was an exercise in frustration: dances sharded and frozen just when a choreographic line appeared and rhythm kicked in. Irwin calls attention to responsiveness by blunting it.

Moschen isn't embarrassed or analytic. In his ninety-minute solo, *Michael Moschen in Motion,* he uses the means of art, especially visual, abstract art, to reshape aesthetic boundaries, and he lets us see his rapture. He gazes at his crystal balls with the love a dog-person lends a pet, a parent a child, and we're reminded there is no getting over the beauty of certain natural facts. He juggles flashily, two balls in each hand, then four in the air at once. A ball is allowed to roll down an arm and under his chin, then glide across his hand and around his fingers, so it seems weightless. The ball, appearing suspended in place as Moschen dances away from it, makes sport of time—the pull that etches lines on the face and draws blood from the brain, downward.

In the course of the evening, Moschen cavorts with hoops of varying sizes; he balances one, eight feet in diameter, on his lip. Metal rods zigzag like crazed compass points. A pliant form suggesting a bicycle tire by Dali is juggled like a giant piece of pasta. And two solid, S-curved shapes become elk antlers, then formal Adamesque designs.

Despite the high-toned press coverage Moschen attracts, his work is playful, provisional. Opening night, he clowns with a child who is sitting near the front and whose yelps of delight are a beat behind everyone else's. Early in the show, he works with silicon balls, bouncing them on the stage and against the exterior and interior walls of a ten-foot-high triangle. The pings alternately accompany and counterpoint David Van Tieghem's lissome electronic score. Sometimes the balls move so fast they leave comet-tailed afterimages, and the collective effect synthesizes computer graphics, percussion, and juggling. Sometimes the balls weave patterns that surprise even Moschen. But he isn't unnerved by accident.

It delights him as much as control, and a good deal of the magic of his work comes from the tension he establishes between discipline and improvisation. Physical skill grounds Moschen, affording him the peace that makes experiment possible. Practice and technical skill are the raw materials with which he shapes his art, looking to other practitioners for sources. Fan dancers and Loie Fuller's light shows are remembered in his pieces. In the second half of the performance, working with sculptural forms designed by John Kahn, Moschen's work alludes to Klee, Kandinsky, Miró, and Calder. The week I saw Moschen, I attended a show of Diebenkorn works at MOMA, and I was struck by the way both artists—Diebenkorn with erasures and pentimento, Moschen with increasingly complex variations on themes—expose their fascination with geometry, physics, and architectural forms (Diebenkorn's lattices and grids), and also their striving for originality by playing and testing until a new note is struck.

Penn and Teller: Leger de Mainia

December 1987

Penn and Teller did their comedy/magic show for a year at the Westside Arts Theater, got an Obie, and got famous. They've moved to the cozy—for Broadway—Ritz and added one bit. Teller's in a tank of water, wearing his customary gray suit and red tie. He's holding his breath, and he's prepared to stay submerged until Penn finds a card an audience member has written his name on. Penn has shuffled it into a deck, and of course can't find it, won't find it. The seconds tick away as Penn's megaphone mouth touts Houdini's breath-holding record (five minutes, 45 seconds). After a while, he bangs on Teller's tank. "You broke the record." Teller's deadpan stare—part Buster Keaton, part Kubrick space-baby—is visible through his diver's mask. After six minutes, Teller waves the key he's holding, the key to the lock that secures the tank. Penn finally tries the lock and discovers it won't open. He shrugs. Teller's body turns, a lifeless float. Penn taps the glass again. "Brain dead."

It's a trick. Teller stays in the tank for more than 11 minutes and doesn't die. The stunt is beautiful. Teller's illusion of breath-holding, his and Penn's sleights of hand—Teller winds up with the missing card *under* his mask—are exactly what they're meant to be: magic.

Penn and Teller don't make you jump through high-art hoops to get to the crowd-pleasing stuff. They revel in freak shows and sleaze. Penn, self-described in his radio ads as "the obnoxious one with the stupid haircut," *is* aggressive and *does* look weird. The head atop his tall, hulking body sports a braided rattail behind and a flowing frizz mop in front. The hipness lacing his nonstop rap skates on corniness. One minute he calls himself and Teller "two eccentric guys who've learned to do a few cool things"; another minute, before eating fire, he milks our sympathy, explaining that, each night, a teaspoon of poisonous fluid is also swallowed. But both tacks are calculated. Penn is the carny barker, luring the sadist in us to gawk at the Seal Boy and the two-headed fetus. He's also one of the freaks.

The show lets us indulge our taste for gore and pain over the safety net of the performers' mastery. In one stunt, Teller—the silent, nimble partner—is straitjacketed, then hoisted upside down above the stage. His head points at a bed of wood spikes. He'll crash unless he can escape before Penn finishes speed-reciting "Casey at the Bat." In two other pieces, hands are fake-pierced, and gooey fake blood spurts. And in the evening's tour de force, Teller swallows two dozen embroidery needles and six feet of thread, then, from his gullet, extracts the same number of needles *knotted* on the thread.

In some of the duo's most gleeful bits they lead us behind the scenes of a trick. First, they do the famous "cups and balls" routine—their hands, like the hands of chefs, are athletes. Then they do the trick again, with plastic cups, explaining every feint and pass. But this is a trick, too, for their intention isn't to demystify their powers but to make us marvel at them all the more. Seeing the works of this trick is like glimpsing the gears and jewels of a precision watch.

The skill of these men asks us to wonder about such devotion to craft: the hours spent developing card moves and shifting fire inside the mouth. Under their weird exteriors lurk true weirdos. Their compensation, aside from fame, fortune, and dancing groupies? During their show, they get to hold all the secrets. We are forever left out, but this is the price we pay for such satisfying gawking.

Gory Details

April 1991

At the beginning of *The Refrigerator Tour,* Penn & Teller's latest spectacle at the Eugene O'Neill Theatre, a crated and rope-bound box, said to contain a 450-pound Amana, swings above the magicians. It crashes on them with serious noise. Something heavy is definitely in the box, or so it seems. But Penn and Teller spring up unharmed from beneath a tarp. Perhaps, at the last second, they've substituted dummies for their bodies, then whisked them away before surfacing. The secret behind the trick is intriguing; each illusion in their arsenal requires a combination of mechanics and muscle control, ranging from the diabolically simple to the painstakingly intricate. But even more compelling is the lunatic poetry of that blank box, freighted with menace and fears of dismemberment. Penn and Teller make horror hilarious without making it disappear.

Since teaming in 1975, they've had lengthy runs on and off Broadway, done several TV specials, and made the movie *Penn & Teller Get Killed.* When not working live, they can come off stagy, the primary exception being their shots with Letterman, who enjoys being spooked by them (they once loosed a thousand roaches onto his desk) and ups the ante on their wit. Before seeing *The Refrigerator Tour,* I wondered if the partners were tiring of their personas: aggressive Penn threatening to detonate, Harpoesque Teller twisting his passivity into feats of physical mastery. No need to worry: They've grown keener, more reflective.

The show, featuring several new bits, is a comic monologue in which stunts illustrate themes. Some sequences are thrillingly unfathomable. Teller cuts the petals of the shadow of a flower, and an actual blossom is denuded. Every sleight-of-hand, false cut, and misdirection—all before our eyes and yet undetectable—presents reality as too manifold to grasp, except in staggered fragments.

Penn and Teller study annihilation. In one classic piece, a blindfolded, knife-wielding Teller uses his "psychic" powers to impale Penn's hand as he reaches for cards. In another vignette, a live duck, placed in a shopping bag, awaits pressing beneath a pendulous anvil. And later Teller, swinging from a trapeze, plucks the ingredients of a baloney sandwich from the snaggle-toothed jaws of a dozen leg-hold animal traps.

The tricks acknowledge that the world is painful. The ubiquitous pulleys, harnesses, and ropes invoke the pleasures and risks of violence and passivity. But while Penn and Teller flirt with danger, they don't submit to it. Their mission is preparedness. Each sequence ends with escape, resurrection, a display of mastery over chaotic forces—including loneliness and the anxiety of being damaged. Yet the triumphs come laced with poignance. Supernaturalism, denying as it does the finality of death, is scorned. We're exhorted to sharpen our senses and dodge capture, all the while contemplating actual helplessness and inhaling the smell of real, inevitable mortality.

One of the pair's wonders is their ability to create, within a tightly choreographed and scripted show, an atmosphere of spontaneity and taboo-bashing. These days, there's even more premeditated disruption, including Teller poking through the restraints of his silence with occasional outbursts at Penn, such as "Shut up." Their work is a commentary on partnership, the alliance of self-described "eccentric guys," who feel outside the loop of sociability and invent secrets no one else can know.

In "Cuffed to a Creep," one of their most eloquent pieces, Teller sneakily handcuffs himself to perfect-stranger Penn, and their ensuing struggle riffs on the strains of mutual dependency. They cut even more sharply against their established roles in "Burnin' Luv," in which Penn leaves the partnership to eat fire with glamorous Carol Perkins, and Teller, sitting apart, accompanies them on a piano. The scenario is sexy and Oedipal, in a word, hot.

A few days after seeing their performance, I join Penn, thirty-six, and Teller, forty-three, in their Midtown office, unremarkable save for the sign on the refrigerator: "Disease Control Center, Specimen Transfer Unit." Penn says that nothing they do onstage is dangerous; their goal is control. He explains that two ducks work in the show and, when not appearing, swim in an inflatable pool at the theater. But he zealously blocks my attempts to ferret out the secrets of the refrigerator stunt, which, from his perspective, is as graceless as wishing to look up a Scotsman's kilt (another challenge I'd take on).

Teller suggests I'd be disappointed by the trick's guts, which he calls "ugly," just as he was dejected to discover that Bach had lifted several melodies for *The Well-Tempered Clavier* from the composer Johann Casper Ferdinand Fischer. I explain I'm not an idealist, that, to the contrary, process and influence are just as alluring as finished work, but this argument buzzes like a gnat around the elephant of Teller's resistance.

The rest of the conversation roams through magic art. On stage, Penn and Teller set up a tension between their roles as sleazy con men and the perfectionism that shines out in their moves. Off stage, all that's left is devotion. Teller extols women magicians of the past—among them Adelaide Herrmann, Talmer, and Mademoiselle Patrice—and wishes more women performed today, to loosen "the boys' clubby thing," a monolith of males "afraid of social contact." Penn rails against scammers who, using tricks, pretend to divine thoughts and move objects with their minds. "If we had no morals, we could be doing evil things and making a lot of money," he says. The best magic, Penn and Teller insist, is "making a career out of doing what you love."

Kuni Leml: Between Two Worlds

July 1984

"The boy is perfect," crows Reb Kalman, the Matchmaker, to Reb Pinkhos, his wealthy client, extolling Kuni Leml, the proffered groom. "The boy can scrimp," Kalman goes on, "but since he isn't farming, does it matter he's a shrimp?" In addition, Kuni is blind in one eye, deaf in one ear, and has a hump, a stutter, and a limp. Never mind, Reb Pinkhos agrees; he's a pious Hasid, thus right for daughter Carolina, whose head and heart have been snatched by the tutor, "Max Nobody, son of Nobody." Will Carolina marry Kuni, or will she and Max happily ever after read Tom Paine in the pantry, Darwin at dinner, and Pushkin in the parlor?

Avrom Goldfadn's original play *The Fanatic, or The Two Kuni Lemls* (1880)—a perennial hit in the Yiddish theater—is a love song to life beyond the ghetto, a celebration of change under Czar Alexander II's reign, when Jews studied, traveled, and entered professions as never before. Ironically, a year after the play was written, Alexander was shot, anti-Semitism grew ferocious, and battalions of Russian Jews, Goldfadn and his audience among them, fled to the States. This first-ever English adaptation, under Ran Avni's direction, is a wry, spare, 1980s reading of 1880s modernity. In *Fiddler on the Roof*—similarly about the clash of old and new—when the cast sings "Tradition," we're meant to feel weepy for *mikvah* baths and guilty about eating lobsters. Change is mainly seen as painful and destructive. *Kuni Leml,* on the other hand, has a raw, nervy tone. The future may be chaotic, the play says, but there's no virtue in sticking to the past for its own sake. The direct and honest *Kuni* expands Max's humanity, but Kuni gains more. By acting on his desires instead of following Hasid law, he suddenly feels at home in his skin. He's no longer a shmendrik.

The production is impeccable. Raphael Crystal has incorporated some of Goldfadn's tunes and lyrics into his score, which, like everything else in the piece, is both a homage to and conversation with the past.

Nahma Sandrow's swift dialogue keeps the farcical machinery well oiled. The play is mostly sung, operetta-style, and Richard Engquist's lyrics are part social history, part stand-up comedy. In "The World Is Getting Bigger," a tribute to Flaubert, Mendel, and Marx, Max and his fellow students rhyme demonic and Abraham Lincolnic. My favorite couplet is from "A Little Learning," Pinkhos's lament for his daughter's education, in which he sings, "She serves peculiar dishes./ She wouldn't give me knishes."

The acting and singing mesh elegantly with the production's witty tone. Daniel Marcus and Jack Savage harmonize sweetly in the double parts of the Russianized Jewish students, Yasha and Sasha, and as Yankle and Simkhe, Hasidim in kingergarten dress-up beards. Mark Zeller's Reb Pinkhos is forever pacing, brandishing an index finger, and reversing his direction. While one side of him waves a red flag at the locomotive of social change, the other side tells him to clear the tracks before getting squashed. Gene Varrone, as Kalmen, and Susan Victor, as his daughter, Libe—the girl who wants a husband just like Kuni—resist the temptation to ham these stock parts. Barbara McCulloh (Carolina) has a sprightly soprano and is wonderful dropping French phrases in Odessa street conversation. And the two Kunis—Stuart Zagnit, as the real one (his *payes* look electrified) and Scott Wentworth, as Max-impersonating-Kuni—do slapstick turns, among others, the Harpo-meets-himself mirror sequence. This is stylish musical theater with a minimum of cost and a maximum of brains.

Shlemiel the First

July 1994

In Isaac Bashevis Singer's *Shlemiel the First* (Serious Fun! at Lincoln Center), sex is rekindled when a married couple pretend to be strangers. In trucking with *Yiddishkeit,* is the Serious Fun! festival snuffling for that block-ticket temple audience? Could be. But the delight of this piece isn't folk wisdom; it's the lineage of foolishness. Fast-paced and ingeniously staged by David Gordon, *Shlemiel the First* treats its audience to old vaudeville shtick by way of new vaudeville panache and reimagined simplicity. Robert Israel's set, Catherine Zuber's costumes, Zalmen Mlotek and Hankus Netsky's music, and Arnold Weinstein's lyrics are skewed with irony that strokes rather than sneers at the piece's sources. The cast of nimble clowns—Larry Bloch, Marilyn Sokol, Charles Levin, and Remo Airaldi—encompasses Yiddish theater, burlesque, the vaudeville of the Marx Brothers, Danny Kaye, and such movement-theater pranksters as Avner the Eccentric and Bob Berky.

Rhyming "Pennsylvania" with "I'll explain ya" and zooming around in black frock coats and fake facial hair, the antic denizens of Chelm are deathless, acrobatic Grouchos. In this Jewtopia, the actors cross-dress, women toot sweetly in the klezmer band, and brothers descended from Africa trippingly sing "Rumania."

BETTY: Best Betty

July 1990

Think of girl gangs . . . composed of princesses. Think of Bette Midler . . . before she became a Disney character, when, as the Divine One, she channeled Mae West, bawdy and bold. Think of girl bands, like the hellzapoppin' combo in *Some Like It Hot* and the real-life International Sweethearts of Rhythm, an interracial ensemble that blew tight, swinging tunes during the forties. Think of the Andrews Sisters with rich fantasy lives, unfurling and unchecked. And you have something of BETTY, the group that slithers past categorization at the Ballroom.

BETTY consists of twin sisters Amy and Bitzi Ziff, who don't inordinately resemble each other, and Alyson Palmer. The trio is a band, knowing and relaxed with each other and with their instruments. They sing three-part harmonies that are thrillingly woven and mellifluous, then take jolting twists. And they're partial to hard-driving rock rhythms with punk, new wave, and Caribbean beats; most of their tunes are composed by the threesome.

BETTY is richly comic, part home movie, part artful contrivance. It's a dream pajama party, with every wish of wildness and silliness indulged. Diversity is prominently featured. The Ziffs are diminutive and pale-skinned. Palmer is statuesque, her complexion café au lait. Bitzi's mane is red, Amy's blond, and Alyson's brown, but they're all frizzed, and electric current seems to flow from the tendrils. The performers are wired, connected to one another, yet each projects an individual persona. Bitzi, boogying solo and flashing a sleek midriff, is an earthy imp sporting a slender nose ring. Alyson, wielder of the bass guitar and master of electronic gadgetry, is a glamorous wizard. And Amy, who does most of the talking and delivers monologues between musical numbers, translates the associations, mannerisms, and verbal tics that trail the trio like jet streams.

Favored themes are standards of pop—love gone sour and feelings of freakishness—but they're freshened with puns and double entendres. In "Go Ahead and Split, Mr. Amoeba Man," the women quip, "I can't divide my love again." In "First Date," about a happening that doesn't, they croon, "I shaved my legs for nothing." After the song, Amy stares out. "You weren't feeling sorry for us in that last number, were you?"

"D.C. Dog," a punk anthem to "problem pets," provides Bitzi with the opportunity to lift her leg and mime peeing. "Wolfwoman" celebrates the hungry, hairy appetites women carry inside. At one point, Amy declares, "I can't decide whether to ride girls or boys." Long take. "Bicycles, that is." In two surreal sequences, she becomes the cigarette-toting "tough girl" in every women's prison movie.

References whiz by, but an intelligent, foxy tone is sustained, and this, above all, lifts the evening from a revue to a work of theater. The name BETTY evokes Betty Crocker, concocter of brown Bettys and conjurer of all that's homey and secure. The women of BETTY hold the stage, their skilled hands on the controls; they are delighted with each other's company. They are anti–Betty Crockers, and yet, as Amy is fond of saying, "not." BETTY is homey, a sister act, with inside moves and code phrases. "Understood," the women continually beep at one another.

The pleasures and tensions of being part of a group—even a group of outcasts banded together—are paraded. The urge toward individuality is countered with a yearning to meld into a united, harmonic voice. Sisterhood is at times an amulet, at others an albatross; in one bit, parasitic twins are described. These women refuse to lop off portions of themselves, but there's no piety in their stand and no exclusivity in the pleasure they generate. BETTY satirizes insider humor, letting everyone in on the joke.

I met BETTY for lunch in a dive of their choosing near their duplex apartment on the Lower East Side. They've shared it since moving to Manhattan in 1988. The three are twenty-nine and met in Washington, D.C., ten years ago, when the sisters were forming a band and advertised for musicians. All three grew up abroad, children of men in the diplomatic service.

Off stage, they're equally voluble and available. At school, Bitzi was the wild girl. One hot day, miffed that boys could bare their chests, she organized the girls in her class to rip off their blouses and run through the grounds. "I was raising my hand, offering some perfect answer," recalls Amy, "when I saw my sister dart by. I was horrified but supportive." When Alyson entered the twins' lives, a third dimension was added and an artistic collaboration charged.

The women come across undefended, excited about their involvement, and ambitious to succeed. They know their worth, these daughters of the women's movement. "Sure, we fight," says Alyson, "and we each have personal insecurities. I look in the mirror and see Bullwinkle moose. But we have this other thing. BETTY takes away the doubts."

Slant: Bias Cut

December 1995

Perry Yung was riding his bike one night, wearing his leather jacket and letting his freak hair fly, when he stopped at a light beside a Chinese delivery guy. "In Cantonese he says, 'Working late, too?' He sees Chinese and bicycle, so I must be doing the same thing as him, and I thought, if *he* assumes this, probably everyone does. Then I wondered about him, zigzagging across the city. What is his life about?"

These questions percolated in Yung, who, with Richard Ebihara and Wayland Quintero, all thirty-one, make up the performance troupe Slant. A couple of weeks ago at La MaMa they debuted their first piece, *Big Dicks, Asian Men,* a satirical revue as raucous as it is deadpan, as unironed as it is deliberate, as piercing as it is self-exposing. In the tradition of the Chicano clowns of Culture Clash and the gay card sharks of Pomo Afro Homos, Slant pledges allegiance to nakedness, pulling down the underpants of the tribe and flashing to all voyeurs. In their case, the tribe is hyphenated Asian men, living in a culture that mostly cancels them, and, when it doesn't, allows either mysterious villains or subservient geeks.

Dicks is a pent-up explosion that is deftly calibrated. The big dicks unfurled are wit and individuality, dry humor and slapstick, dancer-buffed bodies and rock 'n' roll hearts. In the opener, the three, who look nothing alike, are hauled in for a lineup when a woman complains she's been sold a fake Gucci bag. A voice directs them: "Say, 'Gucci, Rolex, Obsession . . . best deal.' " They're told they don't sound "Oriental enough," and the cop is confounded when Ebihara speaks with an English accent.

Music and movement interludes—drawing on the actors' training in voice, martial arts, and dance—propel the comedy into moody improvs. Singing the ballad "No Menus Please!" the trio circle the stage on tiny tricycles, injecting poignance into their vaudeville: "Nothing is ever quite as it seems/We litter your halls with our family dreams." As sumo wrestlers stuffing to put on weight and exchanging girlfriend advice, they cavort nude but for their genitals, although enormous facsimiles—harking back to Chinese and Japanese erotic cartoons—are finally wielded after the three, in another sketch, undergo penile enlargement surgery.

"The police lineup is partly an actor's joke," says Quintero. "We all audition for the same parts. I've played Korean, Cambodian, Japanese, Puerto Rican. In a way it's freeing, but it also means that the differences among Asians aren't noticed. A white actor would really have to learn a German accent, but all a Japanese actor has to do to play Chinese is talk high up in the throat and singsong."

"We wanted a loose form for the cultural baggage," says Yung. "I constantly get confronted with racial comments. 'Hey, Bruce,' or 'Jackie Chan.' " Ebihara chimes in, "I get Judge Ito." In the show, a character talks about the rarity of seeing a black woman with an Asian man. "I had a black girlfriend," says Yung, "and we were stared at. We were seen as an exotic mix, but it's also that blacks and Asians aren't supposed to like each other, the 'model minority' thing that supposedly hurts blacks. The pain has become our material."

Slant is a balcony for their imaginations, a couch for their psyches, a map for the countries within this country. Ebihara, who grew up in Ohio and sang with the Cleveland Opera, is third-generation American on one side and fourth-generation on the other, but his mother was born in an American internment camp for Japanese-Americans. Quintero was born in the Philippines and raised in Hawaii, where Filipinos "were like blacks, under the Japanese and Chinese." Yung was born in San Francisco, where his parents, Chinese immigrants, conversed entirely in Cantonese. "My father bought a Chinese restaurant in Texarkana. I was the only Asian in my school."

For their next piece, they plan to work the irony that while in the West Asian men are wimpified, in Asia machismo rules. "We want to try drag," says Ebihara, "play with the image of Asian men as effeminate, in straight and gay worlds." Yung is working on a piece in which he transforms himself into a Sharon Stone type—"change from an Asian male, the least desired sexual persona in the culture, to the most desired."

Humiliation is the swamp that hasn't drowned them. At the end of *Dicks*, the suspects are booked and do a dance with their pants around their ankles. Strip searches and bondage are conjured, but we also see strangeness and grace. The three remain themselves—angry but not righteous, candid but not back-patting, sexy but not truckling.

CHAPTER EIGHT

TV: Comedy Tubular and Wired

David Letterman

Sitcoms generally weary me. The dialogue is like panel on a talk show, people waiting to drop punch lines that pretty much anyone on any show could deliver. These shows have ruled network programming most of the last ten years: *Cosby, Murphy Brown, Cheers, Roseanne, Home Improvement, Friends, Frasier, Seinfeld.* Though they repeat like dogs circling a worn spot on the couch, they have their moments.

I'm tickled by the belligerent feyness of David Hyde-Pierce, who plays Kelsey Grammer's brother on *Frasier,* by the pitiless contempt Sarah Gilbert sprays at her nearest and dearest on *Roseanne,* by Christine Baranski's dry disdain for sobriety on *Cybill.* What an amusing family these three would make. And looming transcendently is *Seinfeld,* the antisitcom, celebrating failure and disconnection.

Most sitcoms champion family, whether nuclear nests of parents and kids or workplace gangs of reporters and cops. *Seinfeld*'s solitaries huddle from a sense of shared desperation. No one outside the foursome quite speaks their language, because the rest of the world seeks to be adjusted, satisfied. *Seinfeld*'s landscape is mined with menace and defeat: a place where men need bras to contain their sagging pecs, where Elaine's co-workers jeer because she dances weirdly, where Jerry's car acquires a stink so ferocious he has to abandon it on the street. The show's motto is: Hell is other people. Loneliness, in comparison, doesn't look so bad.

No other TV comedy has matched *Seinfeld*'s stoical, mordant disaffec-tion, and during the past ten years, sketch comedy and variety shows have mostly lain like loxes. *SNL* never measures up to *SCTV*'s wry skewer-ing of the medium, and the show in recent seasons has devolved into a loop of beer-and-vomit humor. In better days, Mike Myers created inef-fable sillies, among them pretentious, Eurotrash film critic Dieter and pop culture savant Wayne. Al Franken's Stuart Smalley, whose inner child had run amok, tweaked confession as sewage, while copping to the pleasures of navel gazing.

The most dramatic shifts in TV comedy have been the rise of cable and the late-night wars. The fists of Carson in late night and of the big three networks in TV broadcasting were pried open by Carson's retirement and by the alternative programming beamed on cable networks—in com-edy, especially HBO and Comedy Central. HBO, corporate- and dollar-driven though it is, has backed independent minds, from Tracey Ullman, to Dennis Miller, to Eric Bogosian, to John Leguizamo, airing solo evenings, talk shows, stand-up hours, and series such as *Dream On* and *The Larry Sand-ers Show*. Comedy Central's animated series *Dr. Katz*, written and performed by Jonathan Katz, is an ingenious running joke, with real stand-ups doing couch duty and the doc's life, with his deadbeat twenty-three-year-old son reeling on behind the scenes. Wanting peace before leaving the house, Katz embraces his recalcitrant scion and croons, "Who loves you?" No response. Doc: "It's not a trick question."

■ ■ ■

This chapter begins with a poke at *Thirtysomething*, which I describe when it was fresh out of the chute and, to me, at its most irritating. It stands as an interesting marker in the culture of AIDS hysteria. With its open-ended narrative it had its hooks, but it remained determinedly retro, reflecting the Reagan/Bush eighties, a postcounterculture, it's-hip-to-be-square soap.

The next piece scrutinizes HBO as benevolent/opportunistic daddy of Comic Relief. Then follows a profile of writer Eddie Gorodetsky and the kick-off of The Comedy Channel, which shortly would merge with Ha!—there really *wasn't* a need for two twenty-four-hour comedy networks—to form Comedy Central.

I write about three shows cobbled not by committee but a unified vision: *Life and Loves of a She-Devil*, *Sessions*, and *Northern Exposure*. The first two were miniseries, but *Northern Exposure* had a spirited run for its money, a comedy motored by a utopian social view and emotionally revealing dialogue. The counterculture remained kicking in this Hollywood dream factory.

The rest of the chapter reports on Letterman, Leno, and the talk show wars. Often in this book I cuff Letterman for his dominance in stand-up. Stories are legion about his Captain Queegish obsessions: eating the same sandwich every day for lunch, guzzling coffee and candy bars to pump up his energy, excoriating his performances so mercilessly he wafts a cloud of gloom and hysteria over his workplace. But since Leno has assumed control of *The Tonight Show*, he has become unwatchable: the joke sprays that beg for acceptance, the nervous head tics, and, most grating, lifting wholesale the kind of shtick on remote locations that Letterman patented.

I never thought I'd hear myself say this, but I have to admit I'm getting to like Dave. I wrote a snide piece about him, got up in the form of viewer mail. I stand by its points—it was composed right after Letterman had closed the $41 million deal with CBS. Many critics like the crazier, meaner, NBC Dave, but I found it difficult to watch his rage. For a while on the new show, as he pulled ahead of Leno in the ratings, he seemed almost cheerful, almost interested in his guests. Almost.

Then in the summer of '95 Leno got first crack at interviewing Hugh Grant after his arrest for public sex with a hooker, and Leno began to lead in the ratings, an edge he's maintained. Go figure. Letterman isn't a happy puppy. He fired his longtime producer and friend Robert Morton and off camera has returned to his infectiously depressed state. I still like the show. Something has come loose in Letterman for the better, a way to continue without being top dog. There's less urgency to be smart-assed, hip-asdisaffected. He laughs more at other people's humor, and he's found two natural comedians in Rupert Jee, the deli guy around the corner, and Manny the Hippie, chanced upon when the show visited San Francisco.

Paula Poundstone took a misstep with her talk show, whose cancellation may rank among the quickest on record. It was a parallel-universe nightmare reverse of what Rosie O'Donnell would pull off in the fall of '96. O'Donnell's genuineness cuts through the sludge of her obsessions: the infantile star worship and pop culture ticker tape she spews.

I quite liked the late-night gigs of Dennis Miller and Jon Stewart, short-lived though they were. Miller was quickly rescued by HBO, where he continues to thrive. Stewart has made a deal with Miramax and, like Greg Kinnear, is adding a movie career to comedy. But Stewart is most faceted as himself: smart, curious, and improvisational.

The last piece honors *The Larry Sanders Show*, a comedy landmark. Pure and mean as hell, it represents the best of uncensored cable, the funniest, best-made TV show in the decade.

Yuppie Chow: *thirtysomething*

October 1987

A Steven Bochco knock-off, *thirtysomething* tries to imitate the tooled originals—*Hill Street Blues* and *L.A. Law*, but on this program, instead of feeling characters within a developing story, we get bundles of attitude and fifty little epiphanies in an hour.

One tiny scene builds to a laugh, another to tears. Or there's a fight, a confession, a reverie, a parting, a reunion. It's like getting your foot caught in an escalator and having your head thump, thump, thumped along the steps. Michael (Ken Olin) and Hope (Mel Harris), who love each other and their new baby, are supposed to be two choices among an array of options. The other types include Elliot (Timothy Busfield) and Nancy (Patricia Wettig), a settled married couple; Ellyn (Polly Draper), a single exec sans personal life; Melissa (Melanie Mayron), a waning sex goddess; and Gary (Peter Horton), a long-haired Peter Pan. For a while it seems they'll get equal time. As it turns out, they superimpose a picture of diversity.

The focus is on the happy couple. The other characters orbit them, popping into view to show they yearn for Hope and Michael's life. Melissa feeds their seven-month-old daughter, Jane, and declares she wants to keep the kid. In another scene, Ellyn brags about having twenty-seven people "under" her at work, then confesses she's jealous of Hope. Teary-eyed, Hope turns to Ellyn and says, "*I'm* jealous of *you*," but we don't believe her. *Thirtysomething* paints her life—dirty diapers and messy kitchen withal—as devoutly desirable.

Hope has quit her job to stay home with her child, and she's presented as brave for resisting Ellyn's exhortation to go back to work. Michael likes this arrangement more than his "integrity"; he's a partner in a small advertising firm, and, to support his family, he courageously acquiesces to a client and concocts a shabby campaign. You might think these two would be worn out from all this heroism, but they endure yet another trial. Their friends, the arrested cases, urge them to go camping—to hire a babysitter and have fun. The couple tries to accommodate: Michael has a fantasy about sex in the woods; Hope interviews a parade of baby-sitters. In the end they stay home, in the suburbs, because they don't really want to leave.

Michael and Hope keep repeating, "We're so lucky." They're surrounded by panic. It shoots from the eyes of their single friends, fueling a mantra in the couple, unspoken but discernible in all their rationales: If we can just get clean enough, straight enough, simple enough; if we can just forget about adventure, exoticism, and risk; if we can just escape the city and its denizens—the poor, the druggy, the freaky, all those who remind us of our doubts and nasty cravings—then we'll be safe for life. The show's milieu is white, moneyed, heterosexual, and IV-drug free. Still the characters utter the words "family," "marriage," "commitment," and "home" as if casting spells, as if praying. They've succumbed to that spreading secondary infection, the one that gives people license to cave in to their terrors about aloneness and otherness and call it fear of AIDS.

Comic Relief: Causes Célèbres

March 1990

At Radio City Music Hall, as the Comic Relief telethon was winding to a close, Whoopi Goldberg, Billy Crystal, and Robin Williams announced that the event had raised over \$3.5 million. An hour earlier, at midnight, Andrew "Dice" Clay, hosting *SNL*, had declared he was donating his earnings to the homeless. He said it sheepishly, as if embarrassed to be caught out of his braggart character. There they were, the week's two big stories in comedy, momentarily converging.

About Clay: the man has fat thighs, the kind that rub together and make pants rustle, the kind that wear out fabric near the crotch, and yet this schlub has the temerity to insist he's virile and that women are mindless. What is that? You have to be amazed at the permission he grants himself to strut under such challenged circumstances. On *SNL*, stripped of his slurs for national TV, he proved bland, save for a single apt description of Sinéad O'Connor (who'd refused to appear on the show with him) as "a cute bald chick."

As for Nora Dunn, who'd also protested Clay's hosting on feminist grounds with a no-show, she arrived at Comic Relief not as a performer on the roster but as a guest at the press room. Typical of the media's bent to trivialize feminism, most reports skewed Dunn's stand so it seemed she was against raunch rather than bigotry. She might have explained the difference. But she was introduced with the coy prohibition that she'd only field questions about the homeless. Hoping to skirt the charge of grandstanding, she came off appearing to do just that, but hey, self-promotion is hardly unknown at Comic Relief.

In a TV interview last week, HBO chairman/CEO Michael Fuchs said, to this effect, it was great to help others, but when you could also assist yourself, well that was dying and going to heaven. In its four-year existence, Comic Relief has earned over \$16 million, every cent of which has funded a national network of health care facilities for homeless people. HBO, with the aid this year of Canada Dry, has covered all expenses—\$2,063,710 for 1990.

But the show, with its enormous audience, superstar hosts, and good-guy image, has also become the premier "please-book-me" comedy event of the year. Who does get booked? Nearly all of the performers have solid ties to HBO. The nation's largest subscription network produces, among this year's lineup, shows starring each of the three hosts, as well as Elayne Boosler, Bob Goldthwaite, Alan Havey, Richard Lewis, Steven Wright, Robert Wuhl, Rita Rudner, Paula Poundstone, and many more. HBO gets to write off the production costs of Comic Relief as charity, at the same time gaining five hours of promotion time for its talent.

With only four minutes alotted to each guest, the sets, indeed, amounted to little more than trailers. This year's program was well oiled but generally tame, with periodic exceptions. Robin Williams scowled, "I'm Bernhard Goetz. I don't have any spare change." Unpredictability flared when Rick Overton goaded Bob Goldthwaite to lop off his shoulder-length sweaty, Ben Franklin mane "for the homeless." Thank you, Rick. And light glinted off Steven Wright, who admitted he went through a stop sign: "I don't believe everything I read."

Thursday's nontelevised benefit for Comic Relief, held at Caroline's, was sillier, wilder. Booed for a foolish pun, Bob Saget came back, "No, you were right to do that, I feel cleansed." He Grouchoed, "My wife is a saint. She's Gandhi. She walks around in diapers and won't eat." Goldthwaite went on a tear, upending Axl Rose for telling gays to go back where they come from: "What country is that, Homoslavia?" He pointed to a banner emblazoned with the logos of HBO and Canada Dry and spouted "Comic Relief, brought to you by major corporations forcing people to live in the streets."

Back at Radio City, in the expansive green room—tables adorned with rubrum lilies, Thai food catered by Tommy Tang, chocolate truffle cake topped with whipped cream and raspberry puree—hands shook hands that feed themselves. "Agents, managers, lawyers, and publicists," chanted Rick Newman, a manager/producer/restaurateur who had, earlier in the week, hosted a lavish party for participants in Comic Relief. There, as here, deals hatched, sniffed the air, and rose, smiling, toward the ceiling.

Stars, blinking into the space illuminated by their celebrity auras, moved about flanked by female slaveys, each wearing, around her neck, a photograph of her charge that was captioned, "I belong to _____." I chanced upon Joan Rivers, vampy in black, with tresses moussed and snakey. "You look beautiful," I said. "Oh sure," she returned. "No," I persisted, "you really do, and you should believe it." Her assessment of female flesh seemed as unremitting as Dice Clay's. She shook her head, meeting my eyes. "It's too late."

This scene, with its absence not of pain, but of want—of any trace of the predicament being etched and campaigned for on stage—was disturbingly detached, yet entrancing, as luxury always is and is imagined to be by those barred from it. Behind me a man mused, with understandable cynicism, "For five hours, I'm eating cake and drinking wine—for the home-less."

Laffs on a Loop: Writer Eddie Gorodetsky Fuels the Comedy Channel

November 1989

When HBO debuts the Comedy Channel on November 15, it will launch continuous humor programming. That's 8760 hours a year soliciting laughs, chortles, and moans if need be. Eddie Gorodetsky, thirty-three, is the head writer for this project, the man whose sensibilities and inner life will be packaged and beamed to eleven million cable subscribers—with more to come once the network is available in Manhattan.

Gorodetsky's face is round and soft but his eyes can slit mischievously. With his short hair, rotund form, and ubiquitous T-shirts, he seems to have fashioned his image on the cartoon character Sluggo. Except for his right bicep, on which resides an alter-ego tattoo: a conga player drawn in the style of twenties deco artist John Held, Jr. "The guy's jacket is plaid," he says, pointing to a pale gray pattern on his arm. "I wanted the contradiction of a *subtle* tattoo. I considered a Jackson Pollock, but I thought it would look like a rash."

The rash quip, fusing an art world reference with anxiety about appearance, is typical of Gorodetsky's comic bent. A media junkie indiscriminately consuming pop culture and scholarship, he grafts private obsessions onto public icons and myths. The process gives him a charge, though he can't say why. Nonetheless, his talent for pastiche has won him writing jobs on TV's most influential comedy shows—*SCTV, Letterman* and *Saturday Night Live*—as well as gigs developing material for innovative clowns like Don Novello, Martin Short, and Penn & Teller. With his inventory of experience, it's not surprising HBO would trust him with the Comedy Channel. If the venture attracts the MTV viewership to which it aspires, Gorodetsky's style of humor could swarm psyches more persistently than any comedy previously known.

At HBO's press preview last week, he stood in the background, watching nervously and smiling modestly when introduced. The next afternoon, we had lunch in a bar down the street from the channel's 23rd Street studio. Gorodetsky comes across genial and observant; in the recesses lurk dreaminess and a taste for the illicit. His voice is loud and sonorous, the kind of radio baritone that could fill the room of a lone listener and promise companionship. "I do a lot of phone sex," he growls. "If this job doesn't work out, I can always fall back on 907 numbers." He's worked in radio, but Gorodetsky often depicts *himself* as a solitary, lost in fantasy, eager for a visiting voice.

He grew up in Providence, the son of a liquor salesman of Russian Jewish origins. He has three older sisters, the nearest being ten years his senior. "I was an afterthought, a mistake, a last blast of potency." His mother died when he was twelve. "Ouch, ooh, the Freudian implications." He hasn't been in touch with his family for years. "Every falling-out has thousands of versions: what each of them thinks, what you tell yourself in the dead of night. We never got along. I can be stubborn, and I'm not looking back."

At school, he hung out with the guys he thought cool; most were black. Alone in his room, he binged on electronic media and read *Superman* comics. "I learned how a complicated piece of action could be broken into panels, in other words how to write for TV." With equal gusto, he devoured "the standard miserable kid syllabus: juvenile delinquent novels, *The Bell Jar, Nausea,*" as well as a series of C. S. Lewis novels called *Chronicles of Narnia,* "about kids who find a secret world in their closet." He became enthralled by Chandler and Hammett. "I got a sense of people using language playfully, like a cowboy swinging a rope. No one I knew carried a gun. My environment was suburban, and here were these urban scenes, midnight jazz blowing over sweaty bodies. It was more than sexy. It was *passionate.*"

The Comedy Channel is a projection of Gorodetsky's enduring dreams, startling because it's so unusual for one vision to prevail in TV. The Comedy Channel is evolving, but to begin with, four host/characters will do shtick and serve as video jockeys, introducing two- to three-minute comedy clips culled from movies, sitcoms, variety shows and concerts. "I don't like stand-up that much," Gorodetsky confides. "That's a guy at the podium, lecturing. It's real distancing. A bunch of strangers sit in the dark and laugh because group psychology takes over. MTV was clever when it started. There was this windowless, limbo environment. Where does it hap-

pen? No place but some TV land. I wanted to create physical locations, inhabited by people who could knock on your door, and you would let them
in, and they would sit on your bed and say, 'Let's hang out.'"

In their customized sets, the hosts, who offer sample bits at the press
preview, constitute a Gorodetsky mindscape—an Eddie incarnation of
Genet's *The Balcony*. Tommy Sledge, an over-the-hill PI, slinks around a
dusty office and talks in the hard-boiled patter of noir pulp. The Higgins
Boys & Gruber—two overweight goofs and a dry, slender friend (a Letterman type pretending to suffer but secretly reveling in the *Animal House* antics of his sloppy pals)—loaf in the kitchen of their postcollegiate
California ranch house. Rachel Sweet—she talks with a Victoria Jackson
whine, sings rock 'n' roll, and takes classes at Columbia—presents a running diary of her New York whirl. And urbane Allan Havey—a scene of
the Brooklyn Bridge is painted outside his picture window—sasses cultural
trends and gender wars. (Havey has the most edge. He's at lunch with
Mother Teresa, and the check comes: "I'm not picking it up. In New York,
okay, but we're in Calcutta.")

Gorodetsky describes an amusing bit planned for Rachel Sweet's show
called "celebrity math," the brainchild of writer Mark O'Donnell. For example: "Bela Lugosi, plus Elvis Presley, minus a hundred and fifty pounds,
equals Keith Richards." Or: "Betty Boop, times Nancy Spungen, equals
Cyndi Lauper." In another O'Donnell caprice, three intersecting circles
are drawn and labeled: smart, ugly, and rock star. At the convergence of
smart and ugly is Sartre; of ugly and rock star, Ozzy Osbourne; of smart
and rock star, Sting; and of smart, ugly, and rock star, Bob Dylan.

Gorodetsky dotes on the cultural artifacts that have stirred and entertained him. Milton Berle makes a guest appearance at the press preview
and proves long-winded; yet Gorodetsky finds his mere presence touching.
He cares about comedy's history. He's attracted to frank emotionalism.

Still, the limitations of his approach are already clear. The Comedy
Channel may not exist in a physical limbo, but it feels like a hothouse. That
intensity is Gorodetsky's aim: "I see it as a terrarium. I put together all this
creative stuff, close the lid, and hope something interesting will grow." The
format, however, is self-referential, a series of clips and cues triggering
memories and a sense of excitement without a point of view.

He believes he is channeling the shared consciousness of "everyone
who grew up with TV." He believes this although there are no minorities

working in any creative capacity at the Comedy Channel, and, in addition to Sweet, there is but one woman writer on staff, Margaret Webber, who collaborates with Rich Hall, a contributor. As things stand, women are represented by a performer whose remarks, even when saucy, are delivered in a baby-girl bray.

When I mention this to Gorodetsky and Stu Smiley, vice president in charge of programming, they look as if I've stirred them from sleep. They say, "We're just getting started." But the omissions are conscious. Judging from the cast and material, the Comedy Channel is reaching out to the same demographic as launched MTV—to a white, male, middle-class audience—and neither Gorodetsky nor his superiors have the will to buck the prevailing marketing strategy.

In future, the hosts are promised guests, and Richard Belzer is slated to conduct a weekly political round table, but Gorodetsky isn't keen on TV conversation or politics: He's not voting in the mayoral election. Missing in his airless, hermetic videoscape is a sense of spontaneity and of being in the world—feelings that stand-up comedy generates. Missing is comedy that heightens our sense of reality. Gorodetsky's material derives its charge by associating with already famous images; it refracts borrowed light—much of which, originating on TV, was ersatz to begin with. The work tends to nostalgize and reassure, even when the surface bristles.

The best bet lies in Gorodetsky's sense of perversity. At lunch he tells the dirtiest joke he knows: "A guy is fucking a chick and gets bored. He says, 'Turn over, I want to fuck you in the ass.' She says, 'Isn't that presumptuous of you?' He says, 'Isn't presumptuous a big word for an eight-year-old?' "

Flaming Creature: *Life and Loves of a She-Devil*

June 1987

The BBC treatment of Fay Weldon's comic novel *The Life and Loves of a She-Devil* (A&E) achieves a level of oddness and ingenuity rarely seen on TV. Our heroine is Ruth (Julie T. Wallace): six feet tall, hefty, and mole-covered—four hairy ones surround her mouth. She eats rice pudding from cans, chaffeurs her kids through suburbia, and labors over meals. Her husband Bobbo (Dennis Waterman) is a successful accountant with a basset-hound look appealing to women. To reel him in, rich, glamorous romance novelist Mary Fisher (Patricia Hodge) needs only to flare her nostrils and raise a brow. At the beginning, she may want him as material for her next book, but she gets hooked.

What does Ruth want? What did Medea want? After Bobbo moves into Mary's mansion—perched atop the Dover Cliffs—Ruth goes wild. Rage, like a bloody kiss, stirs her from sluggishness and focuses her intelligence. She sets fire to her own house, dumps her children with the lovers, and begins a picaresque journey. Bobbo has told her she thinks in clichés and that Mary is a creative artist. Ha! She has in mind a poetical revenge.

In this tale, old-fashioned man-hate and female self-pity are gotten up as a woozy feminism drunk on goddesses. Ruth sees it as an antidote to Mary's toxic romanticism, and we're meant to take it seriously, too, although it's unintentionally lampooned. Ruth wants not only to humiliate and destroy her archnemesis; she wants to become her. Feminism isn't a wish for a new game but for a turnaround, where plain women crack the whip.

The feminist tangle, however, detracts little from the story's pleasure and even adds frisson when Ruth becomes a political lesbian. She and her lover, a fellow odd-woman, embezzle money from Bobbo's company (Ruth still has the keys), then transform themselves from frumps (Ruth loses the moles) into the prosperous, dressed-for-success proprietors of Vista Rose, an employment agency "for women with unused talents."

The script crackles in the segment when Ruth tells Bobbo's parents the truth about her marriage, and the father, so thrown by candor, ladles soup off the carpet, then eats the fuzzy brew. Mary is dealt a blow when her novel, based on the affair with Bobbo, is rejected for being "too realistic." And abandoned by their mother, Ruth and Bobbo's son and daughter turn into punks—but not before the boy takes a turn dressing in Mary's lingerie.

Kinkiness and irreverence rise to witty heights in two send-ups of the law and church—there is a flavor of Swift and Thackeray about them. After framing Bobbo for swindling his company, Ruth goes to work for the judge assigned to his case. He's into S/M. She smiles while he beats her bare ass, because with each stroke, he agrees to increase Bobbo's sentence by a year. In another incarnation, Ruth becomes housekeeper and confidante to Mary's confessor; she's turned to religion since Bobbo's imprisonment. Wishing to dash her last support, Ruth seduces the priest, then sics him onto Mary's scent. He's like a dog who's just discovered liver.

The actors never betray their soap-opera masks. Dennis Waterman's Bobbo, who doesn't quite understand why Mary wants *him*, lets vanity get the better of his senses every time. He's a perfect sleazeball cuddling Ruth and describing his lover's parties—"They have a Japanese quality; nobody talks loud." Patricia Hodge's Mary walks an edge between cynical manipulator and dupe of her own philosophy. Mary: "I want the flame of my life to be snuffed out." Priest: "Even when you're suicidal you're still romantic." Mary: (Eyes cast down) "I know."

In the marathon role of Ruth, newcomer Julie T. Wallace is unflagging, becoming all things to all people to attain her goal. Dressed for seduction, with boobs jiggling and lips smeared gash-red, she's a female drag queen, the embodiment of *She-Devil*'s dizzying mood. For the plastic surgeon she convinces to mold her into a double of Mary, she plays a Galatea willing to oblige the man in his fantasy of motherhood. She smiles indulgently at the woman doctor who accuses her of becoming a blond doll, a male fantasy. In voice-over, Ruth growls to Bobbo and Mary, "I have all the power and you have none. You are where I once was." She says she's completely fulfilled. What's to argue? Every woman needs a calling.

Sessions: Candid Camera

October 1991

The tube flashes psychotherapy as inspirational message: In twelve steps you shed compulsions and emerge reborn. Dr. Ruth and Dr. Joyce sermonize, while their fictional counterparts—Bob Newhart and Alan Thicke, et al.—dispense bromides as punch lines. Sitcoms make shrinks look patronizing and fraudulent, or they cast patients as wimps. Absent from the airwaves and most movies is what actually transpires in the office: the patient's gradual self-illumination. Busting this taboo is *Sessions* (HBO), developed and cowritten by Billy Crystal. The series is remarkably ungiggly, its concept simple: a guy and his shrink alone in a room.

Dan Carver is the guy—forty-two, a lawyer, married, two children— played by Michael McKean. Gloriously vain and vapid as a Brit rocker in *This is Spinal Tap*, here McKean looks like Corbin Bernsen unraveling into the angst-ridden dishevelment of Michael Keaton. Dan talks to his shrink,

Sidney Bookman (Elliott Gould), but there is plenty more action: flash-backs, memories, even flashbacks within flashbacks. We see dreams, sexual fantasies, and the truth that tap dances while Dan evades.

Crystal's work has often had a pinched side, addressing white men in their forties for whom baseball is more real than women. Crystal's women are mommies. They smile indulgently and say, "Go find your smile." What makes *Sessions* larger is that while Dan talks like Crystal, Bookman sees the Crystal cosmology as subjective. Crystal's peasant Jews have always been his master strokes: scrutinized but not left bleeding. Crudeness unfurls on *Sessions*, too, but it's only the medium where Oedipal conflict blooms.

The series tracks ordinary misery. Dan hasn't wanted to have sex with his wife, Carol (Linda Kelsey), for over a month. His parents come for a visit and noisily go at it in the next room; Dan listens, his ear to the wall. Dan is ashamed he masturbates, has a wet dream, hates the fact that his sixteen-year-old daughter, Annie (Jennifer Crystal), is going on a date.

These sequences are spiked with Crystal stand-up. Annie's date arrives in the form of a six-foot penis. Dan conjures himself masturbating in the bathroom as a kid, and his father is outside with a mike, reporting the hours that have passed. Dan tells Bookman he spent "quality time" with his son, while in the reality unreeling in his head he tosses a baseball desultorily, wedges a wireless phone against one ear, and tells his partner, "Look, if he wants to sue, we'll sue."

Humor doesn't let the viewer off the hook; nor do episodes end neatly. One installment fades with Dan asking Bookman, "I don't want to sleep with my mother, do I?"

Dan begins one session describing a dream in which he's tied to a bed while two voluptuous women lick and mount him. For a while he's aroused, but eventually he's frustrated, because he can't touch the women in return. Bookman asks what he's tied with, and at first Dan thinks the question irrel-evant. He closes his eyes, pictures neckties, and uses the word *haberdashery*. Bookman comments on the term and Dan recalls his father using it. But it's not until the end of the session that Dan remembers giving his father a tie for Christmas and being rebuffed when he asked for a hug. "If your father held back expressing love, that doesn't mean you have to," offers Bookman, who sees the dream in a positive light. "You're happy at the beginning be-cause you're passive and infantile, but then you want to join in, untie the ties, take part in your whole life."

In another session, the shrink observes that Dan, who says he doesn't enjoy masturbating, is always in jeopardy of getting caught. He suggests that his patient make plans to do it when the house is empty.

Sadness snakes through the series, butting against comedy but not canceling it. The doctor helps his patient recognize his smell, hear his voice, see his shape. "You're supposed to make me feel better," whines Dan. "Who says?" returns Bookman.

The Big Thaw: *Northern Exposure* and the Unrepressed

September 1991

We should all be so lucky to end up shanghaied in Cicely. Joel still misses Zabar's, but he's stopped *hocking*. Recently, when he had the chance to fly home, he stayed put. Of course, there *was* the matter of Maggie's death dream, in which Joel buys it in a plane crash. No one takes Maggie's death vibes lightly, what with the demise of four of her boyfriends. And there was the threat of Joel's replacement doc, a guy claiming to be Jewish but whom Joel insisted was a shill because he was blond and easygoing. He turned out to know the precise meaning of *naches*, and Ruth Ann was baking him cookies.

New York was never as far from Cicely as Joel believed. In Cicely, granted, there's no swirling garbage underfoot or panhandlers demanding reparations for not mugging you. Cicely's population is a mere 850, but it's not small-minded, only scaled down so people can talk. New York, at its best, is freedom—anything goes, nothing is alien because everyone winds up there. Everyone winds up in Cicely, too. A Tolstoy-spouting Muscovite. A Viet-vet gourmet chef impersonating Bigfoot. A couple of gay guys in the market for a bed and breakfast.

In this northern exposure, the top of the head lifts off. Anything can be said. Everyone listens. Desires are hatched in order to be gratified. There are no voice-over asides, because spoken language is unrepressed. Joel is a fish out of water not because he's hip, but because he isn't. Cicely is knowing—part satellite-dish effect, part fancied zeitgeist. Joel's bagels arrive from New York, and Alaska native Marilyn tells Maggie that the special ingredient is the water. Dishes at the potluck supper include shiitake mushrooms and sun-dried tomatoes. When Joel says *farkakte*, no one needs a definition.

There are places like this, sort of, in Alaska—Homer, Cordova, towns where the radio is lifeblood and a lot of fisherpeople have advanced degrees. But Cicely is a mindscape, where hip flows from being porous, not judging. Maurice is slapped for his assumptions. He's bothered that Cicely was founded by two lesbians who stalled out in the woods, but Chris tells their true story on Founders' Day. In Cicely, there is space to be imperfect and time to learn. When Maggie's patronizing father visits, we see that she's fled north not because she's already tough but to acquire independence. Joel keeps discovering he's generous, keeps developing a taste for difference.

Folks in Cicely have a tendency to cooperate; others are all they have. Ed is served french fries that taste like shrimp, and he asks for cocktail sauce. During the ice melt, Holling is dying to pick a fight: "I need to cause some pain. I need to hurt somebody." Responds a café customer: "I'd like to oblige you, but I have a five hundred dollar deductible on my health insurance." Boundaries aren't big in town. Ed doesn't knock. Gossip is culture. When Elaine dumps Joel, Marilyn reads the letter and soon everyone consoles Joel about his smashed plans. When Chris loses his voice and Maggie agrees to sleep with him so he can recover it, dozens gather outside her house for the event.

The trashing of privacy drains eroticism. On the other hand, solitude is permitted, enjoyed. No one in Cicely lives in a nuclear family, and when Maurice tries to create one by adopting Chris, it's a bust. Chris, who obtained his divinity degree by answering an ad in *Rolling Stone*, improvises the town's ceremonies. The only rituals that are meaningful are the ones made up.

The best alliances in Cicely are mismatches. Maurice craves Barbara Semanski, a state trooper and boxing champ. After riding spaceships for NASA, he feels safe, for the first time, in her embrace. Holling is sixty-three, an adventurer who stopped hunting after he dreamed that all the animals he'd ever killed were packing heat and gunning for him. To please Shelly, nineteen, he decides to make his Johnny fashionable and undergo a circumcision. In honor of the pending surgery, Chris programs the overture to *Fiddler on the Roof* on his radio show. Shelly, who ran away from a marriage in which meals were expected on the table and clean laundry in the drawers, thinks Holling macho for devising the circumcision. But when Joel, to everyone's relief, cancels the operation, she decides his turtleneck is bitchin'.

Joel and Maggie only imagine they're a mismatch. They're so alike they each think the other is a barbarian, and their violent fantasies make them hot. When they finally do go at it, they're animals: thrashing, sucking, clawing. It redeems the chronic tease that threatens to supplant real with cute.

The sentimentality of communal togetherness is repeatedly spiked. The longed-for family of one's choosing is shown to be fleeting, continually rearranging itself because of human fickleness, movement. No community can stave off danger, the citizens of Cicely are reminded. Did you ever see a show more attuned to death? Maurice's brother dies. An unknown man departs in Joel's office, and the town lends him an emotional funeral on a lighted pyre. Maggie's *fifth* lover, Rick, expires on a collision course with a falling satellite. "Life is dangerous and unpredictable," Chris tells Ed, as they contemplate the vast Pacific Northwest spaces. In Alphabet City, risk glints up in crack vials. In Cicely, it comes in a swirling sky that, in the flick of an eyelash, can hurl a bush plane into a glacier. Says Chris at the funeral, "It's that solitude in death that's our common bond in life."

Next season the spirit of Rick comes back as a dog. Return visits are also planned for the Bigfoot gourmet, Maurice's throb Barbara, and Chris's black half-brother. Here is a show that celebrates individuality and experimentation in what Chris calls our "pathologically normal times." Here is a comedy that can't let go of mortality, an hour-long weekly with almost no action. Characters are shaded and stay that way. Segments are organized around thematic motifs and counterpointed with musical scores. And the People are watching. Audience share has been consistently above twenty, sometimes reaching twenty-five. The People aren't supposed to dig references to Jung. Places like Cicely aren't supposed to understand *mazel tov*.

Medium Leno

December 1988

Although Jay Leno's career is cruising faster than anyone's in the comedy derby right now, he still tours colleges and I caught him last week at C. W. Post's packed Tilles auditorium. Leno's velvety shock of hair is getting grayer; his double-breasted suits, enfolding a hefty frame, are more chic than ever. His big face, with its oversized jaw and plastic expressiveness, is canny and good-hearted. But his act is disappointing. At two hours—a length meant to justify $25 tickets—it's way too protracted, especially for Leno's rambling style. He lopes from subject to subject with an unaltering, sweetly pissed-off bemusement that is so assured he doesn't bother with transitions.

He's funny, most often during the first hour, pointing up illogic that's beamed into the culture like microwaves. The show *Crime Stoppers*, which invites the audience to help apprehend felons, offers this caution about a criminal: "Be careful, he's armed and suicidal." "There's a problem," Leno quips, "that's going to take care of itself." He approves the quick thinking of a man on trial for providing drug-free urine to people undergoing tests: "I just sell the stuff, I don't know what people *do* with it."

Leno's social conscience cuts through media hype with amusing results. He calls McDonald's idea of employing the elderly side by side with teenagers their "cradle-to-the-grave minimum wage program." To raise money for worthy causes, he wishes people would vote for progressives so he won't have "to stand in ditches holding hands with Morgan Fairchild and Robert Blake." About the expiration date on Wonder Bread: "You should live so long." About the comfort of multiplex cinemas: "Theater? Excuse me, the cement bunker at the end of the mall."

But with the exception of the muck he rakes off corporate America, Leno's subjects are commonplace: fast food, airlines, Elvis. Leno is likable for telling the truth, but he tells only a part of it. He defends the poor, but he has no other concrete politics. He doesn't mention the election, Central America, or even Gorbachev.

He's awkward with women, femmeness. Teasing two guys in the audience, he predicts that, after the show, they'll "drink some beers and beat up homos," taking it for granted that neither man is gay. There are as many females as males before him, but when Leno questions people about their cars, he addresses men. Later, inquiring about the work people do, he speaks to twenty males and only four females, all of whom are "pretty lady." He comes off not as a man who dislikes women but as one who has nothing to say to them.

I wouldn't have predicted this diffidence from his TV appearances. The tube likes Leno; it's a better medium for him than the stage. He's sharper doing short bites on *Letterman* and, subbing for Carson, drawing material from the day's news. Interviewing guests, he listens. He's curious and unpatronizing, which makes him free with kids.

But part of his TV success derives from what makes him bland on a live stage. His politics are murky because he aims at broad appeal. He's slippery, one minute ripping into junk food toxins, the next hawking chips in

Dorito commercials. (For all Letterman's tortured romance with merchandising, he refrains from selling products.) Leno's insides are masked. Reminiscences of family life are limited to gentle satires of his frugal parents, and he seldom refers to his wife. He's shy, self-protective.

For some stand-ups—Sandra Bernhard, Richard Pryor, Richard Belzer—comedy is a conduit for libido. Performing is a hit on the audience, a goose. For another set of comedians, smart-mouthing is an end run around sex. It's no accident that the jocular men—and they are all men—with staying power on TV project almost no eroticism: Carson, Cavett, Letterman, Leno.

Carson is the perpetual coy boy. When his true feelings about women pop out, they're lewd; women are creatures you wed because they're idle, then despise because they're predatory. Cavett's libido is channeled into envy; his competitiveness has killed him on the tube because it's so glaring it disturbs, like sex and violence in their more naked forms. Sex embarrasses Letterman; he says and shows this every chance he gets.

Leno, baffled by sensuality, waxes priggish. To him, females who wear makeup are always bunnies, flyweights. A California woman he knows refers to her live-in mate as "my lover." "I hate this," he rails. "Okay, let's see you *do* it right now. Bring in the hoses." Condom ads make him so twitchy he claims, incorrectly, that the United States makes a bigger deal of them than any other country—in fact, Britain has waged a tougher campaign for their use. Worse, Leno irresponsibly disparages rubbers before college kids, in need of information and protection.

The bluff, shy guys who've made it on late night have the same tension in the shoulders, the same tightness in the voice, the same remoteness in the eyes. Medium cool is programmed to be chilliest before bed, to lull you past the stimulating conflicts of consciousness.

Viewer Mail

December 1992

Dear Dave,

I don't blame you for being steamed when you got passed over in favor of Jay. Some people say you weren't supposed to care about the corny *Tonight*

Show and that you would have become the butt of your own joke, because, like, you're making fun of talk shows, which must be a little bit weird, since you've done one every night for ten years. I guess you would say, "Not really," that you were goofing on them. But I know you would have done *your* thing at eleven-thirty, instead of trying to do a Johnny, the way Jay is and coming off so lame he's making even terminal Johnny—when he would say things like, "That's wild, I did not know that"—look wacky. You would have bodysnatched *Tonight*; the show would have kept its name but talked weird.

Anyway, the point is you got *passed over*. You can't let that happen, or you're a pussy. I know you like to come off as Mr. Outside and make fun of corporations like GE and that pushing for top place on the totem pole *does* make you look pretty corporate yourself, but, hey, it's a guy thing as much as a corporate thing, even if it's not easy to tell them apart. Besides, I know what you want isn't really the job but winning, and, boy, did you make out: $42 million from CBS, and getting NBC to sweat all over Jay, and nailing your own eleven-thirty spot!

Now, I'm only telling you this as a friend, Dave, but has anyone mentioned that you've started to look like Dustin Hoffman at the end of *The Graduate*, when he sits on the bus with a blank expression on his face because he put his heart and soul into winning Katherine Ross, even though he really didn't know her or care that much about her (or anything else except not being fucked with), and now he's got this ton of responsibility on him? I mean you were saying you were bored with the show before you fought to keep doing it, and now you sure have to keep doing it, don't you!

You know, Dave, I think it isn't so much a winning thing with you as a fighting thing. Which is okay, because you can always be pissed off. It doesn't matter that you're very rich now. You were plenty rich before, and you did pissed off great. The greatest!

Some people think a person has to be a little bit of a masochist to go on your show if they are anything other than a babe who makes you drool or a comedian who makes you feel like you can make or break their career. And you'd be the last one to contradict that, because you know how you like to look right in the camera and say you're not interested in anything, really, and how you make us believe you, even though you're trying to be humorous. That's what you're trying to do, isn't it? I guess that's why it doesn't matter if you like doing the show. You make it pretty obvious there's nothing else you'd rather do, so you might as well stay put.

And I can understand why you act distracted whenever someone takes time to do their own thing. I mean, it's your show. Like the other night when Don Novello was doing Father Guido Sarducci and everyone was laughing at this play he was writing called *Late for the Last Supper,* and then he wanted to make a few predictions for the new year, and you cut him off and said, "I'll make a prediction, you'll be in a cab in ten minutes leaving this studio." Boy, did the color drain from his face.

I think you do this stuff because you hate to see anyone be too enthusiastic about their work, because it, like, embarrasses you when they show they want anything too much. That's why you dump on fat people, because, man, their hunger is right out there. Can't miss it! And you hate when people blow their own horn, because it's sort of like begging to you, you know, trying to win your approval and hyping their stuff. That's why you make so much fun of advertising.

But it's weird, Dave—have you noticed that ads are sounding like you? I mean I think you've had more influence on ads than on anything else, maybe. There are all those fake top 10 lists selling stuff like milk, and that Subaru guy who sounds just like you and is real nervous and suspicious that someone might trick him, because he doesn't want to look like a dufus, and he says, "I don't care about torque, I don't even know what is. I got the money, I want to know what to drive."

So, Dave, what about suing these people for ripping you off? Although maybe you don't mind, because it's sort of like they're advertising you, ha ha. I know you don't need the dough, but there's a principle, and what's gonna happen if people can't tell the difference between a goof on something and the thing itself? Like when someone who hates selling stuff sounds just like someone who loves it? Between us, Dave, maybe you like some of those fakey things like talk shows and TV ads a little bit yourself. It's okay. I won't let on.

But having ads steal your jokes—it puts a burden on you to think up new stuff. Not fair! But, Dave, don't worry about it. It's not that big a deal. Now, don't get me wrong. You still do funny top 10 lists. Like the other night, in "Top 10 Things to Get You Kicked out of the Inauguration" when you said, "Telling Chelsea you wrote, directed, and starred in *Annie Hall.*" That was good. And another night in "Top 10 Signs That Roger Clinton Is Going to Be Trouble" when you said, "Let's face it, if Clinton were a Corleone, he would be Fredo." Dark, man. Edgy. Stuff like this doesn't happen on *all* your shows, but we don't care!

Man, the eighties were great for you, with all those tired old white guys running the country. Reagan and Bush. You looked hip just by being young, even if you were a white guy who would eventually get old and tired. Those days were perfect for you, the way you were angry and didn't care about anything. I mean, who *could*? And I know you weren't angry about the world, or anything. Everyone knows how you hate political comedy and would hardly ever let one of those guys on the show.

But don't worry if Clinton makes people feel hopeful about the country and they get all mushy about being involved and stuff. Everyone will still have plenty of reasons to be resentful, and who better than you to carry that torch? It's great when you've had a bad day and bully Paul. I mean, who wouldn't like to beat up some little guy once in a while? And even though you've got job security with CBS, you still don't have to like what you do. Like what in life isn't stupid? Believe me, there are plenty of guys who don't like their jobs, if they actually have one. And we don't care that you're making a bundle, because you know and I know, Dave, that no one can pay you enough for a job you hate.

Yours truly,
Your Biggest Fan

Fun with Rupert: Hanging with Letterman's Neighbor du Jour

December 1995

Letterman is in love—not the smarmy, protective number he pulls with babes. No, for the past year or so, he's been haunting the Hello Deli on West 53rd Street, a crammed closet of a shop, where co-owner Rupert Jee beams a siren song of accommodation. Rupert is the secret sharer Dave sends out to pester people, now that he's too recognizable to do it himself.

On the surface theirs may look like one of Dave's bully/stooge setups—the sort he enacts with Paul Shaffer or Larry "Bud" Melman. When Letterman began culling his new neighborhood for found characters, at first he glommed on to Mujibur Rahman and Sirajul Islam, the souvenir salesmen from Bangladesh, because he could make comedy out of *their* top/bottom dance—Mujibur's reflexive upstaging of the more recessive

Sirajul. Letterman smacked down Mujibur, while Sirajul aroused the sort of tender sentiments Letterman usually reserves for dogs. Though it's appealing to see working guys getting a break, part of what Letterman finds funny is their cultural dislocation—their accents, deferential politeness, and seeming blankness amid his references. Letterman still stalks New York as a big, wide-eyed white boy from the Midwest.

When he poked into the Hello Deli, he may have imagined that Rupert Jee—who is thirty-nine, of medium build, and of Chinese parentage—would be a variant on the souvenir guys, but as soon as they interacted something else became apparent. Though Rupert was willing to enter Dave's playpen without cynicism or embarrassment, he was not only hip but stooge-proof. From his debut spot, when he walked into the Ed Sullivan Theater to riotous applause from Dave's robotic audience, his ease and game attitude simultaneously tamed and disinhibited Letterman. Everyone knows how to go on Letterman: act relaxed but not slick, willing to indulge Dave's fantasies but not self-abasing. Rupert seemed assembled with the program installed. He is that being for whom Letterman has been searching throughout his career: the naturally gifted, unselfconscious entertainer.

In the show's recent week in L.A.—meant to boost ratings—the freshest footage came not from the local talent but from Rupert, who was flown in. In his classic bits with Dave, Rupert dons fake glasses and wears the casual garb Letterman prefers off stage: baseball cap, T-shirt, and shorts. While Dave sits in a car, holding a walkie-talkie, Rupert, equipped with a hidden camera and an earpiece, hits on strangers and repeats whatever Dave says. The sentences don't exactly issue from Dave's mouth, either, but from one of his alter egos: the slow-witted lunk who knows no social boundaries—a drunk Gump. (Who is this emanation? Dave's dad? Dave's idea of his mother's worst nightmare?)

In the funniest passes, Rupert flays pomposity or becomes deliciously moronic. On Muscle Beach, he asks sunbathers, "Is David Hasselhoff here?" To a dignified man he takes for Kenny Rogers, he proclaims, "Got to know when to hold 'em, know when to fold 'em." And in the lobby of CBS, he informs a suit, "I'm Dan Rather's nephew."

He orders an ice-cream cone with six scoops, then confides, "I'm lactose intolerant." At McDonald's, told there's no such thing as a five-pounder, he orders twenty Quarter Pounders, explaining, "I'm trying to build my own five-pounder." At a Soho boutique, a beautiful saleswoman says she's from France, and Rupert chimes in, "Me, too. Where in France?" She: "Lyons." Rupert: "Me, too. Where in Lyons?" She names a street. Rupert: "Me, too. You know what I miss most about France?" She: "What?" Rupert: "The french fries."

Letterman tells the audience, "This guy is lucky to be alive," but he loves placing Rupert in peril. Rupert asks people to pay him for doing deep knee bends and for sprawling on a desk at CBS. He insists that a tall, black guy is Ed Bradley, though the two look nothing alike. He goes up to customers at McDonald's and asks if they are named Jimmy, and when a frustrated bouncer picks up the phone, Rupert taunts, "Who are you calling, Mayor McCheese?"

Rupert doesn't get clocked because he doesn't come off as menacing or as an outsider to New York. Comfortable with the city's ethnic stew and deviant acts, this puppet has more street smarts than the man in the car. Letterman relies on Rupert's skills, which free him to take comic risks. He can push Rupert without worrying he will crumble or seem too vulnerable, and he can be cruel, because Rupert is doing his dirty work. Rupert, too, is liberated to wildness for which he doesn't have to assume responsibility. His performances are juiced by the doubleness of the position; he's a provocateur but he's unprotected; he's in on the overall joke but caught unawares by each line; he plays voyeur with strangers at the same time that he's an object of the audience's titillated regard.

■ ■ ■

When we meet at his deli, he says that at first he'd hoped Letterman would pass him by. "The night he came in I was scared the whole time, numb. Afterward, I thought, 'Oh good, now I can relax,' but word went around this wouldn't be the last time." We sit at a little table. A woman nearby is eating a Letterman sandwich, stuffed with turkey and cheese. She's from Arkansas and wants Rupert's autograph. Every few minutes someone makes the same request or asks to take a picture with him. He's gracious, patient.

Originally, one of the staff writers was slotted to play Dave's mouthpiece, but at the last minute Rupert got a call. "I've been a pretty tame person. I had never done anything wild, and I wanted to see where it would take me. My career path has not exactly been a straight line."

Rupert's parents, hailing from Guangzhou, raised their five kids on the Upper West Side, and at City College he bounced from biology, to oceanography, to architecture, to economics. In one job he bought maternity dresses for a retail chain, then landed a position he found fascinating—negotiating contracts with oil companies for Y. K. Pao, "one of the four richest men in Hong Kong" and owner of the largest private fleet of super tankers. Next he designed and manufactured young men's fashion wear in partnership with May Chinn (they're not an item, and Rupert is single), who continues to be his partner at the deli. "Our clothing company was so hot people were saying we would be the next Jordache. Then the recession hit." Rupert had always wanted to work with food. "I felt the key was making really great sandwiches." He and May bought the shop the year before Letterman arrived, by which time they had become entrenched.

Although Rupert recently auditioned for the part of a deli guy in a movie, he's philosophical about his probable fifteen minutes. And although he isn't trying to make a killing from his exposure, he's letting the bounty wash over him. He sells souvenir T-shirts, though he thinks his face on them is too big. "Last year, when I was sent to Puerto Rico. I sat by the pool, drinking piña coladas, and realized I hadn't had a vacation in ten years."

Rupert says that working with Letterman still intimidates him, but Letterman is real to him. Rupert is savvy about Letterman's anxiety around the corporeal, such as the buzz he gets from saying *meat*. One sketch involved Rupert touching various meat cuts in the deli, and in an ongoing bit Rupert informs guests they have one of Dave's blue cards stuck to their ass. "I think the word *ass* is very powerful to him: the Big Ass Ham and his routine with Dick Assman."

How does Rupert feel when Dave acts the rube with minorities, the way, in one sequence, he has Rupert address a Latin delivery man as *Pepé*? Rupert says he hasn't yet squirmed. "I've always been good at bearing provocation when it was thrown at me. The truth is, I'm concentrating so hard on making something happen, on giving the audience a degree of danger, I don't think about anything else.

"When you do these things on the streets, you kinda get hooked. Dave doesn't laugh a lot when he's on location. He's too involved. The first time I heard him laugh at what I was doing, it was intoxicating. I felt: If he's laughing, it's gotta be pretty good."

The Perils of Paula: *The Paula Poundstone Show*

November 1993

Just as Warhol said that ordinary objects could be art, Letterman says that ordinary people can be entertainers. Of course Warhol had to be the one designating the found art, and on Letterman's show, shtick that may look spontaneous depends on the host's ability to transform his subjects into *something*—usually something tense. Is Meg going to submit to a shampoo? Will the telephone operator, or the doorman, or the cabbie explode at Dave's moronic demands? Dave's model isn't public access TV, although he's satirized/appropriated some of its filler—lugubrious, blank staring; camera sweeps of the studio and streets. But you need to be Letterman to do Letterman, and even then it's hit or miss. Dave has never maintained that ordinary people should have *their own TV shows*, and he is laughing all the way to the bank as the confusion mounts.

Something weird is afoot. Imitating the dreariest aspects of public access has become a style, as if the absence of talent and structure were engaging. It's like performance art that sells self-promotion as self-revelation. *Watch me because, well, I want you to.* The late Chevy Chase show, Conan O'Brien's show, and Leno's bland soup of borrowed ingredients all trade on this plea. They have taken *Wayne's World* and *Coffee Talk* not as satires but exemplars, at the same time stretching out the formats and draining them of wit. These shows are infomercials without the Thighmaster.

The hour-long *Paula Poundstone Show* (ABC) is the latest and sorriest clone. Poundstone can be charmingly irreverent. Her election coverage for Leno, pulling planet-friendly guns on good ol' boys, was sharp. But she has a mushy side, wanting to be liked and protected. In the stand-up world, she's been a mascot in the boys' locker room, chucked on the chin because she isn't sexually threatening. She exudes no sexuality at all, with her tomboy galumph, bow ties and vests, and squirmy discomfort in her flesh. She crouches awkwardly on a stool, her body offering the bargain, *I won't pick on you if you don't probe me.* It's an invitation to get smacked and the least likely affect to make chaos jump through hoops.

Her debut show was a study in ineptitude: pointless shots of the production crew and endless unfunny chitchat with the audience. Did these people try out for the Letterman audience and get the hook? Inside a closet sat an expert on recycling who popped out to inform us that telephone books clutter landfills. We were supposed to be amused because she twinkled? Lots of remotes: economists on a Disney-esque ride, spouting lines from the likes of Adam Smith; Sam Donaldson reading from Maurice Sendak's *Where the Wild Things Are*. (Don't ask.) A long segment was devoted to the ratings required for Poundstone to remain on the air, with viewer shares represented by Oreo cookies, so that she would be adorable in her special pleading.

The six members of a British a cappella girl group called the Mint Juleps were the only rehearsed and talented guests. They were terrific, offering cascading, melodic doo-wop and Afro-Caribbean harmonies, but they were allotted only one full number and otherwise relegated to the ten-second spots leading to commercials. More than anything, they highlighted the surrounding waste and execrable judgment.

Rosie Complexion: *The Rosie O'Donnell Show*

July 1996

The buzz goes that Rosie O'Donnell is a big hit because her show harks back to a simpler time, the era of Mike Douglas and Merv Griffin—before Oprahfication and the big spill. In fact, she's delivering the realness that talk shows fake. Disclosures on those programs are staged, ritualized, about as spontaneous as high mass. O'Donnell is all gut, and viewers are responding to her authenticity. She is New York: goony for Broadway musicals, hip to queerness and the polyglot melt. The casts of *Rent* and *Noise/Funk* have already performed sets, and though these shows are hot, they also declare her taste. When Fran Drescher was a guest, a remote picked up her parents, Morty and Sylvia, reviewing early-bird specials in south Florida, the best deal—with all courses lustily described—earning a four-knish rating. The Dreschers were back the next week and are slated for an eating campaign through New Orleans. O'Donnell isn't beaming out white bread to the heartland but raisin-walnut pumpernickel.

She teases that her show is totally original, introducing her band leader as Doc Severinsen, referring to her producer as Gelman, shattering windows with a tossed pencil. Sure her format is a late-night variant—with

guests performing and trotting over to the desk for a chat. But her daily
hour, broadcast live, isn't like any other, because it's much less shtick-driven,
emanating almost entirely from her personality. She does an opening
monologue, but she's never had a knack for the practiced timing of telling
jokes. She doesn't act funny, is, rather, ineffable, riffing off conversations,
tunneling back, rootswise, to George Burns and Groucho.

A couple of years ago, Paula Poundstone fashioned a nighttime hour
around her personality, and it bombed. She gave off no libido of any kind.
The atmosphere had no edge. O'Donnell, too, is sexually masked; she
comes across all gut but not the entire gut—like a lot of comedians. Often
overt sex dissolves comedy. Id-rocking comedians, male or female, are
rare. Jon Stewart is flirtatious but not turned on by himself. And there is
Dennis Miller, who is as helplessly vain as he is acerbic. Libido wafts off
him, but in most comedians it's shadowy, and sexual starving is part of
their bond with us. They admit they get no satisfaction, and we let them
stand apart, diddle us.

O'Donnell isn't sexual but is plenty libidinous, diving into appetite,
hoisting her smarts and bents. The large women of daytime—Oprah, Carnie Wilson, and ex-fatty Ricki Lake—are humiliated by their bodies.
O'Donnell calls herself fat and neither weeps nor apologizes for liking
food. She isn't about to trade her authority for a seat at a twelve-step sisterhood. Internal voices don't censor her. She breaks into song and impressions whenever she feels it, her head a satellite dish receiving beeps only she
can detect. She's telling Vanessa Williams she liked *Eraser*, because she
could follow the plot, when a subliminal aside shoots out of her mouth, "I
didn't need Cliff Notes, like for some summer movies I won't mention . . . Tom Cruise . . . because we want him on the show." Another day
Donny Osmond calls her fat, and in almost every subsequent program she
nails his boorishness, punctuating the dig with a Betty Rubble cackle.

She's hog-happy with her hungers, whether for Drake's cakes or TV
trivia—O'Donnell is Joan Rivers without the self-loathing. Is there a sitcom
theme song she cannot summon, a twenty-year soap plot she can't unfurl?
Susan Lucci comes on, and O'Donnell wants only to truffle for nuggets
about Pine Valley. When first guest George Clooney quips, "I'm here because Madonna couldn't make it," O'Donnell snaps back, "That's true,"
then asks if he's scared about being the third Batman in his upcoming
movie: "You know, like being the second Darren on *Bewitched*."

Her show plays like an extended Kmart commercial—those improvisational gems, concocted with fellow Noo Yawker Penny Marshall, the depressed, laconic counterpart to O'Donnell's ebullient street kid. The commercials are sly, seeming more genuine than the programs they interrupt and casting women who act like backyard neighbors but whom everyone knows are showbiz big shots. O'Donnell doesn't falsify either side of herself; she works the tension. Like every original, her art combines the recognizable and the skewed.

She wants acceptance but doesn't truckle, admonishing her live audience, "Don't clap unless you mean it. This isn't *Sally Jessy Raphael*." O'Donnell is principled—following the O. J. verdict, she condemned the soft-pedaling of violence against women—but she isn't pious, recently dissing Kato for lying at the same time acknowledging his charm. Besotted by her adopted son Parker, she gushes without patting herself on the back, à la Kathie Lee. Skirting sentimentality, O'Donnell revels in her guests, and the lineups have been impressive, from buddies Janeane Garofalo, Dana Carvey, and Martin Short to talk-show forebear Virginia Graham, looking heroically Jurassic and sassing spryly. O'Donnell's guest lists have sparked the denied rumor that *Live with Regis and Kathie Lee* started a booking war with the new show, refusing guests who came on O'Donnell's program first.

People go on *Letterman* in a state of fascinated terror, not knowing whether the host will fawn over, yawn at, or bite them. Many of the guests on Regis and Kathie Lee strain against leaking condescension at their hosts' platitudes. Rosie, clearly, has made friends in entertainment, and audiences are responding with similar affection for her big, smart, heartfelt, unembarrassed presence. What has paved her success isn't a yearning for simplicity but an openness to what is independent, urban, unmarried, imposing.

Dennis Miller: Obit for a Talk Show

August 1992

Free Dennis Miller from cancellation hell! Phone, write, run your fingers through your hair. Sure, he poached Letterman shtick. And he could get flopsweaty during interviews. But gone was his past smugness and in its place generosity paired with intelligence, plus the most surprising guests on late-night TV, Mary Ellen Mark, Susan Faludi, Harry Crews. Not since Cavett has there been a talk show host who read books; but Cavett couldn't stop competing with his guests. Miller was responsive, unashamed to be informed, exuding a sexual self-confidence that gave him room to appreciate others. He squealed and collapsed with pleasure at Dana Carvey, David Spade. Surreal references careened from a brain on random scan. A depressed Jon Lovitz, entering unannounced, was "Stepfording out." Miller even managed to find a bright side to the Thomas/Hill hearings: acting work for Danny Glover and Alfre Woodard. While Carson was smarmy, Leno sexless, Letterman contemptuous, and Arsenio treacly, Miller was endearingly self-mocking. After a large dog licked his own genitals, Miller mused, "If we could do that I wouldn't have to host a talk show." Alas, for his fans, he'll have time to practice.

Miller's Tale: Miller as a Stand-up

November 1992

Now that Leno isn't strong-arming guests into exclusive appearances on *Tonight,* can't Dennis Miller have another show? Give him Letterman's old slot! We just elected a president who likes books, the mirror, and fucking; Dennis is the perfect host for the Age of Clinton—a fool for words and interested in other people.

Bereft of desk, Dennis is once again standing, albeit on a concert stage and before TV cameras, in *Dennis Miller Live From Washington, D.C.* (HBO). Since his chat show stint, he's more confident and fluid, his hour gig a testament to crisp writing and delivery. No props, impressions, songs, guests, just Dennis and his roving, monkey-cam mind, yoking improbables in a way that lends the folly du jour historical context. He nearly has a brain hernia trying to conceive what Izzy Stradlin had to do to get kicked out of Guns 'N' Roses: "Hey, Slash, do you want to quit shooting heroin into your cock, we're gonna vote on Izzy over here, he forgot to return one of Axl's casserole dishes from that gangfuck, sorry Izzy, you're just not G 'N' R."

Dennis is still a snob and a xenophobe, carping at cabbies who smell bad and at the same time tweaking minorities and women for being sensitive to jabs. But mostly he slices the powerful, listing the qualifications on planes that stipulate who can sit next to an exit door in case of a crash in water: "Item eight, 'You must not be Ted Kennedy.' " Dennis is self-mocking, confessing he sometimes has to "fake an erection" and then "sell it" to his wife: "Oh, honey, little Casper took a Percodan, don't read anything into it." The Miller key is shared idiocy, sublime regression.

Hot and Bothered: Miller on HBO

May 1994

Just as Dennis Miller is about to dive off the deep end of self-admiration, he senses he's being an asshole. He takes issues seriously—especially those that touch him personally—but not his opinions. Calculated but endearing, he is passionate about the world and self-revealing. So of course he's now on HBO, in a six-part series of taut half-hour shows, *Dennis Miller Live*. In each, Miller riffs on a theme—violence, celebrity, etc.—in a monologue and in dialogue with a guest, then caps off the evening with deep captions of news photos, à la his "Weekend Update" routines.

Bearded now, and looking like Manson at Canyon Ranch, Miller is increasingly anxious about *the mob*, all those dimwits he used to sneer at for shopping at Kmart but who are now imagined carrying assault weapons. As Beardman, nerd avenger, he acknowledges the broadened poverty base under Reagan/Bush, then races into the woods to pound his chest and beat a drum for blood. He boosts the death penalty, not as a deterrent to crime, but as a fucking catharsis—never mind that sissy shit about cycles of abuse and punishment stoking cruelty. But he slaps himself for being hysterical by interviewing Senator Bill Bradley, who inserts that the barbarian frequently isn't at the gate, but at home, committing domestic crimes—half of the women murdered in the country are killed by male spouses.

Miller is at his most generous allowing others to shine. He plays straight man to Jim Carrey, who presents an oily rap on the perils of fame while demanding a sandwich from his minions—and kicking it away when it arrives without mustard. As keen as ever, too, are Miller's nose for the zeitgeist and his baroquely fanciful references. Musing on the award to Rodney King of $3.8 million, he puns, "Can't we all get a loan?" He dubs

Clinton "the Stu Sutcliffe president," observing that at Nixon's funeral, among the former heads of state, he looked like odd man out. And noting the upcoming twenty-fifth anniversary of Woodstock, Miller channels Wavy Gravy and intones, "People, people, there's some bad Prozac going around." This comedian needn't be so worried about Lorena Bobbitt et al., because his power isn't dangling, but safely lodged in his head.

Going to Bed with Jon Stewart:
Talking with Late Night's Slinkiest Host

March 1995

Jon Stewart is the sexiest, most soulful apparition haunting late-night TV. He flirts with women and men with equal abandon, even hitting on inanimate objects like the Pez dispensers and dolls he turns into puppets. The message isn't that he's hoping to fuck his guests after the show but that he wants to twirl them around his fingers while the cameras are running. Seduction tames the world for Stewart and calms him down, and he is so successful at it guests fling themselves on him, or cuddle him, or rear up with unprecedented rambunctiousness. *Wings* star Steven Weber spanked Stewart with a shoe. Jennifer Tilly slapped him, then kissed him passionately. William Shatner lifted Stewart in his arms and held him on his lap, prompting Stewart's crack, "Bill, you're about to go where no man has gone before." Part of that moment's giddiness was that Stewart wasn't trying to escape Shatner's embrace but to mine his own discomfort for comedy.

Try to imagine Letterman being spanked. Being *touched* spontaneously. Leno being spanked. Carson. Cavett, or Parr. Late night has been a vast Jell-O mold of sexual inhibition, encasing guys with stiff walks and unarticulated body parts, pasty men who joust for power.

Enter *The Jon Stewart Show* (UPN), a program nursed on goofy bits à la Letterman but whose host is temperamentally the anti-Letterman. So far the show, which debuted in September, hasn't garnered competitive ratings, and the suits have been restless, already sacrificing head-writer Fred Graver. The new Paramount network, which owns the talker, is nonetheless pledging support, and it pumped in money during February sweeps for a week of taping in L.A. Over the phone, Stewart's producer, Madeleine

Smithberg, says, "Paramount wants wider appeal. What does that mean? We don't know."

Yes we do. It means Urkel and Pamela Anderson, a book-free zone. Stewart has made nice to Urkel and Anderson, but the show slips in authors, among them Paul Rudnick and Jim Carroll. Eric Bogosian appeared the other week, and Danny Hoch has been booked. The musical acts are adventurous, a mix of grunge, funk, and blues groups, including the Mighty Mighty Bosstones, the Gin Blossoms, the Breeders, White Zombie, and local house bands like the New York Blues Experience. While Letterman enjoys nothing so much as using household names such as Regis Philbin and Tony Randall as ball boys, Stewart goes in the opposite direction, showing appreciation for fringe raconteurs like Johnny Legend—wrestling manager and psycho-Santa film archivist—and for novelty acts, including a septuagenarian cheerleader who executes perfect splits, a rotund man who deftly impersonates Patsy Cline, and a violin-playing contortionist.

The show reels between the stoned insouciance of *Wayne's World* and the edgy self-awareness of *The Larry Sanders Show*—baring flop sweat and weltschmerz. When he's unsteady, Stewart dumbs himself, weasling past controversy and sneaking in his sentiments indirectly—a tendency he cops to when we talk. Dick Clark, alluding to Tipper Gore's campaign against rock lyrics, spouts, "Don't get me started on politicians' wives who want to get their husbands a job," and Stewart passes up the opportunity to air the issue, merely chiming in, "Oh, my friend, I admire what you said."

The dumbing courts the live audience, mainly composed of the hormonally challenged, whose preoccupations are in sync with the warm-up comic Mark Cohen—his spiel the night I attend consists of lame dick jokes. This raw infantilism is worlds from Stewart's regression, projected in the Land Rover seats and Nok Hockey table installed on his stage and in his jeans-and-sweater wardrobe. His set isn't a specific place like Wayne and Garth's rec room but a headscape, suffused with longing and a sense of displacement in ordinary life. Stewart excavates emotional arrest.

He hasn't yet achieved the conversational authority of Dennis Miller or Richard Belzer, but Stewart grows more idiosyncratic each day. Even feigning blandness, he can be devilish. Comedian Brian Regan does a pedestrian act, and Stewart slaps him with this embrace: "Come on over, have some water, you earned it, worked hard on the doughnut bit, a lot of facial

expressions." Greeting Penelope Ann Miller, he croons, "You smell wonderful," adding, as she curls into the compliment, "is that Charlie?"

But Stewart is funnier letting his true colors fly. When Lorenzo Lamas,
with his big hair and teeth, speaks contemptuously and ignorantly of
Arabs, Stewart tugs on the beast's forelock, inquiring, "Is Islamic actually a
language?" Another night, he mentions with chagrin that the death penalty
has been reinstated. The audience cheers, as if they've been offered free
pizza. Stewart is shocked, and you can see something rising up inside him.
Smiling beatifically, he calls the audience "bloodthirsty maniacs" and reminds them, "You don't actually get to *do* the executions."

In the scripted bits that are de rigueur on late night, Conan O'Brien
remains a study in forced hipness, while Stewart, sailing at once above and
beneath embarrassment, reaps pay dirt from the most ridiculous premises.
He rides a truck mounted with a Port-O-San and invites people at Planet
Hollywood to take a piss. His "No-Money Theater" re-creates classic texts,
using Pez dispensers in all the roles. He impales Kathie Lee Gifford in his
retrospective, "Up Front and Frank," playing a dead-eyed Kathie with
chest hair poking from a scooped-neck dress. And in homage to Rolonda
Watts, Stewart airs *Jon in the Afternoon*. Dripping sincerity, he testifies, "Our
show is like an onion. On the outside it's rough, but when you peel away
those layers, it turns out to be white, moist, and acrid."

Stewart harkens to a younger Woody Allen (if Allen were good-looking), not only in his physical uninhibitedness but in his Jewish self-reference.
Is there another comedian in his early thirties who thinks about his Jewishness more compulsively? Born Jon Stewart Liebowitz, he amputated his
last name not out of Jewish self-hatred (as some have suggested), but to un-
load some family baggage. He milks the disparity between his Gen X,
slacker livery and the old-world dybbuk whirling inside. When a French
plane is hijacked by Islamic fundamentalists, he counsels the passengers,
"Don't order the bagel and brisket." During the holidays, when a Christmas tree is placed on the set, he shrinks back "Not too close! It's like Kryp-
tonite for Jews, it sucks the energy out of you."

For Stewart, Jewishness is bathed in melancholy, coloring his vision of
himself as a rambling loner. "Welcome to my life," he intones, "every night
scotch and Tom Waits." Jewishness bids him to follow dark passages once
rafted by Lenny Bruce. Riffing on O. J. Simpson's response to letters he's
received, Stewart growls, "Who does he think he is, Dear Stabby?"

■ ■ ■

More than anything, the sexual wash Stewart paints over everything makes him irresistibly watchable. Letterman is gripped by a self-dislike that erupts in his know-nothing, blue-color malcontent character. Letterman would feel terminally humiliated to be goosed. Stewart is continually extending his behind and drawing power from that looseness.

Lean and compact at five-foot-seven, dark-haired and handsome with a sculpted face and direct gaze, Stewart trades on his physical powers to extract what he wants from people, at the same time depicting himself as puny and awkward—no threat, often the clichéd short, hairy Jewish nerd. The manner could register as coy, if Stewart weren't convincingly confused. Sometimes he is bizarrely out of touch with reality. He's growing a goatee that early on looks like a Chia beard, when Jason Priestley appears on the show with the same arrangement of facial hair. Stewart gazes at him, spellbound. "You look like me after the surgery . . . the cheekbones, the nose," as if he, Stewart, were a homunculus, instead of a man more vividly attractive than Priestley.

The flattery is a way, too, of flirting with Priestley. There has never been a show with more open, homoerotic dander. It flies spontaneously from Stewart, with none of the overhearty camping straight men usually affect when copping feels off each other. One night, Stewart entices a cameraman to give him a kiss, then sighs, "There's nothing like the feel of mustache on mustache." Last week, Lara Flynn Boyle, frustrated by her inability to titillate Stewart, asked, "How come everyone thinks you're gay?" He did a wide-eyed take, a Groucho spin around the stage, and shot back: "Just because I gave one guy a hand job doesn't mean I'm gay!"

One of Stewart's most beguiling routines is inviting guests to his "special place"—his version of the kids' cave in the living room, made out of sheets and chairs. Robin Leach is guided to a posh table, where he seems at first to be suffering Stewart. Eventually relaxing, he concedes: "I see you went for a decent bottle of champagne." Stewart: "We had a coupon." Smiles seductively. "This is the best prom I've ever been on." Leach: "I'm pleased to be dating you." Another night B. D. Wong asks Stewart if he wants to see his navel ring, and Stewart shoots, "I'd love to . . . finally I'll score with *someone*."

He's as puppyish with women, skirting smarm with easy rapport, especially around daredevils like bicycle racer Missy Giove and jocks like Gabriela Sabatini, whom he challenges to an aggressive Ping-Pong match. Stewart doesn't have to feign interest in women; it's installed. And it affords him room to tease and play. With both sexes, he's working out his sexual feelings, whose lack of clarity gives rise to restless, quaking comedy. He is everyone's trick, and also no one's, a Pan, piping but not giving himself over.

His sexual attractiveness derives from a lack of vanity, a grace and un-selfconsciousness about his ability to entertain. He simply does not see himself as alluring. But since his inner image is no longer manifest, he keeps its totem on stage, embodied in his announcer, Howard.

Howard Feller, with his flowered shirts, halo of bad hair, and assertive front teeth, is the Jon puppet. He sits on a stool in his own niche, and Stewart doesn't schmooze with him in a prescribed way; his presence is sufficient, he doesn't need to speak. On any other show, Howard would be a "kick me" stooge. His magical aspect here—and the essence of the show's strangeness—is that Stewart treats him with reserved respect. Howard is the wound at the heart of all comic invention, the damage from which we cannot recover or tear our eyes.

■ ■ ■

Off stage, during a meeting that lasts for several hours, Stewart's intelligence remains undimmed by the beer and cigarettes he methodically consumes. He doesn't strive to charm but gets naked psychologically. He is one of those people for whom adulthood is salvation, because childhood was withering.

"My father broke up with me when I was nine," he say, referring to the time when his father left home and then married another woman, with whom he had a child. "I wasn't told anything true about what was happening. He was a dad, and my older brother and me were little sportniks, always outside, and then he was gone."

From then on, Stewart's mother, a teacher of special education, raised her sons alone, in suburban New Jersey. "She pulled herself up by her bootstraps and did everything for her kids," remembers Stewart. "She was young, and it must have been frightening to have that responsibility." Even before the split, Stewart felt that his father, a physicist, and his brother, who was interested in economics, shared an intellectual bond from which he was excluded. The shearing off between Stewart and his father accelerated through the years—the father guilty and numbly jealous, the son gleefully outing family *mishegas* in his club act—so that when, a few years ago, Stewart landed his first shot on *Letterman,* his father could only pass this gallstone: "I always thought they picked more experienced people."

Now Stewart speaks without acrimony, partly because bitterness is what he has vowed not to duplicate. He depicts his grandfather and father as feeling buffeted by circumstances and disappointed with their lives, a fate he has already averted. "No one expected anything of me, and I grew up with a very poor image of my body. I was disappointed in my size, expecting to grow bigger and taller and hoping to play pro basketball. My friends were twelve guys in jockstraps. I didn't date until college, partly because my skin was bad—I was Dermatologist Boy. My first sexual experience was in the backseat of a car, only I was in the front seat, *driving.*"

In high school he found soccer and made it a passion. "The whole reason I got into sports and then comedy was to overcome mediocrity. My parents said I couldn't stick to anything, and there I was kicking a ball against a wall, day after day."

At William and Mary College, he played soccer and consumed the drugs and *Gilligan's Island* reruns that would equip him for stand-up. After college, he worked as a bike mechanic, a porter in a bakery, and as the fool in a research lab conducting encephalitis tests—his job was separating live, thirsty male and female mosquitoes. Stand-up bit him during a stint using puppets to teach school kids about disabled people, a gig in which he honed his prop-wielding skills. "I was twenty-four. I had been suppressing my intelligence. Comedy was something I wanted to make, and it was a fit."

He traveled for six years—getting juiced on gladiatorial bouts on stage, sleeping them off in a blur of Ramada Inns. Opening for Sheena Easton, he told masturbation jokes to Vegas droids, whose hands darted only toward slot machines. "In stand-up, I show my game face," he says, meaning he tries not to hedge or truckle. One night at Stand-Up N.Y., he attacked the ban on gays in the military—"You know what the army's really afraid of? A thousand guys with M16s going, 'Who you calling a faggot?'" A drunk heckled, "That's why you're not in the Army." "It really made me angry, so for the rest of the set I cruised him and flirted. He was defenseless, and as I walked off the stage, he grabbed me. A bouncer had to pull him off. It taught me never to pick on a guy in the aisle," he says smiling. "But seriously, I saw how wickedly powerful my words could be."

He landed the hosting job on Comedy Central's *Short Attention Span Theater,* then hosted MTV's short-attention-snagging *You Wrote It, You Watch It,* and in 1992 launched MTV's first talk show, a hit from the get-go and the prototype of his current playpen. "It's not yet clear what we're saying," he acknowledges, wanting the show to be more relevant, within its confines. "Talk shows are basically infomercials—people selling their wares, their careers. Guests wouldn't come on unless we let them sell." He worries that his audience doesn't want to see his "game face." "They're thinking, 'It's twelve-thirty, so dance, little moron.' "

He sounds as if he's apologizing for loving a medium so money-driven, but in truth he is smitten by his mass audience and by the craft of late night. "At first, the audience doesn't know who you are. You let them see your traits, your normal range, so they can be surprised by deviations. Natalie Merchant came on when I was starting. She's a musician. She wasn't comfortable talking and I was so inexperienced I didn't know how to ease her pain. Whenever I doubt myself, I return in my head to William Shatner. It let me know what was possible in the moment. I thought, 'If I just let go and enjoy myself, I can do this.' When Robin Leach was patronizing me, I thought of him as being in his snob character, but I went home thinking, 'I'm not going to let that happen again.' "

"In the worst-case scenario, I get canceled. I'll feel bad, but I will know how much I enjoyed this. There is so much pleasure in having a creative outlet every day that's structured. I am the baby and the father of this organization. All these people come in and bust their asses for a lot less money than me. How could I not be grateful?"

When the conversation turns to his personal life, he says, "I'm so much up the asshole of the show, I barely know what's going on in the world, much less have time for a relationship." I say, "Oh, bullshit," and he admits he doesn't know what he wants. "My brother is married with two kids. He's the flag bearer, so my parents have grandchildren." Stewart speaks tenderly and with protectiveness about a woman with whom he lived, describing the painful end of their connection. "It's dangerous to have people count on you. I'm less solid as an intimate." He says there is pleasure in this life "from hard work," but not joy. "Joy takes you off your foundation. It breaks all the rules." In one week, he went from the exaltation of appearing on *Letterman* to the terror of being in L.A. during the big earthquake. "It would have been nice to have someone to call."

He says his parents are not allowed to attend tapings. I say his father's voice is there anyway, coming out of his mouth when he rakes himself and shows dad he hasn't gotten so far ahead—isn't really successful, sexy, and likable. Stewart admits he's not quite as simian as he makes out. "I do have a hairy ass, but it stops at the fertile crescent at the base of my spine."

As we leave the restaurant and Stewart heads home to the Greenwich Village apartment he shares with two cats, he says, "When you drink beer, after a while all you want to do is keep drinking it." The same could be said about Stewart. His show isn't about anything but his singular charm, which has been throwing more shadows lately, reference-surfing—despite the blankness of his live audience—over Newt and newly discovered cave paintings in France. *The Jon Stewart Show* will live or die by its host. Paramount, get off his hairy ass and let this garden grow.

Mean Business: Garry Shandling Skewers Fear and Loathing on the Network Trail

December 1992

Garry Shandling looks pained. Chronically. He's ordered a rare burger; and it's well-done. His girlfriend says he's remote. His favorite jacket . . . well, there's grease on the lapel. From the burger. Sigh. Not to mention the ozone layer and mortality. The pain is mostly in the mouth, with its fleshy, disappointed lips. And in the eyes, poised for a wince. Shandling understands this face, knows how the fear of humiliation can turn into a bludgeon. Shandling has used this insight to surmount his anger and doubt, turned them into subjects. The result is *The Larry Sanders Show* (HBO)—a shrewd satire of talk shows with a dazzling ensemble cast—which may well be the hippest, funniest take ever on the pecking order.

Sanders is charged with giddy license, a sense of possibility arising not from stagey shocks but from pointed truths. The series—its cameras poised to pounce on unguarded moments—is an unmuzzled gloss on repression and on the devil-brokered bargains and slipping authority behind it. *Sanders* is HBO's most exuberant fuck-you to the networks, a dance on the grave of centralized power.

When it debuted in August, the series, co-created with Dennis Klein, inspired raves. Now, after thirteen episodes, an expansive, cohesive vision has emerged. Larry Sanders, played by Shandling, is the golden-boy/lackey at an unnamed network owned by Unideck Electronics—read Letterman, pampered/dissed by NBC, minion of GE. He jousts for ratings in the post-Carson frontier, a mediascape at once lawless and energized, a breeding ground for paranoia and the hunger to stay alive. His trademark is holding out an invisible remote control and urging, "Do not flip around." When the show's producer, Artie (Rip Torn), hears mention of CNBC, he grouches: "What the hell is that? What does that mean? My TV stops at thirteen, where it's supposed to."

Most of the action unfurls behind the scenes; *Sanders* is a showbiz confidential, its nose trained on power, its characters archetypes worthy of Molière. Atop the show's pyramid hunkers distant-father Larry. On the air, he isn't as irascible as Letterman, rather closer to Leno, blanding himself out in his monologues, curbing his competitiveness with his guests (who are real celebrities, playing themselves and hyping actual projects). He is cripplingly self-conscious, a man who worries that his ass looks fat, a creature struggling to be decent but who would always sell out for a punch line. Not sex, not money, not intimacy—nothing makes him feel as alive as a laugh. He can simulate connection *only* before cameras; during commercials, he sinks into stony silence, stranding the gulls on his couch to stare bleakly into space. He's so terrified of self-exposure, he's never invited longtime ally Artie to his home. When his wife, Jeannie (Megan Gallagher), arranges a dinner and informs him, "It's at your house," Larry gets a hunted look and wishfully asks, "What is that, a new Chinese restaurant?"

As for sidekick Hank (Jeffrey Tambor), there is no turd he will not swallow with a rueful grin. Hank—former cruise director and current endorsement junkie/bimbette hunter—is the Ed McMahon who guffaws as Carson ridicules his drinking while obscuring his own, who plays the sport in a feigned friendship requiring he accept barbs.

Head writers Jerry (Wallace Langham) and Phil (Jeremy Piven) are geeks turned tormenters. Among themselves, they curse Larry's delivery for blunting their brilliance, then separately draw him aside to backbite each other. When Larry has William Shatner on the phone, they challenge, "Get him to say 'Klingon,' " then huddle around the speaker phone so their snickers can be heard.

This world is Animal House, *Sanders* pointedly documents. When Jon Lovitz and his female satellite dine *chez* Sanders, the men relive their club gigs, oblivious that the women are sitting by silent and glum. The female regulars, in addition to Jeannie, include Larry's assistant, Beverly (Penny Johnson), Hank's assistant, Darlene (Linda Doucett), and the talent booker, Paula (Janeane Garofalo)—team players lacking even parking space on the influence totem pole. Darlene, an aerobicized mommy, is Hank's ideal, but overworked Paula and Beverly, the only African American on staff, shoot off smart mouths in private.

With the least at stake, they are the least snowed, functioning as the show's chorus. One night before a taping, a depressed Jeannie says to Larry, "Do you know that I sleep all day?" And Beverly, feeling implicated, remarks to Paula, "We fetch for him all day. We create the atmosphere he takes home to her." When, at last, a woman with clout does enter—network exec Melanie Parrish (Deborah May)—she's so desperate to measure up in the locker room, she hurls threats and insults (shades of Leno's Helen Kushnick?), outcruding even the actual penis people.

Paranoia saturates the atmosphere. In almost every episode, someone's head rolls or a character fears being replaced. Everyone feels tangential, assumes that pod replicants are waiting in the wings. Their egos stroked one minute and clobbered the next, the characters are unable to gauge their sizes, seeing themselves one minute as scurrying rodents and the next as gigantic talents. "I'm a day away from being the funny weatherman in Tucson," Larry whines, serious enough to hawk Garden Weasels when the sponsor insists. On another show, he returns from a two-week vacation after three days, a nail-biting interval during which guest host Dana Carvey has raked in big ratings.

Fear of the ax distracts the characters from taking stock, but when, occasionally, the buzzing quiets, they are filled with melancholy. Cynicism, they see, doesn't protect them from midlife malaise. The inanities of talk shows are continually paraded: bits with wild animals, the youngest X and the oldest Y, banter about last night's audience. Yet this gig is the brass ring for Larry, Artie, and Hank, men who sense their mediocrity but have no urge for more challenge. When Larry complains that, since he doesn't own a Garden Weasel, endorsing it would be unethical, Artie's eyes fill with alarm and he cautions, "Don't start pulling on that thread, or our whole world will unravel!"

With all its unmasking, though, *Sanders* doesn't come off mean-spirited. It is generous, permissive, overflowing with antic detail. Even when it snarls at real people, the targets are padded with status and fame. Most shows would settle for one plot line per episode; this one routinely weaves together three. The writers—including Shandling, Paul Simms, and Maya Forbes—are reference junkies far from recovery. Artie keeps replaying Larry's flirting with Mimi Rogers, and Larry gripes, "Christ, it's like making me watch the Rodney King tape." Hank auditions for substitute host, and Artie counsels a network chief: "Go easy and don't mention Rupert Pupkin." When Artie says the network is pushing Donna Mills, Larry groans, "Donna Mills, even Kiss is working without makeup."

The dished and dishers alike come clean. It's as if Hollywood has waited its lifetime to flash underbelly—even to look unattractive. Family man Billy Crystal admits putting business first. Robin Williams screws up his timing and dies. Nice-girl Carol Burnett, prodded to do a Tarzan sketch, bitches to her assistant about Larry's bad acting, and, during a commercial, she whispers loud: "Get a longer loincloth. I saw your balls."

Even innovative sitcoms—*Murphy Brown, Seinfeld*—present cartoons with shtick that's repeated over and over. On *Sanders*, doubleness rules, and the characters are drawn with increasing richness in seemingly marginal exchanges. During Burnett's appearance, Larry freaks out, killing two tarantulas that have been placed on his arm. Afterward, we see Artie weave his devilish spell: "You finally got to do a sketch with Carol." Larry (miserably): "It wasn't a sketch. It was a massive, spastic fuck-up." Artie: "Tomato, tom*aa*to, it was broad physical comedy. It made the Ed Ames tomahawk throw look like a big piece of shit." Larry: "Really?" Artie (sadistic glee washing over his face): "Until you sent that poor creature to a fiery death." Larry: "But in a funny way." Artie: "Very funny." Larry: "Want to watch the tape again?" Artie: "Atta boy."

Hank generally crouches on Larry's other shoulder, piping up as conscience. When Larry bumps David Spade for appearing on Leno's show first, Hank reminds him of his own scrabbling days. When Larry admits, "I've turned into an asshole," Hank responds, "Have a good time with it," causing Larry's face to freeze in dismay. But poignance never turns maudlin here; it remains laced with gritty truth. Hank finally explodes at Larry for his sniggering: "What about the time I chipped my tooth on the bathroom urinal? What the fuck is comical about that?" Larry is tempted to be a mensch, but his resolve melts. Slowly, he exhales, "It was a back tooth, Hank. Don't know how you did it."

■ ■ ■

Shandling himself is straddling excitement and anxiety when I reach him by phone. "I'm glad the series was picked up," he enthuses, then worries, "but now we have to deepen the characters, especially Larry, find out why he even *has* a personal life, since he keeps running away from it." Shandling measures his words, as if each is a bubble he wants to examine. Unlike Larry, he doesn't sniff extensively before revealing his thoughts. He's evasive only once, halfway through the conversation: "Er, I'm going to call you back on another phone. In five minutes." I think: He's getting in his car. He's reluctant to look like an L.A. cliché. The phone rings. "Are you in your car?" Shandling: "Behind an Arrowwood truck, on my way to an agent."

A part of Shandling would like to store the praise he's received and live off it, go camping or something, because exploring Larry means that his source, Garry, goes back on the couch. That he's willing is what distinguishes him from his creation. Shandling understands that exposure is funnier than protecting himself, and he wants to dramatize the struggle.

Shandling: "Next season, Larry has to look at what he is or the show won't be interesting. He surrounds himself with yes men, and there are a lot of other temptations. You get all this recognition, and the pay is great, and it's not exactly digging ditches. But when I was hosting *The Tonight Show,* I got to a point where I had to ask myself: 'Do you really want this as a career, dealing with momentous decisions like whether Michael Bolton is going to do one number or two?' "

Stone: "Larry lets in the truth when he absolutely has to, like when his job is on the line."

Shandling: "He's going to feel that urgency with women. He's unhappy enough to ask why he would choose a wife like Jeannie. It's very common in showbiz, women without lives of their own who devote all their attention to their husbands. So many men need women to revolve around them. But it's not just that Jeannie is frustrated with Larry, I think he resents *her*, and he will think about why. I want to bring back Melanie Parrish. She's a good authority figure for Larry to clash with, and we can explore what makes a woman become that angry."

Stone: "What does Larry really think of Hank?"

Shandling: "He believes Hank is the best man for the job. He loves him."

Stone: "*Loves* him? When he constantly mocks him?"

Shandling: "Oh, come on, you can be mean to anyone."

NAME INDEX

A

Abalou, Migaly, 172

Agnew, Spiro, 70

Airaldi, Remo, 233

Allen, Gracie, 5, 79

Allen, Randy, 164, 198

Allen, Steve, 7

Allen, Tim, xxiv, 200, 215–216

Allen, Woody, xxiii, 4, 9, 24, 28,
    78, 80, 83, 113, 218, 271

Altman, Jeff, 204

Altman, Robert, 83

Ameen, Mark, 126–127, 140–142

Ames, Ed, 279

Amis, Martin, 72

Anderson, Eddie, 5

Anderson, Laurie, 86

Anderson, Louie, 126

Anderson, Pamela, 270

Andrews Sisters, 233

Angelos, Maureen, 190, 192, 193.
    See also Five Lesbian Brothers

Ann-Margret, 46

Arcade, Penny, 101

Armitage, Carol, 97–98

Arnold, Roseanne. See Barr,
    Roseanne

Arnold, Tom, 33

Arquette, Cliff, xxv, 57, 58, 88

Askin, Peter, 113

Athey, Ron, xv, 101, 102

Avner the Eccentric, 233

Avni, Ran, 231

B

Bacall, Lauren, 171

Bailey, Pearl, 46

Baird, William, 53

Baker, Howard, 36

Bakker, Tammy Faye, 78

Ball, Lucille, 5, 81, 107

Ballet Trocadero de Monte Carlo,
    160

Balletta, Dominic, 103

Balthus, 148

Bankhead, Tallulah, 185, 198

Baranski, Christine, 238

Barbette, 94

Barentyne, Ross, 176

Barr, Roseanne, xxiv, 33, 78, 126

Barrows, Sydney Biddle, 88

Bartenieff, George, 97

Bass, Eric, 201

Bassey, Shirley, 109

Bayoul, Oksana, 82

Beamon, Bob, 137

Beazey, Jeff, 179

Bee Gees, 38

Begelman, David, 18

Behar, Joy, xxviii

Belanger, Michael, 178

Belushi, John, 4, 7, 58, 69, 81

Belzer, Richard, xxv, xxvi, 27, 42, 43, 78, 248, 256, 270

Benchley, Robert, 218

Benigni, Roberto, 209

Benny, Jack, xxviii, 4, 5, 9, 19, 48

Benson, Robby, 113

Berger, Suzy, 196

Berky, Bob, 233

Berle, Milton, 13, 58, 200, 247

Berman, Shelley, 4

Bern, Alan, 201

Bernhard, Sandra, xii, xix, xxv, xxvi, 24, 25, 26, 28–33, 89, 115, 162, 195, 196, 197, 205, 212, 256

Bernsen, Corbin, 250

Best, Pete, 216

BETTY, 233–235

Black, Lewis, xxvi, 35–37

Black Eyed Susan, 159

Blair, Dennis, 60

Blake, Robert, 255

Bloch, Larry, 233

Bloolips, xix, 165, 166, 178, 185, 188

Blue Man Group, 102, 103

Bob and Ray, 85, 215

Bobbitt, Lorena, 81, 269

Bochco, Steven, 241

Bogosian, Eric, xxvi, 94, 95, 98, 103, 104, 114, 120, 239, 270

Bolger, Ray, 67

Bolton, Michael, 280

Bono, Sonny, 84, 88

Boocock, Paul. *See* Premium Bob

Boosler, Elayne, 243

Borg, Bjorn, 216

Borgeson, Jeso, 207

Bornstein, Kate, 147

Boskovich, John, 31

Botha, President, 64

Bourne, Bette, 185. *See also* Bloolips

Bowie, David, 30

Boyle, Lara Flynn, 272

Bradley, Senator Bill, 268

Brand, Jo, 202–203

Brandenberger, Stormy, 173

Brando, Marlon, 106, 115, 134, 165

Branner, Djola, 185, 186. *See also* Pomo Afro Homos

Bread & Puppets, 201

Breeders, 270

Brice, Fanny, 58

Broderick, Matthew, 87

Brook, Peter, 222

Brooks, Albert, 61

Brooks, Mel, xiv, xxvii, 4, 41, 82, 126

Brothers, Dr. Joyce, 250

Brown, Julie, 81–82

Brown, Ron, 103

Brown, Tony, 223

Brown, Trisha, 99

Bruce, Lenny, xiii, xviii, xxv, xxviii, 7, 8, 9, 17, 24, 25, 27, 52, 56, 104, 217, 271

Buckley, Lord, 3

Buffalo Bob, 87

Burden, Chris, xv

Burnett, Carol, 58, 81, 279

Burns, Diane, 115

Burns, George, 4, 5, 18, 78, 79, 265

Burroughs, William, 164

Busch, Charles, xx, xxv, xxviii,
    161, 178, 179, 198
Busfield, Timothy, 241
Bush, Barbara, 77
Bush, George, xvii, 12, 13, 19, 36,
    48, 50, 60, 76, 77, 138, 240, 259,
    268
Butler, Brett, 200, 202

C
Caesar, Sid, 4, 58, 202
Cagney, James, 211
Cale, David, 94
Cambridge, Godfrey, xviii, 4
Camicia, Jimmy, xix, 159, 171, 176,
    177. See also Hot Peaches
Candy, John, 58
Capone, Al, 22
Capote, Truman, 214
Capri, Dick, 6
Captain Kangaroo, 72
Capurro, Scott, 196
Carey, Robert, 178
Carlin, George, xviii, 4, 24
Carr, C., xv, xx, 163
Carrey, Jim, 61, 86–87, 268
Carroll, Jim, 270
Carson, Johnny, xxiii, xxiv, 6–7,
    239, 255, 256, 257, 267, 269,
    277
Carter, Rosalynn, 77
Carvey, Dana, 266, 267, 278
Castro, Fidel, 18
Cave, Jim, 139
Cavett, Dick, 22, 256, 267, 269
Chan, Jackie, 236
Chandler, Raymond, 246

Chaplin, Charles, xxiii, xxviii, 4,
    60, 68, 107, 218
Chase, Chevy, xxiii, 263
Cher, 78, 79, 208
Chicago, Judy, 30
Chinn, May, 262
Chrysis, International, 159, 165,
    177
Chucklehead, 201–202
Chung, Connie, 134, 160
Churney, Russell, 188, 217
Clark, Dick, 270
Clarke, Martha, 222
Clary, Julian, 166, 187–190, 200,
    217
Clary, Robert, 85
Clay, Andrew "Dice," xxvii, 40,
    213, 214, 243, 344
Cline, Patsy, 270
Clinton, Chelsea, 258
Clinton, Hillary, 197
Clinton, President Bill, xvii, 60,
    197, 267, 269
Clinton, Roger, 258
Clooney, George, 265
Coca, Imogene, 4
Cockettes, 159
Cocteau, Jean, 168
Cohen, Jaffe, xxi, 166, 183, 184.
    See also Funny Gay Males
Cohen, Mark, 270
Cohen, Myron, 4
Cohn, Roy, 17
Cohn, Sam, xxv
Coleman, Amy, 177
Colette, 146
Collins, Joan, 188

Como, Perry, 168
Cooper, Gary, 168
Cooper, Tommy, 224
Coppola, Francis Ford, 70
Cosby, Bill, xviii, 19–20, 73
Covan, Ellie, xxviii
Coward, Noël, 3
Crawford, Joan, xx, 177, 178
Crews, Harry, 267
Crimmins, Alice, 88
Crimmins, Barry, 212
Crisp, Quentin, 160, 161
Crocker, Betty, 234
Cronyn, Hume, 29
Crosby, Bing, 158, 215
Crosby, Gary, 215
Cruise, Tom, 16, 265
Cruz, Migdalia, 121
Crystal, Billy, xxvii, 34, 78, 80, 85,
    91, 242, 250, 251, 279
Crystal, Jennifer, 251
Crystal, Raphael, 231
Culture Clash, xvii, 202, 222, 235
Cunningham, Merce, 97
Cuomo, Mario, 42
Curry, Tim, 160
Curtis, Jackie, 159
Curtis, Jamie Lee, 133, 135
Custer, General George, 64
Cytron, Sara, 165, 180–182, 184

D

Dahl, Arlene, xxvi, 198
Dali, Salvador, 226
DANCENOISE, 164
Dangerfield, Rodney, xxv, 14–17,
    20, 41, 208, 212, 215

Danson, Ted, xviii
Darling, Candy, 159
David, Larry, xxiv
Davidson, Jaye, 56
Davis, Angela, 7
Davis, Bette, xx, 62, 164, 177, 183
Davis Jr., Sammy, xviii
Davis, Mark, 196
Davy, Babs, 190, 192, 193. *See also*
    Five Lesbian Brothers
De Niro, Robert, 112
De Palma, Brian, 112
Dean, James, 115, 165, 168
Decroux, Etienne, 220–222, 223,
    224, 225
Dee, Jack, 216
DeGeneres, Ellen, 126, 162
DeLaria, Lea, xix, xxi, 166,
    196–197
Dell, Tom E., 73, 74, 75
Delon, Alain, 106
Dennis, Charles, 97, 98, 100
Diamond, Neil, 149
Dibbell, Dominique, 147, 190,
    192, 193. *See also* Five Lesbian
    Brothers
Dickens, Charles, 3, 88
Diller, Phyllis, 12–14
Dinkins, Mayor David, 27, 49
Divine, 88
Donaldson, Sam, 264
Doucett, Linda, 278
Douglas, Mike, 264
Draper, Ruth, 3, 58
Drescher, Fran, 143, 264
DuArt, Louise, 61, 78–81
Ducommun, Rick, 211

Dukakis, Kitty, 38
Dulles, John Foster, 17
Dumont, Margaret, 23
Dunaway, Faye, 178
Dunn, Nora, 243
Durst, Will, xxv, xxvi, 42–43, 78
Duvalier, 42–43
Dylan, Bob, 60, 135, 247

E
Easton, Sheena, 274
Ebihara, Richard, 199, 235, 236, 237. *See also* Slant
Eckoff, Sally, 97
Edelman, Richard, 201
Edelstein, Lisa, 162
Edwards, Clarence, 109
Edwards, Jango, xxv, xxvi, 205, 207–208, 209, 210
Eichelberger, Ethyl, 159, 161, 191
Eisenbach, Helen, 193, 194
Eisenhower, Dwight David, 8, 17
Eisenhower, Mamie, 83
Elliott, Kenneth, 178
Ellis, Albert, 52
Elovich, Richard, xxviii
Elvis. *See* Presley, Elvis
Engquist, Richard, 232
Epperson, John, xix, xxvi, 27, 33, 45, 46–47, 104, 161
Essmann, Jeffrey, xxvi, 61, 87, 89, 90–91

F
Fabray, Nanette, 46
Fairchild, Morgan, 255
Faludi, Susan, 267

Falwell, Jerry, 91
Farley, Chris, 58
Farrakhan, Louis, 27
Feller, Howard, 273
Fellini, Frederic, 209
Fenley, Molissa, 97, 103
Ferrante, Frank, 22, 23
Field, Crystal, 97
Field, Minnie, 99
Fields, W.C., xxv, xxvi, 57
Finley, Karen, xix, xxi, 89, 90, 94, 100, 101
Firestein, Harvey, 59
Fischer, Johann Casper Ferdinand, 230
Fisher, Robert, 22
Five Lesbian Brothers, xix, 164, 190–193
Flaherty, Joe, 58
Flanagan, Bob, xvi
Fleck, John, xxi
Fleisher, Julian, 158, 161, 163, 165
Fo, Dario, 224
Foerster, Rand, 35, 37
Fogelberg, Dan, 38
Fonda, Henry, 78
Fonda, Jane, 18, 30, 78
Forbes, Malcolm, 18
Forbes, Maya, 279
Forbes, Steve, 10
Ford, Betty, 63, 77
Ford, Gerald, 55
Foster, Jodie, 196
Foxx, Redd, xviii
Francis, Connie, 46
Franciscus, James, 85

Franken, Al, 239

Franklin, Benjamin, 244

Freeman, Brian, 186. *See also*
Pomo Afro Homos

Friedman, Budd, xxv, 41, 205

Friedman, Silver, 35

Frohnmayer, John, xxi

Fromme, Squeaky, 55, 88

Fry, David, 60

Fuchs, Michael, 243

Fuller, Loie, 226

Funny Gay Males, xix, xxi, 165,
182–184

G

Gabor, Zsa Zsa, 79

Gaines, Bill, 52

Gallagher, Megan, 277

Gandhi, Indira, 117

Gannon, Frank, 207

Garbo, Greta, 175

Garcia, Jerry, 202

Garland, Judy, 34, 159, 177

Garner, James, 38

Garofalo, Janeane, xxv, 81, 266, 278

Gazzara, Ben, 62

Gearheart, Della Mae, 166

Gelbart, Larry, 4

Gershwin, George, 108

Giancana, Sam, 56

Gifford, Kathie Lee, 266, 271

Gilbert, Sara, 238

Gin Blossoms, 270

Giove, Missy, 273

Giraud, Tiye, 102

Gittings, Barbara, 158

Giuliani, Rudolph, 27, 48

Glaser, John, 179

Glass, Philip, 100

Gleason, Jackie, 45, 58

Glover, Danny, 267

Gobel, George, 215

Godwin, James, 102

Goetz, Bernhard, 244

Goldberg, Whoopi, xvii, xviii, xix,
31, 59, 62–63, 78, 89, 115, 242

Goldfadn, Avrom, 231

Goldthwaite, Bob, 20, 243, 244

Gomez, Marga, xiv, xvii, xxii

Gomez-Peña, Guillermo, 222

Good, Sandy, 55

Googooly, Jeff, 81

Gorbachev, 48, 76, 255

Gordon, Davis, 232

Gore, Tipper, 270

Gornick, Vivian, 146

Gorodetsky, Eddie, 240, 245–248

Gottfried, Gilbert, xxv, xxvi, xxvii,
61, 62, 87, 89, 91, 203

Gould, Elliott, 251

Graham, Billy, 117

Graham, Virginia, 266

Grant, Hugh, 60, 240

Graver, Fred, 269

Gray, Spalding, xxii, xxvii, xxviii,
25, 127, 128–129, 150–156

Gregory, Dick, xviii, 4

Griffin, Merv, 264

Grodin, Charles, 7

Grosz, George, 117

Grotowski, Jerzy, 98, 99, 100, 121

Guevara, Ernesto "Che," 202

Guillony, Preston, 55

Guns 'N' Roses, 267

Gupton, Eric, 186. *See also* Pomo
   Afro Homos
Gutmacher, Benito, 95, 105–107

H
Hackett, Buddy, xiii
Hagen, Uta, 36
Hagman, Larry, 216
Haig, Alexander, 18
Hall, Arsenio, xxiii, 166, 267
Hall, Rich, 207, 216, 248
Halliday, Andy, 178
Halston, Julie, xxviii
Hamadi, Mohamed, 18
Hammett, Dashiel, 246
Haney, Kevin, 214
Harding, Tonya, 81, 82, 123
Hardy, Jeremy, 214, 216
Hardy, Oliver. *See* Laurel and
   Hardy
Harris, Mel, 241
Harris, Rennie, 223
Hart, Gary, 71
Hasselhoff, David, 260
Havey, Alan, 243, 247
Hayworth, Rita, 165, 168
Healey, Peggy, 190, 191, 192, 193.
   See also Five Lesbian Brothers
Hearst, Patty, 7
Heatherton, Joey, 88, 214
Held Jr., John, 245
Hellman, Lillian, 88
Helms, Jesse, xxi, 102, 148, 219
Helmsley, Leona, 10, 81
Hepburn, Katharine, xxv, 78, 79,
   168
Herman, Dave, 73

Herman, Pee-wee. *See* Reubens,
   Paul
Herrmann, Adelaide, 230
Heston, Charlton, 18
Hicks, Bill, xxv, xxvi, 25, 44–45,
   200, 217–218
Hills, Bruce, 203
Hinckley, John, 42, 50
Hines, Mimi, 46
Hirschfeld, Dr. Magnus, 158
Hitler, Adolf, 70, 71
Hoch, Danny, xxvi, xxviii–xxix,
   93, 94, 95, 96, 102, 103, 114,
   115–124, 270
Hockenberry, John, xxii, xxiii,
   136–138
Hockney, David, 184
Hodge, Francis, 99
Hodge, Patricia, 249, 250
Hoffman, Abbie, 7, 50, 53, 54, 55
Hoffman, Dustin, 79, 80, 257
Holly, Buddy, 139
Holman, Bob, 115
Holtz Jr., Lou, 87
Hoover, J. Edgar, 17, 56
Hope, Bob, 5, 12, 13, 158, 214
Hopkins, Bruce, 175
Horton, Edward Everett, 158
Horton, Peter, 241
Hot Peaches, xix–xx, 159, 164,
   170, 171, 172, 173, 176–177
Houdini, Harry, 227
Houston, Whitney, 202
Houston-Jones, Ishmael, 99
Howell, John, 100
Hoyle, Geoff, xxvi, 201, 222,
   223–225

Hsieh, Teching, xv
Hughes, Holly, xx, xxi, xxii, 25,
    125, 127, 146–150, 164, 165, 168,
    169, 170, 173, 191
Hurlin, Dan, 149
Hurston, Zora Neale, 108
Hurt, John 160
Huston, Michael, 202
Hyde-Pierce, David, 238

I

Iobst, Anne, 164
Irwin, Bill, 200, 222, 225, 226
Islam, Sirajul, 259–260
Israel, Robert, 232

J

Jackson, Jesse, 186
Jackson, Michael, 46
Jackson, Victoria, 247
Jagger, Mick, 30, 60
Jarmusch, Jim, 209
Jee, Rupert, 241, 259, 260–262
Jennings, Peter, 86, 109
John, Elton, 213
Johnson, Lyndon Baines, 53
Johnson, Penny, 278
Jones, Tom, 33
Joplin, Janis, 177
Jourdan, Charles, 30
Judas Priest, 38
Julia, Raul, 111

K

Kael, Pauline, 150, 151
Kaelin, Kato, 266

Kafka, Franz, 40, 67
Kahn, John, 226
Kamali, Norma, 30
Kaminsky, Mikhail, 220
Kantor, Thadeusz, xii, 99, 220
Katz, Jonathan, 239
Kavner, Julie, 84
Kaye, Danny, 67, 158, 233
Keaton, Buster, xxiii, 59, 144, 227
Keaton, Michael, 250
Kelly, Gene, 106
Kelly, John, 94, 102, 161
Kelly, Patrick, 131
Kelsey, Linda, 251
Kennedy, Bobby, 7
Kennedy, John F., 7, 17
Kennedy, Ted, 38, 268
Kerrigan, Nancy, 81, 82, 123
Kesey, Ken, 53
King, Alan, xiii, 6
King, Danny, 165
King, Martin Luther, 7
King, Rodney, 268, 279
King, Yolanda, 121
Kinison, Sam, 40, 213
Kinnear, Greg, xxiii, 241
Kipper Kids, xxvi, 104
Kirkpatrick, Jeane, 36
Kirkwood, Carla, xxviii
KISS, 279
Kissinger, Henry, 36
Klein, Calvin, 29, 31, 222
Klein, Dennis, 277
Klein, Michael, xix
Klein, Robert, 24
Klezmatics, 201

Kline, Kevin, 82, 113

Koch, Mayor Ed, xii, 26, 49

Koch, Philip, 175

Kohan, Jenji, 84

Kolodner, Arnie, 178

Koop, C. Everett, 50

Kornbluth, Josh, xxii, 127,
144–145

Korshunov, Georgi, 220

Kovacs, Ernie, 7

Krassner, Paul, 27–28, 49–56

Kron, Lisa, xxii, xxiii, 170,
180–182, 190, 191, 192. See also
Five Lesbian Brothers

Kubrick, Stanley, 227

Kulp, Nancy, 84

Kurt, Elvira, 196

Kushnick, Helen, 278

L

La Gran Scena Opera company,
xxv, 160, 175–176, 178, 198

Lake, Ricki, 33, 265

Lamas, Lorenzo, 271

lang, k. d., 160

Langham, Wallace, 277

LaRue, Danny, 177, 178

Latham, David. See Premium Bob

Lauper, Cyndi, 73, 247

Laurel and Hardy, 158

Laurel, Stan. See Laurel and
Hardy

Lauren, Ralph, 31

Lawrence, Mal Z., xxviii, 5–6

Leabhardt, Thomas, 221

Leach, Robin, 272, 275

Leary, Denis, 26, 37–39

Leary, Timothy, 33, 53, 88

Lecoat, Jenny, 211

Lee, Bruce, 236

Lee, Peggy, 26

Lee, Spike, 113

Legend, Johnny, 270

Leguizamo, John, xiv, xvii, xxvii,
95, 96, 110–113, 114, 239

Lemon, Brendon, 160

Leno, Jay, xxiii, 240, 254–256, 257,
263, 267, 269, 277, 278, 279

Leopold, Tom, 85, 214

Lepkoff, Danny, 99

Letterman, David, xxiii, xxv, 133,
207, 229, 238, 240, 256–262,
263, 266, 267, 269, 270, 272, 277

Levin, Charles, 233

Levy, Eugene, 58

Lewis, C. S., 246

Lewis, Gary, 74, 75

Lewis, Jerry, 4, 29, 158, 213

Lewis, Richard, xxvii, xxviii, 126,
133–136, 243

Liberace, 75

Lily, Bea, 58, 88

Liman, Arthur, 85, 86

Limansky, Ilya, 220

Linkletter, Diane, 88

Little Richard, 46, 87

Livington, Jennie, 161

London, Becky, 178

Long, Adam, 207

Lorre, Peter, 64

Lovitz, Jon, 267, 278

Lowe, Rob, 71, 211

Ludlam, Charles, xx, 159, 161, 170, 178. *See also* Ridiculous Theatrical Company
Lugosi, Bela, 64, 247
Lundquist, Monisha, 89
Lynam, Chris, 216
Lypsinka. *See* Epperson, John

M

Maddox, Lester, 64
Madonna, xviii, 34, 81, 161, 185, 265
Magee, Rusty, 35, 37
Magnuson, Ann, xxviii, 133
Mailer, Norman, 52, 55
Malley, Mike, 205, 206
Man Ray, 222
Manchester, William, 53
Mandel, Howie, 20
Manilow, Barry, 38
Manny the Hippie, 241
Manson, Charles, 54, 55, 56
Mapplethorpe, Robert, xxi, 162
Marceau, Marcel, 208
Marcos, Ferdinard, 70
Marcos, Imelda, 43, 81
Marcus, Daniel, 232
Margolin, Deb, xxviii, 165, 167, 168, 173
Margolis, Keri, 223
Mark, Mary Ellen, 267
Marlowe, Theresa, 178
Marsden, Les, 22
Marshall, Penny, 266
Martin, Colin, xix
Martin, Darnell, 123
Martin, Dean, 158

Martin, Steve, xxiii, xxv, 41, 58, 80, 81, 82
Marx, Arthur, 22
Marx, Chico, 22
Marx, Harpo, 22, 57
Marx, Groucho, xxi, 5, 9, 21–23, 27, 34, 53, 56, 76, 135, 265, 272
Marx, Miriam, 21
Marx Brothers, xxv, xxvi, 4, 23, 104, 190, 202, 233
Masina, Giulietta, 107
Mason, Jackie, xxvi, xxvii, 4, 6, 19, 27, 31, 47, 48–49, 91
Matchanov, Bakhram, 220
May, Deborah, 278
May, Elaine, 28
Maya, Frank, 196
Mayron, Melanie, 241
Mazar, Debi, 33
McCambridge, Mercedes, 177
McCann, Brenda, 55
McCarthy, Joseph, 17
McClure, Jessica, 50, 62–63
McCulloh, Barbara, 232
McGraw, Steve, 73
McKean, Michael, 250
McKeown, Allan, 82, 84
McMahon, Ed, 6, 277
McWilliams, Danny, xxi, 165, 182–183, 184. *See also* Funny Gay Males
Meany, Kevin, 200, 210–211, 212, 213
Meese, Ed, 36, 43
Mell-O White Boys, 108
Melman, Larry "Bud," 259
Melton, Sid, 215

Meltzer, Richard, 54
Mendoza, John, 215
Merchant, Natalie, 275
Merton, Paul, 189
Midler, Bette, xviii, 6, 63, 233
Mighty Mighty Bosstones, 270
Miller, Dennis, xv, xxvi, 239, 241,
   265, 266–269, 270
Miller, Penelope Ann, 271
Miller, Tim, xix, xxi, 97, 100, 222
Milli Vanilli, 38
Mills, Donna, 279
Minette, 159
Minnelli, Liza, 34, 78
Mint Juleps, 264
Mitchell, Joni, 32, 94
Mlotek, Zalmen, 232
Molière, 277
Monk, Meredith, 222
Monroe, Marilyn, 29, 178, 198
Montano, Linda, xv
Montoya, Richard, 202
Monty Python, 58
Moore, Mary Tyler, 29
Moranis, Rick, 58
Morris, Jim, xxvi, 60, 75–78, 212
Morse, Robert, 214
Morton, Bob, xxv, 240
Moschen, Michael, xxvi, 200, 222,
   225–227
Moulton, Charlie, 97, 100
Mr. Rogers, 72
Mr. T, 50
Mull, Martin, 61, 85, 215
Muppets, 72
Murphy, Eddie, xvii, xxvii, 19
Murray, Bill, xxiii, xxiv, 7, 58

Murray, Madalyn, 52
Myers, Mike, xxiii, 239

N
Nabokov, Vladimir, xvii
Nelson, Willie, 78
Netsky, Hankus, 232
New York Blues Experience, 270
Newhart, Bob, 213–214, 250
Newman, Paul, 18
Newman, Rick, 244
Niven, David, 87
Nixon, Pat, 168
Nixon, Richard Milhouse, 8, 17,
   18, 60, 91, 269
Noriega, Manuel, 43, 212
North, Oliver, 43, 85
Novello, Don, xxv, 59–60, 68–70,
   245, 258
Nulman, Andy, 203, 208

O
O'Brien, Conan, 263, 271
O'Connor, Sinéad, 243
O'Donnell, Mark, 247
O'Donnell, Rosie, xxvii, 241,
   264–266
O'Hara, Catherine, xxv, 58, 78,
   80
O'Keefe, John, xxii, xxvi, 138–140
Olin, Ken, 241
Olson, Steven, 37
Onassis, Jacqueline Kennedy, 11
Orlandersmith, Dael, xvii, xxvi,
   95, 96, 113–115
Osbourne, Ozzy, 247
Osmond, Donny, 265

Oswald, Richard, 158
Overton, Rick, 216, 244

P

Paar, Jack, 7, 269
Page, Patrick, 225
Pain Boy, 102
Palin, Michael, 83
Palmer, Alyson, 233, 234, 235. *See also* BETTY
Pangborn, Franklin, 158
Pao, Y. K., 262
Papp, Joseph, 97
Park, Chung Hee, 70
Parrish, Melanie, 281
Pashalinski, Lola, 159, 170
Patrice, Mademoiselle, 230
Patrick, Robert, 99
Pearl, Minnie, 66
Pedretti, Mike, 199, 200, 219, 221
Penn & Teller, xxvi, 222, 227–231, 245
Perkins, Carol, 230
Peron, Evita, 81
Perot, Ross, 60
Perr, Harvey, 99
Phace, Hapi, 165
Philbin, Regis, 270
Philips, Emo, xii, xxv, xxvi, 57, 59, 66–68, 203, 204, 207
Phranc, 149
Picasso, Paloma, 33
Pierce, Charles, 177, 178, 198
Piñero, Miguel, 115
Piven, Jeremy, 277
Poe, Edgar Allan, 212
Poindexter, 43

Polanski, Roman, 211
Polivka, Bolek, 200, 219
Pollock, Jackson, 245
Pomo Afro Homos, xix, 166, 185–187, 201, 235
Poundstone, Paula, 126, 212, 241, 243, 263–264, 265
Premium Bob, 104–105
Presley, Elvis, 38, 208, 211, 247, 255
Priestley, Jason, 272
Prowse, Juliet, 175
Pryor, Richard, xi, xiii, xvii, xviii, xxii, xxv, xxvi, 8–9, 10, 19, 24, 130, 256

Q

Qaddafi, 36
Quayle, Dan, 49, 76
Queen Elizabeth, 10
Quintero, Wayland, 199, 235, 236. *See also* Slant
Quinton, Everett, 161

R

Radner, Gilda, 81, 107
Rahman, Mujibur, 259–260
Ramis, Harold, xxiii, 58
Randall, Tony, 270
Raphael, Sally Jessy, 266
Rather, Dan, 86, 260
Reagan, Nancy, 11, 43, 50, 77
Reagan, Ronald, xvii, 12, 13, 18, 29, 36, 42, 43, 48, 50, 60, 61, 62, 64, 75, 76, 77, 85, 91, 152, 240, 259, 268
Redford, Robert, 18
Redgrave, Vanessa, 18

Redmond, Michael, 211
Reduced Shakespeare Company,
  The, 207
Reed, Donna, 178
Reed, Lou, 212
Reese, Mason, 210
Regan, Brian, 270
Reiner, Carl, 4
Reiner, Rob, 61, 85
Reneaud. See Reno
Reno, xiv, xix, xxvi, xxviii, 25, 26,
  33–35, 90, 101, 102, 197, 212
Reubens, Paul, 60, 68, 70–73
Richards, Keith, 38, 60, 216, 247
Rickles, Don, 6, 29, 126
Ridiculous Theatrical Company,
  xx, 159
Rivera, Geraldo, 160
Rivera, José, 109
Rivera, Sylvia (Ray), 159
Rivers, Joan, xxv, xxviii, 3, 6,
  10–12, 28, 73, 78, 79, 244, 265
Rivers, Melissa, 11
Roach, Hal, 158
Robertson, Pat, xxi
Robeson, Paul, 36, 42
Robinson, Meghan, 178
Rochester. See Anderson, Eddie
Rock, Chris, xvii
Roeg, Nicholas, 31
Rogers, Kenny, 260
Rogers, Mimi, 279
Rogers, Will, 3, 88
Rolling Stones, 43, 209
Rollins & Joffe, xxv
Rose, Axl, 267
Rose, Peter, 97, 98

Rosenn, Eno, 207
Rosenthal, Rachel, 222
Ross, Katherine, 257
Rosse, Wilhelmina, 170, 171
Roth, Philip, 9
Rousseve, Dave, 103
Roy, Jack. See Dangerfield,
  Rodney
Rozon, Gilbert, 203, 208
Rubin, Jerry, 50, 53, 54
Ruby, Jack, 134
Rudner, Rita, 243
Rudnick, Paul, 270
RuPaul, 161, 162
Rush, Michael, xix
Russell, Mark, xxix, 94, 97–103
Russell, Theresa, 33
Russinyol, Luis, 176
Russo, Vito, 158, 160, 161

S
Saban, Stephen, 210
Sabatini, Gabriela, 197, 273
Sacharow, Larry, 121
Saget, Bob, 244
Sahl, Mort, 17–19, 36
Sales, Soupy, 71
Salinas, Ric, 202
Sanders, Barry, xv–xvi
Sanders, Ed, 53
Sandrow, Nahma, 232
Sarducci, Father Guido. See
  Novello, Don
Sarler, Carol, 216
Sartre, Jean Paul, 247
Savage, Eleanor, 149
Savage, Jack, 232

Schechner, Richard, 119
Schiff, Stephen, 207
Schimmel, Robert, 26–27, 39–42, 203, 204, 210
Schlamme, Thomas, 84
Schultz, 18
Schwartz, Gary, 105
Schwartz, Glenn, 203, 205, 207, 210, 213–214
Schweitzer, Albert, 68
Schygulla, Hanna, 30
Scorsese, Martin, 28
Scott, Angela, 126, 129–131
Scott, Bon, 104
Seale, Bobby, 7
Seinfeld, Jerry, xxiv, 122, 123, 162
Sellers, Peter, 58, 83, 107
Sendak, Maurice, 264
Severinsen, Doc, 6, 264
Sexton, Lucy, 164
Shaffer, Paul, 85, 202, 214, 259
Shafransky, Renée, 151, 154, 155, 156
Shakespeare, William, 111
Shamir, Yitzhak, 18
Shandling, Garry, xxiv, xxvii, 276–281
Shatner, William, 269, 275, 278
Shaw, Peggy, xxv, xxix, 157, 164, 165, 167, 168, 169, 170–175, 180–182. See also Split Britches
Shear, Claudia, 127, 142–144
Shearer, Harry, xxv, xxvi, 27, 61, 78, 80, 84–86, 193, 214
Shepard, Sam, 99
Sherman, Joanna, 219
Shiner, 99

Shore, Dinah, 22
Short, Martin, xxv, 58, 78, 80, 82, 245, 266
Siegel, Bugsy, 22
Siff, Ira, 160, 176, 198. See also La Gran Scena Opera company
Siguenza, Herbert, 202
Simms, Paul, 279
Simo, Ana, 172
Simon, Carly, 50
Simon, Neil, 4
Simon and Garfunkel, 65
Simpson, Mona, 146
Simpson, O.J., xvii, 123
Singer, I. B., 9
Singer, Isaac Bashevis, 232
Skelton, Red, 58
Skira, Stephanie, 99
Slant, 199, 235–237
Slayton, Bobby, 202, 204
Sledge, Tommy, 247
Slick, Grace, 87
Smalls, Derek. See Shearer, Harry
Smiley, Stu, 248
Smith, Adam, 264
Smith, Bessie, xviii
Smith, Bob, xxi, 166, 183, 184. See also Funny Gay Males
Smith, Jack, xix, 159
Smith, Margaret, xxv, 89, 90, 126, 129, 131–132, 203
Smith, Mike, 89, 90
Smith, William Kennedy, 71
Smithberg, Madeleine, 269–270
Sneed, Pamela, 147
Soderberg, Steven, 155
Sokol, Marilyn, 233

Soma, Andy, 89, 90

Souter, 49

Spade, David, 267, 279

Spencer, Dr. Robert, 53

Spiderwoman, 164, 170, 172, 173

Spielberg, Steven, 63

Split Britches, xix, xxix, 163, 164,
    165, 166–168, 170, 173, 191

Springsteen, Bruce, 43

Spungen, Nancy, 247

St. James, Margo, 53

Stanwyck, Barbara, xx

Starr, Stevie "The Regurgitator,"
    204, 205, 206, 207, 210

Stein, Daniel, 222

Steinberg, David, xxiii, 24, 126

Steinbrenner, George, 76

Stelarc, xv

Stern, Howard, 56, 134

Stewart, Ellen, 97

Stewart, Jon, xxiii, xxiv, 40, 241,
    265, 269–276

Stiller, Ben, 87

Sting, 247

Stoklos, Denise, 95, 107–108,
    222

Stone, Sharon, 237

Stradlin, Izzy, 267

Strasberg, Lee, 178

Streisand, Barbra, xviii, 6, 31, 63,
    78, 79, 198

Stuart, Lyle, 52, 55

Sullivan, Ed, 8, 200

Sutcliffe, Stu, 269

Swados, Elizabeth, 118

Sweeney, Steve, 212

Sweet, Rachel, 247, 248

T

Talking Heads, 105

Talmer, 230

Tambor, Jeffrey, 277

Tandy, Jessica, 29

Tang, Tommy, 244

Tate, Sharon, 54

Taylor, Elizabeth, 62

Taylor, James, 38

Taylor, Robert, 34, 175

Tenuta, Judy, xii, xxv, 203, 204,
    207

Teresa, Mother, 247

Thatcher, Margaret, 43

Thicke, Alan, 250

Thomas, Dave, 58, 214, 215

Tiegs, Cheryl, 10

Tilly, Jennifer, 269

Tim, Tiny, 210

Tingle, Jimmy, xxvi, 25, 200,
    211–212, 213

Tomlin, Lily, 26, 58, 89, 179

Torn, Rip, 277

Torr, Diane, 165

Toth, Lazlo. *See* Novello, Don

Townsend, Robert, 130

Tracy, Spencer, 78, 168

Travolta, John, 144

Trillin, Calvin, 27, 47–48

Tropicana, Carmelita, xxv, 164,
    170, 173

Trump, Donald, 18, 36, 79

Trump, Ivana, 79

Tucker, Michael, 84

Tucker, Sophie, 4, 13

Turba, Ctibor, 200, 219

Turner, Jim, 60, 73–75

Turner, Tina, 29
Twain, Mark, 3, 88

U

Ulay, xv
Ullman, Tracey, 81, 82–84, 239
Urban Bush Women, 102

V

Vaccaro, John, 159
Valiant, Prince, 67
Van Tieghem, David, 226
Vance, Danitra, 95, 100, 108–109, 115
Vanilla Ice, 118
Varrone, Gene, 232
Vaughn, Stevie Ray, 38
Veidt, Conrad, 158
Vera-Ellen, xxvi, 198
Victor, Susan, 232
Viola, Lou, 204

W

Waits, Tom, 271
Waldheim, Kurt, 36
Wallace, Julie T., 248, 250
Walters, Barbara, 77, 78, 79, 80–81
Warfield, Marsha, xvii
Warhol, Andy, 33, 159, 160, 263
Waterman, Dennis, 248, 250
Waters, John, 87, 88–89, 163
Watts, Rolonda, 271
Wayans' brothers, xvii
Wayans, Damon, 27, 45–46, 47
Wayans, Keenen Ivory, 27
Weaver, Charlie. *See* Arquette, Cliff

Weaver, Lois, xxv, 157, 164, 165, 166, 167, 168, 169, 170, 172, 173, 174, 175, 180–182. *See also* Split Britches
Webber, Andrew Lloyd, 202
Webber, Margaret, 248
Weber, Bruce, 31
Weber, Steven, 269
Weil, Mark, 220
Weinberger, Casper, 18, 64
Weinstein, Arnold, 232
Weiss, Jeff, 164
Weldon, Fay, 248
Weller, Peter, 37
Wentworth, Scott, 232
West, Mae, xviii, xxv, 57, 117, 208, 233
Westenhoefer, Suzanne, xxi, 166
Westheimer, Dr. Ruth, 250
Wettig, Patricia, 241
Wheeler, Jed, 100
White, David, 100
White, Marvin, 186. *See also* Pomo Afro Homos
White Zombie, 270
Whitehall, B. T., 179
Whynot, Tammy, 174
Wilde, Oscar, 3, 190
Wildbaum, Paul, 219
Wildmon, Donald, xxi, 148
Williams, Cara, 215
Williams, Karen, 195
Williams, Robin, xxiii, xxv, 59, 64–65, 82, 202, 242, 244, 279
Williams, Vanessa, 265
Wilson, Brian, 75
Wilson, Carnie, 265

Wilson, Robert, 98, 99
Winfrey, Oprah, 265
Winters, Jonathan, xxv, 4, 211
Winters, Shelley, 79, 80
Wolfe, George C., 108
Wolfe, Tom, 88
Wong, B. D., 272
Wong, Joni, 170
Woodard, Alfre, 267
Woodbury, David, 99
Woodlawn, Holly, 159, 160
Wright, Steven, xxv, 59, 65–66, 212, 243, 244
Wuhl, Robert, 243
Wynans' brothers, xvii
Wynette, Tammy, 29

Y

Young, Susan, 170
Youngman, Henny, 4, 15, 65
Yung, Perry, 199, 235, 236. *See also* Slant

Z

Zagnit, Stuart, 232
Zaloom, Paul, 201, 219
Zeller, Mark, 232
Ziff, Amy, 233, 234, 235. *See also* BETTY
Ziff, Bitzi, 233, 234, 235. *See also* BETTY
Zipper, Allen, 84
Zuber, Catherine, 232

ABOUT THE AUTHOR

LAURIE STONE has written about comedy and drama for *The Village Voice*, and is the theater critic for *The Nation*. She is the author of the novel *Starting with Serge* and her collection of literary memoirs, *Close to the Bone*, is forthcoming. In 1996 she received the Nona Balakian Excellence in Reviewing Award from the National Books Critics Circle and she is the recipient of a grant from The New York Foundation for the Arts.